SHAKESPEARE AND THE MATTER OF THE CRUX

Textual, Topical, Onomastic, Authorial, and Other Puzzlements

Robert F. Fleissner

The Edwin Mellen Press
Lewiston/Queenston/Lampeter

Library of Congress Cataloging-in-Publication Data

Fleissner, Robert F.
   Shakespeare and the matter of the crux : textual, topical, onomastic, authorial, and other puzzlements / Robert F. Fleissner.
     p. cm.
   Includes bibliographical references (p.   ) and index.
   ISBN 0-7734-9622-X
   1. Shakespeare, William, 1564-1616--Criticism, Textual.
I. Title.
PR3071.F57 1991
822.3'3--dc20   91-37508
                                                                            CIP

A CIP catalog record for this book
is available from the British Library.

Copyright © 1991 Robert F. Fleissner

All rights reserved. For information contact

    The Edwin Mellen Press   The Edwin Mellen Press
            Box 450   Box 67
     Lewiston, New York   Queenston, Ontario
        USA 14092   CANADA, L0S 1L0

                The Edwin Mellen Press, Ltd.
                  Lampeter, Dyfed, Wales
             UNITED KINGDOM SA48 7DY

          Printed in the United States of America

In memory of my sister-in-law,
Norma Klein Fleissner,
psychoanalyst's daughter,
author of adult and young adult fiction

"Thou smilest and art still"
—Matthew Arnold, "Shakspeare"

Table of Contents

List of Illustrations i
Foreword iii
Preface ix
Acknowledgments xv
Part I: Shakespearean Cruxes in General 1
    Chapter 1: A Survey of Leading Textual Cruxes in
        Shakespeare 3
Part II: Identification Cruxes 21
    Toward Solving the Problem of the Companion to *Lost*
    Chapter 2: Much Ado about *Love's Labour's Won*:
        Shakespeare's 'Missing' Comedy 23
    The *Sonnets* and the Cryptic Inscription
    Chapter 3: The Case of the Embarrassing Em Space: A Textual
        Solution to the "W. H." Mystery 67
    Toward the 'Faithful Wife' Subgrouping
    Chapter 4: Marital Loves Encompassed: Sonnet 116 in Relation
        to Donne's "A Valediction: forbidding mourning" 101
Part III: The Textual/Philosophic Crux 123
    The Meaning of "Meane" in *Romeo and Juliet*
    Chapter 5: Friar Laurence and the Aesthetics of Ethics in the
        Star-Crossed Tragedy 125
Part IV: The Topical Crux 143
    The Mar-text Original in *As You Like It*
    Chapter 6: Sir Oliver, Contaminator of the Text, and Marlowe 145

Part V: Two Key Cruxes in the Most Tragic of Plays 161
    The Biographical Crux
    Chapter 7: The "Base-Born" Connection: The Bastard in *King Lear*, Shakespeare's Brother Edmund and His Son......................163
    The Textual Identification Crux
    Chapter 8: "And my poore Foole is hang'd"—Figuratively or Literally?..175

Part VI: The Authorship Crux 195
    Did Shakespeare Have a Hand in the Best of the Apocrypha?
    Chapter 9: Elizabethan Hydropathy: The Domestic Relation of *Arden of Faversham* to *The Merry Wives*................................197

Part VII: The Crux of Cruxes..229
    Did Sir John Falstaff Really Babble of Green Fields?
    Chapter 10: The Submerged Heraldic Emblem in Falstaff's Last Moments..231

Appendices...241
    Appendix A: "New tricks": Special Effects in the *Odcombian Banquet*, *Volpone*, and the *Sonnets*.....................................243
    Appendix B: Retabling Green Fields: Submerged Resonances in Milton and Heywood 249

Conclusion 257
Select Bibliography 261
Index...279

List of Illustrations

The order of the plays in the First Folio compared with the order in Meres's *Palladis Tamia,* showing how *Love's Labour's Won* was 'misplaced' 65

The 'Dedication' to Shakespeare's *Sonnets* from Q1, 1609 ed. 69

Otto van Veen, *Amorum Emblemata,* introd. Stephen Orgel, p. 237 112

Otto van Veen, *Amorum Emblemata,* introd. Stephen Orgel, p. 39 113

Excerpt from *Henry V* in *The Guild Shakespeare,* Volume 6, edited by John F. Andrews 230

Excerpt from *Henry V* in *The Guild Shakespeare,* Volume 6, edited by John F. Andrews (Editorial comments) 240

Foreword

For almost four hundred years William Shakespeare has challenged the acumen of scholars, beginning with Francis Meres whose *Palladis Tamia,* published in 1598, put him in first place among English dramatists. Meres' book is still an important source for students of the Shakespearean canon. Shakespeare has inspired more research, explication, and argument than any other author in history; he is a gold mine, and sometimes a mine field, for critics.

Dr. Robert Fleissner has for many years investigated those facets of Shakespeare's *œuvre* that have prompted much scholarly debate. In his latest book, *Shakespeare and the Matter of the Crux,* he has distilled and often extensively reworked some of his previously published criticism, to which he has added new information and interpretation. A leading specialist in Shakespearean puzzles or "cruxes," he offers the reader the most comprehensive and copiously documented survey of the subject. To my knowledge, no other scholar has brought together, examined, and tried to solve so many Shakespearean riddles between the covers of one volume.

Fleissner is primarily a textual critic, though willing to discuss Shakespeare's family members, relatives, and associates. He speculates on a possible connection between William's youngest brother Edmund, an actor who fathered an illegitimate child, and Edmund in *King Lear*. He observes that Arden, the family name of Shakespeare's mother, is identical with the name of the forest in *As You Like It*. But despite a penchant for biographical conjecture, he focuses mainly on Shakespeare's text. Biography attracts him chiefly for the light it may shed on the writings.

A good example of Fleissner's textual criticism is provided by his fourth chapter, in which he examines thematic and verbal parallels between Shakespeare's Sonnet 116 and John Donne's "A Valediction: forbidding mourning." The reader comes away from this lucid explication with a heightened awareness of relationship between the two poems, and a deepened understanding of both.

In another groundbreaking chapter, Fleissner suggests a convincing solution to a mystery created by Francis Meres when he listed *Love's Labour's Won* among Shakespeare's comedies. Since the play is missing from the canon, scholars spent much time in fruitless search of the lost treasure. Surprisingly, the author argues that the play never disappeared and that it is known to us under a different name, *Much Ado About Nothing,* which he regards as a sequel to *Love's Labour's Lost.* He thinks that it was originally called *Love's Labour's Won: Much Ado About Nothing,* and he gives a plausible explanation why the title got decapitated. By showing connections between characters in *Love's Labour's Lost* and *Much Ado About Nothing,* he lends his theory textual support. Sometimes close reading yields astonishing fruit.

At the beginning of his tenth chapter, Fleissner writes that the Hostess' account of Falstaff's last moments (*Henry V,* 2.1) contains "the most time-honored crux in literary history." Contrary to most critics, he favors the wording of the passage as given in the First Folio and considers Lewis Theobald's emendation of it a mistake. Ephim Fogel and Leslie Hotson, both leading Renaissance scholars and Shakespeareans, also hold this view.

In the First Folio version, the Hostess says of the dying Falstaff that "his Nose was as sharpe as a Pen, and a Table of greene fields." Lewis Theobald, whose edition of Shakespeare was published in 1733, saw "Table" as a typographical error caused by the printer's misreading of the script. Accordingly, he changed it to "his Nose was as sharpe as a Pen, and a' babbled of greene fields." The emendation was widely accepted, as it seemed consistent with the Hostess' statement that Falstaff moved his hands as if playing with flowers. George Lyman Kittredge, in his notes on *Henry V,* praises "the correctness of Theobald's marvellous emendation of the Folio reading." By contrast, Fleissner downgrades Theobald as "a notorious emendator." He thinks it highly unlikely that the Folio printer would have misread "babbled" as "Table" had "babbled" been in the script. The verb "babbled" would have been in lower case, whereas the noun "Table" was apt to be capitalized by the compositor. (In Elizabethan typography, nouns were often capitalized as they still are in German.) In Fleissner's view, a beginning "b" would not have been taken for a "t." His conclusion is that "table," not a form of "babbled," appeared in the manuscript from which the printer worked. Moreover, he maintains that "Table" was synonymous with "picture," a meaning that survives in the word "tableau." By his interpretation, the nose of the heavy-drinking Falstaff suggested a picture of green fields, and he adduces evidence from ancient medical literature that a green or yellowish-green complexion was associated with a disease later diagnosed as cirrhosis of the liver.

Who is right? Although the supporters of Theobald's emendation are in the majority, there is strong opposition, with Fleissner as one of its most vigorous spokesmen. Unless the questions raised by the opposition—Fogel, Hotson, Janowitz, Fleissner—are not satisfactorily answered, the problem of Falstaff's deathbed scene cannot be put to rest. In my opinion, what the author designates as "the crux of cruxes" is unlikely to be resolved in the immediate future.

Fleissner gives much attention to Shakespeare's wordplay, especially his puns. In contrast to critics who feel that the greatest English writer should have curbed his punning, the author shows an Elizabethan relish for the fun and challenge of wordplay, occasionally using apt puns that need no apology. It is precisely his pleasure in verbal virtuosity that allows him to enter so fully into the spirit and language of Renaissance England. More than most scholars, he is able to live imaginatively in the mind that created *Romeo and Juliet, Hamlet, King Lear,* and the *Sonnets.* Accepting verbal acrobatics as characteristic of Elizabethan and Jacobean style, he realizes that Shakespeare without puns would no longer be Shakespeare. As M. M. Mahood has demonstrated in *Shakespeare's Wordplay* (1957), hundreds of puns appear in his work. Only the author of *Ulysses* (1922) and *Finnegans Wake* (1939) challenges him for first place among wordplayers in British literature. Shakespeare's exuberant punning is an essential component of his art. To my mind, anyone who hates puns cannot fully appreciate Shakespeare or his contemporaries—or, for that matter, James Joyce. I am pleased that the author recognized the value of Shakespeare's wordplay instead of trying to play it down.

A self-confessed nominalist, Fleissner is keenly interested in onomastics, or the study of names, as attested by his two recent books, *Ascending the Prufrockian Stair: Studies in a Dissociated Sensibility* (Peter Lang, 1989) and *A Rose by Another Name: A Survey of Literary Flora from Shakespeare to Eco* (Locust Hill Press, 1989). Both of these studies abound in onomastic explication. In *Shakespeare and the Matter of the Crux*, he focuses his microscope on the names of characters and places in Shakespeare's work, including Othello, Shylock, Falstaff, Cordelia, Lear, Sir Oliver Mar-text, and Arden. Whenever possible he traces the etymological roots of names.

Finding the name Othello absent from Cinthio's novella on which Shakespeare based his Venetian tragedy, Fleissner reviews many possible sources of the name. The most plausible of the given alternatives, it seems to me, is Thorello from Ben Jonson's *Every Man in His Humour* (1598), a comedy in which Shakespeare acted. According to the author, Shakespeare may have switched the letters around to produce Othello from Thorello, as he later probably shifted the letters of "cannibal" to form Caliban. The explanation makes sense.

I am especially impressed with the author's analysis of the name Lear, which he scrutinizes in the light of etymology and folklore. By relating it to the Germanic adjective "le[e]r" (empty), he links the name to a major theme of the play. The idea of nothingness or emptiness looms large in *King Lear,* the darkest of Shakespeare's tragedies.

In the chapter titled "Sir Oliver, Contaminator of the Text, and Marlowe," the author proposes Christopher Marlowe as a source of the name Oliver Mar-text, the bush priest in *As You Like It* (1599). While agreeing with those who think that the name suggests Martin Marprelate, he believes that it also evokes Marlowe, whose sensational murder at a Deptford tavern in 1593 was of great interest to the London public. Accordingly, Mar-text is a conflation of Marprelate and Marlowe.

Fleissner uses onomastics in examining *Arden of Faversham,* a domestic drama based on an actual crime. Usually regarded as the best of the Shakespeare Apocrypha, this tragedy was probably a collaborative effort by several playwrights, one of whom may have been the young Shakespeare. As the author observes, the leading names in the play have too many biographical connections to be satisfactorily explained by coincidence: Arden, Greene, Will, Shakebag. On both stylistic and onomastic grounds, one may assume that Shakespeare had a hand in the work. A separate chapter, "Elizabethan Hydropathy: The Domestic Relations of *Arden of Faversham* to *The Merry Wives of Windsor*," establishes links between the tragedy and the comedy which some readers may consider watertight.

In the chapter titled "The Case of the Embarrassing Em Space: A Textual Solution to the 'W. H.' Mystery," Fleissner's talents as critic, scholar, logician, and literary sleuth converge in a remarkable effort to decipher the cryptic dedication of Shakespeare's *Sonnets* to Mr. W. H., an enigmatic figure never identified to everyone's satisfaction, though scholars have spilled oceans of ink in propounding the claims of one candidate or another. After analyzing the dedication in microscopic detail, Fleissner offers a tentative solution. But I will not reveal it, since doing so would spoil your pleasure in following his detective work to its logical denouement. I will limit myself to brief comments on some of the textual puzzles he has labored to unravel.

When Shakespeare's *Sonnets* appeared in print in 1609, he was forty-five years old and the most celebrated dramatist in England. His collection of 154 sonnets constitutes his most important writing besides the plays. Since it marks a pinnacle in the world's lyric poetry, one wants to learn all one can about the sources that inspired it and the circumstances surrounding its publication. As soon as one examines these matters, however, one is confronted by problems. The title page does not give the poet's full name, only a hyphenated variant of his surname: Shake-speare. Unlike other sonnet sequences of the period, as, for example, Sir Philip Sidney's *Astrophel and Stella* (1591), Henry Constable's *Diana* (1592), Samuel Daniel's *Delia* (1592), Michael Drayton's *Idea's Mirror* (1594), and Edmund Spenser's *Amoretti* (1595), Shakespeare's has no descriptive title, but is simply called *Sonnets*. In view of the unconventional title page and other textual evidence, Fleissner believes that the book was published without Shakespeare's official authorization.

The title page is problematic, but the dedication is a veritable maze of mysteries. Normally a dedication is written by the author, but the one that appears in the *Sonnets* was not composed by Shakespeare but by Thomas Thorpe, the eccentric publisher-printer whose initials are appended to it. By quoting from

Thorpe's writings, Fleissner shows that the man had an irrepressible penchant for idiosyncratic wordplay—puns, alliteration, cryptograms, anagrams, syntactical oddities, and typographical quirks—all of which may be found in the dedication to Mr. W. H. As set up on the page, the dedication suggests an inverted pyramid; one is reminded of George Herbert's shaped poems. All of the letters are capitalized, and there is a period after every word. An eye-catching gap or "em space" separates the initials W. H. from the next word in the line, which is ALL. This lacuna, according to Fleissner, holds the clue to the identity of the man to whom Thorpe dedicated Shakespeare's *Sonnets*.

Thorpe honors W. H. as "the onlie begetter" of the *Sonnets*. As Fleissner interprets the word, "begetter" does not refer to the person who inspired the poems but to the one who obtained them for the publisher; "begetter," then, is practically synonymous with "obtainer" or "procurer." As he is quick to point out, if "begetter" meant "inspirer" then the word "onlie" would be incorrect, since at least three sources of inspiration are reflected in the *Sonnets:* the aristocratic young man, the Rival Poet, and the Dark Lady.

The fact that W. H. is addressed as "Mr." virtually rules out any nobleman as dedicatee, since Thorpe would have used "Sir" for a person of high social rank like a knight. This consideration adds weight to the thesis that W. H. was not the young aristocrat immortalized by Shakespeare's poetry. But then, *who* was W. H.? In attempting to solve this riddle, Fleissner has vigorously exercised his powers of analysis, interpretation, and deduction, and I invite you to do likewise as you pursue his labyrinthine argument to its conclusion.

Enjoy!

Dr. Alfred Dorn
June 24, 1991

Preface

Some of the most tantalizing puzzlements in Shakespeare studies have involved cruxes: textual mainly, but also biographical, authorial, onomastic, and generally interpretive. So far, although numerous articles have appeared in the Shakespeare journals and elsewhere on these problems, no book of stature has dealt with the issue in a comprehensive or specialized manner. Indeed, few, if any, scholars might be considered specialists in crux-solving. Over the course of years, however, because my research on the greatest poet and dramatist in English has revealed a tendency in this direction, I eventually decided to compile my current thoughts in a single volume. Because most of my earlier studies are available in the standard annuals and journals already, I do not generally repeat myself but rather summarize past research in a cursory manner in the first chapter as well as preview the rest of the book.

A few partial exceptions stand out. One of the leading chapters deals with the familiar "Master W. H." identification, and I offer a supplement to my article hitherto available in *Res Publica Litterarum* (University of Kansas). My reworking is substantial, and the results are rather different from the original paper because I revise essential elements in the argument (namely apropos of the relevance of Dr. Hall's brother William and especially that of the Aldine Ovid, which was the focus of the first article, even justifying, in effect, its inclusion in *RPL*). I also take into account the recent *PMLA* article on the subject (Jan., 1987), to which I had a response (Oct., 1987). The first Appendix relating to this problem is then entirely new. Likewise, I have dealt with the identification of *Love's Labour's Won* somewhat briefly before in *Shakespeare Survey,* and my present chapter on the topic is based on that but with extensive elaboration and, with luck, new insights. (The offhand criticism that because *Love's Labour's Lost* ends with a year having to intervene before the matches can be finalized, Shakespeare could have written his *Love's Labour's Won* as a sequel to relate what happens after that 'lost' year strikes me as clever but too cavalier to be taken seriously, especially when not a scrap of information can be documented in support of that assumption.) Thus, all the chapters are essentially hitherto unpublished essays.

The organization of the crux-solving is, to a certain extent, chronological but not entirely so. It starts with an early comedy and the sonnets (many written, if not published, originally in the early Plague Years of 1592–94, though apparently with a few notable exceptions), progresses to an early tragedy, then to a later comedy, and deals with two approaches to perhaps the most tragic of the great plays, *King Lear*.

Not to be ignored is the crucial issue of the Apocrypha, most of which are commonly assigned late dates. But an early such play, one of the most time-honored cruxes throughout the centuries, is said to be the best of them, *Arden of Faversham;* the crux is in determining its precise authorship. In reconnoitering this drama, once again, as possibly apropos of Shakespeare, we shall be taking into account some startlingly 'new' material, including mainly thematic and onomastic connections with *The Merry Wives of Windsor*. The leading parallel between these two domestic plays, as they were called, is what may best be termed 'Elizabethan hydropathy,' namely the use of water as a therapeutic device to cleanse a rascal of his impurities symbolically. It will be shown that this therapy was not merely stock and certainly not anachronistic.

Since the title of the book allows for some leeway, certain matters which are not strictly aesthetic can be covered with impunity: aspects of the identification of Master W. H. and the eccentricities of Thomas Thorpe (also dealt with in an Appendix) and the psychobiographical concern with the origin of Edmund's name in *King Lear*. Finally we cope with the knotty problem of the report of Falstaff's death, coincidentally enough also apropos of *The Merry Wives*. (The Appendix on this problem is then less an afterthought than essential to the argument.) That concluding chapter confronts the timely subject of the interrelation of emblematics and heraldry to literary study. My transition to Falstaff's death in this chapter may appear abrupt and simply unchronological, but it at least is fitting to end with one of Shakespeare's most famous characters and his own end.

But there is another method of organization besides the loosely chronological, namely a thematic one which is more subtle; because consistent transitional elements are not "built into" the discussion in the chapters themselves, it will be of help to discuss the more abstract arrangements here. The first major grouping is captioned "Identification Cruxes" mainly because the vital question of identity in some ways always comes first. For example, one of Shakespeare's earliest plays, *The Comedy of Errors,* is recognized as a study in 'mistaken identity.' This grouping is then followed by the textual crux (the most common understanding of what a literary crux is, especially to bibliographers) but also in terms of a new ramification, namely 'philosophic' placement in terms of intellectual history. Yet the surprise is that the particular crux invoked is one hitherto unheard of in the annals of scholarship. The same is generally true of the next major division, "The Topical Crux," where I treat hidden meanings in the Mar-text name in a manner hitherto unacknowledged. Thus Parts III and IV are linked in this capacity. In order to end in a resounding way, the next three Parts are meant to be well-known in content and particularly provocative. The link between Chapters 6 and 7 is obviously onomastic as is that with the eighth chapter (Lear's Fool having no name other than that). Another hidden transition is that between autobiographical elements in *As You Like It* and *King Lear* (again linking Chs 6 and 7), which is a subject then broached again in Ch 9. How else then to end but with a crux to beat all the others, namely that in *Henry V*? As a further matter of transitional emphasis, *entrées* to the chapters are provided in the Table of Contents but then, for aesthetic reasons, not in the book proper.

Regarding the format of the book, MLA style is used as much as convenient, though a distinction is made between quotation marks, to indicate actually cited material, and single quotes (commonly designated 'inverted commas') to set off words and phrases not directly quoted but used in a special sense. The main reason for this distinction is tonal, but the purpose is partly that it can also serve to avoid ambiguity between what is actually quoted and what is not. Although the original Renaissance spelling and typography have been adhered to as much as possible, the *u* and *v* have been normalized for the sake of greater readability. Occasionally a letter or paper cited is not fully documented because of inadequate or inaccessible bibliographies, because (like Hobday's exciting, though modest, work on *Arden of Faversham*) they remain, to my ken, still unpublished, and because some authors have simply not responded to queries. Occasionally documentation has been, as inobtrusively as possible, interpolated in the main body of the text rather than in more ostentatious footnotes (especially allusions and cross-references to other chapters and the like). Finally, I confess to a penchant for occasional alternative expressions for the names of some authors, notably the Great Man himself. By some standards perhaps, such onomastic circumlocutions may appear unnecessary, as elegant variations, or even arch, but the tedium of oppressive repetition appeared to me in advance to be a greater flaw and hence a deterrent; I have done my best, however, to avoid having my penchant result in too obvious stylistic mannerisms. Readers have raised the caveat that my occasional attempt to divert may be taken amiss, but at least I have tried to label my style adequately. When America's leading Shakespearean, Samuel Schoenbaum, allows himself to refer to Meres's listing of Shakespeare's plays as a "Meres Nest," as he does in print, perhaps I have some justifiable precedent for a few similar turns of phrase and so invite the patient readers to bear with me if they get exasperated. (Is there, moreover, anything really arch about a Shakespeare journal, to suggest an analogy, being called *The Upstart Crow*?) After all, wordplay was part of Shakespeare's own style, and making incidental scholarly use of it upon occasion is perhaps better than, say, applying the modern abstraction *sex* to Shakespeare studies when no record of its usage to mean anything but gender can be found prior to Donne's "The Extasie," which is late for Shakespeare, and even there the assertion underscored is that "it was *not* sex" (italics added). As essentially a nominalist, I find such misapplication in modern criticism annoyingly anachronistic, and it hardly helps to say that once in a blue moon Shakespeare himself was that way, romantic though it be.

    I do confess, though, to utilizing certain expressions upon occasion which may appear more modern than Renaissance but only when I have been at a loss to find equivalent historical terms which say the same thing (for instance, in my passing reference to Shakespeare having plausibly 'kibitzed' in the rogue scenes in *Arden of Faversham*, thereby understandably contributing an element, however inadvertently or minor, to the structure); likewise, I have attempted from time to time to translate some modern idioms and put them back into a Renaissance setting by adding historical interpolations in my diction to try to give them the proper contextual flavor. These turns of phrase may be more characteristic of my own style than of style, say, as convention as such, but in some cases seemed tonally unavoidable and were not meant, in any event, to be obtrusive. It is nearly impossible, as anyone would admit, to speak to modern readership exclusively using the language of the Renaissance period alone. It is another matter, of course, to reintroduce ideological concepts which only became trendy in a much later time period. That sort of anachronistic 'rewriting' appears to me to be indefensible.

As for my incidental notations (mainly past scholarship on the popular culture pastiche level) to the exploits of Mr. Sherlock Holmes apropos of his 'solving' mysteries in the crux field, admittedly some personal therapy is here involved, yet enough precedent for this can be cited. For one thing, Arthur Conan Doyle himself was an extremely versatile writer, given to dramatic effects, and he hardly hesitated incorporating allusions to Shakespeare even in his detective fiction. The most obvious example, of course, is the familiar shibboleth "the game is afoot," which derives from the Henry plays. It occurred to me that conceivably my references to my own ventures in this line might better be deleted altogether from this book, lest some readers find such allusions comical or at best too satirical to take seriously. Granted, a certain lightheartedness is at times present that way, but faithful Conan Doyle devotees do take these matters seriously indeed, however playful their entourage. As Ecclesiastes has wisely phrased it, "To every thing there is a season" (3.1).

For aesthetic reasons, references to my previous publications for the most part will be cited in notes to Chapter 1 but not at all in the Select Bibliography. The reader can thus be spared seeing what might be taken as an arrogant listing of my past works under my name all at one time. Infrequent references to a piece or two of mine later on can easily be tracked down, if need be, in the clustered notes at the bottom of pages in the initial chapter.

Apropos of those who have helped me with this book, let me thank here the most important of the various scholars who have been of great assistance to me in making some sensitive decisions, some involved in proofreading early drafts, including Eva Horvathy of my Department, my Department Chairperson Terry Glass, Terry Otten and Robert Parker of Wittenberg University, particularly Nicholas Ranson of the University of Akron and David George of Urbana

University; likewise Ephim Fogel of Cornell, Alfred Dorn of CUNY, Cecile Cary of Wright State University, and Michael Marsden of Bowling Green State University. Two editors of relevant journals have likewise helpfully contributed their time and energy: James R. Andreas of Clemson University and editor of *The Upstart Crow;* Thomas Gasque of the University of South Dakota and editor of the journal of the American Name Society, *Names.* I am particularly grateful to Dr. Giles Dawson, associated with the Folger Shakespeare Library, for having taken the time from his busy paleographical schedule to survey the entire manuscript in late draft form. To all, many thanks.

R. F. F.

Acknowledgments

The diagram following Ch 2 has been duplicated and reset from *Shakespeare Survey* 27 (Cambridge University Press, 1974) with the permission of the editor, Dr. Stanley Wells. The reproduction of the 'Dedication' to the *Sonnets* following Ch 3 is from the 1609 edition (Q1) based on the copy in the Yale Elizabethan Club, where it was duplicated for *Shakespeare's Poems: A Facsimile of the Earliest Editions* (Yale University Press, 1964) 241. The emblems at the end of Ch 4 were examined in person at the University of Glasgow Library's collection of emblemata; they appeared in Otto van Veen's *Amorum emblemata figuris aenis incisa* (Antwerp, 1608). For practical purposes, the pictures here are taken from Otto van Veen, *Amorum Emblemata,* introd. Stephen Orgel (Garland Publishing Co., 1979), pp. 39 and 237, with permission. Because the reproductions are not claimed as unique, and because the van Veen collection scarcely is to be found in a unique repository (being available also, for example, in the University Library of Göttingen), this procedure has been followed. The reproduction of pages from the Guild Shakespeare edition of *Henry V,* ed. John F. Andrews, 348-49, is with the permission of the Doubleday Book Clubs, Doubleday and Co., New York City, and Dr. Andrews. The reproductions are at the end of Ch 10. For the copyright declaration, please turn to them.

PART I

SHAKESPEAREAN CRUXES IN GENERAL

Chapter 1
A Survey of Leading Textual Cruxes in Shakespeare

Over the course of the centuries, certain focused textual problems have been uncovered in Shakespearean study and, for want of a better generic label, have been designated cruxes. They have led to innumerable interpretations. It is easy to imagine the poet looking in and smiling as scholars have battled each other over them relentlessly. Hence the allusion in my epigraph to Matthew Arnold's familiar "Shakspeare" poem (so spelled in MS) with its apt sphinx-like smile. Still, the key memorable line there ("We ask and ask:—Thou smilest and art still . . .") is ultimately superseded by the sonnet's last three words, "that victorious brow," meaning that the human mind is at times capable of overcoming the curious obstructions of creativity.[1]

One connotation of Shakespeare's imperturbable smile may be that he held back his wisdom, allowing others to hang themselves through carelessly reading in their own views, but keeping his final intent in abeyance. This could suggest that his meaning was often enough ambiguous or even ineffable and thereby akin to the nature of the Almighty.[2] Although admittedly the full effect of his

---

[1] Brit. Mus. Add. MS. 37772, f. 44. For the full text of the original document, see R. Fleissner, "Arnold's 'Shakespeare' Textually Revisited: Accidentals—or Clues?" *The Arnoldian* 8 (1961): 62-8. The title in the manuscript is spelled differently, and the last line ends with "that Victorian Brow"—partly underscored for effect.

[2] The danger of Shakespearolatry is always with us: a caveat to be reckoned with. (All references to Shakespeare are to Harbage's Pelican edition with text taken from the Hinman edition of the First Folio of 1623 and the Yale Elizabethan Club ed. of the poems unless otherwise indicated.)

significations may never be completely intellectualized, let us not subscribe to the all-too-fashionable position that we are thereby incapable of analyzing much of it objectively with real profit. Such a pessimistic view is not only cynical but also subversive; moreover, it is neo-Kantian, in effect, suggesting unhistorically that his meaning was like that of the philosopher Kant's *Ding-an-sich* (or *inner essence*), remaining secret forever. Such an attitude is surely not in keeping with his dramatic intent, which was clearly to communicate. Too blandly do some modern, refractory critics claim that an author's basic meaning is unascertainable; all too often do they thereby bypass fundamental historical contexts in favor of implanting their own critical pursuits, even when anachronistically. Thus, for example, one literalist (Blake) has actually gone so far as to assert that Hamlet's "flesh," in his first soliloquy, is "too solid" because it tells of his being overweight. Yet, as E. E. Stoll has indicated in a key historical article, context as well as theatrical history reveal that we have no supportive evidence that the Prince was obese; on the contrary, most spectators have imagined him (based on his presumably lithe performance on stage) as active enough and even slender. His being "fat" (5.2.276) may mean only *sweaty*.

The present analysis of cruxes involves different kinds of such problems, ones best broken down in terms of the following criteria: (1) textual cruxes, both major and minor, considered in previous studies of mine, and hence not given full treatment here; (2) 'new' cruxes broken down into various subdivisions. The latter includes categories which, on the surface, may appear not to be primarily textual, and yet they all have some kind of textual bearing: identification problems such as whether the title of an apparently long-lost play may really be an alternate one for a comedy already in existence; plausibly spelling out the name of the cryptic 'dedicatee' labeled "W. H." in the 'dedication' to the *Sonnets;* considering if key meanings of words in probably the most famous sonnet, no. 116, relate to his wife, as they definitely do in no. 145 (if only because of analogous indebted meanings in a similar poem by John Donne); the philosophic crux (relating to the bearing of the textual *meane/means* issue on the problem of moderation in the story of *Romeo and Juliet*); topical problems (whether textual allusions to Mar-text in *As You Like It* relate to Marlowe, who is cited so much in the play, topically, as well as to Marprelate); problems in *King Lear* (whether the name of Edmund harks back to Shakespeare's brother, an actor with the same name, and possibly his son). Also we shall consider whether the famous "poor fool" reference at the end of this tragedy should be taken literally or figuratively, whether any textual proof supports the authenticity of *Arden of Faversham* as at all bearing on Shakespeare's hand; finally, we can ponder the most famous textual reading in the plays, the Hostess' "Table of greene fields" allusion in *Henry V*.[3] Because the specifically textual involvement in some of these cruxes may be debatable, the term "textual crux" is avoided in the main title of this book, and the various chapters are grouped under pertinent sub-headings: identification cruxes, philosophical and topical ones, cruxes in *King Lear,* the authorship crux involving internal proof, and the most famous crux of them all ("a Table of greene fields"). These can be subdivided even more into such groups as onomastic and autobiographical cruxes and as the final appendices dealing with more specialized, technical matters relating more indirectly to the main chapters.

It is appropriate to deal first with noted textual issues considered previously. Because they are some of the most talked about, reviewing them again in detail might not amount to good economy, and so they are not examined *in toto* here. Especially noteworthy has been the "sallied," "sullied," or "solid" flesh problem in *Hamlet* (1.2.129), as I have pointed out in detail elsewhere.[4] Suffice it to say now that the late Fredson Bowers' approach favored the Q readings (*sallied,* considered as a variant of *sullied*) over that of F. My own defense of "sullied" has been on 'new' grounds primarily, drawing from certain historically alchemic connotations of "sallied" or "sullied" as opposed to the flatter, later reading of "solid." To sum up the problem, the Prince, in referring to the composition of his flesh in metaphoric terms (somewhat like the Hostess alluding to Falstaff's greenish pallor

---

[3] See my "Falstaff's Green Sickness Unto Death," *Shakespeare Quarterly* 12 (1961): 47–55; "'A Table of Greene Fields,' Grasse-Greene / Table, and Balladry," *Shakespeare Jahrbuch* (East) 112 (1976): 143–9; "Putting Falstaff to Rest: 'Tabulating' the Facts," *Shakespeare Studies* 16 (1983): 57–74; "Sir John's Flesh was Grass: A Necrological Note on Falstaff and the Book of Isaiah," *American Notes and Queries* 24 (1985): 8–9.

[4] "Hamlet's Flesh Alchemically Considered," *English Studies* 59 (1978): 508–9; "Hamlet's Flesh Revisited," *Hamlet Studies* 4 (1982): 92–3. See also the chapter on the flesh crux in my book *The Prince and the Professor: The Wittenberg Connection in Marlowe, Shakespeare, Goethe, and Frost—A Hamlet / Faust(us) Analogy* (Heidelberg: Carl Winter, 1986) 69–80, 144–48. For a parody of the problem, see my "Sherlock Holmes and Shakespeare's Second Most Famous Soliloquy: The Adventure of Hamlet's Polluted Flesh," *Thalia* (Univ. of Ottawa) 10.1 (1988): 43–47.

in her description of his nose being a "Table" or picture of greenery), either is stressing his feeling dirtied for one reason or another (most likely because of his mother's all-too-hasty remarriage) or is emphasizing how he would like his very flesh to melt or decompose and turn into a new form, even as in his more famous soliloquy he yearns for death. But also implicitly he suggests that human flesh in general is sinful. Bowers argued that "sallied" must be right because Q also has the reading "sallies" (meaning "sullies") elsewhere, and because they were set by different compositors, they evidently were not misprints. F. W. Bateson's response that it is by no means unheard of for different compositors to make nearly identical mistakes strikes me, in this particular context, as not very convincing.

The next critical, textual problem of import is most probably the "base Indian/Iudean" issue in *Othello,* 5.11.347.[5] Although the earlier reading ("Indian") is preferable again on textual and this time phonic grounds, for "Judean" will not scan properly in context, Shakespeare could conceivably have changed his mind later and revised. But the evidence here again is opposed to his having done so (as with "solid"). For example, at the time of writing no proof has emerged that the word *Judean* even existed in print or was a standard usage in the year *Othello* was probably composed. If he revised, then we would have two arch-texts, as E. A. J. Honigmann has suggested. But, even as I write, new evidence suggesting that *Indian* was a misprint for *Iudean* before *Othello* may have surfaced.

First of all, the scanning problem cannot be easily dismissed. Probably "Indian" was pronounced *Injun,* even as *Medicinable* in the same context was contracted to *Med'cinable,* with the result that the scansion was something like this: "Like the base Injun, / threw a pearl away. . . ." (For this point, I wish to thank David George.) Good source material for this image can be found in Nashe and other writers, even, as I have pointed out elsewhere, in Shakespeare's own

---

[5]"The Three Base Indians in *Othello,*" *Shakespeare Quarterly* 22 (1971): 80–82 (albeit only the Constable Indian is considered a truly plausible source); "Othello as the Indigent Indian: Old World, New World, or Third World?" *Shakespeare Jahrbuch* (East) 114 (1978): 92–100; "A Clue to the 'Base Júdean' in *Othello,*" *Notes and Queries* NS 28 (1981): 137–8; "The Case of the 'Base Júdean' Revisited," *The Upstart Crow* (Univ. of Tennessee, Martin) 6 (1986): 44–53; and especially "'Base Júdean' in *Othello* Again: Misprint or, More Likely, Misreading?" *Notes and Queries* NS 35 (1988): 475–9.

work. Another word in the immediate context, *tribe,* likewise calls for *Indian* much more than *Judean.* Because Oriental Indians have seen the tragedy as one of caste, the adjective "base" has relatively low-keyed significance, appropriate in this context in which, as Eliot said, the Moor was trying to cheer himself up. But if "base" modifies "Judean," the allusion would have to be to Judas and have the meaning of *wicked.* This would make Othello's speech at this point anti-climactic, for what could be thought worse than a Judas-figure? With "Indian," *base* need imply *dark* and *lowly,* not *evil* or *ignorant.*

Yet some critics prefer "Judean" because it would seem to have more moral meaning in this context, Othello having acted like a Judas in killing his wife after kissing her and then taking his own life like the arch-betrayer. Because of other religious allusions in the tragedy, such a reading cannot be totally dismissed, but it still has major limitations. First of all, the phrase as a whole, "the base Judean," would have lent itself to anti-Semitic interpretation (as with the word "Judas-Jew" in the poetry of Herbert), which would be wise to avoid. Secondly, from a Christian point of view, the Moor's allying himself with a dark-skinned native of India in terms of universal brotherly love is perfectly in keeping with the overall historically religious context found in the tragedy, so a Judean need not enter the picture to retain the religious aura. Thirdly, biblical passages can be taken out of context to support 'preacher's license' in all kinds of ways, so that making Othello out to be a Judas-figure bent for hell (as resonant already in his very name?) is perilous. For instance, because base Othello "threw a pearl away" in this context, it has been argued that the allusion must be to Christ as the "Pearl of Great Price" in the Bible (Matt. 13.46), but it could just as readily be to a good woman whose price is far above, not "rubies" in the Genevan text Shakespeare used, but "pearls."

Nonetheless, in a fairly recent letter to the editor of the *Times Literary Supplement,* Stanley Wells pointed out that Richard Knolles's *The General Historie of the Turkes* is so probable a source for the Venetian tragedy that scholars can base the *terminus a quo* for the play on the date of his book, and in checking into the section of that work dealing with Othoman (one presumed prototype for Othello's name, not found in the Italian novella upon which Shakespeare based most of his plot), very near those passages telling of one

Michael Cossi (who, in turn, could have provided Michael Cassio's name in the tragedy), I stumbled across the following passage:

> All which fatherly kindnesse he forgetting, went about most *Iudas* like
> to have betrayed his aged father.   (Knolles 166)

Although the noun *Judas* was assuredly not uncommon then, this context offers perhaps two specific foundations for the "base Iudean" reading: First, it uses the phrase *"Iudas* like," which is akin to "like the base Iudean" (the complete phrase being compositorily isolated in parentheses); secondly, the Judas-like betrayal of a close member of the family is thus recounted in both Knolles and Shakespeare: a father in the former, a bride in the latter. To my mind, though, in spite of these parallels, they are still insufficient for fully substantiating the F reading. For one thing, it is hardly definite that the chief source for Othello's name had to be about Othoman; as I have pointed out elsewhere, and shall do here again later, it could better derive from *Otho*. Further, the best overall source for the crux, as has been pointed out by various scholars of late, is most likely in Nashe, where the context cites Indians, not Judeans (Tobin).

Another such crux that has engendered an inordinate amount of controversy, though it is far less controversial, is the "dram of eale" reading in *Hamlet,* 1.4.36. Previously I have engaged myself here in only one short note,[6] which defends a conservative position once more, namely the viewpoint that *eale* means both *ale* and, in terms of wordplay, an implied contraction of the word *evil* (*e'il*). Some of the ramifications are cited by Hilda Hulme in her valuable study of Shakespearean textuality, but her reference to "eale" as a variant of "yele," meaning beer yeast, has struck at least a few other critics as rather strained. The "eale" problem is textual, in any event, in a somewhat different sense from some other textual problems in that we do not have two variant readings thereof; it appears in two quarto versions only.

A word can also be said for what might be called the 'merry Arden' crux in *As You Like It,* 1.1.7–8. The issue is whether a hint of Shakespeare's mother's maiden name, Mary Arden, crops up invertedly and presumably inadvertently in

---

[6]"That 'Dram of Eale' Again: Textplay in *Hamlet,*" *American Notes and Queries* 21 (1983): 98–9. According to the Variorum edition, this key phrase is found only in the second and third quartos. But it is incorrect, because Q3 does not have "eale," but "ease."

the collocation of the early words "Arden" and "merry" in the comedy. They appear almost next to each other. The problem is biographical and psychotheological more than textual; I have examined it in the annual *Marianum* (published by the Pontifical Faculty in Rome), and again in a recent book dealing with onomastics.[7] (No suggestion of Shakespeare himself having been a Catholic in his adult years is at issue; the wise critic, however, has recognized that his mother and probably his father followed that faith at least at one time.) So relevance of such text-play, to coin a term, depends upon a number of prime factors, such as whether it would have got across adequately on the stage and whether two key words, *merry* and *Mary,* were then sufficiently close in sound to allow for such casual phonetic blurring. They certainly appear to have been virtually homonymic. If not, they would have been pronounced enough alike to allow for clandestine name-play, which often takes the form of latent, blurred associations.

As far as textual cruxes as such dealt with in this study go, the main one involves what might appear, but only superficially, to be a relatively minor issue in *Romeo and Juliet:* whether Shakespeare used *mean(e)* in the sense of a principle of moderation (as in the sense of the Golden Mean) or to denote *instrument* (5.3.240). It has become something of a commonplace to assert that this youthful tragedy deals with the need for temperance. The import of this crux is rather more extensive than it may at first appear in that it bears on the central issue of whether the hero would "denie" or "defie" his stars (5.1.24). Strategic critical shibboleths, such as 'Voluntarism versus Determinism,' enter the picture.

Cruxes involving onomastics deserve special attention. Among the most puzzling enigmas have been those regarding how the dramatist acquired names for characters and titles for plays. The main concern here is not so much with the etymology of names as such, but with coming to terms with the names Shakespeare originally used and then their contextual significance. To begin, some previous onomastic studies may be considered.

---

[7]"'Arden and . . . merry' / Mary Arden: Calling on Shakespeare's Mother in *As You Like It,*" *Marianum* 44 (1982): 171–7; see also my book *A Rose by Another Name: A Survey of Literary Flora from Shakespeare to Eco* (W. Cornwall, CT: Locust Hill, 1989) Ch 1, for a somewhat revised version. (My main focus there is still literary criticism.)

The most time-honored onomastic crux in all of the dramas, aside from the origin of Hamlet's name, which led to a book-length study in etymology, is probably the source of the name *Shylock*.[8] Articles on this tantalizing subject were extant already in the earliest pages of one of the oldest of learned journals, the Oxford *Notes and Queries,* and in other well-known English periodicals such as *The Gentleman's Magazine* and *The English Historical Review,* appearing in the middle of the last century. My own contribution contended that the name was originally English, not foreign, the best source for it being the analogous, venerated, recusant name of *Shacklock.* (Curiously enough, that name has been found to be most likely one source of that of another famous literary character but a figure who appeared much later, namely Sherlock [Holmes].) Whatever the main source of *Shylock,* the name was hardly based on that of Caleb *Shilocke,* as hitherto surmised (for example in the Arden edition of *The Merchant of Venice* and elsewhere), for the latter name arrived on the scene only after the fact. Hence *Shilocke* was derived from *Shylock,* not vice versa.

In a study of the etymology and connotations of King Lear's name, I next broached the subject of Nihilism versus Emptiness, of whether the playwright would have been cognizant of the anagogic idea of a spiritual emptiness waiting to be filled with grace, as evident in St. John-of-the-Cross's Dark Night of the Soul, the early English *Cloud of Unknowing,* and ancillary studies,[9] and hence the relevance of Old English *lǣre,* which then turned into *lear(e)* in Elizabethan times, meaning *empty,* both akin to the German adjective *leer.* Tracing this origin back shed new light upon a tragedy nowadays sometimes considered absurdist or downright non-Christian (pessimistically Christian from William Elton's perspective) in significance. Granted, other possibilities of deciphering the etymology of *Lear* may be germane (for instance, its harking back to the Celtic *Lyr*), but any presumed connection with *lear*ning seems after the fact, and thereby based more on, let us say, the 'learning' of the presumed etymologist than what the play itself reveals. Indeed, this arena of study is fraught with obstacles, and Murray Levith's 1978 book *What's in Shakespeare's Names* caused some

---

[8]"A Key to the Name Shylock," *American Notes and Queries* 5 (1966): 52–4.

[9]"Lear's Learned Name," *Names* (American Name Society) 22 (1974): 183–4.

controversy to this effect. But the engaging popularity of onomastics has scarcely diminished if the various name societies with their frequent meetings and journals serve as any indication. The overall danger of *Volks-etymologie* (etymologizing which is 'folksy' in nature), in any case, remains all too evident; many scholars are often not trained enough onomatologically to get behind the cursory folk meanings of names for their linguistic sources. Yet not all onomastics *is* etymological.

My previous onomastic studies have focused on such names as *Falstaff, Othello,* and *Arden*. The first issue, whether *Fastolf* or combinations like *fall-staff, fats-laff,* and the like, not to leave the often-hyphenated name of *Shake-speare* out of the running too, can be set aside. Likewise, the last: whether the name of *Arden* echoes Shakespeare's mother's maiden name not only in the Forest of Arden of *As You Like It* but also in the anonymous domestic tragedy of *Arden of Faversham,* on which more later. Let us consider here the special interest of the Moor of Venice, his unusual name, an original one with the dramatist.

Although he drew upon Cinthio's Italian novella for much of the plot of this tragedy, the name *Othello* is conspicuous by its absence there. It is likewise notably non-Italian, unless perhaps derivative of some form of dialect. It seems more like a cognate from some other name about which the tragedian read. If so, the most likely sources would be either the name of *Ottoman* (also spelled *Othoman*) in Knolles's *Historie of the Turkes,* as cited earlier, or at any rate just as likely, that of Otho I, Emperor of Rome, a name not to be confounded with that of Otho I, Emperor of the Holy Roman Empire and honored generally as Otho the Great. Since the time that my study on *Otho* appeared, incorporating the notation that a contemporary of Shakespeare, Francis Bacon, cited him,[10] some more evidence thematically favoring this etymology has come to light. First, the play itself speaks of "filching" a name (3.3.155–61), thereby inadvertently opening the way for such borrowing in reality. Secondly, it so happens that Otho's career has conveniently parallel aspects with the noble Moor's.

To begin, Marcus Salvius Otho (A.D. 32–69) was Emperor of Rome during the time of Nero, who took it upon himself to live with Otho's spouse, Poppea

---

[10]"The Moor's Nomenclature," *Notes and Queries* NS 25 (1978): 143.

Sabina, for about a decade. Such adultery naturally led to a break-up of the Otho-Nero comradeship, but even then the Emperor declined to divorce his gorgeous wife. The overall situation apropos of *Othello,* where the Moor has trouble with *his* better half, owing to her indiscretions so soon after marriage in defending Cassio, who, he thinks, because of Iago's machinations, is having an *affaire d'amour* with her, is analogous. Similarly, Othello is credulous as well. Like Otho, the proud hero does not seek a divorce, let alone separation. His alternative method of coping is hardly requisite to rehearse here, but in any event he acted in a petty way compared with Otho and so might be thought of as truly a diminutive Otho in this respect, thereby as an Oth-*ello* (accommodating an Italian diminutive normally not used with proper names). Secondly, Otho, like Othello, was once enslaved and then liberated. Finally, both leaders stoically stabbed themselves during the finale. Otho succumbed with the same kind of weapon, a dagger, and by a bed as well, with the fatal instrument concealed under a pillow, even as the Moor applied a pillow to asphyxiate Desdemona.

Strong competition exists in that various other candidates for the Moor's name also emerge. Probably the most prominent has been that of *Othoman,* whom we may feel inclined to dispense with right off, since he was a leader of the Turks, whom Othello is to engage in combat. Even though it is likely enough that Othello was first a Muslim before his required conversion when he married an Italian Catholic (the play's subtitle, *The Moor of Venice,* signifying as much), he still castigates the Mohammedan as a "circumcised dog" (5.2.55). It is more likely that his being called a Moor was owing largely to his skin complexion being dark, or his having 'black blood,' than to his being identified with Muslims in any contextually germane manner. (The etymology of the word *Moor* confirms this.) It would appear not only coincidental but rather strange if Othello were named directly after a celebrated leader of the Turks.

Another onomastic candidate not easily to be dismissed is Thorello from Jonson's *Every Man in his Humour,* Shakespeare having acted in a production of that comedy. Thematic analogies between the plots of the two plays have occasioned recent research (McDonald). Plausibly Shakespeare could have switched the letters around, even as *Caliban* amounted to an orthographic shifting of letters in the word *cannibal* (a variant being then often spelled with a single "n"), and other partial anagrams can be cited. Yet one of the earliest correlations was uncovered in 1869 by B. H. C. in *Notes and Queries:* The allied name of *Othelio* was found registered in Venice in 1606. Since Othelio happened to be an attorney, however, his career would at any rate hardly link with the Moor's bellicose one, and so this parallel, on balance, seems only accidental.

One of the technical problems has been with regard to the first three letters of the Moor's name: Were they originally Greek or Germanic? The Hellenic *theta* comes readily to mind, but other linguists have defended a Teutonic origin of at least the *Oth* syllable. For example, *The Oxford Dictionary of English Christian Names* relates the name *Otto* back to the Old English adjective *ead,* meaning *rich;* evidently this scrap of information led an intrigued scholar, in an article directly following mine in print, to posit that likewise "Othello is an Italian name (of Teutonic origin) meaning 'rich'" (Macey). He defended this etymology on the grounds that the Moor was of royal blood and called his wife a pearl, indeed in mercenary terms as one "richer than all his tribe." Consequently, if the name *Otho* is relevant here at all, it might point to the German emperor *Otho* (an old spelling of *Otto*), whose dates were much later than those of the Roman ruler and incidentally concerning whom Keats later wrote a play. Apparently from this false association, the quaint or curious notion arose that the name of the Moor of Venice was actually based on an old German soldier's name.[11]

In any event, if the earlier *Otho* was the basis for the name of *Othello,* the Teutonic connection would hardly also hold, but then the Greek etymology could appear just as likely. Compare, for instance, such a Greek name as *Otheitiuium* (that of a berry), if only because a strawberry becomes a leading symbol in the play, appearing on Desdemona's memorable handkerchief. On this basis, it has been urged that Othello's name and designation may best derive geographically from the Morea: "With regard to the origin of the name nothing definite is known. . . . It has been held that the 'Otelli del Moro' were noble Venetians, originally from the Morea, whose device was the mulberry—perverted in the play into a strawberry, upon the handkerchief" (Stokes 240–1). Curiously enough, *moro* in Italian can mean both *mulberry* and *black Moor*. Then again, a certain Christofalo Moro was the name of a heroic Lord-Lieutenant of Cyprus, who in

---

[11]"Addendum: Chasing a Ghost," *Names* 24 (1976): 75–6.

1508 returned to Venice. In any event, since it appears that Shakespeare invented the term *Ottomites* in the play (2.3.161), it is not unlikely that he thought up that of the noble Moor as well, whereupon we should be hard pressed to discern the main source. The Avon bard's inscrutable smile, surmounted by that impenetrable, victorious brow, seems in this instance in complete control, leaving us without a definite answer in terms of literary history.

The first major onomastic concern in this book is the identity of a 'missing' play, namely *Love's Labour's Won*. The inverted commas around the descriptive term 'missing' have no bearing on Eric Sams's controversial edition of *Edmund Ironside,* which he dubbed *Shakespeare's Lost Play,* although most critics doubt that the stylistically mediocre drama later is Shakespeare's. It was, moreover, never truly 'lost' to begin with. No: The intent behind using quotation marks around *missing* is to imply that although *Won* (as it will henceforth be largely abbreviated) has been presumed to be the title of a lost drama, it may rather amount to an alternate title for a comedy the canon already possesses. Whereas this chapter got its start with forerunners in the *Times Literary Supplement, Shakespeare Survey,* and *English Studies,*[12] considerably more material has now been adduced in the way of evidence and argument. Because presuming to add anything, in whatever mode, to the Shakespearean canon would seem to be of greater moment than any other endeavor (the risks being commensurate with the challenge), this chapter perforce comes second.

The next major concern here with nomenclature is with the identity of the enigmatic Master W. H. in the so-called 'dedication' to the *Sonnets*. This inclusion is of very special interest at this time owing to the fairly recent "W. H." controversy in *PMLA,* which happened to entail a response of mine.[13] Although

---

[12] *"Love's Labour's Won* and the Occasion of *Much Ado," Shakespeare Survey* 27 (1974): 105–10; correspondence entitled "Much Ado" in the *TLS,* 1 August 1975: 874; 24 May 1985: 579; "Shakespeare's *Carte Blanche* —Appropriated by Marston," *English Studies* 56 (1975): 390–2. See also my "'Love' in Tennis," *American Notes and Queries* 10 (1972): 89.

[13] "The Case of the Embarrassing Lacuna: A Textual Approach to the W. H. Mystery," *Res Publica Litterarum* (Univ. of Kansas) 3 (1980): 17–29; "A Sherlockian Treatment of the Mystery of the Dedication to Shakespeare's Sonnets," (Bowling Green University) 6.1 (1985): 57–66 (rpt in *The Sherlockian*); correspondence in *PMLA* 102 (1987): 839–40. See also "A Plausible Mr. W. H.," *Notes and Queries* NS 16 (1969): 129.

this little textual puzzle does not, strictly speaking, involve Shakespeare's own creativity, its inclusion is justifiable if the meaning of my subtitle is seen in a broad light. The argument includes many new items and then is supplemented with additional material in the first of the appendices.

The third major concern here with onomastics is with the cognomen of Sir Oliver Mar-text in *As You Like It* (based on my paper for an international Marlowe event in England). Akin to my earlier study of the name *Arden,* the inference is that Mar-text's name (hyphenated in the First Folio) and role entail topical meaning that goes beyond the commonplace Martin Marprelate associations. This approach is admittedly oblique, but the inferential evidence is worthy of cautious consideration, particularly since this play, perhaps more than others, is permeated with clandestine political and autobiographical allusions. In defense of such a topical approach, I claim that the comedy's title definitely implies that the playwright was trying to accomplish what appealed to his audience rather than that the audience was automatically given *carte blanche* to do with the work simply what it wanted. Too many modernistic productions have based themselves upon the wrong heuristic assumptions in this regard. The hint of satire in Mar-text's name is of much modern interest, too, though the parodic approach is fraught with encumbrances, notably the peril that the wary reader will look askance at what he reads as critical parody-hunting.

A final onomastic approach comes in the section on *King Lear,* the tragic density of which has so often obfuscated the scholarly world. Its very fabric seems august and permeated with raw material for the literary archeologist. Does the key figure of brother Edmund have autobiographical relevance? Such a fair number of Edmunds figured in Shakespeare's background and reading in one way or another that it is perilous to try to pinpoint where he might best have had recourse to the old forename. Edmunds are to be traced in history books and religious tracts as well as literary writings. But the insinuation that this resonant name in its context derives particularly from his own family background is at least worth taking up, if only for its psychobiographical import.

Throughout, cruxes not specifically associated with onomastics but still having autobiographical and textual relevance are considered. Included in the first section is a study of sonnet 116 in terms of the theme of the 'Faithful Wife.' A few other sonnets might also be placed in this category; it is tempting to posit a subgrouping. But the more intriguing association is textually with John Donne's "A Valediction: forbidding mourning," which has so often also been taken as about his spouse. The evidence suggests that Donne pilfered a bit from Shakespeare, an alignment which helps to shed light on the probable meaning on some of the terms in no. 116.

To turn to *Lear* again, the section on this tragedy of tragedies ends with one of the stickiest problems in interpretation: the King's stirring exclamation "And my poore Foole is hanged!" (5.3.306). A good bit of new information is here adduced to material already in print, which includes my notes in the "Critical Forum" section of an Oxford journal, a paper for a Shakespeare session of the MLA, another paper for the seminar on imagery in *King Lear* at the International Shakespeare Association Congress in West Berlin in 1986, and so on.[14] Of particular value has been an article (that appeared, about the same time as my West Berlin paper, in *Review of English Studies*) which provided striking new evidence that Lear did not believe that Cordelia had been hanged or was deceased when he uttered his crucial line (Williamson). More recently (1989), a leading scholar has likewise defended the *literal* reading of the line, which is my own penchant (Everett, *Young Hamlet* 80-1).

This interpretive crux relates to the earlier study of the meaning of "meane" in *Romeo and Juliet,* though there several textual variants come into play as well. The intent of that chapter is not meant to be on friar-bashing, as it were, although a number of recent articles have criticized the professionalism of the leading cleric in that tragedy. Having had especially friendly and profitable associations *en passant* with Franciscans myself in years gone by, I see the emphasis more on the inherent need for classical, as opposed to strictly "Christian," virtues, those of moderation.

An entire section is devoted to the old apocryphal warhorse *Arden of Faversham.* Begun as a paper read at the second Ohio Shakespeare Conference (University of Dayton, 1978), and subsequently selected for the printed

---

[14]"Lear's 'Poor Fool' as the Poor Fool," *Essays in Criticism* 13 (1963): 425-7; "Lear's 'Poor Fool' and Dickens," ibid. 14 (1964): 425; "Lear's Proletarian Fool," *Shakespeare Newsletter* 27 (1977): 2. (The last item was based on a paper for Special Session 255, The Modern Language Assn. of America annual meeting, Chicago 1976.)

Proceedings,[15] it incorporates material from my entry in a special volume of the *Dictionary of Literary Biography* edited by the late Fredson Bowers.[16] In delving into the plausibility of Shakespeare's at least partial involvement in the final composition of this domestic tragedy, I choose to put the notion of a single author up for question if only because of the inherent differences in the textual style. For instance, Arden exemplifies punning and low comedy mixed with melodramatic effects; professional murderers hold forth in high-flown poetry; the play has elements of immaturity conflated with solid structure and evidence of craftsmanship in other respects.

More and more, however, it has come to be recognized that numerous 'echoes' of this play appear in Shakespeare's writings and by no means only, or perhaps even mainly (as has been thought), in *Macbeth*. I am indebted here to C. H. Hobday's British paper *"Arden of Faversham:* A Case Reopened," unpublished at the time of writing and to which I refer with his kind permission. Such echolalia need not mean that the master playwright was necessarily in any way responsible for the earliest script, because he may only have acted with it. Yet in the final version, in the collaborative formation of what can be called an 'actors' play,' his 'touch' may at times still be present. In any event, leading names in the tragedy have a seemingly striking and thus possibly more than coincidental connection with those relating to his family: *Arden, Greene, Will,* and *Shake* (the standard abbreviation given there of *Shakebag*). In this respect, this chapter relates also to those dealing more specifically with onomastics.

Nonetheless, numerous textual parallels have been discerned also in Marlowe (not so many any more are claimed to be in Kyd). Still, no other evidence exists that Shakespeare and Marlowe in any respect collaborated. In fact, they were very likely not collaborative but the Rival Poets. Relevant here is the chapter on *As You Like It,* where allusions to Marlowe are brought to the fore. Whether the reference to the Forest of *Arden* in that comedy is purely coincidental will have to be considered. In any case, the chapter on the Faversham play in this book represents an entirely 'new' approach, although once again stressing the import of internal

---

[15]"'The Secret'st Man of Blood': Foreshadowings of *Macbeth* in *Arden of Feversham,*" *The University of Dayton Review* (special Shakespeare issue) 14 (1979/80): 7–13.

[16]*"Arden of Faversham," DLB* 62 (1987): 361–64.

evidence. Although Samuel Schoenbaum has argued that authorship can scarcely be determined on the grounds of such proof alone, other notable textual scholars, such as Ephim Fogel of Cornell, have not entirely agreed.

The final major chapter deals with the crux of cruxes, the Great Crux, or the subject of the most textual controversy: Mistress Pistol's reference to Falstaff's death and his nose being like "a Table of greene fields" in *Henry V* (2.3.16–17). Again it is Ephim Fogel who deserves the credit for stressing the import of this Folio reading, though numerous editors and critics have since done their best to discourage him. My own attempts to defend his position appeared in standard Shakespearean journals[17] but have hardly discouraged Gary Taylor in his new Oxford edition of the play from demoting the Folio reading in favor of Theobald's emendation "'a babld of greene fields," which is probably the most famous emendation of them all as well. In presenting new information now favoring "Table," perhaps I should clarify certain points at the outset, for most readers will doubtless be prejudiced in favor of the emendation owing to the latest scholarship relating to Shakespeare's handwriting (Dawson). The first point is that those who argue that the "Table" reading can be explained as an *erratum* on the grounds of the compositor having misread Shakespeare's penmanship are begging the question. They *assume* that the Folio reading is in error, and only then do they posit reasons to account for it. The second point is that no record exists of Shakespeare having ever used the word *babbled* (however spelt) in print elsewhere. The third point is that the capitalization of "Table" indicates that the compositor most likely set the noun deliberately and not accidentally. (Comparable is the capitalization of nouns in German.) Other subtleties will be discussed in the chapter itself, which then has an important but more speculative follow-up in the appendices.

One crux that has been deliberately omitted from this book is that of the identity of the so-called Dark Lady of the *Sonnets,* an age-old problem on which, largely owing to my teaching environment, I have expended much time and speculation and have centered a number of articles (one of which a colleague

---

[17]See n3.

translated into Spanish).[18] The reasons for bypassing this fascinating female now are not to be misconstrued as ungallant, so they might best be summed up here. First, the problem is almost entirely an autobiographical one and hence not directly related to literary issues as such. It is even more this way than the Edmund matter, where we have at least definite literary nomenclature to go by. Although the issue bears some tangential affinity to the identity of Master W. H., the difference is that there the problem is *strictly* non-literary (yet introducing the greatest poetry ever).

Secondly, my approach has been to consider the Dark Woman as racially non-Caucasian, a view espoused already in the last century by a German scholar (Jordan), not to mention in this one by Anthony Burgess in a popular book on Shakespeare, several novels, and published interviews. Indeed, he expressed the hope to me when he was a Visiting Professor of English at the City College of New York, where I used to teach, that he then expected to make a film out of Shakespeare's life and have a prominent African American—who just happens to be an alumna of the university at which I now teach—play the role (Warner Bros. reneged on this). Yet admittedly the Dark Lady could have also been Welsh in her darkness or of Italian lineage (giving passing credit to A. L. Rowse's questionable candidate, Emilia Bassano Lanier). Lastly, no solid evidence exists that the mysteriously dark mistress was more than a figment of the poet's imagination, so does it really matter? Most probably, Shakespeare did not directly authorize the publication of his sonnets and may also have suppressed their republication (see the chapter on W. H.), so she may well have been real enough, but, in any case, something has to be left for a future project.[19]

This book by its very nature provides a new approach to Shakespeare studies: in-depth consideration of specific cruxes almost for their own sake.

---

[18]"That 'Cheek of Night': Toward the Dark Lady," *CLA Journal* 16 (1973): 312–23; "Herbert's Aethiopesa and the Dark Lady: A Mannerist Parallel," ibid. 19 (1976): 458–67; "Shakespeare's Sonnet 137," *Explicator* 35 (1977): 21–2; "William Dunbar's Sultry Pre-Shakespearean Dark Lady," *The Upstart Crow* 3 (1980): 88–96. The last was read at the annual CLA meeting in Washington, D.C., in 1979. It was translated by William Felker as "La Dama Negra en la Poesia de William Dunbar" for *Káñina* (Univ. of Costa Rica) 5 (1981): 111–14.

[19]Other essays of mine to be cited *en passant* include *"Brassica Hirta: Non Sanz Droict* Re-echoed," *The Coat of Arms* NS 5 (Autumn, 1982): 81–4; "Donne and Dante: The Compass Figure Reinterpreted," *Modern Language Notes* 76 (1961): 315–20; "The Malleable Knight and the Unfettered Friar: *The Merry Wives of Windsor* and Boccaccio," *Shakespeare Studies* 11 (1978): 119–20.

Whereas previous book-length studies have focused on various textual issues in a limited capacity, such as Hilda Hulme's work on lexical problems cited earlier or that by Paul Jorgensen (called *Redeeming Shakespeare's Words*), no book of any length has taken major (as well as a few minor) cruxes at large and considered them for themselves. (Jorgensen's work, incidentally, dealt mainly with words that act as running metaphors in the plays and so is not directly apropos here.) Only one volume has tackled the issue of such cruxes head on at all, an antiquated and rather inaccessible compendium by Benjamin Gott Kinnear learnedly entitled *Cruces Shakespearianae*. It is far too dated and limited in its approach to be acknowledged in any more detail in the present work.

PART II
IDENTIFICATION CRUXES

Chapter 2

Much Ado about *Love's Labour's Won:* Shakespeare's 'Missing' Comedy

The proposition that a label like *Much Ado About Nothing* was initially an alternative title for another drama, such as the so-called long-lost *Love's Labour's Won,* a play ascribed to Shakespeare by both Francis Meres and a bookseller's list, is worth careful reconsideration for the reason that no more rewarding pleasure may befall the true Shakespeare scholar than the recovery or identification of a purportedly missing item from the canon. And in no other comedy by the playwright, not even *The Taming of the Shrew,* is found such stress on the winning of love as in *Much Ado.* Such, at any rate, is the present thesis.

In this chapter, let us, first, summarize the major *Ado/Won* correlations set up by scholars thus far and then consider any new pointers available in favor of this purported titular reassignment. In so doing, we shall concern ourselves with the following matters: the ethical issue involved in the choice of a respectable dramatic title; psychological, theological, and pedagogical aspects; the initial registration of the comedy, its inherent wordplay and title-play, and various other textual concerns; problems involving secondary versus alternate titles; finally, other proposed reassignments for the 'missing' play and title. As for the demurrer that *Much Ado* is simply a worthwhile title to retain because it aptly characterizes Claudio's prominent but unnecessary fuss in his marriage ceremony, we might respond that such fretting actually alludes to much ado about a great deal, at least if we bear sensibly in mind Don John's association with Don John of Austria, an affiliation which now is said to have historically prompted the play's basic entanglement (see H. Richmond). The notion that the old title which we have had to put up with for so long is finally in need of replacement or at least being alternated with what purports to be an older one need not be ruled out or scoffed at. An open mind is always salutary.

I

All such ado is a good bit to expect when the record would seem to indicate that the only 'smoking gun' available for purposes of identification is simply the mysterious title, *Love labours wonne,* with apparently not a word of new text to accompany it. Still, should we decline to try to accommodate the title to a play already extant, do any very reasonable alternatives remain? We might momentarily chance the opinion that a play from Shakespeare's richly productive middle period merely melted into what he called "thin air"—an unthinkable proposition. The recently published controversy surrounding the *Edmund Ironside* manuscript might also be enlisted, insofar as that drama was discovered only at the end of the last century; but, in any case, that problem differs from that of *Won* because, if the former play is at all Shakespeare's (which is doubtful), it might derive only from the time when he was involved mainly in 'apprentice' work. True, the title of at least one other of his supposed plays represents a vanished work, but that seldom-cited collaboration, *Cardenio,* was very late, and insufficient evidence exists that it was even partly by him. How so? Because no truly adequate reason appears for trusting the eighteenth-century claim that a play partially by Shakespeare was adapted by Theobald for his *Double Falshood.* The bulk of evidence, as augmented by Theobald's purported adaptation, argues for, at best, the style of Fletcher, not Shakespeare in addition (rather than, say, an imitator's). The allusion to Shakespeare in the *Stationers' Register* was clearly inserted as an afterthought following an end-stop and does not appear to be at all reliable. We have no evidence that the Stratfordian ever took an interest in Cervantes, the source of the Cardenio story. Also it is reasonable that more plays by Shakespeare said to be absent from the First Folio may have been simply early drafts of other dramas there represented. At any rate, to presume that another title, like *Cardenio,* rivals *Won* in being that of another missing masterpiece is to mislead the unsuspecting reader. Such, at least, is a worthwhile caveat.

Next, let us consider that the master dramatist may simply not have composed a work entitled *Love's Labour's Won* to begin with; that Meres, who cited it in 1598, simply erred or referred to a work then in progress (an unlikely event). Edward Hubler once raised the issue of an error, but then the subsequent finding of a bookseller's stocklist, with the title represented again, ruled out that theory but substituted a new one by T. W. Baldwin no more satisfactory.

For what it may be worth as a temporary digression, this notable discovery was regrettably left unmentioned in the new Penguin edition of Edmund Crispin's ingenious mystery story *Love Lies Bleeding,* which concerns itself with the finding of this 'lost' play. (Although, granted, such popular-culture treatment of a serious matter may initially produce at best arch or critical smiles, it can at least also be enlisted *en passant* as ingeniously germane to this discussion.) Curiously, the story does mention tentatively linking the title with *Much Ado* and does not cite the main rival candidates, *All's Well* or *The Shrew,* in this connection (Crispin 151), yet the author's inventive suggestion toward the end, that *Love's Labour's Lost* simply needed a sequel—hence *Love's Labour's Won* arrived on the scene and was then presumably unsuccessful (as often enough sequels are) and thereby unpublished (253)—is pure, unadulterated conjecture, however pleasant it may be to meditate lightheartedly. Crispin does note that some other plays, for example Jonson and Dekker's *Isle of Dogs,* have also evanesced (see Sams), yet it is far more unlikely that a successful 'middle period' play went agley. (True, the Folio did omit a couple of plays in which Shakespeare had a hand, but they were only late collaborations.) Yet we can 'learn' from Crispin.

The presumption that *Won* could have been a successful sequel to *Lost* which then easily acquired another title does, however, make good sense. A suitable contention is that *Won* was not what the dramatist merely *elected* to write, but instead a work which, for one reason or another, came to be registered in print with a variant title.

A further alternative inference to be first considered before trying to identify positively our 'playless' title is that the dramatist did not truly *want* (or need) a sequel to *Lost,* for that way we could pass over that problem altogether. Yet, in doing so, we might feel somewhat intellectually thwarted, especially when we take into account Jonson's precedent in setting up similar brother-sister plays, like *Every Man in* and *Every Man out,* as well as such complementary dramas as *A*

Knack to Know a Knave set off against *A Knack to Know an Honest Man*. We should, moreover, be leaving in the lurch one of the great Shakespearean mysteries without a semblance of a solution. Doubtless any plausible clues that are presently available to help point to a rational explanation for this identification mystery deserve at least passing scrutiny, if only because such an enigma never fails to tantalize the literary sleuth, not to mention the world at large. In any event, certain aspects of the problem, at least, are not merely speculative, and the responsible thing to do is to concentrate on them. So let us first scrutinize some of my past findings on the problem, supplementing these when possible.

My first examination of the identity of *Won* (*"Love's Labour's Won* and the Occasion of *Much Ado"*) was arrived at as follows: After trying cautiously to dispense with other previously suggested identifications of this 'lost' play for various express reasons, I fastened on *Much Ado* as clearly the best option. The main rationale evidently escaped some reviewers and critics, namely the extremely arresting affinity to be drawn between the order of the plays in Meres and that in the Great Folio. (See the diagram appended at the end of this chapter.) For instance, this rationale bypassed the critic for *Shakespeare Survey* and thereby the evaluatory examination in detail by G. Harold Metz, who then relied on that earlier evaluation in giving my argument rather short shrift (5). He made a big point of saying that I see *Won* as a subtitle but that, though I state that "a number of Shakespeare's ... comedies have similar 'flippant' subtitles" (105), I do "not enumerate them" (8). Now, aside from the most obvious example, *What You Will* (the subtitle for *Twelfth Night*), *Measure For Measure* was given the somewhat flippant, alternate title of *Beauty the Best Advocate* (in 1699), the plausibly Shakespearean (?) *Iphis and Iantha* was likewise fatuously subtitled *A Marriage Without a Man*, and even *The Merchant of Venice*, which was considered a comedy in the Folio, was originally registered with the subtitle *The Jew of Venice*, which may be considered a bit casual, too, insofar as it hardly sums up the mainstream of the play, Shylock not even appearing in Act V. (*As You Like It* meant "what the audience wants," was not flippant.)

In a word, it appears that the Folio arrangement came into being directly by way of Meres, even though his 'coarse' or hodgepodge listing was clearly not chronological and hardly of the playwright's own devising. The order of the Folio has been dubbed and deflated as "that repository of coarse distinctions" (Berry

25), but the basic question is *how* it came to be that way (not so much *why* it should have been so). One fairly plausible answer is that it simply deigned to follow the order in Meres.

Naturally the extent of these parallels has to be limited to the plays cited by Meres, for he did not name them all. In the parallel arrangements, we can readily detect that the title of one of the comedies is conspicuously out of alignment. Then if it is reinstated in its natural position, corresponding to what the parallel lists would require, we find that the title *Love labours wonne,* as Meres termed it, is situated directly opposite *Much Ado About Nothing* in the Folio. The proposed correlation bears good factual weight, therefore, is not merely random speculation, though some skeptics might at first find it no more than coincidental. The only serious animadversions which might arise regarding its import concern the plausible reason or lack thereof for any such parallel listings. Why, one might inquire, should Heminges and Condell, Shakespeare's fellow actors and shareholders who set up the order of the plays in the Folio, have elected to follow the lead of a relatively little known, seemingly hack writer like Meres? For if they did not deliberately take after him, the arrangements would amount to little more than a singular set of chance parallels. Such an eventuality, one without any acceptable explanation, would be rather more startling in itself than our attributing the parallel order merely to the Folio having been, let us say, 'a mirror of Meres.'

Such puzzlement, not directly addressed in my earlier research, deserves some candid response now. First, an odd misassignment in the Folio could well have occurred because the titles did not quite correlate. Heminges and Condell apparently did not have any inkling that *Much Ado* might have originally been penned as *Won;* or, if we say that as the dramatist's fellow actors, they might be expected to have known, let us add that they simply preferred the published title, which, after all, from a theatrical point of view, may have seemed more sensibly low-keyed. Or, as Leslie Hotson has pointed out, an abrupt title like *Love's Labour's Won* could even have suggested an imprecision, since it was *de rigueur* to speak of love's effort as finally or duly accomplished, but not precisely as 'won.'

Now why exactly would they have so formally imitated Meres? Why should they *not* have, let us respond with a *tu quoque,* if they were prompted by none other than the master of form, Ben Jonson himself? For it is reasonable enough that this famed challenger in wit-combat at the Mermaid did have something vital to do in bringing about the Folio order (though this tradition has been challenged by Samuel Schoenbaum). Several pieces of evidence spring to mind. Most noticeably, *The Tempest* was placed first rather than last, where it should normally be expected, at least in terms of the development of Shakespeare's dramaturgy. And why first? Probably because, in part, it accorded best with Jonson's acclaimed predilection for the classical 'Unities.' Another reason could have been the very popularity of the play then, although such stress on 'relevance' or 'timeliness' seems like a relatively odd or at least minor criterion for editing or for scholarly procedure in general. The Folio plays, moreover, were prefaced with the superb Jonsonian eulogy on Shakespeare which dutifully acknowledged his debt to Meres itself, most notably in the mention made of Ovid. Thus Jonson is said to have echoed "Meres's tribute, that 'the Muses would speak with *Shakespeares* fine filed phrase, if they would speak *English,*' by praising the poet's 'true-filed lines' (68), and he extends Meres's suggestion that Shakespeare be compared to great classical playwrights" (van den Berg 210), a point also made in John Davies' epigram "To our English Terence, Mr. Will. Shake-speare." This also appeared in the Folio.

The printing of the Folio followed in the wake of the fine example of the first edition of Jonson's plays, its only predecessor, as has been duly recognized (van den Berg). Proceeding further, we observe that in 1616, the year of the Stratfordian's death, a marked gap occurred in Jonson's productive activity, one which has reasonably been connected with the commencement of the editorial labors involved in the compilation of the First Folio under the direction of the Pembroke group. Especially intriguing with regard to Jonson's possible hand in the contents of the Folio and their relation to the Meres order, then, is the suggestion that "the exclusion of *Pericles* from the First Folio may reflect Jonson's aesthetic judgment, if in fact he played a strong editorial role in the project" (van den Berg 207). W. W. Greg and others proposed that Jonson was even the author of the prefatory letter generally attributed to Heminges and Condell, and the implications of this thesis would further support my argument. This aesthetic thesis needs to be given due weight in terms of a recent scholarly tendency to reject *Pericles* as being, in whole or in part, non-Shakespearean

(Thomas 448–50). It would perhaps add further credence to the matter of why other doubtful plays, like *Edmund Ironside* or *Cardenio,* were excluded as well.

Further, Meres's import must be recognized for what it was. He was actually not altogether a 'hack writer'; he had, indeed, a certain scholarly reputation, having received two degrees from Cambridge, one from Oxford, having been both schoolmaster and rector, and finally but above all having first properly assessed Shakespeare's title to fame. His *Palladis Tamia* means "The Housekeeper of the Goddess of Wisdom" (Pallas Athene), an appropriately wise, domestic, modest, hardly merely hackneyed or servile designation. Is it then too much to assume that Heminges and Condell in effect wanted to follow the lead of Jonson himself in paying tribute to Meres by further accepting the latter's order of the plays? Hardly so. Or, better yet, Jonson himself could have had some editorial hand in the Folio arrangement. A critic or compiler like Meres could do worse, one might fancy, than following the bidding of Athene's own housekeeper. Or should it be contended that Shakespeare's fellow actors would more readily have followed their master's own order? But then they would not necessarily have known of that. In any event, clearly they did not apply themselves to the master dramatist's workings in seriatim fashion because the plays are no more presented in the order in which he wrote them than in the order of their own chronology. In fact, as far as the author's own intent was concerned, the assemblers would scarcely seem to have known what they were about, having placed *The Tempest* as a curtain-raiser rather than at the end, even carelessly omitting *Troilus and Cressida* from the Table of Contents altogether. And how, it might be further asked, could a truly collected edition of the master's works have come off the press without his narrative poetry and sonnets? Was, then, the edition not somewhat hastily devised? Such anomalies were, however, hardly inordinate sins of omission or commission because the actors' conscientious interest was evidently centered almost entirely on what they considered to be the internal accuracy of the plays themselves, though this may have led to some alarming misreadings, like Othello comparing himself to "the base Judean" when that phrase simply did not scan in context. But, whatever the cause, the parallel orders in Meres and the Folio represented something more than an adventitious overlapping, the result being, to accommodate our Elizabethan-like punning figure of speech, 'A Mirror of Meres.'

In this connection, two other points in my earlier published research on the subject should be recapitulated and recast. Both deal with the issue of occasion as focused on in the title of my initial article. The initial point was that the comedy was originally registered as *Much Ado* rather than as *Won* because of incidental in-house jesting. Granted, it was a rather curious example at that, though scarcely was unusual by Elizabethan standards. The idea was that the clientele of the Mermaid could easily have entertained themselves by linking the title *Much Ado About Nothing,* which can lend itself to farcical exaggeration by its very nature, of course, with the play's having been technically "staied" in A.D. 1600—hence allowing for some convenient, even pictographic title-play, namely upon the form "Ad oo" (then so spelt). The inherently playful paronomasia might be decoded as follows: A D [16]00. (On such usage apropos of *Venus and Adonis* and *The Rape,* see Franson.) In a word, the "Nothing" of the title makes a certain amount of pictographic sense when taken literally as a reference to the year of registration, and pictography, in point of fact, was, for what this may be worth, in the process of coming into its own as literary byplay. Not very much later it developed most conspicuously in the hieroglyphic or 'shape' poetry of George Herbert. In sum, trivial or irrelevant though this modish stylistic mannerism may appear to modern critics, it went over well enough in the Renaissance and so should be finally given its due here. Granted, it can also be overrated if taken too far or by itself alone.

Supporting this thesis somewhat was Hotson's discovery in his leading book (1949) that Shakespeare named, as a trustee on a parchment indenture, one William Johnson, a vintner who became host of the Mermaid Tavern; Hotson then proved that John Jackson, also mentioned in the document, was a member of the "fraternity of the Mermaid" (76–140). It is thereby reasonable to aver that Shakespeare frequented the Mermaid often enough and would scarcely have been apodeictically opposed to such tavern jesting as has been proposed. Again, for what it may be worth, other attempts to justify the likewise seemingly flippant title of *Much Ado About Nothing* have been legion, ones which have been, to some modern minds at least, rather hard to assimilate, some even rather gross in conception. (One of the directors of the BBC television series on the canon I heard lecturing at Oxford on this title. He saw it as analogous to Pauline Reage's notorious, modern-day novel *Story of O,* if only because of the supposedly hidden, vaginal implications in both titles.) Yet most probably the general over-popularity of the present-day title does not relate actually to the possible undercurrents of an obscene jest so much as to the oft-acclaimed Englishman's innate love of litotes or the low-keyed effect. How much more of an understatement can one get, after all, than "Much Ado About *Nothing*"? Such 'justification,' however, hardly makes up for the commonsensical reaction that such a title was simply too farcical to have been the main one, at least as initially desired by the master draftsman himself. After all, certain jests can really be taken too far—spatially, that is.

Yet how may we assume that such neat numerical double-play provided an acceptable opening gambit for Shakespeare's theatrical company? Is it not because, as spectators, we all believe somewhat in the magic of numbers, especially in the curious appearance-reality calculus of the nought? As a valid response, let us say that if any play of his must be somewhat discussed as dealing with aspects of number lore, it would most probably have been the work to which *Won* was the evident sequel; for reference to numerology is explicit in *Love's Labour's Lost* (see, for example, 3.1.88–90, 94–97; 4.3.206–7, 337–42), more so probably than in any other play of his. Indeed, the name of the key figure Berowne was based, according to the erudition of Frances Yates, on that of the esoteric Giordano Bruno, the Renaissance Neo-Pythagorean mathematician who happened to be resident in England at the time (95–99; see also Beyersdorff). Berowne himself, moreover, has been duly imagined as the prototype of Benedick in *Much Ado,* and H. Richmond finds both men founded on important figures in the French court.

Analogous number-play occurs in the latter comedy (or sequel) in terms of the well-recognized but probably vastly overrated verbal double-play upon "nothing." What has not been observed so far is that, in context, the paronomasia is not merely upon "no thing" (homophonic then, as is well known, with "nothing"), but also upon *"one* thing," thereby setting up the important contrast between *one* and *null,* a connection I dubbed the 1/0 factor previously, as duly operative in the suggested titular quibble

Love's Labour's *Won* / Much Ado About *Nothing*.
(1)   (0)

The essential point then is this: After the well-known phrase said to have a bearing upon the titular word *Nothing* —namely, "Note, notes, forsooth, and nothing"—

Balthasar produces musical notes and sings, "One foot in sea, and one on shore, / To one thing constant never . . ." (2.3.54–60). Note the conjunction of *nothing* and *one thing,* a collocation which was clearly not merely adventitious and could easily be grasped by the usual alert theatergoer.

Further let us proceed. A conscientious, authoritative student of Renaissance number lore, Alastair Fowler, uncovered not long ago sensitive numerological elements elsewhere in Shakespeare, for example in the order of the *Sonnets* (for which he fairly recently won the acclaim of Kenneth Muir in the latter's article on "The Order of Shakespeare's Sonnets"), and then in what he deemed the key structural role of the number sixteen in *The Winter's Tale* (see his "Leontes' Contrition and the Repair of Nature"). The sensitive reader can scarcely avoid thinking back on how sixteen happens also to figure as an element in the proposed 'A.D. [16]00' quibble. Should it be countered that Shakespeare would not readily have been supportive of such curious pursuits, or, if anything, might have been tempted to parody them instead, this point may be partly conceded. But in any event, whether the number-play was meant seriously or satirically, its ludic import appears to have some bearing upon the identity of *Won,* at least as regards intellectual history, and so may be overlooked only at the playgoer's or reader's peril. Sixteen was, after all, the marriage number, the tragedy of Romeo and Juliet surely resulting in part from the heroine's being underage. A multiple of this key number figures as well in sonnet 116 (see Chs 4 and 5).

Further revelations derive from the registration of the play as *Much Ado,* ones augmenting the import of the timed 'occasion,' as discussed in my previous articles. We might recall here that the drama happened to be the very first by Shakespeare to be registered, and hence could then all the more easily have been offhandedly *mis*registered, and was not assigned in the *Stationers' Register* to the full name of the author, moreover, but cited only as having been devised by one "master Shakespere" (Halliday, *Companion* 326). Such relative informality suggests that what was abbreviated in one instance (where *William* was left out) could have been also shortchanged in another. In brief, *because* the Christian name was deleted, the first (or original) part of the play's title might likewise have been. Flippant negligence, for whatever reason, or lack of such, in one respect, would account for much the same in another case.

Omission of the initial title would have been either a matter of someone's intent or an accident, more likely the former; in any event, it could readily have been caused by the dramatist's not having registered the play himself, thus accounting for the dropping of the author's first name, for such a deletion would hardly have been effected otherwise. Indeed, it is plausible enough that the registerer or clerk might simply not have been aware of it. The same point, analogously enough, has been brought to bear on the *Sonnets*. Since they also were registered without their author's full name, or the kind of formal title all other sonnet sequences warranted, the poet most likely failed to see them to the press and hence would not have proofread them, accounting thereby for certain textual inadvertencies (Rostenberg, but see Duncan-Jones, who objects). It might seem a bit curious that Shakespeare himself would have been capable or culpable of promulgating an offhand but rather disconcerting full title if it were only *Much Ado About Nothing*. Is it not likelier that he permitted it, if at all then, as a casual subtitle (akin to *What You Will,* the more-or-less lackadaisical *sub*title of *Twelfth Night,* which had at least the hidden virtue of harking back lightheartedly, if perhaps subliminally, to the dramatist's forename by implicitly connoting "what you [would have from] Will")?

If the omission of the playwright's full name from the *Stationers' Register* may be taken into valid account in coping with what could be called the decapitated title of the play as it was registered, then the use of one of his subtitles later even as a main title likewise deserves to be considered. This link became then the subject of the second earlier essay of mine on the problem ("Shakespeare's *Carte Blanche:* Appropriated by Marston"), one in need now also of some revised recapitulation.

The point is that if Marston later appropriated the Shakespearean subtitle *What You Will* as his main title, then a helpful precedent emerges for considering yet another subtitle as having been likewise promoted as a main title, namely *Much Ado*. Such presumed interplay may appear at first only coincidental, but now perhaps for several bonafide reasons it should not be totally written off. First, let us recall that John Dover Wilson once held the shrewd notion that *Twelfth Night* was "first produced in the late autumn of 1599, under the title of *What You Will*"—a very important example of the separation of subtitle from main title— "and that it was then given again at court before the Queen on Twelfth Night,

1600." Exactly why? Wilson inferred "that it had to be renamed because it would have been hardly polite to present a play at Court with an off-hand label like 'What You Will'" (*Happy Comedies* 164). That was a sensible, valid inference, one with which more critics should concur. Now, whereas this separation of main title from subtitle is clearly arresting, the *reverse* situation also occurred insofar as *What You Will* was used as a main title (albeit not at court) following the turn of the century. Let us examine the rationale.

Marston's appropriation of the subtitle *What You Will* as his main and only designation is perfectly obvious from the Induction to his play. There a reference to the title is followed by specific allusion to his predecessor, namely to Polonius' notorious generic categorizings: "Ist Commedy, Tragedy, Pastorall, Morall, Nocturnal or Historie?" (Wood II, 223). When we couple this allusion with the probability that Marston likewise borrowed from the name and character of Malvolio in *Twelfth Night* when he invented his own malcontent, namely Malevole of *The Malcontent* (1602), we may begin to feel our ears perk. For was not Marston, in turn, following the precedent of his mentor, whose earlier play was published under a subtitle rather than main title, that is as *Much Ado* rather than *Love's Labour's Won*? At least an even chance exists that he was; no other comparable precedent suggests itself. Clearly any evidence for *Love's Labour's Lost* as the companion piece to *Much Ado* ought also to prove of value in terms of Marston's *What You Will* being a comparable follow-up.

Such allusions to Shakespeare in Marston do indeed exist; in point of fact, they almost stand on their heads for proper recognition. For example, Marston's comedy contains reference to the pedant Holofernes of the *Lost* play: "What is your name?" is answered by *"Holifernes"* (designated thereafter "a scholler"). Should the reader quibble that the name simply takes its origin from Rabelais once again, he can notice that the celebrated longest word in Shakespeare, again from *Lost,* is parodied, in appropriately staccato fashion, in Marston's verily unpronounceable mooncalf of a word, "Honorificac-cac-cac-cacuminos" (Wood II, 256, 272). Further, small-talk follows about sonnets (which also happens, of course, to have been incorporated in *Lost*), and the fairly unusual phrase "Keele it" clearly echoes the same expression in 5.2.913. Because these parallels are so suggestive, should we not also expect to have an implicit, indirect allusion to the *title* of *Love's Labour's Won* (in part) in *What You Will* ? If so, it could plausibly represent a ludic allusion to *Much Ado,* considered as *Won*'s presumed alternate title, and not amount to a verbal echo as such.

Consider the evidence. We are confronted in Marston with an unusual amount of quibbling again on the abstraction *nothing,* following a phrase which may just as well have been used as a signpost pointing to the source of inspiration: *"What You Will,* as nothing." That could also connote *being,* in part, *Much Ado About Nothing.* The titular quibbling is clear enough. If, however, Marston had the latter comedy at the back of his mind in this instance, that would have been entirely subliminal. Notice how the parley then develops in the Marston play:

Meletza. As nothing, how will you valew my love.

Lampatho. Why just as you respect me, as nothing, for out of nothing, nothing is bred, so nothing shall not be any-thing, any-thing bring nothing, nothing bring any-thing, any-thing & nothing shall be *What You Will,* my speach mounting to the valieu of my selfe, which is—

Meletza. What, sweete?

Lampatho. Your nothing, light as your selfe, sencelesse as your sex, and just as you would ha me, nothing.   (Wood II, 280)

Although such wordplay was widespread in Renaissance times, the Stratford "upstart" easily had a hand in starting up this somewhat curious fashion, however inadvertently.

A final early publication of mine on this problem begs for momentary reconsideration now too. Written in response to Samuel Schoenbaum's politely low-keyed recognition of my *Shakespeare Survey* essay in his review in the *Times Literary Supplement* ("On the Page and on the Stage"), my follow-up letter to the editor dealt with certain additional factors favoring the identification of *Won* (entitled "Much Ado"—also in the *TLS*). I there concisely itemized them in seriatim fashion since Schoenbaum duly had specified that my points would have had greater effect if expressed more potently, in a more compressed format. Some of these points hinged on the tie-in between *Lost* and *Much Ado* when considered the same as *Won,* for example minor parallel references to black skin pigment in the two plays (*Lost,* 4.3.242–64; *Won,* 3.1.63–64), abstinence from women in *Lost* and 'confirmed' bachelorhood in *Won.*

What more can be adduced? To begin, both comedies, as reflected in their complementary titles, were effective in their day as suitably 'stylized' creations (the inverted commas added advisedly). Shakespeare's plays may be called stylized in their own way in a certain sense, but hardly in the one used in general by modern-day producers or by historians of stylistic modes in the arts. The key word *Labour's* relates to this point of style, which is notably self-conscious in its euphemistic references in *Lost,* even as it is a bit contrived in the sequel—hence, in effect, 'labo*red*.' The mannered, as well as Manneristic, qualities of *Lost,* evident already in the emphatic titular alliteration, which has a certain affected aspect because love is not really or totally forgotten at the end, complement the conventionalized plot and characters of the sequel, for instance in its so-called patterned trio: Claudio, Benedick, Don Pedro (traditionally seen as lover, heretic against love, and reasonable man). Such complementation is artistically more noticeable between these comedies than among many other plays in the canon and in itself sets forth a memorable kinship that augurs well for the later play's being a variation on the theme of the earlier.

To some extent, true, this affinity between these two amorous comedies has already been noticed. Clifford Leech, for one, commented with his customary commonsense, "It is . . . difficult to believe that an audience going to see *Love's Labour's Won* would not expect a play with an ending diametrically opposed to that of *Love's Labour's Lost*" (149). In this respect, he courteously and cogently differed with Leslie Hotson. In any event, the *Lost-Won* opposition does not rule out complementarity of some sort, particularly given the applicability of the magnetic principle of polarity in nature, namely that opposites attract, the earth itself having around the turn of that century been discovered as being a great magnet. The first play ends with a year having to ensue before the marriage can be prudently consummated; the second concludes with a dual marriage on the spot. Love's labor is clearly more decisively 'won' in the later play when that is considered as *Much Ado*.

That the second play is a true sequel to the first has likewise been carefully treated in the New Variorum edition of *Much Ado*. In turn, the New Variorum edition of *Lost* duly specifies that "the assertion is time-honored that in Berowne and in Rosaline we have the predecessors of Benedick and Beatrice" (xviii). Further, a recent study adds valuable additional linkage, contending that "since Berowne at least was directly modelled on the historical Charles de Gontaut, duc de Biron (not to discuss the complex precedents for the Princess, Katherine,

Maria, Longueville, and Dumain), we may be encouraged to feel that the later warring lovers are less unprecedented than we are usually told" (H. Richmond 56, 61). (The assumed association of Benedick and Beatrice with figures in Castiglione is played down.) This study notes, in addition, that in "Colynet's history of France (which also affords parallels for both *Love's Labour's Lost* and *Henry V)*, there is a disturbing seduction scene in which the lover of some ladies of the Guise faction is dexterously excited to 'exalt the Church' and serve the cause of honor by killing a man they feel has slighted them" (60–61).

Even more straightforwardly, Wilson remarked cogently that "the whole Beatrice-Benedick plot with its brilliant flyting is clearly a development of the *Love's Labour's Lost* manner, so clearly that many critics have supposed that *Ado* is simply a revision of *Love's Labour's Won,* the lost twin" (122). Here we appear to get nigh the truth. Yet we need not unduly complicate matters by finding *Much Ado* a mere "revision" of the "lost twin"—unless (and this point may be rather consequential) Wilson was aptly intuiting that the title of *Much Ado* constituted the very, and perhaps only, portion that happened to have undergone some sort of revision (or was the result of one). With such qualification in mind, let us enroll Wilson in our camp as providing a splendid hint for the proposed title-shift. His further views are welcome as well. He likewise considered Benedick a more mature Berowne, linked Beatrice with Rosaline, even as did the Variorum. Still, one of the most clear-cut correlations he disregarded: that of the two obtuse constables involved. Evidently Master Constable Dogberry in the later play harks back, although somewhat less as an amusing figure *per se,* to Constable Dull of the earlier one. This constabulary hence was united. Or we might say that what was tedious in the earlier comedy thus became more lively in its intended comic quality in the later one. Could it then be that this similarity has not been seriously discussed before simply because it is so obvious? It appears that way.

Overall, a key connection is that even as *Lost* commences with a set of gallants who studiously determine to avoid the lures of the fair sex for a grueling three-year period, owing to their conscientiously devoting their energies to learning, so *Much Ado* starts off with analogous coteries: not only a confirmed bachelor type this time, but a complementary confirmed maid. Although these labels are 'characteristic' ones, they should now be properly qualified in context: Clearly Benedick and Beatrice were confessedly in love once and, at heart, at the outset of the drama still are. Thus Shakespeare doubled his effects. But whereas, at the end of the earlier play, a year must still intervene before the love relations can be formally consummated, appropriately at the finale of *Won* a double wedding is effected. Don Pedro's gallant effort in bringing Benedick and Beatrice into "a mountain of affection" in seven days, and thereby having her wed at the same time as her cousin, achieves results. More such studious winning of love is extant here than in many another comedy of the time (*The Merchant of Venice* possibly excepted). The contrast between *Lost* and *Won* could hardly be more self-evident, setting the scene for more structured interrelations to be discussed in the later sections of this study.

In now summing up a vital concern at the end of this introductory section, we have to bear in mind the proper perspective. What counts primarily as factual, historical evidence is the fascinating parallel in Meres and the First Folio (as noted in the appended diagram). The purported 'excuse' for the original use of a fatuous title like *Much Ado About Nothing,* because it could have been based on a tavern jest, although a bit more complicated, is decidedly secondary in import. It must finally be remarked that a distinguished critic, Sidney Thomas, has also of late referred to *Love labours wonne* as "probably an alternate title for a genuine Shakespeare work" (188).

II

Schema

t_1 = double title (e.g., *Twelfth Night, or What You Will*)
t_2 = secondary title (e.g., *What You Will*)
t_3 = mini-title (e.g., *Much Ado . . .*)
t_4 = subordinate title (e.g., *The Humours of Sir John Falstaff*)
t_5 = alternate title (e.g., *All Is True*)

If Shakespeare's comedies, then, are to be recognized as having a firm moral basis, a description I incline to feel they deserve (following a cue from Kenneth Muir), the seeming appeal of a flippant, offhand, or throwaway title ought to be diminished, or at least put solidly in its subordinate place. For that reason, reconsideration of the authority thus far given the title *Much Ado About Nothing* is past due. In my initial *Shakespeare Survey* paper, I recommended that this title be thought of as originally a subtitle for *Love's Labour's Won,* in much the same manner as, say, *What You Will* was the recognized subtitle for *Twelfth Night.* Since that precise suggestion about a surreptitious subtitle may have seemed at the time unsupported (although I confess I still hanker somewhat for this position, which has its follow-up in Dryden's *All For Love . . . Lost),* I determined to emend my approach a little in my 'addendum,' namely my letter in the *Times Literary Supplement,* suggesting thereby that *Much Ado* may be referred to merely as an odd alternative title. (This was bypassed in the New Cambridge edition's note on my work.) Such a revised stance need scarcely be thought of as necessarily canceling my first, since a subtitle is, in fact, nothing else but one mode of alternate title. Evidence from other examples suggests that the Elizabethan method of selecting and describing titles was considerably varied—even as it is also at variance with present-day procedures. For instance, certain plays evidently flaunted secondary titles which need not have been part of the original full titles. Consider, for example, *Henry IV, Part I,* which was registered with a subordinate description, namely *The Humours of Sir John Falstaff,* one which most probably, however, was not intended as a subtitle. It might better be distinguished from other secondary labels by being termed, let us say, a descriptive 'subordinate title.'

Since the distinction between these terms is new and may be, at times, ambivalent, I now propose the following categories, with abbreviated subscripts following, as easier to handle or at least more structured: double title (t_1), secondary title (t_2), mini-title (t_3), subordinate title (t_4), and alternate title (t_5). By t_1, I mean a play's full title as having, by intention, two designations, one of which may either be, or have been, the second part of the original title. Or it may simply be an alternative title not necessarily always associated with the principal one. t_2 should be self-explanatory; t_3 refers to a shortened form of a title which, for one reason or another, was sometimes used in an abbreviated or curtailed manner. It could, for instance in the case of *Much Ado,* point to an abbreviated form of t_2. t_4 represents a subordinate title associated with the main title, although not necessarily so by the author, and t_5 refers to an alternate title not by necessity linked to the main title at all. Whereas t_4 may have certain 'official' implications, t_5 need not, and its formulation can be looser.

Although, at first glance, such new terminology may appear overly to complicate an already involved methodology, once we fairly accustom ourselves to it, I am confident that it should prove serviceable. The terms are meant simply as useful designations for making distinctive generalizations about title-formation during an age when no established rules existed—hence their apparently somewhat arbitrary or merely descriptive approximations. Yet our understanding of them can still have worthwhile Gestaltist implications. To some critics, for instance, the term *subtitle* is too official-sounding, whereas *alternate title* (t_5) would be preferable. Although it is extremely difficult to ascertain just what would have seemed 'official' to the playwright himself—regardless of whether it really mattered that much to him or his audience—I adhere firmly to the hypothesis that some such distinctiveness was then, as it is now, recommendable.

Plausibly enough, many of the dramas originally had considerably lengthier titles than are now normally assigned to them. The description of plays in the *Stationers' Register* intimates as much. In this connection, let us come to terms with some other instances of t_2 in Shakespearean comedy. As is well known, for instance, *The Comedy of Errors* once had been referred to as *The Night of Errors.* It is uncalled for to infer positively that such a secondary title was no more than a careless slip. Thus, we ought to consider it also as an example of t_5, even though it was most likely never part of t_1. The import assigned to it depends on the extent to which it relates more to t_2 or t_5—in other words, how it might have conformed to the dramatist's considered intent. Indubitably, it relates more to t_2 than, for example, does the title known as *The Jealous Comedy,* if that was indeed another designation, as has been suspected on very little evidence, for this play. One reason is that it represents a kind of t_3 as well, even as *Errors* was t_3 for the drama in Meres's *Palladis Tamia*.

In like manner, Charles II provided several additional examples of t_5 which were never part of t_1, nor may they validly be taken as t_2: He designated *All's Well* as *Parolles,* and *Twelfth Night* as *Malvolio*. In the latter case, the label does still have some bearing on t_1, however, in that it connotatively underscores the difference between main title and subtitle. Thus, it may be associated with t_4 as an auxiliary title. It effects this designation by revealing the contrast between "What You Will" (as subtitle) and "Malvolio" (considered as auxiliary main title); the correlation is achieved through the connotation of "mal-volio," which can imply "bad will." This distinction has a direct relevance to the contrast between *Love's Labour's Won* (as the first part of t_1) and *Much Ado About Nothing* (the second part of t_1) in terms of a titular thematic reversal, but also bears on the implied paronomasia in the last word in each part of the double title, whereby *Won/Nothing* equals 1/0. Again the distinction is serio-comic: The first part of t_1 is serious, the second part comical. Together the two parts balance each other. Analogous is the medieval *commedia,* which was serious, thereby underscoring the moral basis of the comic genre, as related to the modern ludic meaning of comedy, although usually with romantic elements. Such interplay between Parts I and II of the double title works regardless of whether or not we consider Part II an intentional component of the author's or possibly t_2 or t_5. (Because of its thematic import, Part II would represent not merely t_4.)

Now, the idea that Shakespeare initially wanted his play to have a casual main title like *Much Ado About Nothing* is ultimately self-defeating because such a presumption is itself rather too offhand, I would submit, to be considered profoundly. We might propose that *Much Ado* was initially most likely an alternate title (t_5), possibly part of t_1.

Indeed, this view has been effectively insinuated by a leading authority on the Globe, C. Walter Hodges. In a clever fictive study, he described a possible Elizabethan parley along the following lines: A Renaissance gallant observes to his confrère: "Why, look you, only today there comes our Master Shakerags with his new play, which he calls 'Much Ado About Nothing,' or some such title . . ." (144).

Note: *or some such title.* The hidden implications are that a flippant title like *Much Ado About Nothing,* when taken alone, can be rather embarrassing or even contemptuous-sounding. Such nonchalance has had the questionable effect, as Josephine Waters Bennett duly urged in her preface to the Pelican edition (275), of pointing up the dramatist's presumed sense of indifference. Even when taken in its overall context, the title is suspect enough. Geoffrey Bullough, for example, in commenting on the bastard in the comedy, "contemptuously adds that 'Don John is a very small villain to cause so Much Ado'" (II, 71–2). Josephine Bennett's claim, in effect to 'make up' for this implication, however, is not entirely cogent, at least to me, so it is gratifying to have at least the hint of another explanation, that creatively intuited by Hodges. For, although obviously intended as a spirited side-comment, his fictive description does contain grains of truth. His pregnant phrase, "some such title," is more suggestive than apologetic, giving the impression that another title may well be lurking about in the background. *Love's Labour's Won?*

Hodges's reference to "Master Shakerags" is, of course, to Will Kemp's presumed allusion to Shakespeare in his *Nine Daies Wonder* as "My notable Shakerags" (along with echoes of some plays) (30–1). But are we not also reminded that *Much Ado* was originally registered as being by one "Master Shakespeare"? The *Sonnets* were likewise registered as coming from the pen of a certain "Master Shakespeare" (Christian name excluded), and hence probably were not given the title that the author himself would have wanted for them and so may well not have authorized their publication. For whereas most other collections of sonnets were given special labels, like Constable's *Diana* or Sidney's *Astrophel and Stella,* oddly Shakespeare's were given no real title at all. (For more on this, see Ch 3.) The parallel with the present full title, *Much Ado About Nothing,* as being probably not the poet's intended effect as well, is altogether revealing.

To what, then, might Hodges's lame appendage, "some such title," refer? To *Love's Labour's Won?* At this time, veritably the only title available without a play to accompany it and seriously ascribable to Shakespeare was *Love's Labour's Won.* A useful enough precedent for such an identity emerges in *Much Ado*'s having been plausibly the same play as that referred to in the Lord-Treasurer Stanhope's Accounts for 20 May 1613 as *Benedicte and Betteris.* Such a title was hardly one accorded the comedy by the dramatist himself and may best be designated as mainly an imposed descriptive title, or as t_5. Moreover, such an alternate title suggests that even in Shakespeare's own time the *Much Ado About Nothing* effect did not always 'come across' or 'go over,' or was thought simply too jejune. The advantage of considering *Won* as the missing t_2 in Hodges's anecdotal account, then, is that it can also fill slots for t_4 and t_1.

III

At issue now is the more complex, psychological problem of why, if *Won* indeed represented the original main title, it was so easily discarded in favor of a recognizably fatuous, offhand, at best demonstrably throwaway tag such as *Much*

Ado About Nothing. In response, certain validly hypothetical reasons, quite aside from the light, in-house tavern jesting intimated earlier, may offer themselves. Although no urgency arises to renounce the suggestion regarding tavern wordplay as simply too light-weight for serious scholarship—for even such seemingly slight folk traditions can have their laundry-bill-like justifications—the bulk of the added evidence to be here assembled provides whatever extra support may be needed for critical, and thereby more notably serious, approbation.

It is plausible enough, for example, that some of the actors or shareholders of Shakespeare's theatrical company, The Lord Chamberlain's Men, found the terse designation *Love's Labour's Won* rather *too* literal, or blatantly obvious, or unsubtly meaningful. For it may have been simply too much of a giveaway. The average theatergoer, after all, usually hoped to be left in at least token suspense, not be bluntly instructed from the outset of what is bound to result at the play's climax. So a giveaway title like *Won* might all too easily appear to telegraph the punch of the double matrimonial dénouement. For that reason it was assigned, let us say, a back row in this metaphorically pugilistic arena.

Now a plausible objection to such a verdict is that the title ostensibly or supposedly substituted for it could also easily give away the ending, if in another manner. Yet that analogy seems a bit mindless, for *Much Ado,* titularly speaking, tells us literally nothing about the actual amorous entanglements. It serves simply as another, more open-ended catch-all phrase, as the bromide that it has all too often become, one which could readily be relegated to almost any comic or more appropriately farcical situation. True, apologists for this rather silly title sometimes infer that it contains hidden double-play which gives away rather more than the plot, thereby providing a teasing mystery for the playgoer, and hence throwing him off his moral guard.

We shall get to that questionable matter presently. Our main concern first is that a label like *Won* could, for better or worse, have at one time been thought of as rather flatly and unnecessarily previewing the play's ludic effects in a manner which would not have seemed that apparent titularly with *Much Ado.* Whether the same argument ought to be advanced with regard to a modern-day production may be a moot point, although surely a title with a serious comic theme should be intrinsically superior to one with a largely fatuous meaning. That is an assessment that basically overrides other considerations. So, with luck, eventually the original title can be reinstated on the stage or at least on the scholar's page.

Little doubt exists that a comedy with the bluffing, even brash, designation of *Nothing* could have come in for its share of derision, although nowadays many spectators and readers seem to have taken critical novocaine and become numb to the largely farcical implications. The commonplace tendency is simply to skirt this problem of non-meaning by economy, that is by shortening the title lightly, but thereby perhaps all too conveniently, to *Much Ado*. Yet such a bland modernization can too often play havoc with the author's real intent, regardless whether he went along with the shortening if only so as to avoid problems. Although several of Shakespeare's titles have regularly been abbreviated for stylistic reasons, in this instance a secondary result perforce emerges, one which then psychologically has the primary effect, namely the welcome avoidance of the embarrassment of communicating pure meaninglessness. No other title of Shakespeare's has been shortchanged so often both in the classroom and study. Such a general consensus, moreover, would suggest that it in fact *needed* to be curtailed to avoid its otherwise inherent frivolousness. So our present appraisal can rightly be sedate.

Anecdotally speaking, a noted Shakespearean, Clifford Lyons, once conceded the titular silliness to me, but then added, as a nonchalant, offhand riposte, "Why not?" That reflection turned out to be on the dubious side itself. Need we accept as gospel that even what is silly, if embalmed in writings by the master dramatist, has a certain warrant? In any event, fatuity need not be forever enshrined in a nonsensical title. To the leading query, "What is wrong with such a coy label for a comedy if the dramatic action itself is accountable in these terms?" let us concur that this drama is simply not basically a coy one, whereas such an offhand label like *Much Ado* could imply that it is made for the genre of farce. Further, if the Claudio-Hero fussing or misunderstanding be taken as 'the much ado about nothing,' should we not make more of the wittier Benedick-Beatrice encounters? Even the fretting between the first two represents actually much ado about quite a lot when we bear in mind again Don John—that is, his being associated historically with the noteworthy Austrian politician.

Rather than being a farce, then, this comedy points to a stylized forerunner of Comedy of Manners, a standard subgenre which hardly merits any ludicrous kind of categorization. True enough, it still could be urged that titularly *Much Ado About Nothing* was self-evidently not meant to be taken literally, and that such awareness was at the back of the playwright's mind, so that to make such fuss about a mere come-on label seems uninnovative or ultra-conservative. But in response, we can stand our ground by asserting faith in Shakespeare's having fundamentally endowed his plays with moral meaning, so that a purely non-literal title would scarcely tally with his basically ethical intent, what the literary historian is obliged to try at least to approach.

On the other hand, it might be countered further that titularly *Much Ado About Nothing* can paradoxically also lend itself to literal enough interpretation. In short, it makes a limited amount of sense in terms of, first, the obvious wordplay at times on the abstraction *nothing* throughout and, secondly, the implicit scholastic axiom that 'something' in fact can be created out of this 'nothing.' Modern interpretive apologists are quick to settle on the quibbling about nought as a prime instance of the pet Renaissance love of such paradox, with which Shakespeare and his fellows were evidently much involved (Colie Ch 7). Ought we not, then, it might be asked, to summon up also Donne's paradoxical turn of phrase "a quintessence of nothingness" in his familiar "Nocturnal upon St. Lucy's Day"? Nonetheless, the weight assigned critically to this argument from paradox can be too ponderous, as can be seen.

Next, reassess the proposed titular double-play. The presumption that the last word in the title is name-play on the word *noting,* meaning eavesdropping, simple observing of other characters, as well as the making of musical notes, is a commonplace; but it places such a loaded burden on this one little word that it scarcely makes much sense in the end. We would presumably have not merely double-play here but triple-play. That the phonology behind the wordplay was purportedly based on the Renaissance pronunciation of the abstraction *nothing* (namely *nōting*) has received due scholarly acquiescence, yet it is fair to note, too, that prominent word-specialists like Helge Kökeritz (132) and Paul Jorgensen (*Redeeming* 22–42) and Larry S. Champion (206) have also brought its relevance to the drama as a whole into question. First of all, the leading passage usually cited as containing the germane play on words, "Note, notes, forsooth, and nothing" (2.3.54), is in need of being better grasped in its immediate context (Hockey). Although hitherto ignored, a simple verbal contrast between "nothing" (as "no thing") and "something" is clearly implied, for, after Benedick's aside, Balthasar intones, *"One* foot in sea, and *one* on shore. / To *one thing* constant never" (2.3.61–62). Hence *no thing / one thing.* Absence and presence thus correlate, as also perhaps with main title and subtitle.

Such a contrast supports the view that the title of *Much Ado* was somehow affixed to *Won,* not indigenous to the latter title, if only because of the inherent, complementary title-play thereby on *Nothing* and *Won* (=*One*). This correlation I have previously designated the 1/0 factor (*"Love's Labour's Won* and the Occasion of *Much Ado"*). Thematically, the contrast helps to support a numeric effect, the familiar appearance/reality motif. Lest the reader be put off by this label, let us grant that it has led to some rather obtuse or blatant generalizations in the past, but that need not mean that the aptness of this motif should be scotched altogether. After all, the effect of a certain 'illusion of the senses' amounts to a primary deduction from human experience, one that works well enough here, if it be not taken as a be-all and end-all.

The intended titular emphasis was, therefore, hardly on *Nothing per se* (whatever that could possibly mean); thus, *Much Ado,* whether termed a subtitle or alternative title, cannot truly tell us the whole tale. If we bear the immediate context of the crucial "nothing" passage fully in mind, we should be able to dispense with the import given to the discussion of 'nothingness' alone. In any event, any purely nihilistic overview would not do much for the moral reputation of the master connoisseur of human comedy, to say the least.

Another argument which might be leveled against the proposal—namely that Shakespeare was a kind of universal creator writing for "all time," as Jonson elegantly put it, and thereby produced a great deal of ado *ex nihilo* (like God in the Vulgate)—hardly helps to sustain the title as registered. Such an argument, if not considered simply strained, would ultimately militate against that title anyway since ado "about" naught is rather different, in a valid enough sense, from such ado being produced "out of" (*ex*) naught. The old classical adage *ex nihilo nihil fit,* when here imported, serves only to demote the meaning further, the implication then being that any ado truly "about" naught paradoxically provides only additional lack of substance. Because Shakespeare made explicit use of this stoic, Lucretian maxim in the opening scene of *King Lear* (1.1.90), as widely and validly recognized, even reiterated it later in the imagery of the tragedy in a pointed way, we have good enough reason to suspect he would have been cognizant enough of parodic connotations in an offhand label like *Much Ado About Nothing* and so presumably would have wanted to shun them. Should it be ingeniously countered that *ex nihilo nihil fit* is itself naught but a limited pagan maxim, that a fervent or conformist Christian (which presumably Shakespeare was) would have believed that God contradicted such heathen implications in that He indeed originally created the universe *ex nihilo* (whereby the artist presumably creates *in loco Dei*), a theological nicety is on our hands. Yet the commonplace that the Creation was *ex nihilo* notwithstanding, a substantial body of Christian believers have still felt that it was instead brought into being *ex Deo* (from the spirit of God Himself)—a view sometimes said to be upheld especially by the genius of Milton (Adamson; contrast Shullenberger 262–78). (If we cannot solve such a theological conundrum without being specialists in theology, would that not be all the more validity logically for eliminating a title which gives rise to the theological nicety in the first place?)

In any event, Renaissance wordplay was not always like our own; it followed its own rules. It is perilous to apply much modern psychology to times past which upheld the ancient views of Hippocrates and Galen (on which, try my "Putting Falstaff to Rest"). One of the main psychological conventions was, as indicated, the implementation of paradoxical meaning, most conspicuously in the works of the so-called Mannerist period around the turn of the century, such as in the poetry of Donne. Mannerism was descriptive of tension, and witty paradox fostered it with indulgence in skepticism and disharmony. Yet such conventionality would have been a bit late for this play, if we accept Meres's having mentioned it already in 1598. (Early plays like *Lost* and Lyly's euphuistic comedies were essentially more mannered than Manneristic, at least in the more serious stylistic meaning of the aesthetic term which was descriptive of the early seventeenth century in England.)

At this point, it is useful to counter the argument that the comedy was written somewhat later, say in 1599, a view recently espoused again on the grounds that it was not specifically mentioned by Meres (see Shapiro). The theatrical fact of the matter, though, is that Will Kemp played the key role of Dogberry, as clearly specified in the Quarto, where the name of the actor appears in place of that of the magistrate through most of 4.2, and that he left Shakespeare's acting company early in 1599. Thus, it is most probable that the play was written and performed already sometime in 1598, giving Meres the effective opportunity, or at least an even chance, to announce it in his *Palladis Tamia.*

After the turn of the century, in any case, Mannerist style came into its own, as is revealed in plays of Shakespeare's transition period, starting with *Hamlet* (as E. M. W. Tillyard had it). Possibly 1600 amounted to that kind of watershed year, as had been said, one allowing for the encroachment of Mannerist style immediately thereafter for a time, and we might conjecture that the potentially Mannerist implications of a title like *Much Ado* were readily seen as then in fashion and so producing good box-office. That would be another explanation why the comedy would have been registered under such a wild title some time after it was written. But would England's Terence, in his heart of hearts, have wanted to cater to such faddism? Even *Hamlet,* which is sometimes thought of as having its Mannerist moments (having been started about 1601) (see McGinn and Howerton), was composed, as Gabriel Harvey affirmed, for "the wiser sort," by which, among other things, was assuredly meant "the subtler set." The distinction is appreciably philosophic, not merely a matter of catering to fashion, and to try to rule out any implicit 'two-audience' theory behind this, as has recently been attempted by Richard Levin, seems unnecessarily reductive, well-meant though his critical dismissal was.

It is also cavalierly maintained by some apologists for the *Much Ado* label that such a seemingly nonsensical display can make a certain amount of even biological sense in terms of hidden name-play on the female pudendum—almost as if it were in 'yonic' contrast to the hidden 'anality' of such a titular come-on as *As You Like It.* (The backside of the donkey *was* depicted in art of the time.) But compare the following anomaly: One would-be participant for the first of the Ohio Shakespeare conferences, which I chanced to direct with NEH funding at Central State University (Ohio), ventured the view that Cordelia, in her initial double "Nothing" response to the King, was indulging in unconscious yonic imagery (as if thereby curiously exhibiting her anticipation of a Freudian Electra complex). To many sensible scholar-critics, further pursuance of such psychobiology is, however, fatuous; but our twentieth-century, too-often-bodily-oriented society has gaily indulged in such foibles at times, and so some readers may not completely dismiss at least glancing at their innuendoes, overly modernized though at times they may seem to be.

Yet would Shakespeare have been a psychologist *manqué* as well as, let us posit, a would-be philosopher? In answer, a bawdy suggestion, such as the one outlined above, is clearly unduly strained, even thereby a little comedy on its own, for it seems most improbable that his staunch moral fiber, as revealed in other areas, would have permitted him to capitalize on a *risqué* note to such an extent as to indulge in it flagrantly on the titular level. Although traces of wordplay upon "nothing" as a zero or oval (hence, psychologically, vaginal) form may be embarrassingly discernible in *Hamlet,* 3.2.111–6 (Pyles), and a few other places, none of it is startlingly apparent in, or relevant to, this comedy. True, some gross bawdiness is evident enough in *Won*'s companion piece, *Lost,* as well as some other early and relatively immature comedies; so an anteroom of sorts may be left for a few such resonances in *Won* too. Most probably, if apprised of such misinformed readings-in apropos of either *Much Ado* or *King Lear,* the playwright would have turned over in his cerement. Such emphasis certainly seems anachronistic.

Likewise, to say that the wit-combat between Benedick and Beatrice is similarly hinted at by the present-day title may not be too cogent, for such ado "about nothing" is not wholly to be equated with, let us say, 'sweet nothings,' if only because the cardinal relationship in the main plot of the play concerns instead Claudio and Hero (whose very name would thereby ironically point to her being the hero*ine*). Some critics then have professed that the main resonance of the title is in the fretting in which Claudio indulges concerning Hero's supposed betrayal the eve of the wedding. The point would then be that his fussing was, after all, for naught. Yet such accommodation of the controversial title is altogether too superficial, for the most striking contrast is rather with love that is *seemingly* lost (harking back to the forerunner, *Lost*) and therefore has to be finally, hence not merely nominally, 'won.' On balance, the association of the *Much Ado* label with the subplot rather than the Claudio-Hero plot works better insofar as the sweet nothings exchanged between Beatrice and Benedick (although, incidentally, not so very sweet in the play's beginning) relate to the subPLOT in the same sort of way as the *Nothing* label provides a subTITLE. In effect, the full implication of the double title (t_1) would then be as follows: For love to be truly won, sweet nothings are the name of this game (at least in the present world).

Yet, still more psychologically, a recent critic has lightly submitted that the *Much Ado* tag was designed as 'throwaway' and, as such, had several notable titular accomplices among the comedies (Heffner 179). True enough, it is common knowledge that a comic line was often expected to be 'thrown away' to draw proper audience response, but this commonplace is purely incidental with regard to the controversial title, for such a throwaway effect would work just as well with the title considered as t_2, t_3, t_4, or t_5. The titles of the dramatist's other works, moreover, ones which in the past have sometimes been taken as throwaway, might better not be adjudicated as such (however fatuous they sometimes may seem), if only because a worldly genius like the inimitable bard would clearly have been above the crass banality of entitling a play with such a purely trivial or farcical effect in mind. If this sounds too idealistic, consider the proof. Are *As You Like It* and *All's Well that Ends Well* truly throwaway? The meaning of the former is not actually so very flippant although the immediate effect is admittedly offhand, if what it in essence implies is that the originator was modestly reminding his audience that he was simply trying to do what they expected of him. (As Alfred Harbage's own book title had it, *As They Liked It*.) Rosalind's Epilogue inherently confirms this judgment in that she charges the audience "to like as much of this Play, as please you," hoping thereby that "the play may please" (12–13, 15–16). Shakespeare was obviously obliged to play up even to the expectant groundlings in this respect to the extent that he was a sensible individual businessman, not to mention stockholder in the theater, and thus aware of spectators' paying to come, get their money's worth, and be satisfied. But, to qualify that, he would still have been sensitive, and for more than mercenary reasons, to the audience's wishes in the finest sense. Pure frivolity was simply out. (In contrast, a modern review of a production of this comedy about the Forest of Arden was neatly published as "As You Like It?" But in such a case the meaning was accommodated for critical purposes; it questioned, in effect, whether modern actors and actresses can get away with whatever they like on the stage, even if the original meaning is grossly distorted. An English 'programme' for the play I was once handed went so far as to display the backside of a woman, albeit clothed.)

Likewise, *All's Well that Ends Well* need not be taken as really throwaway—even if it may have, as a conscience-stricken lady student happened to fear during my graduate school days at the University of North Carolina, Machiavellian connotations, thereby prompting us to assume the questionable ethic that the end can truly justify the means (thus: "if it ends well, then the means used, whatever, just *have* to be good ones," including here the use of the notorious bed-trick to deceive the too-ardent lover). On the face of it, however, the title of this romance does have a certain subtle, teleological suggestiveness that need not be construed as offensive, even as philosophically it harks back to the familiar Aristotelian principle of Final Causation.

Some critics maintain that Beatrice's bombshell, her command to Benedick to prove his love aggressively, "Kill Claudio" (presumably an emotional hint to "challenge him to a duel"), is the high tension point of the play, making it swerve momentarily toward revenge tragedy, so that the audience needs to be put back at ease with an ultimate reassurance that her command and its aftermath amount on the face of it to much ado "about nothing" in that Claudio and Hero are finally to be reconciled. Yet can we be fully at ease with this 'worked-out' notion for justifying the *Much Ado* label? Beatrice's sharp directive was actually in strict enough keeping with standard love conventions insofar as honor and duty were represented as being in due counterpoint to the exigencies of a love match. (Analogously, one might enlist as a gloss the saying that thereby "all is fair in love and war," were it not for that bromide being almost as egregious in modern parlance as is the "much ado about nothing" dismissal.)

At any rate, although the duel which she challenges Benedick to have with Claudio never comes off, the effect of her entreaty, the main purpose of which is to have Benedick reveal his love for her in a manly way, hardly amounts to much fuss about naught, nor is it a melodramatic turn which needs a purely comic resolution. It is essentially an ingredient of her feminine makeup. For when honor was at stake, an affront such as Claudio's renunciation of his bride-to-be in church would have been taken most seriously. For all its supposed fashionable conformity, it amounted to a shocking offense against tact and taste. Instead of urging, therefore, that her abrupt imperative remark supports the controversial title, let us propose instead that it was meant to hark back to the theme of love's labors being on the verge of getting lost again. Thus its main thrust is to glance forward to the forthcoming dénouement, whereby the labors of Cupid win out or are finally rewarded. Her command also tests Benedick.

With this effect in mind, consider the ways in which the meaning of perhaps the superior title, *Love's Labour's Won,* invests the comedy with truly deeper significance. The main contention here is that the theme of love being finally victorious is essential because of the counterplot: the Don John/Borachio machinations against Leonato's daughter. On the other hand, the Beatrice-Benedick subplot is relative minor, although wittier, mainly representing a foil to the principal action, and so does not correlate as much with the title. We may rightly assume as much, the fame of lady Beatrice's witty characterization of this early Comedy of Manners notwithstanding, for in Shakespeare's pre-Romantic times dramatic action always took precedence over mere character development, decorative gallantry, or simple chitchat. To that extent his work accommodates the standard Aristotelian framework in the *Poetics*.

One advantage of the presumed earlier title of *Won* is that it serves forcibly to set off the import and impact of a character who has hitherto too often been given short shrift: Don Pedro, the so-called 'reasonable man' in the patterned trio. His role is not important in itself but only in that it ensures that love will eventually, if laboriously, win out—not only with regard to Hero and Claudio, but specifically with their witty and lovable counterparts, cousin Beatrice and Benedick. Don Pedro's self-made role becomes, therefore, that of a double matchmaker. On a more classical level, however, he operates as the standard Mean between the extremes of Claudio, as the all-too-conventionally 'correct' paramour, and Benedick, as the stereotypal confirmed bachelor. Since Shakespeare, like so many Renaissance poets, was considerably involved in deploying such a classical Mean in behavior, the critical rehabilitation of Don Pedro as moderator is of major import for properly reassessing what the play mainly concerns. In this vital connection, the titular or thematic paradox of much ado concerning nothing offers no structural relevance and so might better be dropped.

We might compare other plays in which the use, or lack, of the Mean pointedly affects the outcome, notably *Romeo and Juliet,* which exemplifies intemperate behavior and a somewhat incompetent attempt to apply the Mean for remedial purposes. Whereas the Friar once counsels the lovers to behave moderately, objectively speaking his dubious actions or lack of any often belie his intentions, as has more than once been pointed out (Hartwig 82, 107–8, 209; also Ch 5 of this book). In contrast, the significance of the title *Measure For Measure* is partly that a due Mean is to be sought—"Measure" being a common Renaissance synonym for that—although the biblical maxim "Judge not, that ye be not judged" is also duly resonant, as is again well recognized. A further titular meaning is that the play reflects both tragedy and comedy, the label suggesting that these genres are being measured off against one another, with the net result that a form of what used to be called tragicomedy emerges.

Consequently, we can validly applaud Don Pedro's efforts to act as a middle man, even as he fits that way into the tradition of the Mean. After he tells of Claudio's love being "won" for the latter (2.1.267–68), although only nominally so as it turns out, he speaks of undertaking the further "labour" of bringing Signior Benedick and Lady Beatrice "into a mountaine of affection" (2.1.326). These warm words reflect the titular meaning of *Won*. Serving as a foil to him, his unruly bastard brother Don John notably questions whether this labor is truly achieved when he alludes to "sute ill spent, and labour ill bestowed" (3.2.86). Finally, at the end, Leonato likewise echoes the theme and title with his phrase "if your love / Can labour" (5.1.269–70). These close resonances of the original title would be revealing enough, as such literary echoes go, and no other comedy has a title like these; they can scarcely be casually dismissed as merely coincidental. Clearly they better the additional 'echoes' in *All's Well*. Recalcitrant critics who would blithely assign Shakespeare's 'lost' play to yet another script that is extant are herewith challenged to come up with another such meaningful collocation of verbal parallels elsewhere to support such a verdict.

In a manner of speaking, Hotson had his point in observing that an obvious parallel for the title, as related to *Lost,* does occur in *Two Gentlemen of Verona:* "If [the object of love] be lost, why then a grievous labour won" (1.1.33) (Hotson 38). It should be borne in mind, nonetheless, that this analogy hardly supports his anomalous solution regarding titular meaning (namely that the title supposedly warrants the gloss "Love Sorrow is Gained"). And, likewise, *Lost* titularly derives more immediately, as is well recognized, from a phrase in Jon Florio's *First Fruites*. In turn, *Won* originates more immediately from both the Florio phrase and the complementary title of *Lost*. By the same token, we might compare how close verbally the lines "Shee is a woman, therefore may be *wonne,* / Shee is

Lavinia therefore must be lov'd" are to such expressions as "a Doe" (=ado) and especially "this adoo" in *Titus Andronicus,* 2.1.88–89, 93, 98. Curiously comparable collocations may thus be apropos of our titular problem.

Further, a leading point to bear resolutely in mind is that when Don Pedro announces that Hero is "won" (2.1.267–8), the *Won* title is not yet itself won or vindicated, but only hinted at, for she is obtained only superficially at this point and needs to be fully accepted, an event which does not occur until the dénouement, that is, after the effects required for true love have been duly accomplished. These labors are Herculean ones in a valid metaphoric sense, it being no coincidence that explicit allusions to the mythic strong man are extant in both *Lost* and *Won,* thus further helping us to link these two comedies. Although F. N. Lees used the Herculean argument to contend that *Won* is really *As You Like It* (169), that comedy was clearly written later, and in any case the kinship was noticed as linking *Won* and *Lost* as far back as 1860, as noted by A. E. Brae and thenceforth glossed as such in the Variorum edition of *Much Ado* (369–70). In another sense yet, Claudio is the figure who basically has to be 'won over,' so that the winning has to be effected more on his side than on any other. Such complexity, moreover, adds depth to an otherwise seemingly conventionalized or stylized title.

If the eventual winning over of Cupid is the dominant motif, it should come as no great surprise that several critics have found that the key word in the comedy, far from being *nothing,* turns out to be *love* itself. John Russell Brown with Ralph Berry (155) in his wake have commented on the running metaphor of the latter abstraction in this work. Those die-hards who would want to urge that the better thematic term is *nothing,* perhaps because of their stubborn adherence to *Much Ado About Nothing* as a descriptive main designation, have not much of a case, for the use of *love* throughout is ostensibly thematic, whilst the passing allusions to, or word games on, "nothing" are largely ingenious and of minimal import. In effect, then, the comedy essentially represents Much Ado About *Love.* It could even be retitled as such, were it not for the almost cliché-like effect this title would also have today, whereby "Love" is all too often a modern euphemism. Indeed, taken as a titular pastiche, such a substitute title (t_4) has at least, let us say, *something* to recommend it, even if it would never be assimilated seriously as Shakespeare's in the theater. No doubt a modern-day audience would balk at so obvious a shift and squirm at the implicit sentimentality; the substitution would be like taking Cibber's *Love's Last Shift* and translating it literally for the stage, as in effect done once in *La Dernier Chemise de l'Amour*.

Granted, some scholarly exegetes might contend that the ideas of 'love' and 'nothing' need not be so very far removed from each other, for aside from the overplayed and questionably relevant meaning of 'nothing' as then plausibly connoting the female pudendum (cited *en passant* earlier), the zero device has been traditionally related to the circle symbol when considered as emblematic of love's constancy (on which, see my "Donne and Dante"). Again, such an association, however plausible, can lead to grotesque views if greatly overplayed. Shakespeare was hardly writing so symbolically for the proscenium arch. If one likes, moreover, one can playfully relate the nothing/love association even to tennis (a game which happens to be cited in this comedy in 3.2.42), the very term *love* there being used technically to designate a deficiency of score (as submitted in my "'Love' in Tennis"). Curious though this conjunction is, inasmuch as the etymology of the term in the game shows a historical connection rather with the French *l'oeuf* (meaning *goose egg*), the sportive link is very probably no more than anomalous here.

Further, if the *nothing/love* association is related abstractly to Love capitalized and thus even to the divine αγάρη, another issue arises. In itself, such a correlation is plausible enough, to be sure. The New Testament memorably affirms that "God is Love," and medieval tradition (especially in the writings of St. Bonaventura) subscribes to God as "a Circle Whose center is everywhere and circumference nowhere," as thereby having no beginning or end. So the symbol of love in circular terms is finally perfectly rounded out in our understanding of the Almighty. On the other hand, when taken as the zero the circle also designates sheer nothingness. The problem that then emerges is how we are to justify concomitantly a symbol for the Deity which is also just as easily interpretable as the sign of God's absence, and thus of vacuity. If these two designations are merged, the unintentional conclusion could even be that this symbol of the Almighty supports an atheistic thesis.

In any case, this sort of paradox did charm Elizabethan audiences, the purported School of Night notwithstanding, although it is one of the kind in which Mephostophilis would have delighted. The implications of paradox may not be fully ignored. In stark contrast, let us say, to the standard symbol of God in circular form Eucharistically, some modern critics have urged instead that at least God's proclaimed Ineffability might better be captioned as 'The Oblong Blur.' Ironically enough, at least that rectangular geometric form can serve to cancel out the disconcerting ambiguity of the circle symbol; that is, if it points to the Ineffable in terms of the incommensurable Golden Mean Rectangle, based on what Fra Luca Pacioli memorably labeled *La Divina Proportione* (see Ch 5). Comparable also is the old problem of squaring the circle. At any rate, the master dramatist would hardly have wanted spectators to get wrapped up in the intricacies of such theological double-play. And so we have further rationale for not adhering to the *Much Ado* tag, which can pose such problems. Further, the ambiguity inherent in *nought* as analogously synonymous (etymologically, as well as phonetically) with the word *naught* in the bawdy sense of *naught-y* can readily be disposed of as well as simply too coy, at least for the model theatergoer.

One further titular connotation of *Won* deserves special attention. The title, aside from being a variation or further development of the theme inherent in *Lost*, must clearly have had some relation initially, if only in terms of contrast, to the well-known monastic shibboleth known as labor of love. Since, in the earlier play, the decision of the gallants to avoid the company of ladies and devote themselves exclusively to scholastic diligence directly parallels the activity of monks in likewise avoiding the fair sex to concentrate on their own labor of love, reverent worship of God in prayer and work, and thereby not to be beset with ugly sin, the applicability of the medieval phrase to the comedy has aesthetic merit. Whereas in the first play of what we might now call Shakespeare's 'love cluster,' namely *Lost,* the meaning of the titular phrase was twisted about somewhat, so that the final labor of love involved love of women, though postponed for a year in tacit deference, no doubt, to the more reverential meaning of the love/labor collocation, in the follow-up drama of *Won* the theological connotations of the titular expression have a more direct bearing on the action. At least we witness the significance of the climactic scenes taking place within an ecclesiastical milieu, a church being the setting first for a would-be wedding and then a would-be funeral, a ceremonious friar duly officiating at both events. Shakespeare was thus secularizing the religious meaning of 'labor of love' but still fusing the more modern meaning with its clerical signification by having key scenes and reversals occur under the aegis of Holy Mother Church.

In contrast, the applicability of the title of *Won* to other plays is not so noticeable and simply does not invite such a parallel. Sir Edmund Chambers' offhand generalization that "almost any love comedy might bear the title in question" has thus been understandably demoted as "wild" by Hotson (38). Chambers sensibly did, however, at least reject the all-too-common identity of *Won* with *All's Well,* the style of which is usually recognized as much too late for the comedy (for a full run-down of which, see my *"Love's Labour's Won* and the Occasion of *Much Ado"* 107 n2). Worth comparing is Raymond Chapman's proposal that the Johannes de Witt sketch of the Swan Theater reveals a character presumably acting like Malvolio in 'an earlier version' of *Twelfth Night* in 1598, but this is a very tenuous suggestion, for the play represented need not even have been Shakespeare's, for example. In any case, as far as *All's Well* is concerned, the late Eliot Slater recently corroborated the view that *Won* could not have been the same play stylometrically.

In any event, it is generally believed that *As You Like It, Twelfth Night, Troilus and Cressida* (the last being Hotson's candidate, no one else's), and *All's Well* were all written later than 1598 and so could not be the same play as *Won*. To raise the unexpected specter of the possibility of any of these plays having been written earlier in another form is supererogatory when such so-called ghosts can have supposititious existence only. (The way one wit put it, it is quite difficult, as Hamlet ascertained, to discern the nature of a ghost. So too with ghosts in the bibliographic sense.) One favorite assumption nowadays apparently, namely that the 'missing' play was really *All's Well* but in an early version, has to confront the issue of the vast difference stylistically between *Won*'s complementary comedy, *Lost,* and the problem play. Reliable word counts strongly oppose such a correlation anyway. Thus, Metz tells us that "almost all those who cannot accept an early version of *All's Well* for identification with *Love's Labour's Won* object on grounds of style" (4). His further remark that I dismiss the association "summarily" "merely because the association is old, 'having been made in 1764'" (4) is incorrect, and at any rate this chapter is the best rebuttal of him. It might be well to note in passing, though, as Metz does, that Malone first accepted the identification with *All's Well* but then abruptly changed his mind. Probably the identification has lingered and become what Metz calls "the predominant solution to the mystery" largely because of the authority of T. W. Baldwin's book *Shakspere's "Love's Labor's Won,"* which is now dated because he does not take into account sufficiently the stylistic factor.

Another curious assumption has been that *Won* was but a substitute title for *The Taming of the Shrew,* which was oddly not accounted for by Francis Meres though also written by the end of 1598. True, the possibility that *The Shrew* (t3) represents the 'missing' drama deserves some passing inspection. As prominent a Shakespearean as Stanley Wells has recently suggested reconsidering that plausible identity, yet without producing any new evidence and only *en passant* (see his entry in *Shakespeare: An Illustrated Dictionary*). The principal argument against *Won* being *The Shrew* is, however, well enough recognized: the fact that both plays were cited concomitantly in a bookseller's stocklist after the turn to the seventeenth century, as T. W. Baldwin showed in his book. Admittedly, the list referred not specifically to *The Shrew,* but *A Shrew,* on the surface perhaps suggesting a slightly different play. Nonetheless, it is now widely believed that the former comedy was the dramatist's revision of the latter (both therefore being his versions). The strong likelihood is that the bookseller meant to allude to only one *Shrew,* Shakespeare's, whether the early or late draft, and happened casually to dub his assignment *A* rather than the more customary *The* (as a casual title reflecting his casual assignment). Still, the question can be fairly raised: Why did Meres neglect citing one of the two *Shrew* plays in his important listing? And can this important query be adequately answered?

Various reasons are worth momentary entertaining. To begin, Meres likewise failed to cite some other works by the same author (such as the *Henry VI* trilogy); thus the omission of either or both the *Shrew* comedies was no exception. Or he felt that the nature of the *Shrew* was simply farcical and thereby too slight to entertain; he may have believed that it did not warrant the treatment he wanted to accord the *œuvre* of the man he considered England's Ovid. Then he favored a neat, symmetrical arrangement, and the formulaic pattern he set up—six plays of one genre, six of another—could thereby have precluded his registering such a generic straggler as *The Shrew*. This appears to be the most commonsensical argument. *The Shrew,* moreover, was not a complementary 'response' to another play in the sense in which *Won* was to *Lost* in any case. Later it did prompt a reply of sorts in Fletcher's *The Woman's Prize, or The Tamer Tamed.* Because Fletcher collaborated with Shakespeare elsewhere, as is well known (for example, in *The Two Noble Kinsmen* and *Henry VIII*), it seems reasonable enough to infer that he would not have composed a 'sequel' to *The Shrew* if he was aware (as he would surely have been) that that play was *already* a response to another play (that is, represented the *Won* following *Lost*).

These reasons, some of which work together concomitantly, should be cogent enough to rule out the options of Meres's having felt the need to cite *The Shrew* and of others, at that time, having made an identification of the farce with *Won,* the title of which would plausibly suggest a relatively serious treatment of love-making. At any rate, the seemingly coarse management of the *Shrew* plot would scarcely have served to complement the highly sophisticated, euphuistic style of *Lost*. Although some modern criticism of the former would relegate its structure to a higher satirical level than has hitherto been allowed (the play being rather more than misogynist, especially in Kate's last long speech inviting mutuality), it still cannot be appreciated on quite the same urbane level as what can be called the mannered comedy, namely *Lost*. And does it not appear fitter for the sophistication complementing that of *Lost* to be discernible in *Much Ado*? Clearly the one thing that may be holding back such a kinship is the latter *full* title, which, if this chapter has done its job, may now be put on the back burner in favor for *Won*.

Next also briefly reconsider the candidacy of *As You Like It*. If it was composed and produced later than 1598, then it would have to be ruled out as an alternate title of *Won,* and indeed a number of factual points do indicate a later date. First, the comedy presumably contains a reference to the motto of the Globe, *Totus mundus agit histrionem,* found in Jaques' "All the world's a stage" speech, and the Globe did not acquire the motto as early as 1598. It appears rather more probable, let us say, that Shakespeare would have 'echoed' the theatrical motto as part of the occasion of his writing *As You Like It* than that the Globe proprietors would have translated this melancholy figure's pessimistic apothegm for their own money-making purposes. In this respect, we ought not to forget that the familiar first line of Jaques' speech points merely to a dismal catalog of human behavior traits to follow, one which the theatrical profession would scarcely have taken pride in seriously emulating. On the other hand, an alert playwright could easily have accommodated such a motto in Latin, having an apt satirical transformation in mind.

Further, just as Kemp's withdrawal from Shakespeare's theatrical company enables us to date *Much Ado* with some precision, so "the date of Armin's entrance in turn enables us to say that Shakespeare wrote *As You Like It* for the summer of 1600," according to the authority of T. W. Baldwin, who notably added the following: "The date is further narrowed by 'The clownish fool' in motley, Touchstone. Now the fool or jester comes into the company with Robert Armin, who, as we have seen, succeeded Kemp about the spring of 1600. Since Armin did not enter the company before March, 1600, but since Shakespeare wrote a part for him in *As You Like It,* it appears that the play was not written before March, 1600" ("Shakespeare's Jester" 454).

As to the objection that a play with the imposing title of *Love's Labour's Won* would have vanished into thin air—akin to the great globe (or Globe) itself, as prophesied by Prospero—it is not so very believable that one of the master playwright's key, centrally composed dramas, being such an important answer to a leading comedy of his with a similar amatory label and one composed during the rich, productive middle period of his life, would simply have been blotted off the record. As Hotson very aptly intoned, "it will not do to imagine ... that somehow one of the six comedies rated by Meres as 'excellent' has been lost" (37). Or, to state this with a trial dash of wit, his *Won* can no more lie hid or be lost than can his *Lost* (Metz's dismissive title, *"Wonne* is 'lost, quite lost,'" notwithstanding). Indeed, Heminges and Condell have likewise assured us that the Stratford genius's "wit can no more lie hid, then it could be lost" (from their prefatory statement in the First Folio). As Hotson continued, "if a piece well known in 1598 and celebrated by Meres had been missing from their collection of 1623, voices would promptly have been raised in protest" (37). That Hotson himself made an unlikely selection of the 'missing' play ought not to detract from our considering his argument on its own objective merits. The very idea, playfully entertained on television by Samuel Schoenbaum (for Robert Cromie), that someone might suddenly uncover a hitherto unsuspected Quarto containing a brand new script of *Won,* is rather too remote a conception to warrant serious consideration, my esteem for his creditable caution notwithstanding. Granted, many things are 'possible,' but literary history often has to put up with what is, at best, probable or at least plausible.

The other explanation, then, that the play was preserved under an alternate title, is altogether more logical and acceptable. Not only do we have the precedent of *What You Will* as originally being such an alternative, but *All Is True,* the well-recognized, likely secondary title for *Henry VIII.* As Theodore Spencer, for one, observed, *"All is True* was evidently an alternative title" (201). The parallel provides an additional aid in that the initial titular word *All* can be thought of as, and probably was, a resounding contrast to the final titular word *Nothing* in the *Much Ado* label. With both titles as alternates, we can see them both as parallels to other titles. The point is that *All Is True* contrasted not only with Rowley's drama on the same king entitled *When You See Me, You Know Me,* but stood for an oblique, complementary contrast to the meaning of the title of *Much . . . Nothing* concomitantly. Further, new proof concerning the status of *All Is True* has been brought out by William M. Baillie (1979) and H. R. Woudhuysen (1984)—not to mention its appropriation as a main title by the editors of the new *Oxford Shakespeare*.

Another correlation of moment is worth adding: the subtitle of the play most recently reaccredited to Shakespeare, at least by Eric Sams, namely *Edmund Ironside* (on which see my correspondence in the *TLS* 3 Sept. 1982: 947). Sams's case, even if dependent to some extent upon E. B. Everitt's wide-ranging speculations, does not go nearly as far out on a limb as Everitt's, particularly with regard to other, later dramas, and does provide some new, factual evidence in support of the manuscript possibly (but still doubtfully, I think) being an example of Shakespeare's early apprentice work. What concerns us here is the subtitle, *War Hath Made All Friends*. Although befitting the patriotic nature of the chronicle history, this label likewise has a kind of 'flippant,' offhand feeling which can scarcely be taken literally. Evidently the meaning is that "war's calamities have made friends finally out of enemies," but that is a psychological reading-in and not the plain meaning of the subtitle as it stands, which is certainly reprehensible from a Christian point of view. It is arguable as well that, as with *Much Ado* considered as originally an offhand subtitle, the originally intended secondary label for *Edmund Ironside* might be remembered as the true one.

But the claim smacks again of something being trumped up. E. B. Everitt wrote, "Labelled on its outer cover *Edmond* [*sic*] *Ironside,* and generally so designated, this play carries as a headtitle its correct name—A True Chronicle History called War Hath Made All Friends" (149). Yet the point is that if this not so much ironic as flippant designation is 'correct,' then we may be making much too much out of the casualness of throwaway headtitles. Let us thereby consider that, in turn, *Much Ado* was so called because its likewise alternative title was given as a casual headtitle on the stage copy, which was then used for purposes of registration.

The question might finally be raised whether students of Shakespeare ought to be worried about such an imposing array of variant titles and effects. As if in direct answer to this poser, a recent essay on the role of Shakespeare in pedagogy noted "the importance of first teaching students the significance of the *full* titles of Shakespeare's plays: for example, *Othello, 'Moore of Venice'* induces the reader to consider the problems of the 'outsider'" (Maclean 27). Such significance in retaining the complete title of that tragedy happens then to have a bearing likewise on the occasion for perceiving *Won* as complementary to *Much Ado* in terms of main title and subtitle. In recurring to the pictography inherent in this association, notably with the play upon the double "o" effect in "Adoo," as harking back to the year of registration, not merely focusing on the titular *Nothing,* and then being in contrast to *Won* as *One* (suggesting appearance versus reality), we can see a certain parallel in the full title of the Venetian tragedy. In other words, with "*O*thell*o,* M*oo*re" the symmetrical interplay of the letter *o* at the beginning and end of the Moor's name balances the double *o* in the subtitle. Yet, in sensing such playfulness either unconsciously or for the sake of publicity, we need not go so far as to speak of any formal codification, cryptogrammatic meaning, or (perish the intrusion) cipher, all of which have become part and parcel of the anti-Stratfordian baggage. In suggesting such aesthetic interplay, we must be wary lest a cautionary reader infer that such lightheartedness is not to be taken at all seriously. The proper point is that it has a serious enough effect for the uncompromising literary historian. Thus even Shakespeare's laundry bills can have their value, small though the factual elements appear to be, if they can be put to some practical use.

The practical purpose here is that the student can become more sensitive to the interpretation of plot and subplot, title and secondary title, and thereby the complementary stress upon the theme of the labor of love. The love-labor plays are a pair not merely titularly, but because of the way they have come down to us textually. The New Variorum edition of *Lost* thus pairs this play with *Won* on the very first page of its Preface. The two dramas also represent Shakespeare's prime 'closed-world comedies,' a designation set up in serviceable correlation to Northrop Frye's better known formulation of the 'green world' comedies. The main irony in *Much Ado* considered as *Won* is related to the age-old contrast of reality and appearance, and although that generalization has been overused in the past in some cases, that is no reason for neglecting it here. The realness of love's labor being won as opposed to the mere world of the apparent suggested in the throwaway subtitle *Much Ado About Nothing* is what is at stake. Claudio proves less true as a lover than does Benedick, the heretic against love, yet at the end, in both cases, love's labor manages to win out. The love is thus achieved even through a professed antagonism. Since it is ironically 'lost' in church, even after it is initially, if only nominally, 'won' by Don Pedro for Claudio, it has to be ritualistically confirmed. The alternate *Much Ado* subtitle which then slipped in might therefore be largely dispensed with as a modern-day main title, the point being that it is perilous enough to reflect on literature *in vacuo* without its having to be taken verbally or literally that way in addition.

The suggestion, moreover, that *Much Ado* was a mere throwaway title to begin with has, for us, the distinct advantage of allowing us to let it live *literaliter* up to its name. In short, it can even be dropped and *Won* put in its place. Eventually the public would catch on. And such an action would scarcely be a radical modernization. Did not Meres and the seventeenth-century bookseller mentioned earlier already shun the *Much Ado* title because of its inherent flippancy?

True, one of the problems that critics may find in identifying the story of *Much Ado* with *Won* is that Claudio's final 'conversion' may not look, to them, as truly representing the winning of love. But such a demurrer bespeaks a lack of familiarity with the conventions. In effect, Claudio himself is nothing if not a creature of convention, a fact strongly attested to by his seemingly cad-like behavior in renouncing his bride-to-be in church. He wants it to be known that he feels his fiancée has misbehaved the night before and so is unworthy of him, and his justification, though ungallant, is based on a strict code of ethics. If the playwright had not wanted it that way, he would hardly have insisted on the need for publicizing possible *impedimenta* (4.1.10) as restricting a proper religious service. (He brought out the same idea in his most famous sonnet, perhaps thereby the most personal, no. 116, which commences, "Let me not to the marriage of true minds / Admit impediments" [1–2]. See Ch 4.) In sum, since this comedy, even if somewhat formalized in structure, is very plausibly Shakespeare's greatest, being more realistic and serious in its treatment of romantic material than the more fanciful dream-world plays, it ought to have, in the final analysis, proper titular recognition too. That way it would be living up to its name by being doubly *Won*. Yet whether the modern-day public would accept such a reformulation on the page or the stage, if only because of its 'giveaway' nature, is problematic. Imposing it, as with changing Falstaff's name back to Oldcastle (see the new *Oxford Shakespeare)*, might strike some as too élitist. In any case, one of the most authoritative of Shakespeare scholars, Sir Edmund Chambers, has declared that "Shakespeare came to *Much Ado About Nothing,* which some believe to be *Love's Labour's Won*" (131) and on the same page admitted that this play had an early alternate title.

Lastly, it might be seriously objected that the *Much Ado* label, rather than being fatuous, is great—as stage history would indicate. Oddly enough, however, no contradiction is implicit here, for plenty of fatuous titles have gone over well on the boards of the stage, notably of course with the modern Absurdist trend. What should be borne in mind is that the traditional label in question is 'throwaway' and, as such, successful in fact only as a sort of *non*-title. Still another criticism might be that if *Love's Labour's Won* was itself too much of a 'giveaway' title, why could not the same criticism apply to *Love's Labour's Lost*? In answer, the latter title is actually unexpected for a comedy which was intended to end happily and so naturally leaves the audience rather in doubt as to how it will all end. The tonal effect, at least, is quite different in both cases. In any event, the prime evidence favoring "*Much Ado* about *Love's Labour's Won,*" so to speak, is still in the diagram that now follows.

FOLIO ORDER	ORDER IN MERES
The Tempest	
Two Gentlemen of Verona	*Two Gentlemen of Verona*
The Merry Wives of Windsor	
Measure For Measure	
The Comedy of Errors	*The Comedy of Errors*
Much Ado About Nothing	
Love's Labour's Lost	*Love's Labour's Lost*
	Love's Labour's Won
A Midsummer Night's Dream	*A Midsummer Night's Dream*
The Merchant of Venice	*The Merchant of Venice*
As You Like It	
The Taming of the Shrew	
All's Well That Ends Well	
Twelfth Night	
The Winter's Tale	

The order of the plays in the First Folio compared with the order in Meres's *Palladis Tamia*, showing how *Love's Labour's Won* was 'misplaced.' (Reprinted from my article in *Shakespeare Survey*)

Chapter 3
The Case of the Embarrassing Em Space:
A Textual Solution to the "W. H." Mystery

"To the Onlie Begetter . . . M[aste]r W. H."
—Inscription by Thorpe for the *Sonnets*

Of relatively little concern heretofore to Shakespeareans and textual critics has been the extent to which the manager of a Renaissance printing house, Thomas Thorpe, was a notably idiosyncratic tradesman who indulged in anomalous effects, specifically with regard to the oversized spacing in probably the most famous of literary 'dedications,' that to the *Sonnets*. As one commentator had accidentally discovered, this gap or em space calls attention to itself suspiciously: "Incidentally or not, where all other spaces between words of the dedication are closed with full-stops, a blank space has been left between the 'H.' and 'all.' as if to attract the eye" (Brooks 271). Though that commentator is himself hardly authoritative, we might still ask why the em should thus attract the reader. It is certainly out of the ordinary.

One explanation is that it merely stands for a pause, so that it might be thought of simply as an example of Thorpe's quaint little rhetorical flourishes used here perhaps to cover up something concerning the identity of Master W. H. George Walton Williams has suggested the space may be "a device to signify the rhetorical pause after the introductory nomination and before the pre-posited direct object" (190), but I would question this (see Appendix A). Loose type is another possibility of course that may not be dismissed. In any event, Thorpe presumably closely supervised what his printer Eld did and so would have been aware of the gap in advance, and even quite plausibly could have instructed that it be inserted. The effect may be that the extra spacing inadvertently gives itself away, disclosing to the initiated perhaps what it was expected otherwise mainly to conceal. In any case, such an eccentricity should not be ignored, for it ties in with Thorpe's notorious penchant for such verbal clowning elsewhere. In an important matter like this so-called 'dedication,' the manager of the printing house, especially when his initials appear at the end, would most probably have taken full responsibility for such a curious detail of typography even though he would possibly not have been held usually or directly accountable for accidentals or similar minutiae (see Jackson, "Punctuation"; McLeod). It appears that Thorpe's quirkiness prompted deviations from the norm in his printing house, at least in a situation such as this one, but the import of the gap here has hitherto not come to the attention of the scholarly world (save for a few earlier contributions of mine [e.g., "The Case of the Embarrassing Lacuna" and my *riposte* to Foster in *PMLA* CII, 839–40]).

Thorpe's idiosyncrasies were first made something of by Sir Sidney Lee, Shakespeare's well-known biographer. For a useful preliminary study of Thorpe's "bumptious humor," "unctuous, florid style" as well as "high degree of accuracy," but particularly his unwillingness to "forego a pun," see Leona Rostenberg's paper for the Bibliographical Society of America. Her attempt to rehabilitate Thorpe foundered somewhat through her final suggestion that he was beguiled by others who wanted the *Sonnets* published "out of malice to Shakespeare" (152), which was a fanciful idea. (See also Katherine Duncan-Jones's important article, to be discussed more later.) Although her view that Shakespeare authorized the publication of his poems is, in part, plausible, the standard view is still surely that he would not have permitted their being printed in the ordinary sense, if only because of the potentially scandalous nature of their contents, notably with regard to the Youth as "Master-Mistress" of his passion and the Dark Lady. His wife Anne presumably would have had her animadversions, although her being pregnant when Shakespeare married her might imply that she was hardly a prude (see also Appendix A). Likewise because all other editions of sonnets then had regular, attractive titles supplied by their authors, Shakespeare would most probably have been a conformist and have followed suit if he had personally taken them to the printer.

Other cases of how such spacing can affect meaning may now be cited. One that comes readily to mind is the oversized space between the "O" and "rare" in Ben Jonson's famous epitaph in Westminster Abbey, allowing for either one of two readings (or conceivably both): *"Orare* Ben" (Latin for *to pray for Ben*) and "O rare Ben" (meaning he was the 'rarest' of poets and dramatic comedians). The present chapter is to suggest that a textual answer to the problem of the 'dedication' can open up new thresholds, revealing at last perhaps the true solution to the mystery of Master W. H., one on the generally overlooked level of managerial typographical quirkiness, a topic which it is hardly too quirky to consider objectively, although Donald Foster, in his reply to me in *PMLA,* has apparently thought otherwise.

TO. THE. ONLIE. BEGETTER. OF.
THESE. INSVING. SONNETS.
Mr. W. H. ALL. HAPPINESSE.
AND. THAT. ETERNITIE.
PROMISED.

BY.

OVR. EVER-LIVING. POET.

WISHETH.

THE. WELL-WISHING.
ADVENTVRER. IN.
SETTING.
FORTH.

T. T.

The 'Dedication' to Shakespeare's *Sonnets* from Q1, 1609 ed.

I
The Cryptic Cover-Up

Let us first closely inspect the key phrase in question:
M^r. W. H. ALL. HAPPINESSE.
It is clear that the somewhat extended spacing between the "H." and "ALL." (appreciably larger than any other between portions of this or other dedicatory lines) is, to the sensitive reader, eye-catching. So we may posit that it was meant to be that way. The most simplistic excuse for it would be that the compositor, in needing technically to 'justify the line,' in printers' parlance, merely botched the job. But would he have got away with that?

Now, with any other dedication, such an apologia could very likely suffice, but with the Introduction to Shakespeare's *Sonnets,* printed when the poet was beginning to become recognized, such a seeming textual blemish or at least inconsistency is especially hard to accept—even granting the inverted pyramidal structure here which, on the surface, would appear to call for special, irregular spacing with accompanying greater likelihood of error. (A possible accidental error of this type is cited in Appendix A, but even there the nature of the lacuna is open to question. An example of a geometrically shaped passage including numerous extra spaces is also noted, but none of them is at all textually significant.) The idea that the extra em space was merely a 'rhetorical pause' seems unconventional, at least from a printer's point of view, if not necessarily from an elocutionist's. For such a claim to make good sense, other rhetorical examples would need to be extant, and so far to my knowledge none has cropped up. True, it could be argued that the extra spacing resulted from the printer Eld's instinctive awareness that in a more conventional type of dedication what follows would normally appear on the next line, but again even that amounts only to random speculation here.

Considerable care would most likely have been taken in setting up a 'dedication' to one of this poet's works, even if it had to be a special rush job, for which no real evidence exists except for their being printed on the sly and afterwards apparently suppressed till 1640. (In using inverted commas around *dedication,* I mean to show that because it was signed by Thorpe and not the poet himself, it was not one in the usual sense.) Particular care should be taken even today with our more sophisticated and scientific methods of textual analysis, so that we faithfully reproduce the idiosyncratic 'dedication' precisely as it first appeared, making certain that the additional spacing is honestly represented, for this is hardly mere pedantry. In the past, most scholars have avoided duplicating the oversized space for no reason other than ignorance or because it seemed altogether supererogatory, but that is scarcely commendable, standard procedure for good textual criticism. Most likely, in their haste, they were misgoverned. The anomalous, symmetrical pointing throughout, moreover, should be duplicated as well, though that is not very relevant in this particular case. A good precedent for the continuous capitalization and end-stops after each word, incidentally, did exist; it was basic to so-called Roman lapidary inscription and is found in the text of Jonson's *Sejanus* (1603), also set by Thorpe, in a production of which Shakespeare was one of the principal listed actors (Duncan-Jones 157).

Given the import of this out-of-the-ordinary spacing, the lay reader is left with several plausible explanations for it, ones which may serve concomitantly: The printing house's intended symmetrical effect missed its mark, or Thorpe was simply indulging in his 'usual' flair or pretentious bombast perhaps, though its point here may at first appear enigmatic. Initially, an acceptable enough explanation emerges as to why he would have surreptitiously tried to avoid letting the uninitiated reader know who W. H. was, especially if, with his known penchant for wordplay, he cunningly planned to divulge the identity at the same time to the select few as a kind of in-house printing practice, if not quite simply a prank. The rationale behind his action could then be as follows: These sonnets, as is widely recognized, could easily enough have contained choice bits of autobiographical revelations published on the rebound, without the poet's express or at least wholehearted approval; but if, as seems at least reasonable, Thorpe secured such confessional poems (presumably in their approximate right order) from someone sufficiently close to the sonneteer to know that their author, in his heart of hearts, scarcely had anything much to apologize for, he would have wished to acquaint the attentive or inquisitive reader with sufficient information as to the nature of the obtainer, the 'accomplice' involved in the procurement of the poems. Such a circumstance is particularly understandable if the obtainer was a member of the Shakespeare-Hall clan, say the brother of the poet's son-in-law, one William Hall.

That supposition is in itself ultimately too speculative to build on or to take very seriously. (For that matter, another family member whose initials would also fit the bill, William Hathaway, has recently been resurrected again by Barbara Everett, but her view is very controversial, for why would the Hathaway wing of the family want to release the provocative Dark Lady sonnets? If anything, relatives of the poet's wife, Anne, might have wanted to hush these up.)[20]

At any rate, the name of W. Hall, as Samuel Schoenbaum has duly reminded us in his full-length biography (although without mentioning the em space as such), stares straight out from the 'dedicatory' page in these terms: "W. H. ALL." (219). In other words, Thorpe had apparently felt free to indulge in another of his in-house puns. True, Schoenbaum then hastened to qualify his admission by cautioning that the end-stop after the "H" would seem to detract from any anagrammatic reading, but it is extremely important to notice that since anomalous end-stops are consistently used throughout the 'dedication,' amounting to a kind of Thorpean insignia here, such a critical demurrer is of little import. For the argument can easily and validly be reversed: Would not Eld or Thorpe have attached the extra dots not only as a modish-seeming Roman lapidary embellishment, but as a quaint cover-up to conceal the identity of the dedicatee from the uninitiated? Such a view, though stressing Thorpe's idiosyncratic nature, is reasonable. He had his peculiar temperament, was a bit of a prankster in his own right. After all, he had punned in his previous dedication, to Marlowe's *Lucan,* on another obtainer of the document, Blount, and the adjective *blunt,* so why not again? Moreover, he soon afterwards put out an unauthorized text of Coryate's *Odcombian Banquet,* also printed by Eld (1611), and mischievously decided to include all of the prefatory material but none of the text (see Appendix A). Such an analogy would help prompt the usual verdict that his publication of the *Sonnets* was likewise unauthorized, thus allowing for his playfulness.

Previously the few Shakespeareans who had suggested a W. H./William Hall identity have been given short shrift evidently because of, first, the 'dedication's' seemingly anti-Stratfordian or cryptogrammatic effect from this standpoint, and

---

[20]In my reply to Donald Foster in *PMLA* (see the controversy cited in Ch 1), I mentioned the possibility of this William Hall as the obtainer of the *Sonnets,* but only then to demote (but not entirely subvert) the suggestion; yet, in his rejoinder to me, Foster did not pick this up, thinking that I definitely still favored the son-in-law's brother as the leading candidate for W. H.

because of the general bias favoring "onlie begetter" in the preface as "only inspirer" rather than "only obtainer." Let us confront both these issues.

First, the paronomasia, or uncomic wordplay, involved in the proposed identification, namely the premise that "ALL" was meant to perform complementary functions, although a habit found in various guises often enough even in Shakespeare's own writings (enough so to have made him a leading English punster), has made some hardened skeptics distraught, not without some reason, and scowl about the perils of all-too-ingenious Hotsonian or even anti-Stratfordian cryptography.[21] Hardly helping the matter, Hotson's labored and ultimately unconvincing codifications of the name *W. Hatcliffe,* whereby the "-Hat," for instance, was somehow to be picked up from the succeeding line in the 'dedication,' not to mention in the sonnets themselves, have failed to persuade the less indulgent scholars. Normally, critics are expected to raise eyebrows at the unprofessional, 'gamey' implications of any seemingly anagrammatic rendering (*homo ludens* notwithstanding). Strictly speaking, in any case, it must be candidly admitted that the usual anagram or cryptogram, almost by definition, involves transposition and inversion of letters, which is not the case here. The letters are strictly in the same alignment, whether the reading is "W. H. ALL" or "W. HALL"; they are merely respaced in the first instance. So the objection about perverse, inverse codification for the sake of double meaning simply does not obtain. Granted, of course, Webster's dictionary registers two meanings of *cryptogram* as follows: a coded, secretive rearrangement of letters, and any secret message (the second being the derived meaning). Yet if the "H. ALL"/HALL name-play be taken as cryptogrammatic in the second sense, virtually all name-play, rhyming, or punning could fall into this category, and that would be ridiculous. Whether a code is involved is not, however, the main issue here (on Thorpe's interest in anagrams elsewhere, see Appendix A); whether a less subtle cryptic message is, *is*. The latter would scarcely have been *too* bizarre for Thorpe and for Eld thereby to have conventionally followed suit.

---

[21] In this connection, it is amusing enough to recollect Leslie Stephen's key takeoff, "Did Shakspere Write Bacon?" about a proposed hidden cryptogram in none other than Bacon's own works, one 'revealing' that the Stratford man was their true author.

Secondly, regarding the semantics of W. H.'s designation, the key phrase applied to him, "the onlie begetter," would presumably suggest, if taken literally, that the poems were dedicated to none other than their only creator, William s*H*akespeare (*sic*), or to "*W*illiam *H*imself." Hazleton Spencer, for one, effectively disposed of this silly identification: "obviously Thorpe is not dedicating the book to its author" (32). More recently, Robert Giroux has claimed the same. In a word, Thorpe was hardly *that* eccentric. Would he have felt he had the official authority, moreover, to know how to dedicate the book to "the inspirer" especially when more than one was involved? Doubtfully so. It was one thing to be parabolic in one's own little habits, but quite another to go so far out on a limb as to be foolhardy.

Nonetheless, as mentioned briefly earlier, the argument that "W. H." was a misprint for the poet's own initials has been put forward recently by Donald Foster in *PMLA*, precipitating some praise but also expected demurrers in print. The point is that the name of the dedicatee would be almost the last place to expect a printer's error, and Foster's notion that "our ever-living poet" in the preface was God, not the earthly poet, has not found favor (whereas *"the* ever-living poet" might have), for the phrase was most evidently a compliment of Thorpe's to Shakespeare. Comparable was the printed phrase "live ever [Shakespeare]" by Richard Barnfield (Foster 46).

True, some of Thorpe's flamboyant printing techniques were unusual, to say the least. As Brandes pointed out long ago, the printer's term "begetter" is itself, in this context, curiously "far-fetched" (266). It is also seemingly bloated in its derived meaning. As Samuel Butler had sensibly commented, the pompous correlation of "onlie begetter" and "Sonnets" with "only begotten" and "Son" (and reference thereupon to eternity) in the Nicene Creed is too obviously recognized as an accommodation to be merely an odd coincidence. The manager of the printing house was evidently indulging in lighthearted wordplay, catering to his penchant for stilted hyperbole. Without being unjust to Butler, we might add to his *aperçu* the implicit signification that even as the *Son* was be*gotten* of the Father, so the *son*nets were, in the Thorpean version be*gotten* of none other than the one who *got* them for him, namely Master W. H. Hence even more wordplay is evident. But clearly he felt it was not too irreverent for the obvious credal reference. The

Nicene Creed, moreover, says, "begotten, not made"; hence the begetter was hardly the maker, as Foster has imagined.

Foster, to be sure, claimed in print that the religious parallel derives ultimately from the Bible (but the Creed is also indebted to that of course) as well as the *Book of Common Prayer*. He made his point well enough, but to most readers the very ritual-like effect of the inscription would have been more likely to recall the often-memorized Creed than either the Bible itself or the Anglican prayerbook. That is presumably why Butler insisted on the Nicene Creed having been echoed.

Thorpe's indulging in other precious expressions, such as the euphuistic phrase "wisheth the well-wishing" here, indicates that he was altogether capable of further eccentricity of just this caliber, certainly a kind in questionable taste by our soberer present-day standards. Comparable is his punning on *Blount* and *blunt,* as pointed out earlier. That he had paronomasia in mind again in perpetrating the W. H. mystery should not be put past him. Hence his need for the additional em space: Hall's lurking surname would otherwise stand out as a bit too obvious, when he was not that important to the world at large.

As I have noted in passing elsewhere ("A Plausible Mr. W. H."), Thorpe employed the quaint, biblical term *begetter* there in the sense of *producer* or *bringer-forth,* a meaning sanctioned by *OED* and incorporating that of *obtainer* (or *procurer*). The point was, as Dowden already carefully observed, *beget* could have the meaning of *obtain* or *procure* only when "the procurement is the result of producing": "we may 'beget' ourselves a reputation, that is, procure it by producing it" (1055). Thus, W. H. 'begot' the sonnets by producing in the sense of giving birth to them, but metaphorically only, that is *in print.* Foster, however, has contended that, *OED* notwithstanding, the derived meaning of *beget* as *procure* has no precedents. (At the same time, he thought its meaning of *inspire* has none either, but J. Q. Adams has found evidence otherwise. Thus, to my mind, even as Foster was wrongheaded about *inspire,* he was also about *beget.*) Compare "acquire and beget" in *Hamlet* (3.2.7).[22]

---

[22]One of the side issues involved here is whether "W. H." was responsible also for coming up with *A Lover's Complaint,* published along with the *Sonnets* as likewise by "Shake-speare." In the past, the authenticity of this work was more in question. Thorpe could have got access to it otherwise of course but more likely it came with the *Sonnets.*

Biographer Peter Quennell revealed (1963) that he also recognized this signification, one oddly bypassed by countless Shakespeareans; he reaffirmed, in his quatercentenary life of the poet, that William Hall, according to Sir Sidney Lee, "had given the manuscript life by delivering it into a publisher's clutches" (124). Yet this link has not been given its due, largely because Thorpe's inimitable ways have been somewhat overlooked, but also perhaps because of Lee's reputation for wavering. Lee, for example, was known for changing his mind rather drastically. He changed his own name (which was Simon Lazarus originally); he switched from considering Pembroke as the Youth to favoring Southampton; and in spite of his Appendix on "W. H." as W. Hall in his Shakespearean biography, he eliminated this consideration, apparently on questionable grounds, for an entry in the *Dictionary of National Biography*. As a literary historian-cum-folklorist, he was guilty of confusing terms in the printing industry and is hardly considered an authority in discussing stationers. But that did not make him unreliable *in toto*. Samuel Schoenbaum often cites him creditably.

The wrongheaded inference that "onlie begetter" meant "one and only inspirer" has itself unduly inspired all too many Shakespeareans, although it has been sensibly noted, and not merely by the intrepid Dr. A. L. Rowse, that "the 'lovely boy' was not the *only* inspirer of Shakespeare's sonnets, many of which were addressed to his mistress" (Halliday, *Shakespeare* 208). Peter Alexander (94) picked up the idea that Hall's marriage in 1608 could have been what inspired Thorpe to refer to "that eternitie promised by our ever-living poet," meaning that Thorpe wished the marriage to be blessed with a son. Martin Seymour-Smith sized the "begetter" problem up well in his edition of the *Sonnets* by noting that "the dedication of a publisher is more likely to express gratitude for provision of profitable copy than for the rather more obscure honour of having inspired it" (15).

Another issue at stake is the conundrum of W. Hall's own identity. Sidney Lee, as is well known, has been verbally pummeled for his guess that the Hall involved was not only once a stationer's assistant, but identical with a later printer with the same name, the same as the signer of the inscription for Philip Howard's and Robert Southwell's *Meditation*. (The latter provided recognizable emendations.) True, Lee's portrait of Thorpe has been taken to task in general for its relative superficiality, for he hardly investigated the manager's publications other than the *Sonnets*. He also built up for Thorpe "a picture of systematic roguery and sharp practice," a view that had "never been seriously challenged" (Duncan-Jones 152). At times, however, Thorpe was only "something of a prankster" (Duncan-Jones 155), as was true here.

Katherine Duncan-Jones is a keen scholar, but her opposition to Kenneth Muir's position regarding misprints in the *Sonnets* scarcely supports her case that their publication was authorized, a position which is very doubtful. As she shows, Muir "suggested cogently that many of what Lee described as 'misprints' can be more plausibly explained as faithful renderings of the accidentals of an authorial manuscript, though one 'presumably' published without the author's permission"; her idea then is that Shakespeare simply did not trouble himself to "correct the normal crop of errors which appeared in Eld's text" (171). Such a dogmatic verdict, which would make England's leading poet appear regrettably like an incompetent, seems highly questionable. Clearly his *Venus and Adonis* if not necessarily *The Rape of Lucrece* were well proofread. (J. Karl Franson, in a recent note, has strong numerological evidence that the dedicatory pages to both poems were consciously composed with Southampton's age in mind, a thesis based on Alastair Fowler's finding the same number operative in *Venus and Adonis*. Such learned self-consciousness is totally missing with the publication of the *Sonnets*.) The notion that Thorpe faithfully followed accidentals in the manuscript before him need not in itself suggest roguish practice, as such, but quite the contrary. It shows a certain faithfulness, for Thorpe was meticulous.

A tangential problem is whether proof exists that Lee's William Hall had any connection with the Stratford Hall family. Only one scholar in the past had noted in print that the Hall involved could easily have been "related to Shakespeare's son-in-law, John Hall," namely K. R. Srinivasa Iyengar (311), a biographical inference that would naturally come to mind, though his suggestion was given short shrift by others before my earliest published research on the subject. Recently Joseph Boe also cleverly but not quite convincingly picked up the notion. Critics often have been hesitant to venture out very far on such a theoretical, autobiographical limb. For some time the standard documentary account of Shakespeare's family members, that by B. Roland Lewis, did not admit of even any William Hall related to Shakespeare's son-in-law, Dr. Hall (also later of

Stratford). In 1961, however, Mark Eccles did uncover just such a kinship. More on that matter in due course.

For the time being, let us return to another key issue: Why should Thorpe have oddly wanted to conceal, and concomitantly still privately spell out, the name of his accomplice? A logical enough answer is not too hard to come by. To begin, stylistically he was not above such redundancy, to which his awkward inclusion of the phrase "wisheth the well-wishing" attests. As a reviewer of Giroux's book put it, "'Mr. W. H.' is Thorpe slyly hinting at the truth without giving himself away" (Jacobs 373). He liked to play with names elsewhere as in his dedication to another member of the stationer's trade, Edward Blount, wherein he would "purpose" to be "blunt" with "Blount" (presumably itself pronounced *blunt*). Evidently, with the *Sonnets,* he desired to avoid acute personal embarrassment to the Stratford "upstart," who probably had no original intention of seeing these poems published (though, like most good poets, he did revise such works, evidence for which Gary Taylor has commented on in the *TLS*), yet he apparently allowed for their publication if only because of W. Jaggard's pirated printing of them already in *The Passionate Pilgrim.* As Lee has flatly and correctly put it with regard to the begetter in question, "Hall was not a man of sufficiently wide public reputation to render it probable that the printing of his full name would excite additional interest in the book or attract buyers" (92–3). Hence the riddling initials were used for simple, low-keyed reasons of commerce. And yet Thorpe wanted to give Hall somehow the credit this opportunity deserved, so he dreamt up an ingenious way of so doing and one not without some precedent even in his own repertoire. His little typographical trick, the added em space, ironically thus proves to be a cause of embarrassment to the scholars who have ignored it, but in being that it was at least not meant as such for the poet.

Most likely Thorpe would have secured the manuscript *indirectly* from the author with the latter's probably reluctant consent, or at least tacit lack of full approval, in that the lyrics appeared "in a text not very badly printed, but badly enough" (Spencer 31). As everyone concurs, the author evidently did not proofread them. If the poet had *officially* authorized their publication, they presumably would have been registered with his full name and at least with a proper title, not merely so randomly as "a booke called Shakespeares sonnettes." Admittedly, Katherine Duncan-Jones has not found it so peculiar that the poet's full name was not registered, because he was well known at that time and "many of the plays were entered without any author's name at all." Yet the lack of an authorized *title,* at least, would give us more pause, as she herself admits, in that "unlike any other Elizabethan sonnet sequence, this collection had no identifying title or names of participants" (153). As for the lack of names of participants, Shakespeare himself would more likely have had more cause for refraining from naming them than Thorpe would have had for his own reasons of publicity. It is possible, though, that the procurer, if a member of Shakespeare's family (however close or distant), easily drew the line there. On the other hand, if the sonnets got to Thorpe on the sly, as has been often surmised, we have no reason to believe that the identity of the participants would have been known to him in the first place. Certainly he would not have identified the Youth with *Master* W. H., even retroactively, if the Young Man was William Herbert in his early years, if only because in 1609 the Earl would have merited more than cursory recognition in any kind of dedication. So, too, with Southampton.

For what it is worth, the offhand hyphenated label on the title-page, *Shake-speares Sonnets,* although hardly an unusual spelling of his name then, at least also tells that the author himself would hardly have authorized such impersonal orthography. Yet its primary import is that it indicates again Thorpe's peculiar little penchant for spaced-out name-play. As with "W. H. ALL," in effect, so with "Shake-" and "speare." One likely basis for the name game implicit in this break-up of the surname was conceivably in part the desire to verbalize the poet's attainment of a coat of arms fairly recently in which a falcon brandishes a spear. If the cautious reader prefers to find such an explanation a bit mild, he ought to concede that it at least outweighs the outrageous anti-Stratfordian view that a pseudonym would have been implicated by such hyphenation. Granted, a stronger analogy with spacing in Thorpe's name-play is evident in his use of acrostics (see Appendix A), but not to be dismissed so easily is a hitherto unknown pun on "speare" in reference to Shakespeare, recently brought to light by R. C. Horne.

Thorpe's eccentricity is said to be evident also in his decision to dedicate these memorable poems to a lowly stationer's assistant, an underling or minor colleague of his. (Low-*keyed,* at least, his action clearly seems.) Although it appears valid enough for us to believe that if he felt or knew that Hall also happened to be a kinsman of Shakespeare, he would certainly have deemed he had sufficient justification for his seemingly quirky behavior, such hypothesizing does not get us very far. For there may simply have been two William Halls involved, one being the procurer and the other a family member, a plausible overlapping but not requisite.

The most ostensible example of his odd action here is in the idiosyncratic use of pointing, its Roman basis notwithstanding. The curious array of dots that he symmetrically incorporated throughout the 'dedication' nearly gives the impression that he was esoterically engaged in the old-fashioned game of geomancy. Granted, obvious enough artistry presents itself in his inverted pyramidal structure and dot-placement, but no proof exists that I am aware of that any other Renaissance printers indulged in such a mannerism. As Lee long ago suggested, moreover, Thorpe's extraordinary circumlocutions and affectations were characteristic of his ornate work in general:

> Most of his dedications are penned in a loose diction of pretentious bombast which it is difficult to interpret exactly. When dedicating in 1610—the year after the issue of the *Sonnets*—Healey's *Epictetus his Manuall* "to a true favorer of forward spirits, Maister John Florio," Thorpe writes of Epictetus's work: "In all languages, ages, by all persons high prized, imbraced, yea inbosomed. It filles not the hand with leaves, but fills ye head with lessons; nor would bee held in hand but had by harte to boote. He is more senceless than a stocke that hath no good sence of this stoick." (419)

Again the final punning on *stocke* and *stoick,* as with the *blunt/Blount* wordplay cited earlier (and somewhat like "W. H. ALL"), points to his penchant for rearranging, or more specifically respacing without realigning and inverting, the lettering. This is historically akin to Old German 'italic,' an East European phenomenon in general. Even though we know of no evidence that this kind of emphasis was popular in England, philosophically at least (if the idea is at all applicable here), it reveals at least yet another instance of νόμοσ (convention) being based on φύσις (nature). In other words, the use of the added em spacing in order to emphasize something has been a printer's device elsewhere. There was clear precedence for Thorpe's allowance for it.

Since most Renaissance scholars accept the likelihood that Florio and Shakespeare were closely enough acquainted (largely owing to the former's translation of Montaigne's essays which the latter might well have used in manuscript), the analogy quoted above is of no little interest. For example, previously some Shakespeareans have debated whether Florio might not have been the one fortunate enough to procure the poems for Thorpe, thus even prompting the latter's bombastic dedication to him later. Bearing the presumed Shakespeare-Florio connection in mind, we now might see that at least the oversized spacing with "W. H." was most probably not merely a fortuitous oversight (an *erratum*), or self-conscious rhetorical pause by itself, but an analogous, deliberately staged effect. Since the printer Hall was, as Lee assured us, "a careful printer with a healthy dread of misprints," Thorpe as at least a reliable publisher (to whom, for instance, Ben Jonson entrusted material) would most probably have gone out of his way to avoid a curious misprint or spacing without purpose in dedicating Shakespeare's poems to such a meticulous colleague. What Thorpe did was to allow himself to indulge in name-play involving a *seeming* misprint (or rhetorical flourish), and hence a deliberate extra em space, which in effect then turned out to be a learned jest. The appearance of dozens of misprints in the *Sonnets* themselves, then, is a bit of an irony, but not enough of a one to waive a healthy reluctance to admitting one in the inscription. All it means is that the poet did not do the proofreading and probably that Thorpe hastily had to rely on another for the text of the sonnets. (Care for the begetter and carelessness for the author of the poems? And why not? The 'dedication' was the first thing his readers would look at and so deserved specialized attention.)

Regarding the identity of the Master W. H. *per se,* the most publicized candidate recently proposed, Sir William Harvey, has his grave limitations, for "Master" was scarcely a valid variant of the knightly "Sir," regardless of how this candidate (or any other knighted benefactor) was addressed in private, friendly correspondence.[23] Clearly Thorpe's overburdened and pretentious style is at notable odds with the daring supposition that he would have allowed himself to use 'Master' when the normal, official, formal designation was always 'Sir.' It would have been certainly an uncharacteristic let-down for his notoriously obsequious nature if he had deigned to call a knight merely *Master.*

As is widely enough known, Dr. Rowse has promoted the W. H./Harvey affiliation, yet without giving due credit to his own predecessors, notably

---

[23]A. L. Rowse has disagreed in his biography (200)—and elsewhere regarding Mr. (Sir) Danvers.

Charlotte Stopes and the Comtesse de Chambrun (*Discoveries and Reviews* 119–21), the latter telling us that since Harvey was the third husband of the Dowager Countess of Southampton, and since she left "the most considerable part" of her property to him when she died in 1607, establishing him as her sole legatee, it is arguable that her death would have removed the last hindrance to the publication of the *Sonnets*. Curiously, Mme. de Chambrun then failed to mention that another, perhaps more obvious hurdle would also have been removed, namely the infelicity of giving offense to the poet's parents, both of whom were deceased finally by 1609 when these daring confessions reached the press. His presumably religious mother (from the old Roman Catholic Arden family) would most probably have been taken aback, to say the least, by the audacity of the Dark Lady sonnets (Pohl 112), not to mention by any deviate suspicions in earlier ones. Is it not then most reasonable to contend that the poems were intentionally brought to press and published within months after Mary Arden Shakespeare's death in September 1608 than that they were brought to Thorpe only *several years* after the Dowager Countess died? In any case, we have less reason to believe that Harvey would have known of Shakespeare's parents having died than that William Hall would have, presuming here that the latter was truly, and not merely nominally, related to the Stratford Halls (on which, see Section II of this chapter).

A final point is to be made about the Comtesse de Chambrun's reliability in this connection. Her Catholic affiliations doubtless made her more susceptible to belonging to the Southampton camp, even though the case for Pembroke has once been thought stronger. (We need but compare the relative number of pages assigned to the two candidates in the Variorum edition, not to mention Pembroke's own 'Dark Lady' poems.) Mme. de Chambrun erred, as we shall see, in presuming that an up-and-coming money-making printer and then publisher like Hall would not have published *both* Protestant polemics and Jesuitical devotional poetry. Why not? He was a businessman.

It is essential to clear the ground still further of some adverse scholarly debris. Fortunately most candidates for the W. H. role may be dismissed out of hand along with Harvey and Hatcliffe. Spencer thus demolished the pet but misguided view that the initials stood for Shakespeare's patron's name in reverse order: "It is strange that the favorite expansion of 'W. H.' has been into Henry Wriothesley; for there is nothing to connect Shakespeare with the Earl of

Southampton after the spring of 1594" (31). Let us hope that this inverted, *outré* initials argument (a commonplace once found in undergraduate teaching) has been put to rest.

At this point, a brief digression is warranted concerning Robert Giroux's recent thoroughgoing, if controversial, study of the *Sonnets*. His interpretation of "begetter" causes some odd problems. He begins with the flat, dogmatic statement that the meaning of this key word is *inspirer,* "the most obvious and soundest theory" (168). Such an assumption is simply too facile. For one thing, the "soundest" assumption by no means has to be the one which is "most obvious" in the sense of commonsensical. For another, as I have shown, the begetter/inspirer identification is hardly so very sound or likely when impressionable Shakespeare here tacitly admitted to having had more than one source of inspiration. Even leaving aside the Dark Lady, we have the Rival Poet, and other sonnets (e.g., nos. 116 and 145) were conceivably and happily inspired even by his wife, in what I would call the 'Faithful Wife' subgrouping (though not in a Gestaltist sense) (see Ch 4). Giroux goes on to concede that his interpretation conflicts with the evidence, notably with the 'Master' label, when he seizes on Southampton somewhat too readily as the begetter (being the inspirer).

So what is to be done? Giroux offers a number of suggestions. First, since Shakespeare did not write the 'dedication,' the problem can simply be bypassed (but that blatantly avoids the issue); secondly, "one can conclude that Thorpe may have been mistaken, or misinformed" (another escape). But then Giroux provides, inadvertently, the most sensible solution: "One can even surmise that Thorpe really knew who it was, and wanted to hint at it, without giving it away" (entirely, that is); "Thorpe's odd dedication reads like something a book publisher with a commercial motive *and* a printing problem might, under the circumstances, produce" (169). Without even considering the prime candidacy of William Hall, Giroux has independently hit on the same ideas as presented in this chapter. He goes a little far, however, in concurring with William Empson that Thorpe simply wanted to make a complete imp of himself.

Further, for him to say that "Thorpe's motive for writing so cryptic a dedication was that he 'was trying to keep out of trouble,' while at the same time attempting to create interest in a new book" (168–69, citing Empson) sounds a bit like out-and-out chicanery on his part. Thorpe would not have been quite so insensitive or foolish. It is simply unanalytical for Giroux, moreover, to call the 'dedication' merely "weird." The "printing problem" involved that he mentions was deliberately effected, but Giroux's use of the term *weird* appears purely adversarial. Frank Kermode's review of Giroux asserts that the book is, indeed, at times brash. His castigation of Giroux mainly for autobiographical interpretations, however, clearly represents an unhistoricist bias. (In contrast, Lois Potter's review found the book "sensible, well-written, and unstartling" and recommended it "for anyone who is not opposed to the biographical approach in principle") (cf. Ch 7).

The Variorum editor, Hyder Rollins, long ago noted that to read the poems outside of their real-life context is, in effect, to consider them *in vacuo;* so we have a psychological problem similar to that which we had in the previous chapter with *Much Ado About Nothing* as titularly frivolous. A great deal of Giroux's commentary is quite enlightening and helpful, yet it has to be read with great care not only for its style but because its occasionally misleading manner of interpretation and expression can throw one off. For example, for Giroux to state flatly that sonnet 20 is "most explicitly homosexual" (20) is too sweeping, especially when he admits three pages later that the question of whether Shakespeare's friendship with the Youth in the sonnets "was homosexual in a physical sense remains unproved" (23). Indeed. Unless one has a biological bias, when a relation is not physical why bring in the notion of deviancy at all? Even when the Youth is called "the Master-Mistress of my passion" in no. 20, we hardly need take him literally; in truth, an allusion to explicit, normal heterosexuality appears, as everyone recognizes, in 1. 13. Granted, the poet goes out of his way to express a lack of interest in the Young Man's sexual organs, though admittedly part of the reason could be because of the 'boy's' early age, especially if (a big if) he was Pembroke during the Plague Years. This seems at least conceivable on the grounds that Shakespeare was plausibly connected with Pembroke's Men at one point in his early career. As Halliday points out, "It is just possible that Shakespeare was with Pembroke's before joining the Chamberlain's in 1594.... The possibility that Pembroke's son, William Herbert, was the M[aster] W. H. of the *Sonnets* strengthens the hypothesis" (*Companion* 473). But because of the reference to the Youth's father having died in sonnet 13, the Pembroke theory does not appear workable in the long run. So "Master W. H." still points to the obtainer only.

II
Was W. Hall Kin to Dr. Hall?

To what extent could Dr. John Hall and W. Hall of the 'dedication' have been related? That, as the Dane might have intoned, is the intriguing question, at least in terms of biographical criticism. It is also pretty much of a fascinating family conundrum, though the evidence is admittedly rather sketchy at best. Yet, at the risk of snubbing those happy few who feel outside the bounds of responsibly speculative reasoning altogether, let us load the breech once more. In so doing, we can also make every effort to distinguish between valid and totally unwarranted hypotheses. The premise is that any valid new approach which might prove worthwhile with regard to knowing more about the life of England's greatest poet and playwright ought at least to be given a hearing.

In answer to the questions posed above, we might inquire first as to how the physician Dr. Hall could have easily become aware of his father-in-law's poetry considerably earlier than Hall's residency in Stratford, which was only after the turn of the century, would suggest. To begin, in his review of a biography of the doctor, Mark Eccles acclaimed its author, Mrs. Joseph, for her prominent discovery that the record of John Hall's B. A. at Cambridge in 1593/4 was signed by one William Covell, "a fellow of Hall's college who in 1595 was one of the first authors to refer in print to 'Sweet Shakespeare'" (43). This link happens to suggest, then, another kind, one with the likewise sweet, or so-called "sugred," sonnets circulating among the poet's "private friends." Was not Covell probably one of them? So at least some valid, if circumstantial, proof is extant that John Hall, as well as William Covell, could have had access to the love poems (if he had not also read them) soon after they were first composed.

Now this proof can be correlated with Eccles's own valuable addendum to Roland Lewis's biographical documentation on how John Hall had a hitherto 'lost' brother called William, one named after the father (112; see also Lewis II, 588). Actually a family tradition of christening Halls William may well have existed, for the grandfather was also so named. Eccles, moreover, tells of a William Hall of Acton, one of Carlton, and one of Bedford—all related. To these, we shall shortly try to correlate a William Hall of Hackney.

Such a proud succession of William Halls is useful to enlist if only in prompting the view that one member of the William Hall dynasty might very likely have felt some pressure exerted on him to live up to his imposing repetitive name and thus make something special of himself. Such a commonplace attitude is, after all, a perfectly natural one to invoke, not especially speculative in itself. It is tempting then to engage in another coaxing bit of theorizing: What better or more adventuresome way might he have had to make such a name for himself than by gaining vital access to the clandestine "sugred sonnets" of "Sweet Shakespeare" and doing something public with them? If he could get them published, he might easily have said to himself, that would prove to the world that he had justified himself and his name. With at least Dr. Hall's probable awareness of their dissemination, he had a lead. Men of Hall's college assuredly had the English fraternal tradition of sticking closely together, helping each other out, even more so when relatives were involved, in business dealings. So copies of the sonnets could have been almost at his elbow and hence disposal, whereby he could well have sensed an opportunity for success. With these poems, young Hall could make a name for himself, let us say, as an up-and-coming stationer. And, as if in support, Lee has presented evidence that his candidate also called William Hall was indeed an enterprising young printer, though inexperienced to the point that his good fortune failed him after a time (that is, some time after 1609).

Might not Dr. John have seen fit to pass any poetic manuscripts he had or knew about on to his kinsman William? Is such a conjecture really too extraordinary to entertain? Not as a valid speculation, at least, but it is hardly one to count on. Most likely Dr. John would have done so, however, if at all, only after he had established himself as a physician, had had time to add to his appreciation of matters Shakespearean (forsooth), even by contracting to wed the poet's older daughter, and had settled down comfortably in Stratford—in short, after the turn of the century and indeed probably after the entire sequence of the poems was composed. Some of them appeared during the Plague Years but several very likely after the turn of the century, if not long after (see Ch 4). Since his marriage took place in 1607, and since he would soon thereafter have been at least privy to news of the last of the poet's parents dying in 1608, he could at that discreet point have turned the sonnets over to an innovative relative, even plausibly his younger brother William, soon enough for them to be printed by

1609. Should it be argued that John Hall's marriage would naturally have made him think twice about seeing to press poems that his father-in-law had kept fairly private, the proper response might well be that the doctor felt that the poet would be at least secretly pleased at their wider dissemination. Shakespeare could even have acquiesced in, but not formally endorsed, their publication.

Again, it is worth stressing that this Puritan doctor would hardly have permitted for publication material overtly offensive to Shakespeare's father and especially mother before he prudently knew they were deceased. That the mother was of Catholic stock, and possibly the father, and he a Puritan, clearly would have made no difference with regard to such ethical or civil concerns. If anything, his realization that she, at least at one time, revered the Virgin, after whom she was evidently named, would have enlisted his sense of righteousness and appreciation of the piety of virginity even perhaps more from his Puritanical perspective than she from her own. If the poet's wife was not a prude (she was not a Catholic and was pregnant at the time of marriage), that might have helped some. This at least makes as much sense as biographer Fripp's bold claim that the sonnets came from the house of the deceased Earl of Oxford, whose daughter was at one time suggested as wife for Southampton. The point is that "how a MS. from that house could contain the Dark Lady Sonnets is not explained" (*The London Shakespeare,* ed. Munro 1288). The same point has been made apropos of the theory that they came from the Hathaway household.

Now if Dr. John's relative William, probably a *cousin* in this case, let us say, was the same as the stationer's assistant William Hall, the mystery could truly clear itself up, but that may seem too easy. Although such an association is hypothetical at best, *any* new glimmer which might be shed on the provenance of the sonnets ought to be in the record. So let us next ask: Who would have initiated the transaction? Would not the doctor's cousin, if seeking a name in the competitive printing profession, be in need of contacts, and thus desirous of some sort of *coup* firmly to establish, if not settle, his new-found reputation? Hence he could well have pressed Dr. John for any extant manuscript material known to fellows at his college. The distinct advantage of this approach is that it offsets Mme. de Chambrun's charge that a nonentity like the printer William Hall would simply not have had recourse to these poems. Will Hall was a more magical name than she suspected.

Granted, by using Occam's Razor, we might now try to simplify matters and consider that William, whoever he was, somehow got the sonnets directly without having to use Dr. John as an intermediary, but the latter suggestion, on the basis of the few facts we do have, may be more feasible. In any case, now a disclaimer of sorts is in order. It seems unlikely that, in spite of what I once contended in print (see "The Case. . ."), the physician's younger brother was involved. For the printer Hall started out in business in 1577, two years after Dr. Hall was born, and the brother was the youngest of William Hall the Elder's eleven children. But in this connection I must also defend myself again by pointing out that I have already revised my earlier views by implication in my critical exchange with Donald Foster in *PMLA* CII, 839–40.[24]

In the remainder of this chapter, I shall consider some factual, supportive material including, first, the evidence of Dr. Hall's will, whether the reputed relative who did the procuring could have been the same as William Hall of Hackney; second, the proof for the "W." in "W. H." standing for *William,* and last but, let us hope, not lost, that other dedication with "W. H." in it and its fascinating ties with the author Southwell, who himself dedicated a work to "Master W. S.," very likely Shakespeare. It would, in any circumstance, be rather too presumptuous to infer that Dr. Hall's possible awareness of Shakespeare's sweet sonnets already at Cambridge led him to get engaged to a member of the poet's own family. Such a thought may be nice and idealistic, especially if, as I suggest in the next chapter, some key sonnets such as no. 116 deal with the 'Faithful Wife,' but any such inference must ultimately be relegated to the remote category of the imponderables.

In short, let us not say that we can have true faith that W. H. was any relative of Dr. Hall's as well as being the printer with the same name. Given a choice

---

[24] I mentioned there that the idea that W. H. was Dr. Hall's brother was speculative, and I implied that it was also improbable by remarking that it was at least not as *"inherently* improbable" (italics in the original) as the argument by Foster that "W. H." was a misprint for the poet's own initials. In his rejoinder to me, Foster simply asserted that *I believe* that W. H. was in fact "Shakespeare's son-in-law's brother." This exaggeration of his, however, could have resulted from the vagaries of the editing process—that is, if I did not get a chance to review my copy-edited manuscript before it came to Foster's attention and before numerous editorial alterations had been made, some of which I was obliged to correct again in final proof stage. One such final revision involved the italicizing of the adverb *inherently* for obvious effect in context.

between the two Halls, one the kin of Dr. Hall and the other the known printer, the grounds for the printer's candidacy are, in terms of *primâ facie* evidence, far more logical. Such is my main focus. But, in any event, valid hypothesizing can now have its place, as I hope to show.

III
W. Hall's Acquisition

According to the *Dictionary of National Biography,* Dr. John Hall most probably left manuscripts in his will for his son-in-law, so that some Shakespearean materials such as books were very possibly included in what young Thomas Nash inherited. But I would not go so far any more as to contend that the "T. N." scribbled in the Aldine Ovid at the Bodleian, which has Shakespeare's purported signature, refers to this member of the Nash family. The date *presumably* given there, 1682 (hard to read), would simply be too late for him.

These residual papers were ones "which Hall and his wife, as residuary legatees, doubtless inherited in 1616" (Lee, *DNB* XXIV, 70–71). Why has thus far little or nothing been made of the likelihood of a Shakespearean connection? The only explanation that comes readily to mind is that, as Schoenbaum specified, "Shakespeare's play-scripts were not his to dispose of—they belonged to the King's Men" (*Compact* 305). All well and good, but that assignment does not account for non-dramatic material. Since many copies of sonnets were circulated in Renaissance times (as evidenced, for example, also with Constable's *Diana,* as my edition points out), it is unlikely that even if W. Hall would not have got the manuscripts back from the printshop after publication to return to the brother who originally got them for him, Dr. Hall could easily enough have retained his own copy, presumably after having passed on a transcript. (Admittedly, manuscripts were often carelessly used as filler material in binding books, but presumably a printer had *some* say in the matter of which papers to discard and which to preserve.) In any event, it is generally agreed that the copy processed by Thorpe was a transcript from someone other than the poet himself (Wells and Taylor 847).

Dr. Hall would have been duly respectful of the manuscripts of Shakespeare's poetry, not only because of their reputation at that time, and the family connections, but for natural reasons of vanity, because he was an author himself and possessed valuable manuscripts of his own: the medical notes, which had then been published in a number of editions. So, all in all, the items that he purportedly left for Nash could easily have contained a copy of the *Sonnets* in manuscript form. Further, the "study of Bookes" indicated in the will that he passed on to his son-in-law more than likely included volumes from Shakespeare's library; Schoenbaum has seen fit to cite Henri Estiennne's *Mervaylous Discourse upon the lyfe of Katherine de Medicis,* a book from Susanna Hall's library that was recently discovered, as quite possibly an item from her father's collection (249).[25]

The physician's will, at any rate, contains the following description:

It[e]m concerning my study of Bookes I leave them . . . to you my son Nash to dispose of them. As for my Manu=script[es] I would have given them unto Mr Boles if hee had been heere but forasmuch as hee is not heere p[re]sent you may (son Nash) burne them or else doe w[i]th them what you please. (Lewis II, 588)

If the invitation to consider incinerating these papers, Shakespeare's possibly included, seems at all disrespectful, we need but recall that, as a presumably staunch Puritan (like other members of the Stratford Corporation), Dr. Hall valued the 'spirit' and the life beyond more than the 'letter' (thus even more so than *belles lettres*). He honored his manuscript possessions but would hardly have gone so far as to *over*-value them. (For that matter, the composing of literature like plays, for example, was generally deemed an ephemeral occupation in those days, a good reason why relatively few manuscripts have survived.) In any event, as Lewis glosses this portion of the will, "There is no definite evidence as to what 'my Manu=scriptes' included." So at least nothing rules out Shakespeare's papers as having been among them; Halliday, for one, was certain of this: "Hall left Nash his 'study of books,' which must have included some of Shakespeare's" (332).

---

[25]Although I heard Schoenbaum claim in a talk at MLA that this finding would no doubt be taken advantage of by scholars, so far, to my knowledge, naught has been made of it. But that does not mean that the same neglect now holds true for items in Dr. Hall's library. One thing leads to another.

Although several details are still left somewhat in the air, the bulk of this argument works reasonably enough, and the reader has now the main (Tarot) cards on the table. One last one is to be extracted: Might not a certain William Hall of Hackney (now a part of London), who was married nine months before the sonnets were printed, have been related also to Dr. Hall? Was he then the relative who became a printer? Whatever, of the only four William Halls in the record who were born, married, and died between 1502 and 1610, Hall of Hackney alone fits the bill.[26]

It appears reasonable that Thorpe, in his 'dedication,' meant to refer to W. H. as having recently married, as has often been pointed out (even with the Harvey candidacy). True, such records were notoriously incomplete, yet Hackney offers something new at any rate. Does not the fact that it was a locale where priests were known to reside have some bearing also on Southwell's (not to mention some of Shakespeare's mother's) Catholic connections?

Robert Southwell, who was a cousin of the poet's and for whose collaborative *Meditation,* as I have noted, a certain "W. H." (who could easily have been the same printer William Hall) wrote a dedication in 1606, also had Hackney ties. He is known for having been at King's Place there. William Hall's side of the Shakespeare family may well have had ties with Bedford, which is also north of London and not far from Hackney. Thus, Eccles identifies a William Hall of Bedfordshire, who seems to have been the father of both Dr. Hall and another William Hall (Lee 418). At any rate, when Thorpe, in describing himself as an "adventurer in setting forth" the sonnets in print, was evidently likening himself not only to a conventional printer, but to a pirate, we might make the one qualification that he would not have confessed to being a pirate as such if he felt

---

[26]For details, see the Harleian Society's *Reprints of Registers of London Parishes* as well as *Marriage Licenses, London, 1502–1610: Marriage Licenses Granted by the Faculty Office,* etc. For valuable assistance, I am indebted to the writings of Colonel B. R. Ward, who cited four William Halls after examining some twenty-odd volumes of the *Reprints* as well as the other registers mentioned, but noted that only one of these Halls is of value, William of Hackney, who married Margery Gryffyn on 4 August 1608. Two objections can be made to this documentation: that it is probably incomplete and that Col. Ward, the source of the information, was anti-Stratfordian. With regard to the first, we can go only by what we have; as for the second, we have to turn to whoever has probed the facts.

Master W. H. was actually a trustworthy intermediary who represented a fairly close family connection with the poet.

Part of the problem has been that scholars have had a hard time accepting even the option that "W." had to stand for *William*. "For example, it could have been *Walter*," a prominent Shakespearean remarked to me once drily in his Oxford office. Recently, however, it has been revealed that "over 95% of British men in the sixteenth and seventeenth centuries with the initial W were named William" (Ramsey 22–23), a figure based on random samples taken from the *Short-Title Catalogue,* the *Dictionary of National Biography,* and the *Oxford Dictionary of Christian Names*. In a case like this, when we have no smoking gun, we have to rely to some extent on the laws of probability.

IV
Something Rather More than Coincidence

More than mere coincidence is evidently involved, in any case, in the curious dual appearance of the key initials W. H. for men then in the British printing trade. In point of fact, they are to be found in several dedicatory addresses that were issued from the printing house of Thomas Thorpe and his associate George Eld. In 1606, Eld had brought out Robert Southwell's and Philip Howard's *Meditation,* as briefly mentioned earlier, whereby the initials had already appeared on the dedicatory page. This time they stood for the proud procurer and dedicator himself. That these two W. H.'s were one and the same was first broached by Charles Edmonds, whom Lee, at least, thought an "accomplished bibliographer" (400). Edmonds' letter in *The Athenaeum* told of his discovery of the Southwell and Howard *Four-Fold Meditation of the Foure Last Things,* described the state of the fragmentary document, and then of how "W. H." had told of the work having been kept secret but then "through an accident as it were, being brought into the open"; commenting on Thorpe's W. H. with the *Sonnets,* he stressed that "the extreme improbability of there existing two distinct individuals engaged in the same pursuits, employing the same printer, and using the same initials, within the short period of three years, is too apparent to need serious refutation" (529). Yet a refutation of sorts appeared on 1 November 1873, to which Edmonds then had to respond on 22 November at great length. The quibble was made that though the two works had the same printer, they had a different publisher. Edmonds replied that the fact that others could have signed their name with the same initials is not strictly germane to this textual context. Other scholars then joined in the fray, including Lee.

The point is that the very repeated use of such an abbreviation meant that it would be fairly easily understood and that Thorpe was following a 'set pattern' in the Shakespeare dedicatory address. Then to make doubly sure that his select readers would identify the initials correctly, he added the extra em space and spelled Hall's last name out in full. Lee showed that all examples of initials figuring in such addresses suggest a close intimacy between the dedicator and the dedicatee. And what sort of *intimacy,* it can rightly be asked, would Thorpe have had with Shakespeare's *inspirer* (presuming there was only one main one) or, for that matter, with the poet himself? Probably none at all. The textual critic ignores or demotes this solid piece of business know-how from a professional manager's commercial methods only at his peril. What Lee failed to point out then was what later perturbed E. K. Chambers: that Thorpe's fancy in-house procedures could have allowed for a little hidden name-play as well. Although Donald Foster claimed in his *PMLA* rejoinder to me (CII, 840–1) that all the claimants for William Hall base their association on a cryptogram, Lee never mentioned one. Probably Lee was wise enough to realize that no real inversion of lettering was involved at all and hence no bonafide cryptography (as in the anti-Stratfordian mode).

Nonetheless, esteemed critics like F. E. Halliday and most recently Stephen Booth in his new, well-received edition of the *Sonnets,* have felt hesitant to believe in the likelihood that the two W. H.'s stood for the same individual. In contrast, Mme. de Chambrun did think so, but she picked Harvey rather than Hall, rejecting Lee's arguments out of hand as follows: "It was indeed hardly possible that Hall, an unknown publisher, should have had in his hands the manuscripts of the *Sonnets;* it was still more improbable that he should have had the unpublished text of the *Meditation,* when he had specialized in the publication of Protestant polemics" (120). Yet, as the Danish Prince would say, *there* is the rub. For was not Hall mainly interested in good commerce? And when the sonnets were passed around so freely anyway, why should he not have had some access to them? Why should an up-and-coming Jacobean printer have been thus bigoted? Conversely, may not a little intolerance be evident on the Countess' part, not Hall's, in her assuming such a stalwart, dogmatic position? We might remember that Shakespeare's own kinfolk and in-laws consisted of Protestants as well as Catholics.

Is it not reasonable enough that Hall gained access to a contemplative work like the *Meditation* for the precise reason that he had had the experience of dealing earlier with other religious work, whatever the precise Christian denomination? Hall was by occupation a businessman: that is a fact. Whether he was subservient to religious bigotry is so much unwarranted theory. The reason why Lee then avoided pressing his claim for Hall in his entry in the *Dictionary of National Biography,* as Mme. de Chambrun notes, is unclear. True, no connection between the printer Eld and William Hall is in the record, nor any between Eld and Hall's former employer (Richard Bradock), but that at least does not exclude the possibility that a secret one existed.

In any event, the Southwell and Howard manuscript had been procured in a manner quite similar to that in which the *Sonnets* were. Seeing that Southwell and Shakespeare were cousins, though distant (but not so much to prevent Southwell from probably dedicating *Saint Peter's Complaint* to Shakespeare, as has been suggested), it does not seem too remote to consider that Master W. H. got the sonnets in some manner through the Southwell (or thereby family) connections.

At any rate, he announced that he had uncovered "a neglected MS. poem" by the Jesuit, one composed in 1595. But he signed his initials as "W.H." and then Thorpe promoted him to "Master W. H." in 1609. Was there a good reason for this upgrading, or was it a mere courtesy? Lee thought the former view could be substantiated: "In 1608 [William Hall] obtained for publication a theological manuscript which appeared next year with his name on the title-page for the first time. This volume constituted the earliest credential of his independence. It entitled him to the prefix 'Mr.' in all social relations" (418). Herewith we think again of Thorpe's use just before of Edward Blount, who "had already achieved a modest success in the same capacity of procurer or picker-up of neglected 'copy'" (409). Yet Thorpe's use of "Master" was not merely to applaud Hall's rise to prominence, but to serve to contrast the bearer of the initials from the earl to whom many of the sonnets were written and who would have been addressed more distinctively.

As suggested previously, Hall would have felt little compunction in dealing with both Protestant and Catholic manuscripts, especially if he was cognizant of some religious division in Shakespeare's own family (the mother, for example, having been Catholic, the daughter Susanna having married a Puritan, who was a Hall possibly related to the procurer himself). But the essential correlation here is not apropos of Protestant and Catholic polemics as such; it is specifically with Southwell and Shakespeare, Hall being associated at least nominally with their clan.

Mme. de Chambrun believed that W. H. obtained the *Meditation* through Southampton's family connection, a point also made by Stopes and then Rowse, and it is reasonable to believe, as many do, that the Youth of the *Sonnets* was the same Earl of Southampton (because his father had died, as mentioned in sonnet 13). When Howard and Southwell died, the manuscript reverted naturally to their estates; nowadays it is associated more with the family of Howard, who was Earl of Arundel (as in the revised British Museum catalogue), and the Southwell portions are called "emendations" (Chambrun 120). Howard was a noted convert to Catholicism.

Southwell's poetry, incidentally, exhibits some rather striking correspondences with Shakespeare's, which the critic may now overlook only at his peril again. Several notable points of comparison have only recently been documented between the *Sonnets* and *Saint Peter's Complaint*. These may be found in Peter Milward's main book on Shakespeare's background. The parallels he has adduced between these two works have been acclaimed, for example by E. Mackerness, who felt the marshalling of pertinent verbal parallels "convincing" (843). Further, the 'dedication' of the *Complaint* is to "Master W. S." Such a dedicatee points not only to Master W. H., by analogy, but specifically to the man from Stratford himself. This 'dedication' has a concluding request which cogently parallels the rhetorical patterning in Thorpe's 'dedication' to the *Sonnets,* thereby intimating a probable debt to it:

Favour my wish, well-wishing workes no ill;
I move the sute, the graunt rests in your will. (Grosart 10)

Compare Thorpe's own alliterative, euphuistic phrase "wisheth the well-wishing." Also worth comparing is W. H.'s dedication for the *Meditation:* "W. H. wisheth" (Chambrun 200). As Halliday points out, lines in the Epistle to the *Complaint* have been taken as plausible 'echoes' from *Venus and Adonis* and *Love's Labour's Lost:* "Still finest wits are 'stilling Venus' rose ... / O sacred eyes! the springs of living light ... / Sweet volumes, stored with learning fit for saints" (*Companion* 465). Is it not likely then that Thorpe was influenced by Southwell indeed by way of Hall?

The main question is: Would a correct response help in the identification of Master W. H.? In answering, let us take into account the subtle paronomasia in Southwell's phrase "your will," which is analogous to Shakespeare's own familiar indulgence in punning on his forename in the 'Will' sonnets (nos. 135, 136, and 143) as published a year later. In a word, Southwell's "your will" was evidently meant to allude to Shakespeare's will—namely Will's will.[27] The Jesuit probably knew of Will's penchant for punning long before the *Sonnets* were published, and then Thorpe was following both Southwell and Shakespeare with his own name-play on *W. Hall,* whereby for what it is worth three of the four letters in *Will* are also utilized. Actually the names of *Will* and *Hall* have themselves a certain similarity of which Thorpe could have taken cognizance. Aside from *Will*'s being "contained" already in *W[illiam] Hall,* the two four-letter names each end with the same double consonant. The correlation can be diagrammatized as follows:

$$\text{Will} > \text{W[Ha]ll.}$$

In sum, since both Southwell's and Thorpe's dedicatory addresses were colored by what Shakespeare himself initially composed, the name-play on *Will* in the phrase "your will" tallies with Thorpe's own name-play dealing with Hall's name. The effect was contagious. A year later he felt called upon to pun again in the Epistle Dedicatory in the *Manuall* of Epictetus, where he again took a proper noun and avoided the anagrammatic effect of switching letters but 'dropped' one, in effect, in writing: "He is more senceless then a *stocke,* that hath no good sence of

---

[27]Was there also a blurred echo of his own name in contrast (South*well*) if only because his phrase "well-wishing" represents euphuistic punning on "South*well well*-wishing," as it were? This is a fine point, but one not to be pressed.

this *Stoicke*" (italics added). (Lee's quotation of this passages is modernized some.)

Because of the Southwell-Southampton connection mentioned a short while before, as stressed by Mme. de Chambrun, next look for a moment at her preference for William Harvey as W. H. again. Why, we may well ask, would this stepfather of the Earl of Southampton have shown any political acumen in releasing potentially prurient data which could then be construed as socially or ethically detrimental to his stepson? It would scarcely have been becoming for him to wash dirty linen in public (a practice especially inimical to the tasteful English) by announcing to the world his stepson's indiscreet sowing of wild oats with the Dark Lady. Scandal would have been the last thing he needed.

Granted, a remote allusion to Harvey's spouse may be found in *King Lear* insofar as he married someone with the name of Cordelia, but a plausible 'Hall connection' can also be found to offset it: Dr. John Hall's respected medical practice seems to be alluded to; it has been inferred that the reference of whites of eyes as applied to Gloucester's eye sockets was Shakespeare's recollection of his son-in-law's medical prescriptions (Bergeron [1972]).[28]

A final demurrer worth citing is Katherine Duncan-Jones's argument that the two works deriving from Thorpe's press immediately after the *Sonnets* were both dedicated to another man who had the W. H. initials, namely William Herbert, Earl of Pembroke (though, in this case, the abbreviation was not used). Since he was obviously not referred to as *Master,* because he was of the nobility, this coincidence has no real bearing except by way of intriguing contrast. Katherine Duncan-Jones herself did not want to press it.

---

[28]Further, according to a notation I happened to see at an exhibit at Hall's Croft in Stratford, a complementary allusion appears in *Pericles,* wherein the dedicated and wise physician Cerimon may also have been based on Dr. Hall.

V
In Sum . . .

Presumptive evidence therefore emerges for asserting that a certain W. (most probably William) Hall was involved in bringing the *Sonnets* to press. The question is whether he was merely a stationer's assistant, later a printer, or related to Shakespeare's son-in-law, or even all three. Booth has categorically argued that the "stationer's assistant named William Hall in the 1590's and early 1600's" need not have been the same William Hall who "set up as a printer in 1608" (548), yet such animadversion would carry rather far the implication that *William Hall* was not only widespread as a formal name, but, in terms of its initials, in the technical trade industry as in our own populous age. After all, Lee had some pretty fair rhetoric to associate the two Halls: "No other inhabitant of London was habitually known to mask himself under those letters" (419).

It might be further contended that if various William Halls were in evidence, two plausibly even competing with each other in the printing trade, as Booth would infer, why indeed would Thorpe have been so casual as to identify only by his use of initials? In answer, the main point of the abbreviated name for him was obviously so that it could easily be identified if a knowing reader took the trouble. But if two William Halls were competing in the stationer's business, such assignment would have been confusing. It is more reasonable that Thorpe did what he did precisely because two such Halls were *not* operating in the trade.[29] In spite of Booth's reputation as an authority on the *Sonnets,* his gloss that an "early suggestion was that Thorpe's 'Mr. W. H. ALL. HAPPINESSE.' is a *misprint* for 'Mr. W. HALL. HAPPINESSE'" (548—with my italics but his omission of the over-sized em space before *ALL*) is simply misrepresentative, missing the point completely. It is, after all, common knowledge that "all happiness" was a conventional phrase in those days, and commonsense alone should tell us that Thorpe certainly would not have been culpable of such a misnomer, nor has that

---

[29]Booth claimed, further, that another candidate for the W. H. role could have been a certain "William Holme" (*sic*) (elsewhere spelled *Holmes*), but that is of little consequence, for Lee has shown (419) that this candidate "was ordinarily known by his full name" and that we have no indication that "he had either professional or private relations with Thorpe."

been seriously endorsed. Booth was so intent in giving the William Hall claimants short shrift that his demurrer completely lacks cogency.

So here are some points that can be at least fairly effectively established: 1. William Hall, the physician's recently discovered brother, could well have obtained the sonnets in their intended sequence from Shakespeare by way of kinship, either in original draft or copy form, although more likely perhaps the latter, and passed them on to Thorpe, ostensibly to better himself in the printing profession by producing hot copy. (This presupposes that the brother had chosen this career, however, for which no evidence exists.) 2. Another view is that the Hall involved was the same as the stationer William Hall. He could have followed the same procedure as he did with the MS. from Shakespeare's cousin Southwell and as another procurer, Edward Blount, did for Thorpe with a MS. by Marlowe just before. This stationer could also have been related to Dr. Hall, granted, though the name was not uncommon, or he could have had access to the poems through Southampton family connections—the Earl most probably being the Youth highly praised in the MS. 3. In any case, Dr. Hall, along with his fraternal colleague William Covell, had the means of knowing about the sonnets already while he was a student at Cambridge or at least shortly thereafter and could have had good access to them, passing them on to the William Hall involved, presumably (most likely) an enterprising cousin. In any event, some such business connection would most properly explain the anomaly of Thorpe's dedicating Shakespeare's poetry with such ostentation to a fellow-worker or apprentice printer.

4. But regardless of whether one of Dr. Hall's relatives was the same "W. Hall" as the one implied in the 'dedication,' the printer who dedicated the Southwell and Howard *Meditation* offers the best overall candidacy for being the W. H. in the Thorpean inscription. 5. The printer Hall, if he dedicated Southwell's and Howard's work, as appears most probable, certainly draws more support than does William Holme(s), the only other printer on record with the same initials.

It is worth concluding with an irony. Critics have so frequently written of the eccentricities of the special pleader who would seek to identify Master W. H. as almost anyone, but they have failed to arrive at the most obvious deduction: that

Thorpe's own idiosyncratic behavior most likely is what turns the key to correct meaning.

Last of all, some readers are bound to find that this chapter, even with its detective-story-like title, frustrates them because it has very little to do with the sonnets themselves as artifacts. To this charge I plead guilty, confessing that such modern criticism was not my concern. Yet only after the poetry can be placed truly in context, including its external as well as internal framework, can we be historically aware of all its multivalent implications.

Chapter 4

Marital Loves Encompassed:

Sonnet 116 in Relation to Donne's "A Valediction: forbidding mourning":

> "How now shall this be compast?"
> —*The Tempest,* 3.2.57
>
> "Looke how my Ring incompasseth thy Finger"
> —*Richard II,* 1.2.203

The intriguingly analogous compass figure, *mutatis mutandis,* in two celebrated love poems characteristic of the Renaissance—Shakespeare's most famous and Donne's likewise best-known—is the main focus of this chapter. A minor poem of Shakespeare's remote cousin, Robert Southwell, will be enlisted as well to tie in with the last chapter, but mainly in contrast. The emphasis will be again on Shakespeare's *Sonnets,* because the materials shed more light on him than Donne through the connection. A corollary feature will be to see whether Donne's debt to his better can be proved in the process.

I

Let us commence with Donne. As might be expected, his most illustrious metaphysical conceit, the compass image in his better known "Valediction," has acquired its complex renown partly, if not mainly, because literary historians have been in the air about its chief source. The interest in the poem's presumed bawdy undertones is secondary. Ever since Dr. Johnson's cautious appraisal of the work for its noted "ingenuity," its unusual concluding metaphor has been seen representatively as a characteristic product of Donne's subtle inventiveness, yet some Donne scholars find a basis for it in Guarini's Madrigal 96, among them Mario Paz, Douglas Bush, and Theodore Redpath. The last adds: "Again, in Madrigal 37 the poet's heart is compared to a flitting butterfly that burns its wings in the flame of the mistress' eyes, dies as a butterfly, but rises as a phoenix," so that yet another poem of Donne's, "The Canonization," presumably "owed something to Guarini's poem" (63). It so happens that I am on record as advocating a debt by Donne to another Italian, Dante, so the Guarini connection seems plausible to me too (see my "Donne and Dante"). But such a seemingly accepted consensus on Donne and Guarini is bound now to be qualified with H. J. C. Grierson's earlier familiar caveat that the basic compass effect was preëmpted some six centuries before by the Persian sage Omar Khayyam (II, 41), even if then having a much different tenor. Yet perhaps the most immediate source is Shakespeare after all, as we shall soon see.

First, observe a paramount distinction to be kept ever in mind: that between the compass device as such and the circle constructed by it. A meaningful enough genesis for the implicit geometrical figure involved is found in the Paradisal circle imagery of *The Divine Comedy,* and also by implication the idea of the circle as relating somehow to human love in the *Vita Nuova* and the similar geometrical analogy in the *Convivio*. Although Freccero has questioned my identification of the Dantean circle design, preferring to envisage a spiraling effect in Donne as well as Dante, Novarr has taken issue with Freccero, so the matter of indebtedness remains in limbo.[30] What principally counts, in any case, is the concept of circularity as relating to constant love.

---

[30]Whereas Dante's accommodation of the circle image as such was not ignored *in toto* by other Donne devotees, Freccero tried to downplay it; orthodoxly, he observed that human love, unlike Dante's divine form, is incapable of attaining consummate circularity, and he had a point, though Redpath, in his new, revised edition of Donne's poetry, declined to take Freccero's position very seriously. On the other hand, Barbara Everett has recently resuscitated interest in the poem's "spiralling" effect as she called it (*Poets in Their Time* 18).

In any event, Southwell's *Saint Peter's Complaint* (1595) happens to offer what might appear upon first reading more immediate source material. Consider this stanza:

> O gracious spheres, where love the Center is,
> A native place for our selfe-loaden soules:
> The compasse, love, a cope that none can miss:
> The motion, love that round about us rowles.
> O Spheres of love, whose Center, cope and motion,
> Is love of us, love that invites devotion.

At least on the surface, the burden of these lines conforms fairly well to that of the final canto of the *Paradiso,* namely the crescendo which T. S. Eliot once praised as "the highest point that poetry has ever reached" (*Selected Essays* 212), and it bears also in transcendental terms on the *Vita Nuova,* where Love, unlike the lover *manqué,* is likewise depicted in the midpoint of a circle.

But what is especially obvious in the Southwell extract is textual: Some key nouns (*compasse, soules, spheres, motion*) emerge in Donne's poem, intimating plausible reverberation on the anagogic level. Yet perhaps these terms are not unusual enough for that. Historically, we might correctly recall Donne's early ties with Southwell's Society of Jesus, but then he later became disenchanted with the Jesuit order. Still, Donne's habit of imaging to himself in the manner of one who was once a trained and devoted Jesuit links the two poems somewhat and makes the tie-in nearer chronologically as well as topographically (nearer than Persia, Italy, or, say, Belgium, from which came Christophe Plantin's printer's device, which Donne also knew and which has been occasionally enlisted as a Flemish pictorial basis for Donne's compass emblem).

Another candidate to be considered was Joseph Hall, one unrelated to the William Halls of the previous chapter. Already in his notes to his first edition of Donne's *Songs and Sonets,* Redpath observed that "in a [work] printed in 1609, over two years before Donne wrote this poem" (85), Hall had likewise introduced a compass simile. (He erred in that he cited the poem but then actually quoted from Donne's *Epistles.*) So perhaps the exact source of the compass figure is not as important as its context; in any event, Redpath did not play up the link with Joseph Hall, relegating it only to a lowly footnote. It *is* curious that Shakespeare introduced compass imagery in sonnet no. 116, which was published the same year as Hall's poetry was. After all, no. 116 may have been written or added late, not during the Plague Years (1592–94).

But before turning to the sonnet as such, consider the subject-matter of the "Valediction." Does it focus on love, death, or both concurrently? A recent reassessor has contended that death figures here more than love: "Although we must understand science to master the poem, Donne's deathbed scene is its controlling metaphor" (Jahn 34). Its very next sentence, however, shows how the "Valediction" commences with a "peacefully dying man" for "encircled by friends," thereby incidentally arriving at circular imagery alongside the necrological. Whether or not this 'death poem' reading is clearly justifiable, it still reveals an instinctive awareness of the figurative import of the circle device.

In correlating Donne's homilies, we find that death, like life or love, has its cyclical basis. Such geometry, manifesting the spiritual in harmony with the temporal, is set forth in the "Valediction": "As the traveler returns to his mistress, he contemplates a temporal circle. Their reunion parallels the reunion of body and soul at resurrection" (37). But why "mistress"? Biographer Walton, we might well recall, claimed that this poem was bestowed reverently on Donne's spouse when he left her to go with Sir Robert Drury to France in 1611, a likely enough period for meditation and faith (she being pregnant at the time too). In spite of that most probable marital context, some critics have read in unusually bawdy overtones which, under the circumstances, seem intrusive. Aptly enough, Redpath, who stressed bawdy suggestiveness in his second edition, showed that a *wife* is evidently under no stoical obligation to hide her sorrow at her husband's departure (as the poem demands), but surely fortitude against excessive dolor might be encouraged, especially in a sensitive, pregnant situation. Although it is clearly tenable, as has often been claimed, that this poem need not have been occasioned by any specific leave-taking, the subject does recall a commonplace of the Anglican marriage service: "till death us depart" (nowadays rendered "till death do us part"). Redpath has raised strong arguments in favor of Walton's standard reading. He finds the poem expressing "such deep satisfaction that it seems reasonable to suppose that [it] rose out of Donne's marriage" (4). In citing the adverse view that a *wife* need not hide her grief, he added: "I do not find the point very persuasive. There are, surely, marriages and marriages" (261, also xxii). Again: "If it stems from a specific love-relationship at all, I would bank on it being that with Ann" (262). Nonetheless, he made what seems like a major error in this regard. After stating that Donne married Ann "in 1601 or 1602" and that the "Valediction" "could hardly have been written before 1605" (4), he remarked that it "could easily belong to the period of Donne's courtship of his wife" (262). In any case, recently John Shawcross has also reverted to the belief that the poem may well be about Ann Donne: "Contrasting with the sublunary lovers . . . who find love only in sense and bodily parts are (if biographical) John and Ann. . . . The biographical may add another dimension" (60–61). He provided examples of other Donne poems having analogous biographical overtones. On the other hand, he qualified his assertions by admitting that the "Valediction" is also "more than just biographical," and that is certainly true of Shakespeare's sonnet 116 too, as we shall see. But the main point is that such connubial echoing can become vitally significant if the "Valediction" derives essentially from yet another lyric stressing similar marital imagery.

II

The best precedent for the "Valediction" as marital—the legal term *precedent* being admitted advisedly—can well be in what is so often accepted as Shakespeare's love poem *par excellence,* sonnet 116; although with its main charm being in the disarming modesty of its couplet, its merit is more readily apparent in its widely acclaimed universality. It should appear rather charming that what has come to be the most popular item in Donne's work could have been betokened in key ways by now the most widely read of Shakespeare's sonnets. What may come to the fore with the latter is an implicit 'Faithful Wife' motif, or possibly subgrouping, one hitherto undetected in the sonnet sequence, no doubt owing to the motif's submerged nature. Lest this be misunderstood, we may acknowledge the possibility of all kinds of inchoate subgroups in the *Sonnets,* ones that have not yet reached the light, but underscore the fact that in setting up such categories we need not be making any special Gestaltist claims for a formal sonnet grouping. For example, it is perfectly possible that because a number of the sonnets deal with sea imagery, we might have a subliminal pelagic subgrouping too.

Inspect closely the opening lines of no. 116:

> Let me not to the marriage of true mindes
> *Admit* impediments, *love* is not *love*
> Which alters when it alteration findes,
> Or bends with the remover to *remove*.

Observe how aspects of these lines could resonate in the "Valediction":

> Dull sublunary *lovers' love*
> (Whose soul is sense) cannot *admit*
> Absence, because it doth *remove*
> Those things which elemented it. (italics added in both)

And now examine the complementary texts, contexts, and subtexts. In both of the quatrains, a fairly close concatenation of three striking (though commonplace) words stand out: *admit, love, remove*. Because the terms are so often used, their repetition in itself would hardly promote the notion of indebtedness; there must be numerous other similar examples. Still, the close proximity of the words in both cases must also be gauged, notably in that Donne appears, whether deliberately or not, to be so taken by them that he isolates them by putting them at the end of successive lines. (To be sure, conveniently "love" also simply eye-rhymes with "remove.")

True, such placement might seem to amount to no more than a curiosity. But then each poem reveals obvious, neat quibbling on the word *love*, involving internal echoing, repetition of the key abstraction (when *love* is considered as "contained" in *love*[rs]). Further, this sharp, verbal congruency is evident only in a single cluster of three lines in each quatrain. At least such obvious parallels can pave the way for less evident ones.

Next, Donne's clear-cut wordplay on *sense* and *Absence* can be taken as reflecting his more distinguished predecessor's similar penchant for punning and word games. But are there any of import in no. 116? Two that have been given short shrift in the past have some special thematic import, thereby helping to round the sonnet out, namely those on *alters* and *altars* (3, 11) and on *writ* (14), for which see Booth (390). But because Shakespeare is the greatest punster in the language, some such paronomasia may appear almost inevitable. What makes it so special here?

As the opening statement in no. 116 reveals, true love admits to an overriding marital metaphor, hence preparing us for relating the verb *alters* also connotatively to church *altars*. Especially the opening phrase "Love alters" (11) has a ring of marriage altars. But then what about the overall context? Do not the neighboring sonnets center on the Young Man? Yes, but the exact order of some of these poems has always been in doubt, and it is perfectly possible that a work originally written for the poet's wife was implanted as a kind of universal love poem among those relating to the Youth. Both original and final intent count here. As for the antiquated form *writ,* that makes nonsense if taken too literally (obviously the poet *has* just written) and thus could well involve some subliminal legalistic quibbling. Indeed Booth thinks it might convey the sense of a "writ of error" (387). But more clearly it would hint at the standard document required for matrimonial services to take place. It may make more sense for the poet to suggest that if he is wrong in his views on true love, he never really had a "marriage writ" rather than that he never wrote anything. More syntactically, the bald phrase "I never writ" would convey " never made a claim to love," which again could contain legal overtones.

But, in fact, can such marital meaning be extant elsewhere in the sonnet? The opening line, after all, speaks of minds and not bodies. True, yet the introduction of *impediments* in the second line does point to the Anglican marriage service, the prepositional qualifier "to the edge of doom" (12) encouraging a wedded couple to remain together "till death" them "depart." (Comparable, incidentally, are the true lovers parting only through "death" in the "Valediction.") Further, the bond which "lookes on tempests and is never shaken" (6) amply recollects another commonplace from the Anglican service, that about *constantia,* namely "in sickness and in health." And is a wedding ring also involved? Perhaps so, especially if we think of the resonances of the word "compasse" (10). It is generally admitted now that a compass figure reverberates in the sonnet as well.

Yet most of this so far is still pretty obvious. How then is our understanding of the poetry itself importantly affected? The key is in seeing how both poems so closely interweave marital and death themes to the extent that Donne may be thought of as the great poet of death partly by way of Shakespeare. This is a thesis of this chapter. In no. 116 occurs a crux concerning the meaning of "remover" (4), which may allude mainly to the Great Leveler, even as "remove" in the "Valediction" has analogous, mortal reverberations. But "remover" is richer yet and may have more legalistic overtones, suggesting a recalcitrant magistrate, again bringing in the marital meaning (see Piper). In any case, the whole opening quatrain thematically presents a certain preoccupation with canon law in matrimony, prohibited when canonical "impediments" obstruct the way. Comparable is the use of the same technicality in *Much Ado* or *Won* (4.1.10). We think of the marriage act sacramentally, which furnishes further gloss on the key phrase "ever fixèd marke" (5), for that recalls the definition of a sacrament as an outward, physical sign of an inner, spiritual grace (hence "ever" in the sense of *eternal,* and "marke" in the sense of a physical fact). Do we not look ahead toward the "fixt" element in the "Valediction"? No less so than the way we recall how "marriage of true mindes" anticipates Donne's again curiously legal term "Interassurèd [of the mind]" (19). Not unusually, his lyric has other legalistic overtones, for example "breach" (23), suggesting that the "Valediction" may be taken implicitly as a preamble to a formal document of leave-taking, the subject of death itself so often calling for that.

Of all these legal terms, including ones relating to the canon law of the Church, the phrase "ever fixèd marke" in no. 116 is probably richest. One thinks also of a seamark, which reminds us that the Virgin has been venerated as *stella maris* as well. Is there then anything specifically Roman Catholic here? The enigmatic allusion to "Times foole" (9) has been thought to be to the occasion of a Jesuit's having to be brought to trial for reasons of casuistry and the like, thus linking with "remover" as a recalcitrant magistrate balking at an equivocator failing to tell "the whole truth and nothing but the truth." Yet, in implying that Love is not like a Jesuit, not like "Time's Fool," Shakespeare was avoiding any denominational commitment, or perhaps taking to task the Jesuitical allowance for mental reservation as duplicity.

Now, some support for "writ" as having legalistic overtones can be gleaned from the plays, for example "such a writ" in *Henry VIII,* 3.2.340–1 (alluding to the Writ of Praemunire), where Suffolke cites even "th' compasse" of a "Premunire," hence allowing for *two* echoes of legalistic words in no. 116. This is a curious correlation, one worth bearing in mind.

As for Donne's compass then following suit, Redpath himself has conceded that "it is quite possible that Donne may have seen some of [Shakespeare's sonnets]" and not only after the turn of the century but "in the late 1590's" (71). The distinct likelihood that Donne was "among [Shakespeare's] private friends" who had access to the sonnets has been considered by a number of scholars

(David Stevenson, Brother Joseph, F. S. C.; Claudio Gorlier). The "Valediction," moreover, has been specifically compared by analogy with Shakespearean love poetry by MacDonald P. Jackson, the textual bibliographer for *Shakespeare Survey,* in his review of the work of Thomas Clayton (209). His not considering no. 116 has left room for the present essay. To sum up the evidence for indebtedness, what counts mainly is the clue of the *close proximity* of notable verbal resonances plus the more unusual use of the same word to allude to death ("remove"). In a somewhat similar vein, Robert Ellrodt has contended, in a well-received paper at the Shakespeare Institute in Stratford (later appearing in the selected papers in *Shakespeare Survey*), that the Stratford genius was indebted in *Hamlet* to the writings of Montaigne mainly because of the convincing tie-in of verbal resonances from several *consecutive* essays by the French prose artist. The reasoning works well in comparing the "Valediction" and sonnet 116, and a complete survey of the fairly imposing extent of the parallels between the two poems appears in the appended Diagram of Correspondences (p. 122).

Next, reconsider the central argument, that Shakespeare's key sonnet has focused marital meaning as opposed to the view that its format is mainly neo-Platonic. Was it somehow displaced in the sequence? If so, several others may also have been, such as no. 109, as has been suggested, but no. 145 in particular; they, too, may revert to marital love (plausibly the poet's own). The key in no. 109 is the phrase "my Rose" (14), with the stress on *my* (meaning his wife rather than Wriothesley), but the more convincing case is with no. 145. Thus, Stanley Wells and Gary Taylor in their *Oxford Shakespeare* admit that one of Will's "less impressive sonnets—no. 145—apparently plays on the name 'Hathaway'" (xvii). (The fact that it is not so impressive need not be discouraging in terms of his marital interests, however, if we bear no. 116 also in mind. Surely Shakespeare was capable of writing sincere sonnets for Anne at a younger age and then revising them properly to be able deftly to incorporate them into his sequence appropriately enough at a later date.) In any event, no. 145 is curiously placed.

Whether or not the similar-seeming misassignment of no. 116 in a group of sonnets praising the Young Man was a real one offers tantalizing mental aliment. Clearly the phrase "true mindes" would have allowed for such an inclusion. It appears possible that the crux of this matter may hinge, tangentially at least but still factually, on its having been *mis*numbered as no. 119 (a turned number) in the original 1609 edition, as Booth has posited himself (384). How can this be explained? The clerical error appears to have been the result of a certain carelessness deriving from an afterthought. In other words, Shakespeare presumably inserted the poem hastily, and as a result it got misnumbered. In any case, both no. 116 and no. 145 have previously been recognized as somehow rising above those surrounding them, the Variorum editor, for example, conceding pointblank apropos of no. 116 that "[a]ctually the sonnet may have been addressed to a woman" (I, 294). In turn, the *Pelican Shakespeare* finds no. 145 relatively extraneous to the overall Dark Lady grouping in which it is found (1478).

Both nos. 116 and 145 happily provide a sort of normal, natural relief for their respective, overall contexts. Whereas the former offers a seemingly heterosexual focal point amid so many evidently Augustinian sonnets lauding the Youth, the latter would represent a final conscientious reversion to conventional marital union (albeit, as Andrew Gurr posits, possibly composed much earlier), again as a reaction to a relationship, one with the Dark Woman, which may then be ebbing out. Because no. 145 enters the picture at the tail end of the part of the sequence detailing her, it might describe in part a welcome mode of recantation, which was a conventional enough *mea culpa* in Renaissance poetry (found, for example, in the sonnets of Constable, to which Shakespeare was very likely indebted).[31]

In any event, no. 116 has been acclaimed as a universal love lyric and certainly need not be strictly construed as relating only or mainly to heterosexual love (or, for that matter, to male friendship, its placement in the sequence notwithstanding). A recent review-article on a new book on the subject sums up the matter well:

> [Pequigney] wants to limit this poem to the poet's love for his friend, who is not directly mentioned here but addressed in adjacent sonnets. . . . On this and other occasions his interpretation of the sequence as a coherent narrative imposes an unnecessary reduction on the imaginative richness of the language. In individual sonnets Shakespeare developed ideas about time and love in general

---

[31]For some proof of this probability, see my *Resolved to Love: The 1592 Edition of Henry Constable's "Diana" Critically Considered* (Salzburg U Studies, 1990) passim. The point has also been made by Joan Grundy.

>   terms. . . . Sonnet 116 offers a supreme example of this richness. . . . (Cox 486)

Thus to relate this sonnet to a wife is not simply to wrench it out of its mediate context, but to show that its true contextual meaning can overlap.

Such an orthodox position as Cox's is substantiated by the poem's patterning in terms of the emblematic tradition. Very primly associated with the prime sonnet is an emblem which portrays a matronly (or wifely) lady *vis-à-vis* Cupid with quadrant, compass, star, and lighthouse being included in the emblematic insignia. (Her hair being up could signify that she is a bride.) Such a cluster, as most conspicuously included in Otto van Veen's (Vaenius') *Amorum Emblemata* (Antwerp, 1608), may appear only conventional and not depicting influence; however, when another neighboring emblem in this compilation happens to depict the selfsame deity nearly having his "rosie lips and cheeks" literally about to be encompassed by Father Time's "bending sickle" (rather than, be it noted, by the standardized, lengthy scythe), more than coincidence appears involved, as Horst Meller has most notably revealed in detail (46), though he was somewhat anticipated in this vital respect independently by Peter Daly. The sickle is coming close to Cupid's visage, it might be added, though one's first reaction might be that it is about to cut off his wings instead; still, both effects may be present, for the designer's intent is not crystal clear. (See the illustrations on pp. 173–174.)

Now the fact that van Veen's collection appeared after the turn of the century hardly need bear on Meller's favored candidate for the Youth, the Earl of Pembroke, as the esteemed subject of no. 116. Instead it could support this sonnet's differing contextually from its neighbors just because of its having been added in a later year (though plausibly begun in a much earlier one) or as a reaction to too much purely male companionship. Hence Taylor and Wells in their edition (xvii) allow for no. 145 as also having been composed at a different time, in this case definitely earlier. As for the sonnet sequence as a whole pointing to Pembroke (or Southampton) as "begetter," it is clearly dubious, as has often been remarked, that a nobleman would have been unconventionally addressed in a formal 'dedication' like that to the *Sonnets* as 'Master.' Whereas A. L. Rowse thought such an address was often enough proper for someone with the rank of knight, as in Parliament, he cited only different or less formal instances as evidence (*Discoveries and Reviews* 32).

AMORVM.

Otto van Veen, *Amorum Emblemata,* introd. Stephen Orgel, p. 237.

Otto van Veen, *Amorum Emblemata,* introd. Stephen Orgel, p. 39.

As for the dominating marital metaphor in no. 116, recently Hilton Landry has persuasively argued for its import. Regrettably, however, he felt inclined to see the lyric as so much akin to the other sonnets in its immediate proximity that he eschewed the literal marital meaning, thereby making of the allusions to solemn wedlock only a Procrustean bed. Admittedly, the initial Augustinian effect in the first two lines could be supportive of a kinship with surrounding poems focusing on the Youth, yet its imagery has endeared its subject to countless readers of both sexes. For the marital metaphor is too powerful to be limited to a Neo-Platonic vehicle for members of the same gender. Only in recent years, moreover, has homosexual 'marriage' received any formal status even among liberals. The poem thus deserves to be a candidate for even a 'new' subgrouping, that of the devoted spouse. If such a modest compilation (including, say, nos. 109, 116, and 145, to begin with) seems too limited for such a gathering, recollect that it is actually only one sonnet short of the number in the Rival Poet cluster. Yet the point of this chapter is not to try to substantiate such an informal correlation, but only to consider its potentiality. It adds to the dignity of Shakespeare's creativity.

Finally, the marital metaphor is not as technical or specialized as the domineering compass device involved, which provides the ultimate correlation between the sonnet and the "Valediction." Recent critics, including Meller and Doebler, have taken no. 116 formally in fairly strict accord with standard mathematical and navigational devices. Also the purported connection with van Veen's emblems informs us that the specific nautical "marke" in the poem relates to a seamark but not a buoy. Rather it is a *lighthouse,* which then would contain the marital sacrament of wedlock also as its spiritual beacon. As Meller has aptly noticed, Mario Praz overlooked the tiny beacon's import in previously accommodating the emblem to the poem (44). This clue alone strongly sheds light on the debt as well.

More imagery in the "Valediction" now contributes to this already beckoning kinship; not only the bending sickle, as sharply relating to the construction of a circle with compasses, but the concept of the two legs or feet of the compasses being correlatives, one acting as the "remover" in relation to the other stationed circumspectly at the midpoint. The "ever fixèd marke" then gains here in meaning, emphasizing the foot fixed in the circle's center, an effect that Doebler in particular has stressed. Like a set of Chinese boxes, circles are here figuratively discernible within circles, even as with the Dantean circles and gyres cited earlier. The center point in the core of Dante's imagined circles is imperative for constructing one of God or eternity (of which Satan in the ninth circle is a grotesque parody), a figure thus having no beginning or end, thereby meaningfully recollecting the Host in the traditional form of a circular wafer. In brief, the love imagery in no. 116 would further call forth the circle image as a standard symbol of perfect constancy, and thereby ultimately also of Divinity, indirectly once again recalling the Florentine master (even as the "Valediction" does on one level).

Can the Shakespeare-Donne relation function critically? It can show the weaknesses of arguments which do not take cognizance of it. In a recent essay, for example, Jane Roessner explicated the sonnet at some length, but failed to take into account either the emblematic context or Donne; as a result her analysis was vaguer than it otherwise might have been. Relying on Booth's claim that this vital poem still had a confusing, inchoate "tendency to make its matter disembodied, unvisualizable, impossible to locate in space and time" (387), Jane Roessner was misled (332). Yet when the sonnet is seen as bearing on the compass device in the modish *Amorum Emblemata* (albeit magnetic, not mathematical) and pointing ahead to the metaphysical image in Donne, its "matter" becomes clearly enough embodied and visualizable, to the extent of being illustrated, and pointedly locatable. At least it is these things in terms of pictorial space, which is what counts in this context. (Comparable also are the emblematic analogs in Ch 10.)

Further, we might address the meaning of the verb *admit*. Jane Roessner, following Booth for her precedent, contended that the opening imperative urgency, "Let me not . . . admit impediments," is frustrating, enervating, and generally bothersome in that it "disturbingly" suggests no less than a "willful denial" of the *persona*'s "knowledge of impediments" (334). But knowing what we do now, can we say it truly does? Only set the sonnet next to the "Valediction" and see. True enough, *admit* may at first imply *confess to* in Shakespeare, but Donne's usage, when seen as derivative here of the former, prompts the better reading of *allow for,* one then supported contextually. In other words, the speaker is not disclaiming impediments in the sense of denying them, but instead is simply not allowing for them. The effect is uplifting. For if, in the "Valediction," Donne appropriated key words from no. 116, would he not more than likely have accommodated the original function of the verb rather than have capriciously transformed it to suit himself? Thus, with both poems, spiritualized marital communion becomes interrelated, in the process making the reader himself "Inter-assurèd of the mind" and not thereby so disoriented.

Then Jane Roessner somewhat disconcertingly came to another unwarranted conclusion: "For it is not so much that the constancy of love is asserted as that its inconstancy is denied" (335). Such a negative rather than affirmative position neglects the import of the circle metaphor, which tells of *constantia* being rather fully asserted. Comparable is a similar compass emblem in Wither (143). Finding the presence of "the remover" merely "shadowy," Jane Roessner made short shrift of the richness of this figure in terms of legalistic ramifications and the Donne connection; in a word, she bypassed them. Instead of being phantom-like, the removing agent, whether Death or recalcitrant magistrate, provides ironically definite shades of meaning. Finally, when she found the description of the passing of youth here "disturbingly unconventional" (339), she evidently failed to be aware of the perilous proximity of Cupid to Time's sickle as depicted in the emblem, itself a veritable model of iconographic conventionality. This is not to say that her approach was inconsistent or unaesthetic or subjectively simply amiss; it did have a firm foundation in Booth, and some readers find 'ambiguity' in poetry a necessary condition of its richness. Yet a reading of the sonnet in terms of faith, love, and charity (in the sense that Donne's borrowing from it was charitable, for instance) offers at least more stability.

III

To conclude this Donne/Shakespeare collocation, we might take into account a small, but plausibly still significant, biographical factor: John Donne the Younger was also demonstrably aware of Shakespeare's poetry, very likely no. 116 in particular, as has been aptly revealed by Meller and Seymour-Smith. In stressing this, I realize that I can be held accountable for trying to build too much on the adage "like father, like son," but after all, traditionally, sons do learn from their fathers, and so such a debt should not be ruled out. Filial piety is a good touchstone after all.

The rewording of no. 116 by Henry Lawes, Donne the Younger's close friend, for musical accompaniment, as preserved in a seventeenth-century commonplace book of songs and transcribed by Meller, is once again worthy of pause. Although it may have been adapted simply "to please Pembroke" at that time (Meller 59), such a particular occasion need not detract from its originally having been meant as a universal love sonnet, one assuredly based on a happy family life. Even as it was clearly meant as basically heterosexual in appeal, Pembroke was himself known as quite a lady's man. But was Shakespeare also trying to please Pembroke in the sonnet? Possibly so, if, as has been suggested, it was written after the turn of the century, for the earlier sonnets relating at all to the Youth clearly focused rather on Southampton (see Ch 3). This is not, however, to suggest that he switched from one Young Man to another (a novel proposal). So it might be best to settle with the notion that it was Henry Lawes alone who was trying perhaps to play up to Pembroke when he set the sonnet to music.

Nonetheless, Meller has cited "the younger Donne's Pembroke volume," referring thereby to various poems by William Herbert, some of which relate quite unusually and significantly to the Dark Lady grouping (57–59). No. 116, in particular, is said to be 'echoed' in Herbert's lines "Love is not love, but given free; / And so is mine, and so should yours be" (56). We might also recall no. 145 as analogously relevant because of its appearance in the somewhat later Dark Lady cluster but also reacting to it with its recollection of Shakespeare's wife's maiden name *Hathaway* in the phrase "hate away" (13), thus lighting up the otherwise dark grouping. Andrew Gurr first went on record positing the sonnet's hidden autobiographical nature, leading to a follow-up debate.[32]

True, it may be difficult for a few recalcitrant readers to be convinced that sufficient evidence exists to believe that the question of autobiographical name-play there revolves around homophony or punning (rather than orthography or text-play, particularly when a poem which involves eye-rhyme is at issue). Still, if no. 145 could easily have been about the speaker's marriage, as is generally now conceded, so, too, with no. 116. (No. 109 presents more of a tease and has been mentioned in this connection only tangentially.) Both of these poems and their

---

[32]See comments by Hilda Hulme and others in *The Listener* (19 June 1978, p. 839; 6 July, p. 19; 13 July, p. 51; 27 July, p. 116; 3 August, p. 148).

particular placement would concern the need for escaping from an embarrassing immediate dilemma. About the time of no. 145, the Dark Lady's interest had turned in favor of the Youth; about the time of no. 116, the Youth's attractiveness to the speaker could have given him second thoughts about the normalcy of their relationship and hence reminded him of his need to reiterate the constancy of marital vows.

These 'interruptive' marital poems would have made the sequence as a whole morally more acceptable for publication and may have been inserted partly for that reason too, in a word helping to account for Shakespeare's permissiveness in allowing them to be taken to press without much ado at the time. Some thirteen copies, a relatively imposing number for those days, have survived. Granted, he would scarcely have brought them to Thorpe himself for a multitude of reasons (Katherine Duncan-Jones's claims notwithstanding): not only because of their socially indecorous Youth and Dark Lady formats, their informally worded title-page, but because of their evincing few signs of revision and many more of inadequate proofreading (having "beautits" for "beauties," for instance). In any event, like most good poets, he would have been prone to revise his work regardless of eventual publication and so could have easily wanted to slip in several marital sonnets if only for prudence's or conscience's sake.

As for Donne the Younger, it appears rather likely that someone like him impressed by the Dark Lady sonnets—if only by way of Pembroke—would have also been well enough versed in key preceding ones, most prominently no. 116. For instance, Meller has revealed that the Platonic lyric "To a Friend," which was ascribed to Pembroke, deals with a *persona* as one of two friends akin to those in no. 116, whom "something more than bodies" combine (57). Donne picked up on this—not only the Younger but by implication the Elder. Evidently the Younger was interested in no. 116 because the Elder had already been.[33]

It might be claimed that the "Valediction" was basically original in nature, as indicated by Dr. Johnson's finding it full of "wonderful ingenuity," but that argument works another way: It suggests also that the poet was not simply making

---

[33]Plausibly, because John Donne's wife was *née* Ann More, his family might well have taken a special interest in a playwright said to have collaborated in the drama *Sir Thomas More*, the human factor always being a viable catalyst.

use of traditional *topoi* in constructing his most famous lyric, and a major reason why he would not have been was that he modeled his work after Shakespeare's. The two-year proximity in their dating helps considerably. Whereas no. 116 appeared in print in 1609, the "Valediction" was presumably composed shortly thereafter—that is, if Walton's view still be accepted. This would imply that Donne, after meditating on the message contained in no. 116, shortly after it appeared in print, and soon after having noticed the pertinent emblems in van Veen's rather popular emblem collection as being extraordinarily allied, came to terms himself with these emblems, at least on the subliminal level.

After all, some of the verbal parallels between sonnet and "Valediction" are most arresting. Take the word "tempests" in the former as correlating with Donne's own use in the "Valediction." Both occur in the same line (6), which may in itself be merely coincidental, but then there is always the possibility that Donne was aware of *The Tempest,* which was acted the same year that he took leave of his wife to go to France, thereby plausibly providing the occasion for the poem's composition.

What is the state of modern scholarship on the matter of the genesis of no. 116? No less an authority in his time than George Lyman Kittredge once posited (1491) that several of the sonnets in the Young Man sequence are "manifestly addressed to a woman" (Monaghan 68). More recently Carol Thomas Neely has seen no. 116 as one of several sonnets startlingly and "deliberately detached from the particulars of the relationship" with the Youth (83); such an assessment is more positive than Jane Roessner's conclusions considered earlier. More recently yet, Heather Dubrow has neatly underscored Carol Neely's point by affirming that "many other sonnets in the sequence might be described in very similar terms" (59). They could have a telling point if it should lead to greater understanding of marital mutuality in the sequence.

Admittedly one disconcerting minor problem is that sonnets sometimes considered to be relating to the wife (nos. 109, 116, 145) are asunder from one another, not clustered as in the case of the Rival Poet, but Heather Dubrow shows how Booth has demonstrated that the subgroups "often overlap confusingly" (183). Not for nothing have so many scholars taken time to try to rearrange them. On the other hand, one invitingly helpful point is that both wives involved were named *Ann(e)*. Thus, in no. 145, the name-play on "hate away," posited by Gurr, supports similar name-play on the forename *Anne*, "*hate*' ... alterd with *an*" (9)—at least on the level of orthography and phonology, a form of text-play. That Donne was somehow aware of such wordplay, evident in his punning on himself and his wife (e.g., "John Donne, Ann Donne, Un-donne"), provides a final, arresting nexus. Can there be much doubt that in, say, punning on his own name in his Sonnet X (the phrase "to no end" being thought as name-play on "to Donne") he was following Shakespeare's precedent in the "Will" sonnets? In the verses accompanying van Veen's compass emblem, which Donne also may have seen, occurs a possible basis for this: "Undonne by none" (4). This is then supported by other imagery there pointing to both sonnet and "Valediction," e.g. "lovers mynde" (3) and "heav'n and love" (4). Last of all, both Booth (385) and Redpath (71) have seen fit already to have related no. 116 somewhat to the "Valediction," if only tangentially. That being the case, the main purpose of this chapter has been to supplement their findings with Andrew Gurr's analogous, supportive evidence. More recently, Arthur F. Marotti, although agreeing that the "Valediction" was written for Ann Donne, has preferred to date it 1605 rather than 1611, which would probably rule out the posited Shakespeare connection here (at least as based on van Veen), but he still had to confess that "chronology is impossible to prove" (168). To add a final twist, Gurr had posited that the Anne of no. 145 was as yet unmarried; still, insofar as Shakespeare alluded to his mother's maiden name (Arden) in *As You Like It,* he could have cited his wife's too (accounting for "hate away" as resonant of *Hathaway*). The poem may well have been composed at a much earlier date (it does not rank with the majority of sonnets in terms of quality) but then inserted later. (It uses "you," not "thou.")

In a major recent article, Lars Engle devoted special attention to no. 116, which he admitted is "in frequent if unquantifiable use at weddings" (839), to the poems dealing with the Youth, claiming that "in happier sonnets, the particular love of the young man is an object of knowledge and a source of value," and he compared the "Valediction." Engle's fixation on the Youth is evident even in his throwaway assertion that "Donald Foster denies him even his initials" (838). In discounting a connection with Anne Hathaway Shakespeare, he engaged in a verbal clutter which tends to obfuscate more than clarify, proficient though he otherwise is.

For example, he asserted that in no. 116 Love "knows what it is not without being able to say what it is" (839). This negation appears at odds with the very subject of his essay. He felt that the sonnet poses the question of whether "marriage of minds is meant as an alternative to the marriage of bodies" (839) when what is set up may be not opposition but conflation. He spent some time debating the contextual meaning of "Admit," claiming that an effort is made "to maintain discursive purity under duress" (839); however, because he kept in mind the parallel with the "Valediction," he might have seen that Donne's use of the same verb (14) conveys the more positive meaning of "allow for." The result is simplicity itself with no need for imposing the disconcerting notion of "reluctance."

Does the first quatrain truly "evoke the experience of a changeable love" (840), or is that reading in what is not present? Again Donne's appropriation of Shakespearean terms (as in "lovers' love" and "remove," also in close juxtaposition) reveals that the basic conception is positive, not negative. Shakespeare's sickle, which Engle found a symbol of duplicity, anticipates (along with "compass") the triumphant finale of Donne's poem. The sonnet's couplet, which Engle dubbed a "garbled vow" of a deviate marital relation, in truth harks back connotatively to the standard marital writ required for valid heterosexual nuptials.

With so much controversial talk nowadays about bisexuality in the sonnets and even of Donne's tendencies in this direction, even in the "Valediction" with the curious image of erection at the end, the proposed link in this chapter between the two famous poems ought to have a beneficial purpose. Such a marital 'union' can claim its own reward.

Table of Correspondences

Correspondences between Shakespeare's Sonnet 116 ("Let Me Not to the Marriage of True Minds") and Donne's "A Valediction: forbidding mourning":

Shakespeare	Donne
"Let me" (1)	"let us" (5)
"true mindes" (1)	"Inter-assurèd of the mind" (19)
"Admit" (2)	"admit" (14)
"love is not love" (2)	"lovers love" (13)
"remover . . . remove" (4) "to remove" (4)	"remove" (15) "To move" (28)
"bends" (4)	"leanes" (31)
"O no" (5) "no" (14)	"some say, no" (4) "no" (5) "No" (6)
"an ever fixèd marke" (5)	"the fixt foot" (27)
"tempests" (6)	"-tempests" (6)
"shaken" (6)	"trepidation" (11)
"the star" (7)	"the spheares" (11)
"Lov[e]'s not Times foole" (9) "Love alters not" (11)	"a love, so much refin'd" (17)
"lips and cheeks" (9)	"eyes, lips" (20)
"compasse" (10) "sickles" (10)	"compasses" (26) "circle" (35) and the last three stanzas as a whole
"writ" (14)	"wilt" (33) and a few archaisms

Editions used: The Yale University Elizabethan Club ed. of Shakespeare's *Sonnets*
 John Donne's *English Poems,* ed. C. A. Patrides

PART III
THE TEXTUAL/PHILOSOPHIC CRUX

Chapter 5
Friar Laurence and the Aesthetics of Ethics in the Star-Crossed Tragedy

> "Then comes she to me,
> And (with wilde looke) bid me devise some mean[s]
> To rid her from this second Marriage"
> *Romeo and Juliet,* 5.3.239–41

> "Quel poème que l'analyse de Φ!"
> Paul Valéry (Introduction to
> Matila Ghyka's *Le Nombre d'Or*)

Among the unusual textual effects in the youthful, romantic tragedy of the star-crossed lovers, *Romeo and Juliet,* is the matchmaker's incidental but resonant use of the seemingly simple, but basically complex, ethical term *mean* in the last act (5.3.240, 246). Whereas the Second Quarto reads "meane," the 1623 Folio has "meanes." The first time the Friar uses the term, it conveys a clear, dual signification: (1) an instrument (*mean* being then a common enough variant of *means*) and (2) the customary understanding of a 'happy medium between extremes' (henceforth, *Mean*). Whether he intends one or both of these effects deliberately is not so germane, initially at least, as what Shakespeare would have expected the audience to bear in mind, or what Juliet, to whom the churchman refers here, grasped. Although the inherent wordplay has been unnoted by Shakespeareans (hidden as it might initially appear to be), it now deserves some analysis apropos of the play as a whole, but also in relation to other works of the dramatist as well as in terms of the general intellectual climate. For a suitable *entrée,* we can accommodate a well-known phrase derived from Horace, *Est modus in rebus* ("there is a Mean in things"), an adage which, along with his more celebrated *aurea mediocritas* (Golden Mean) from the *Odes* (II, 10), explicitly utilizes the term *modus* as also representing both instrumentality and a principle of moderation, thereby serving as an apposite touchstone for our reconsidering Shakespeare's application of it. The similarity of key terms not only in Latin but English (*mean, means, meaning*) may lend itself at first to occasional ambiguity more confusing than resonating in terms of critical analysis; but, with strict recourse to immediate context, the problem is easily resolvable. Finally, our focus here is not to be simply on a textual crux but on its overall effect, not *merely* on the use of the 'good quarto' of 1599 (probably printed from Shakespeare's draft) as a basis for copy-text.

As a starter, we might interrelate another philosophic problem implicit in yet a further, better known textual difficulty, Romeo's well-known credal utterance: "Then I denie you Starres" (5.1.24). (See Quartos 2, 3, 4, and the Folio.) Spevack's new concordance as well as Bartlett's old one bypass this Folio reading in favor of "then I defie my Starres" (the Q1 or 'bad quarto' rendering). The crux involved seems to be in the implication that if "defie" is warranted, its import is that Romeo turns out to be a determinist in spite of himself. Almost as if recalling Homer's Hector or being proleptic of Milton's Satan, he knows that fate opposes him but resolutely determines to act and trespass as a voluntary agent regardless. In this respect, he behaves a bit like Dr. Faustus in Marlowe's play. On the other hand, if the "denie" reading is preferable, he rejects his destiny as already decreed in the heavens and assumes due responsibility for his actions. The effect then is that he would repudiate, as Cassius happens to in *Julius Caesar* (1.2.140), the pagan or astrologically dire superstition that his fate is ready-made.

The Second Quarto reading of "denie" seems, at first, to be more explicitly Christological and hence more germane. Yet the curious question of whether he is defying or denying being at the mercy of the heavenly bodies is truly subordinate to the larger issue of whether, in any valid sense, he applies the classical principle of the Mean to his social attitudes. His defiance or denial is interpretable, in part, as an immature renunciation of certain innate axioms of nature, ones to which he is bound to be subservient, whether or not he admits to them. For if he rejects such a salient natural design, nature can, in its way, reject or punish him.

Now one point is that he is scarcely in a position to disavow traditional astrology *in toto*. According to some standard medieval and Renaissance cosmologists, a certain literal adherence to star lore was still *de rigueur* enough. Aquinas himself had acknowledged that a modicum of astral influence may obtain in human lives. Indeed, man, it was thought then as now, cannot help but be, to a certain extent, partly a creature of fate or social circumstance. A valid solution to the *deny/defy* crux may, however, ironically reside not in itself in an either/or solution, but more in the tension between the two conflicting readings: Romeo's inability to bring the acts of denying and defying into harmony reveals, once again, his relative immaturity and hence lack of moderation. If it is at all doubtful that the author *needed* to have meant it that way, such a historical reading does not, at least, *contravene* what he deliberately wanted. Because Shakespeare's most important source, in Arthur Brooke, stressed determinism, he was thus making the more voluntaristic dramatic version possibly take a step beyond Brooke's. In this case, "denie" would be a better reading than "defie."

In a complementary manner, the seemingly innocuous little substantive *mean* represents another conundrum, one which coheres in the moral and aesthetic dimensions of the drama, interrelating them, thereby serving measurably to balance out its theme, recalling that way a notable Thomistic maxim, *unde pulcrum in debita proportione consistit* ("all things conjoin in due proportion") (*Summa Theologica,* i quest. 5, art. 4). Comparable was Bonaventura's *Nihil in universo est inordinatum* ("nothing in the universe is not in order") (*Sentences,* II, dist. 6, art. 2, qu. 1). Biblically speaking, the most helpful justification of belief in some number lore (if hardly all) is probably the saying that "the very hairs of your head are all numbered" (Matt. 10. 30). Yet, considered in its historical context, the ethical problem in the tragedy paradoxically links not so much with medieval theology as such (on which, see Curtius' fifteenth excursus, that on "Numerical Composition," as well as Vincent Hopper), but points more in the direction of Protestant reform, thus supporting the commonplace that only a limited faith or conscience fails to adjust to measurable self-appraisal.

Let us revert now directly to the dramatic text itself. In fairly close proximity to the *deny/defy* crux, curiously enough, Friar Laurence's apologia contains the following rather obvious, inherent recognition of a moderating power:

> Then comes [Juliet] to me,
> And (with wilde lookes) bid me devise some *mean[s]*
> To rid her from this second Marriage,
> Or in my cell there would she kill her selfe. (5.3.239–42—italics added)

In other words, her danger was that she might be tempted to take rather excessive steps. The need not merely for "some means" in general but for help which would include due moderate action is clear in the circumstances of her desperate plea, beginning with her immoderate "wilde lookes." Critics have hitherto failed to deal specifically with the hint of a Mean in the "means" requested; hence the textual divergence, evidently because in Elizabethan times *mean* and *means* were often enough simply textual variants. Still, the context clearly demands that both meanings be given their due here. As long as modern editions continue to rely on the Quarto's "meane" instead of the Folio's "Meanes," our path is clear, but when editors elect to follow the first collected edition and append the "s" ending, the nuance relating to measurement is lost in the critical shuffle. Friar Laurence, who incidentally cautions us about the need for apt moderation elsewhere (2.6.14), does not get in his full say.

Now what reason had Juliet to suspect that Laurence might not make use of the Mean with her, so that she had to remind him in her own lady-like manner to do so? In answer, earlier she feared that the churchman was unscrupulous and might even elect to give her a poison (4.3.24). Such anti-clerical or anti-Romanist bias was rampant enough at the time, notably in the plays of Marlowe, Webster, and Ford, though also already in *Arden of Faversham* with its notorious poisoned crucifix. (On the related matter of whether Shakespeare could have had any hand in that tragedy, see Ch 9.) The Friar, moreover, seems almost oblivious of the effect of his own words and uses *Meane* shortly once again in a random manner, almost as if only casually repeating the word:

> Then gave I her (so Tutor'd by my Art)
> A sleeping Potion, which so tooke effect
> As I intended, for it wrought on her
> The forme of death. *Meane* time, I writ to Romeo. . . .
> (5.3.243–46—italics added)

This folkloristic apologia is somehow pathetically ironic. His very word "forme" points to concern with form as appearance rather than substance, and thus with form*ality* rather than classic structure in its truest sense. The catastrophe to follow is underscored verbally through the Friar's echo of the word *meane* inasmuch as

"Meane time" represents an accidental or ironic resonance of "meane" earlier, however subtle this connection. (*Meane* here could be stressed by the actor.)

Consciously, Laurence would hardly have been aware of such a conjunction, but the mathematical implications of Golden Proportionality extend far beyond mere consciousness. In any case, he is scarcely enlightened enough as a learned churchman to attend to the full implications. Unable to perform his clerical duties adequately enough, he is at the same time politically ambitious (on which see Brenner). But the perceptive spectator or reader would link the word *Mean* up with Juliet's allusion to "limit, measure, bound" (3.2.125), which conjures up also a lack of proper time. The Friar's sudden use of the term "Meane time" could therefore remind us of, in effect, a "time for the Mean." Indeed, moderation in behavior demanded a temporal context: "The interrelationship of the seasons to form the basic unit of time and the application of this pattern to human affairs was a Renaissance commonplace" (Heninger 29). Compare also the close association of the Mean, time, and music in Kepler's *Harmonicè Mundi* (Walker). It is therefore hardly astonishing that the Golden Mean Proportion has been related by Ghyka and others to music, whereby, for example, the eight-note octave on the piano relates to the golden ratio of 8 and 5 (eight white keys and five black ones). Shakespeare may have readily been indebted here to Sir Thomas Elyot's *The Governour* with its memorable counsel: "do neither to moche ne to little, to sonne ne to late, to swiftly nor slowly, but in due tyme and measure" (cited by McGuire from the Croft ed.). Dancing ties in with the Mean's relation to music in a very practical, artistic way, as McGuire shows in his article, but Elyot's main point is that proper actions are those which are *governed,* hence involving some structured or even numerical judgment.

Clearly the ironic, passing effect of Laurence's dual use of *mean* did not betray Shakespeare's acumen or that of acuter members of his audience. What Juliet wants is that her ghostly father should provide "some meane," namely admonition which would relate to the Christian but also classical virtue of proper, rational behavior. The spectators thereupon would cathartically be expected to appreciate her deficiencies. Evidently this friar, then, cannot understand the full import of Juliet's behest, or, if he does, he indirectly later confesses to his limitations in complying with it. A sleeping potion is one thing, potentially bad or unnatural enough, but his recommendation that she prevaricate with her parents, especially when she is underage and legally responsible to them, is quite another. He prevaricates with them, moreover, himself. It is difficult to grasp how such careless deviation from the true way relates clerically at all to the principle of moderation in proper behavior. On the contrary, it smacks of emotional excess, Machiavellianism, over-indulgence in feral nature. (He may still be considered a *naïf,* though.)

That a single term like "meane" could have such a widespread, rich, allusive bearing thematically on the tragedy as a whole may strike some over-cautious readers as penetrating unduly beneath the surface. In answer, of course the crux serves mainly as an *entrée.* Yet those who find the main meaning simply occult and therefore out of place for a fourteen-year-old maiden fail to distinguish properly between the occult and the mystical, even as "[e]xpositions of the 'mystical' sense of numbers must therefore not be associated with the occult" (Røstvig, "Ars Aeterna" 45). Similar issues of this nature, or cruxes, however, are generally recognizable in analogous plays. For instance, the familiar textual debate over whether the Danish Prince's "flesh" is "sallied," "sullied" (a variant of it), or "solid" likewise informs us about the central bases of the protagonist's dilemmas and how he operates, notably when we recall Romeo's final parallel line about shaking "the yoke of inauspicious starres / From this world-wearied flesh" (5.3.111–2). If the Prince feels unwarrantedly "sullied"—the reading now usually preferred—we have more overall psychological, if not thereby also theological, grounds for coming to terms with his so-called menacing pseudo-procrastination. (See Lin Tung-chi's "'Sullied' is the Word," though he failed to take into account other recent scholarship.) The Pauline biblical formula about all of nature having fallen along with man may likewise be hinted at, particularly because it was so often stressed in developing Protestant theology (also in *As You Like It*). In the same manner, Romeo's actions may be a result of his tainted flesh, though in the sense of being hasty rather than too deliberative. Hence a single word like "flesh" and its crucial modifier can bear again on the tragedy as a whole.

In complementary guise, if Falstaff, in his dying moments, is not reverting to childish thoughts or slightly irreverent ones in the famous "greene fields" allusion to him, but is instead a veritable picture ("Table," as the Folio tells us) of jaundiced death (as synecdoche and ellipsis in the 1623 reading would allow for), we get a more naturalistic, even Hippocratic, portrait of a dying wastrel (see Ch 10 and Appendix B). Similarly, although in a rather more low-keyed way, the *mean/means* conundrum relates both to plot and character, pleasantly lending itself thereby to what is thought of so often as typically British, namely the subtle value of litotes or verbal restraint. Shakespeare cunningly reveals that Juliet asks for a fit instrument or mode of action involving restraint (a Mean) and then shows how her confessor fails to discern the full implications perhaps because of her 'feminine ambiguity.' In the subtlety of a *modus* which implies both instrument and happy medium, he alerts us to the unrestrained bases of this tragedy of youthful passion.

This key crux, moreover, pertains to the 'philosophy' of the play, particularly as then related to that of analogous tragedies. If *Romeo and Juliet* looks ahead to *Antony and Cleopatra* more than to any other drama dealing with the romantic fusion of contraries (save possibly for the likewise star-crazed *Othello*), one reason is that the Baroque style of the Egyptian-Roman tragedy is found in the *lack* of moderation already decried at the very outset: "Nay, but this dotage of our Generals / Ore-flowes the measure" (1.1.1–2). Comparable is the wordplay on this theme in *Measure For Measure,* the title of which can be glossed in Benvolio's words: "But let them measure us by what they will, / Weele measure them a Measure, and be gone" (1.4.9–10). For the assimilation of measurement with the Mean, a Renaissance commonplace, is of particular aesthetic concern also to *Romeo and Juliet.*

It is of course common knowledge how the Mean is classical in origin, operating in Aquinas and Horace also in the medieval period. Its function during the Renaissance is perhaps best brought out in Pico della Mirandola's *Heptaplus* (1489), which provides "an explicit and emphatic Renaissance statement of the view that poetry should reproduce the order of the universe" (Røstvig in *Silent Poetry* 32). It is but one step from this view to another, that principles of due moderation operate in literature as well as nature. In her work on the sixteenth-century French academies, Frances Yates thus found *Love's Labour's Lost* as containing allusions to "a Neo-Pythagorean harmony of the universe" (264–5).

How then is the Mean operative in the star-crossed tragedy? It points to the vital choreographic resonances, dance imagery being central enough also to this dramatic structure, as we have seen. If measure is truly operative in all human concerns, as Aquinas had maintained, it is literally perhaps most obvious in lovers 'treading a measure' at a dance. Hence the hero-lover encounters Juliet at a masked ball, choreographic imagery becoming metaphorically operative. Elyot had shown how "all qualities incident to man, and also all qualities to a woman lyke wyse appertaynyge" are "knitte to gether and signified in the personages of man and woman daunsinge" (236, 238). Likewise "the measured dance accompanying the song at the end" of a drama "would convey the notion of an ordered cosmos" (Heninger, *Pattern* 50). Do we not cogently recollect the commonplace of how the Renaissance tried to make even all of life a work of art? In any event, since the 'compleat' Renaissance gentleman was supposed to know how to dance, it followed that the measure even of his footsteps would be expected to relate to proper measure in his life taken as a whole: "The specific qualities which Elyot sees as 'knitte to gether' in dancing are less important in clarifying the dancing in *Romeo and Juliet* than is the underlying principle of a mean being generated by the reconciliation of extremes" (McGuire 95). Moderation in all things should thus prevail.

Yet is Friar Laurence truly bent on exercising his clerical duties in terms of such a Mean? "Capulet's abrupt decision to have Juliet marry Paris forces Friar Laurence, a character well-versed in the properties of herbs and flowers, to improvise a plan which calls upon Juliet to imitate the withering and subsequent ripening of plants by seeming to die and then, 'in due tyme and measure,' reappearing as Romeo's spouse" (McGuire 89), yet surely such a charmingly folklorish account of a purportedly moderating friar is troublesome to reconcile with the subtleties of true Christian prudence. (By the same devious and questionable token, the indiscriminate use of drugs might almost be condoned merely because they have their sources in the natural world and so must, in effect, be simply gifts of God.) This is a far cry from Elyot's insistence that maturity is definable as "a meane betwene two extremities, wherin nothing lacketh or excedeth" (McGuire 95), whereby the choreographic metaphor relates rather more to the lovers' immaturity.

Still, treading a measure on the dance floor is not so far off from the mathematical basis of the Mean. Thus, the Mean of temperate action is considered in arithmetical terms in Aristotle's *Ethics,* on which Aquinas commented: "The wise man avoids excess and defect, and wants to find the mean not objectively but relative to us" (Litzinger 141). Compare also his question on "Whether the Moral Virtues Consist in a Mean" (Shapcote II, 488). As an ethical formulation of an aesthetic principle, one devised principally by Euclid and the Greeks, the Golden Proportion was highly influential in the Renaissance, deriving more immediately from Horace's *aurea mediocritas* as in Chaucer's reference to "mesure" in his *Parliament* (304–5) and culminating in Shakespeare. Examples of this moral formula, though often only loosely pointed out, can be helpful in analyzing ethical relations in the plays. In *As You Like It,* for instance, Audrey and Phebe are foils to Rosalind, who then represents a happy medium between extremes; in the same comedy, Orlando serves a similar function between Touchstone and Silvius. More specifically arithmetic appropriations of the Mean can be divined in the internal structure of the *Sonnets,* whereby the octet-sestet division nearly approximates the 8/5 division in the so-called Fibonacci Number Series, on which the Golden Proportion in nature is based. (Its name derives from Fibonacci's *Liber Abaci,* whereby mathematical proportions are originally seen as involved, believe it or not, in the multiplication of rabbits.) Some of Shakespeare's sonnets' meaning patterns are recognizably Petrarchan, such as with the standard "When"/"Then" format. (On this view of the structure of the sonnet form as apparently originally formulated in W. Bähr's paper "Der Goldene Schnitt am Sonnet," see Stageberg's discussion of the aesthetic of the Petrarchan sonnet.) How all this relates to Christianity may be questioned inasmuch as the key number five in the Series has often been related to the five senses and in opposition thereby to the spiritual, yet Thomas Browne made much of the spirituality of the number in his *Garden of Cyrus,* and certainly it has a basis in the cult of the Virgin (May, her month, being the fifth, and *five* playing a key role in the rosary). We have but to think of the pentangle and its significance in *Sir Gawayne and the Grene Knight. Five* was seen as "the type of nature, embracing all things" (Hopper 43). Irenaeus argued that this number "is everywhere manifest in the True Faith" (cited by Hopper 74). The main import of the digit linked it with marriage, strongly cited that way in Chaucer's Wife of Bath's tale, and that would tie in with the star-crossed tragedy, even sacramentally. Classically, it was said to combine the first female and male digits (*two* and *three*). Recently it has been urged that the pentad had *evil* signification to a great degree (see Lee and Berkeley), but such an indictment appears tenuous when one thinks of, say, the sacred use of *five* in the Consecration of the Bread during the Mass (*Hic est enim Corpus Meum*), alluded to in *Everyman,* where stress is placed on the need of one's five wits.

Alastair Fowler has also made much of the pentad as symbolic of justice (as in Book V of *The Faerie Queene*). The clearest use in the Bible is in the Pentateuch, though it might be mentioned that *Jesus* has the requisite five letters. Probably *five* has been looked at askance by some for subliminal reasons in that it comes in between *three* and *seven,* digits with more of a well-known, even superstitious, mystique behind them

In numerous other ways, the Golden Proportion (or Section, as it is sometimes called) is evident analogically in nature and literature. It thus has been symbolized as Φ, prompting, in our time, Paul Valéry's acclamation: "Quel poème que l'analyse de Φ!" (Ghyka 9). Sometimes, following the precedent of Fra Luca Pacioli's *La Divina Proportione,* it has been called 'divine'; ofttimes it has been expressed in terms of pentagonal symmetry and its key digit *five* called the Golden Number. Valéry summed up the mathematical import of the Mean in his introduction to Matila Ghyka's major work, *Le Nombre d'Or,* as follows: "L'équilibre entre le savoir, le sentir et le pouvoir est rompu maintenant dans les arts. L'instinct ne donne que des parties. Mais le grand art doit correspondre à l'homme complet. La Divine Proportion est la mesure généralisée" (9). Comparable is the formula of the Gothic master builder in 1398: "Ars sine scientia nihil" (Ghyka, *The Geometry of Art and Life* xi). The Mean has likewise been seen as derivative of Plato, Alberti, and Leonardo da Vinci (Funck-Hellet 111). We are well reminded of the Renaissance dictum that all of nature can be seen as a work of art. The real problem has been in how to reconcile such a fundamentally aesthetic principle with ethical behavior.[34]

In Shakespeare's time, numerology and the accommodation of Euclidean techniques to the fine arts in general was *à la mode,* as studies on the Renaissance

---

[34] Even in our time, John Dewey has made the following telling point: "'Mean' and 'proportional' are, however, not . . . to be taken over in a prior mathematical sense, but are properties belonging to an experience that has a developing movement toward its own consummation" (40–41). Hence the modern predilection for the 'organic.' On the other hand, this attitude may be understood as not cancelling out the Mean but simply redirecting it. Because the mathematical principle can be expressed only in incommensurable terms, as basic to growth itself, it can hardly be very consciously imitated. A genius like Shakespeare, as well as most Renaissance writers, must have understood this principle intuitively. Too conscious an application of the Golden Mean Proportion may not work well, though at the time of writing the Director of the World Order of Narrative and Formalist Poets, Dr. Alfred Dorn, has invented a type of poetic structure based on the 8/5 Golden Proportion with success, as he has indicated in his international poetry contests.

concern with harmony reveal (see Heninger, *Touches* 234–55). The Elizabethan sage John Dee concerned himself with Euclid's *Elements Geometricall, Mathematicè, Physicè, et Pythagoricè*. Because he was a practitioner, albeit an occult one, of the principle of the Mean, it is of interest to observe that he has been considered a prototype for Prospero in *The Tempest*. Friar Laurence is in contrast to this type; although inclined to do the right thing, he is ineffectual. True, he hopes to reunite the feuding families and thereby reestablish the grace of harmonious relations between people, but the illegitimate, clandestine marriage he arranges actually prompts major *dis*harmony. The "temp'ring" of "extremities" asked for in the second prologue is not affected when Laurence tries to "incorporate / two in one" (2.6.37) (McGuire 96). The lack of overall harmony is symbolized by the extensive use of the figure of oxymoron (1.1.173–8), whereby contraries like love and hate are set up against each other. The suggestion is that opposites may be reconciled only in romantic death.

Much of the overall structure of the play can be revealed in terms of chaotic extremities which embrace no Mean and thereby lack a basis for reconciliation. To some extent, the Friar is but a *pro forma* product of an imbalanced world, yet, in certain respects, he adds tragically to the predicament. Numerous scholars of late (e.g., Robert Stevenson, Battenhouse, Bryant, Edwards, Harcourt, Brenner) have tried to come to terms with this problem in detail, but none has stressed the import of the Mean (and lack of it) as such. Whereas the Friar's main accomplishment, his effecting the Sacrament of Matrimony between lovers, deserves some acclaim, it succeeds only as a by-product of tragic circumstance, and the question of his Machiavellian method arises. In marrying Romeo and Juliet, is he not making the end justify the means, putting formality ahead of true form or substance? His primary dereliction of social duty is seen in his not making use of temperate ethics, the very kind he himself once recommended (3.3.55). In idealistically thinking of uniting warring families, the Friar is thinking of political or social expediency but should realize that the rightful end of an action is a product of the means used, not a by-product. So counsels "Philosophie" (3.3.5).

It was Juliet's request that the Friar "devise some meane" by acting as a suitable go-between for her and thereby be a sensible moderator, not merely a closeted father confessor. Granted, the medieval Church was not always 'practical' in such matters, distinguishing between theology and psychology thereby, but then again that was a cardinal reason for some Protestant reform. In Juliet's use of the verb *devise,* she was hardly expecting or allowing for excessive ingenuity; she clearly hoped to find a way out between having to obey her parents and destroying herself, two horrible excesses. When she found she could not trust her earthly father because of her love for Romeo, she understandably sought refuge in a ghostly one. Elizabethan audiences, ones sensitive to the Anglican stress upon a Protestant and yet 'Catholic' communion, would have at least respected, even appreciated, her desire, whoever her spiritual guidance counsellor was, as would any audience aware of the Church of England's own search for the Mean in its conception of being the *Via Media* (as formulated in Renaissance times by Jeremy Taylor). The Latin phrase is particularly relevant here because it betokens a 'middle way' not only between 'extremes' of Christian faith (say Roman Catholicism, on one hand, and Puritan determinism on the other), but also by intimating that a moral objective can have an aesthetic means, thereby analogically revealing again how the supernatural builds on the natural. As the medieval age had already known, "L'homme, étant un microcosme, doit refléter les harmonies de l'univers: à la musique, 'cosmique' répond la musique 'humaine'" (de Bruyne 66).

In putting the tragedy in deeper perspective, we bear in mind, too, that strictures against minors marrying without parental consent were extremely severe in Protestant England. Thus Peter Martyr had written as follows: "Paule saith to the Ephesians: *Children obeie your parents* in all things. He excepteth nothing, when he writeth so: but saith, *In all things:* Namelie, which they command not against the word of God. And in his first epistle to the Corinthians, the seventh chapter, [it] is most manifestlie declared, that it belongeth to the parents to give their daughters in marriage to husbands" (*Common Places of Christian Religion,* trans. A. Marten [1583] II, 432—as cited by Battenhouse and Dobbins 111–2). Likewise Anglican Bishops Robert Sanderson and Leonard Wright had written of how sin is definable as lacking in a Mean: "There is no more *mean* in this vice, than is in theft, adulterie, and murther" (111).

Now, one type of Catholic then might have been inclined to adhere to the Church as above and beyond the Bible at times and thus to respect Friar Laurence's prescriptiveness as somehow superseding Scripture on fine points. Yet even for a Catholic sensitive about censuring the clergy, he should have seen that if tragedy is about to ensue, then the priest who took it upon himself to put his invested authority above that of the Word of God should have to receive a goodly portion of the blame. In any event, it is well recognized that Shakespeare appears more anti-clerical in this play than does Arthur Brooke in *Romeus and Juliet,* the poem which constituted the tragedy's main source and which was manifestly anti-Romanist, as the author's Preface well reveals. On the other hand, to be fair, it would be disproportionate on our own parts not to retain in mind how the dominant tragic fault resides rather in Romeo, whose behavior is hardly to be cavalierly let go as merely the impetuousness of youth. In any case, he slays Tybalt in anger.

Unlike the Friar, at any rate, Juliet seems bound more by the strictures of nature than dogma. Her appeal is to secular commonsense and reason in her sensible inclination to have the moderate thing done if at all possible. As a strict Catholic, nonetheless, she is obliged to conform to the dictates of her Church's teachings, and so she seeks a solution that might be called, in figurative terms here, a special dispensation. Like Emilia in *Othello,* she presumably could be persuaded to venture purgatory for her love, if not quite for the same reasons. Being but fourteen, she does not know exactly what she should ask for, her appeal thereby being more *conative* in nature than *cognitive,* and thus she qualifies her hope: She can expect no more than "some" Mean. That should surely be good enough for her. (Little does she consciously realize that the conative approach relates directly to the aesthetic of the Mean itself, on which see Wertheimer and Weber.) Evidently the Friar, in his limited way, does not comprehend what we might call her true dilemma: her fundamentally classical and not merely romantic disposition. Or she might be thought of as especially close to the proportion operative in nature.

Should an objection be raised as to her implicit double use of the word *meane* (namely instrumentality as well as moderate action) on the grounds of taste, she can be properly defended. It might be said, for example, she is being disrespectful in her ambiguity, mixing religious and secular values with a clergyman, for she is insinuating that Laurence might help her out in some purely secular capacity. In any case, such play upon words has been a regular staple in Christian tradition. For what it is worth, the Church developed through the ages by capitalizing on the paronomasia involved in the way She was founded, by overtly defending the 'uncomic wordplay' used by Christ in designating Peter Her earthly head. Since the Greek for *rock* is *petros,* and the Aramaic *Kepha* (a word which, in Greek, took the form of *Kephas*) may then be related to *Petros* (Mossman 7–10), Jesus, it can be claimed, had name-play in mind when he notified the Disciple whom He most trusted that He would construct His Church on a combination of Peter's new name (his earlier being Simon Bar-Jona) and a rock-hard, permanent foundation (Matt. 16.18). Although, true, this name-play came to be disputed by Protestant and Catholic alike in Renaissance times, for instance by Milton and Erasmus, it was still widely known and taught, thereby providing a precedent for Shakespeare in having his heroine indulge in similar wordplay on "meane," in particular, let us say, in her making her request of a disciple of Peter for assistance. Should it be averred that she is too young and docile to realize the import of such esoteric implications (a questionable proposition since surely many teenagers have always loved joke books and puns), another precedent for such double meaning may be enlisted. For, clerically, equivocation, which has been defended by the Jesuit order, was indirectly criticized as such in *Macbeth,* 2.3.8. Let us not rule out the plausibility that Shakespeare was already parodying attempts at justification of similar equivocation in the heroine's seemingly naïve supplication in *Romeo and Juliet.* —If only the Friar had taken her words to heart. For hers was an equivocation that had no political overtones and was wholly responsible in nature. Her desire for an instrument to remedy her impossible situation, especially when qualified in the same breath with the implied reference to the healthy restraint of moderation, reveals modesty itself. (What should the Friar have done? That raises an entirely new issue. But the question cannot be seriously asked because it is outside the realm of the plot line.)

No wonder that critic after critic has stressed the underlying point of this tragedy as its revealing the need for a Golden Mean in human behavior. One has tried to sum up this approach in rather too modernistic terms by endorsing the applicability of Fletcher's pragmatic solution, "Situation Ethics" (Pearce 2). Still, the notion behind it is sound: that dogma should correlate with the practical world; the former should be used to complement the latter, not the latter the former. Because "Shakespeare used the career of Romeo to illustrate how 'excess in enjoyment, however pure in itself, transforms its sweetness into bitterness,'" he meant for the play "to teach a lesson in moderation," according to the German critic Gervinus (Pearce 2). But a more recent German scholar has found Laurence mainly a comic figure, arguing, "Mönch ist er nur akzidentiell" (Bartenschlager 100). Similar attempts have been made to find Shylock's Jewishness historically comical rather than anti-Semitically portrayed and hence offensive (and biased to modern sensibilities).

True enough, Laurence does pay some token lip-service at least to man's inherent need for moderate behavior. "Therefore love moderately," he counsels (2.6.14). Yet this caveat is of not much avail when he happens to be the one who initially fails to live up to it. In devising the "means" of a sleeping potion, he provides what is (considering the disastrous consequences) an intolerably extreme solution. Likewise we witness him spending no time recommending religious instruction; he charges Romeo with having been up all night with Rosaline and yet hastily deigns to unite him to the newcomer Juliet the same day; he fails to advise the hero to consult with him upon returning to Verona, tells Juliet that she shall sleep for "two-and-forty hours" (whereupon she awakens much earlier) (Harcourt 68), and in general neglects seeing himself in proper moral perspective, failing to atone for what he did or left undone even when the tragedy has been effected. In turning the lovers into unwitting scapegoats for the main purpose of uniting their feuding families, he clearly reveals his politicking disposition, his questionable dedication to the expediency. We may be reminded of the individual unthinkingly subordinating himself to the State.

Again, the mere *donnée* that he *means well* ironically compensates for his deficiency in not properly applying the very Mean he himself recommends. On the other hand, since temperance was looked upon as more of a secular than theological virtue (as Spenser took pains to elucidate in *The Faerie Queene,* Books I and II), one should not be too dogmatic about a principle which is, in essence, relative, not strictly in accord with Christian dogmatics (though Aquinas' Question LXIV, "On the Mean of Virtue," comes to mind), and often largely ascertainable only aesthetically (and, by inference, often mathematically). Still, commonsense would tell us that because moderation is basic to nature, it has a direct bearing upon the manner at least in which dogma should be imposed. At any rate, since some cognizance of the need for balanced behavior is inherent throughout the biblical Hagiographa, it has enough ethical significance and ought to have even for a churchman versed primarily in the clerical codes.

In any event, the Golden Proportion and its implications were widely known throughout the Middle Ages and Renaissance, so the Friar, if at all representative of Renaissance Man,[35] had every reason to want to examine his conscience severely on this score. The concept gained wide currency through such notables as Plautus, Terence, Cicero, Erasmus, Barclay, Chaucer, and especially Castiglione and Spenser. Particularly memorable is Spenser's "Tempering goodly well / Their contrary dislikes with loved meanes" ("Hymn in Honor of Love"). No less important was Thomas Wyatt's "Of the Meane and Sure Estate." Whereas "Meane" has been glossed there as meaning only "poore" (Rollins, *Renaissance* 942), *OED* provides a more provident signification for us: "the middle condition between extremes of fortune" (sb., I, 1). Stoics like Lipsius related the classic philosophy of "Nothing too much" to Christian teachings and infused much of the literature of the time with their helpful precepts. One clear-cut instance of this is the play called *The Golden Meane* (attributed to John Ford). Imagine a Renaissance audience seeing that drama and then *Romeo and Juliet* in tandem, thereupon debating the import of the Friar's and Juliet's references to the Mean—with the ensuing irony involved.

Hitherto, oddly enough, some critics have placed the burden of the critical blame on the wrong churchman. Friar John is the one ineffectual in getting his message to Romeo, and his competency has likewise been questioned since he *is* able to escape from a plague-ridden house. But denigrating his role serves as misdirection when the real *naïf* is the friar responsible for instructing the minors in such a slipshod manner from the outset. Yet, all the same, Laurence is no less jolly as a character, particularly insofar as playgoers, like all Christians, were expected to love others because of, as well as in spite of, their human idiosyncrasies. One of the many ironies about this play is in the way his limited character has become sentimentalized—way out of due Christian proportion with respect to any positive accomplishments. The unstudied reader or spectator is nearly expected *not* to put him down, almost as if doing so might uncover a hidden, disadvantageous bias. On the other hand, too much attention can be placed

---

[35]It could be argued that the Friar was not meant to be representative of such but in universal terms he still stands for the Body of Christ and might thereby be thought of as *deus* (if also somewhat *ex machina*).

on the limitations of the churchman alone, for the play has faults and immaturities on a much larger scale. As has recently been documented, this drama "has been faulted for its dependence on coincidence and on causes external to the protagonists for conditions that bring about the tragic outcome"; moreover, "critics have encountered difficulty in their attempts to reconcile the purity of Romeo and Juliet's devotion to each other ... with the play's equal insistence that their relationship is a form of idolatry—ultimately leading both lovers to acts of desperation that audiences in Shakespeare's time would have considered far more consequential than do modern audiences" (Andrews 306).

As I have intimated earlier, Shakespeare appreciated the import of the Mean well enough throughout his works, and *Romeo and Juliet* serves as a stepping-stone for recognizing the applicability of the Golden Mean Proportion elsewhere. Yet sometimes its formulation may indeed lead to valid disputes. Does, to take an example, Prince Hal truly represent a symbolic or latent Mean between the extremes of Falstaff and Hotspur (gluttony and wrath)? For is it not also rather plausible, in terms of E. E. Stoll's notable stress on the theatrical over and above real-life psychology, to envisage Sir John himself as a Mean between the debilitation of the Prince and the impetuosity of Henry Percy?

Whatever the right answer, the principle of moderation is basic to nature and hence natural law, even as the Golden Mean Proportion has been found operative in biological forms, from nautilus sea shells to maple leaves to the morphology of plant growth. It has been maintained by Zeising that this mathematical formula is "die beste Vermittlung zwischen absoluter Gleichheit und Verschiedenheit" and, in more modern terms by G. D. Birkhoff, that the aesthetic measure of an object, M, is proportional to its orderliness, O, and inversely proportional to its complexity, C; hence $M=\frac{O}{C}$. Never should this Golden Proportion be confused with the modernistic bromide which tends to identify it with a form of mediocrity, a position possibly attributable to a superficial influence of Aurelius' use of the Mean in his *Meditations*. As Shakespeare reflects in one of his later, mellower dramas, where he also makes the same correlation between (1) instrument and (2) Mean, as with the Latin *modus* and (if I have proved my point in this chapter) Juliet's "meane":

> Nature is made better by no meane,
> But Nature makes that Meane.　　　(*The Winter's Tale*, 4.4.89–90)

So should it be in the tragedy of lovers wracked not only by inauspicious stars but unplanned and mishandled human foibles. Agreed, this is hardly a novel thesis in Shakespeare criticism, yet the ethical-aesthetic, even (by implication) numerological, approach broached here provides an innovative perspective. It might be contended that the burden of the chapter deviates somewhat from the story line at times, in so doing detracting from, say, the character of Friar Laurence himself. Admittedly, but he functions mainly as a *deus ex machina* anyway. He is not even himself aware of all the overtones of his remarks and actions, for example in his use of the opener "*Meane* time" (5.3.246). Further, to question whether the physical action of dancing on the stage would call to the random spectator's mind the association of treading a measure and acting in due proportion is, with all due respect to young lovers, finally anti-intellectual. Granted, "the play's the thing," but Shakespeare, let alone Hamlet, was rather more interested in enhancing the powers of the mind than in mere foot exercise for its own sake on the boards of the stage.

PART IV
THE TOPICAL CRUX

Chapter 6
Sir Oliver, Contaminator of the Text, and Marlowe

Is not the hyphenated name of the bush-priest in *As You Like It,* Sir Oliver Mar-text, in a comedy alluding to Robin Hood at the outset (1.1.108–9), a kind of incidental theft of the name of *Marlowe*—as well as *Marprelate*? If it was based on anyone's name, it would most probably have had for its prototype more than a pseudonym, and a hidden Robin-Hood-like allusion to thievery for altruistic motives could imply a more subtle, onomastic theft. In short, Mar-text's name could well have represented a conflation of more than one familiar topical allusion in a comedy filled with such meanings. If it reflects back not only on the Martin Marprelate religious controversy, as has been widely acknowledged as a source, but also on the playwright's probable Rival Poet, it most probably would have had a more forceful, yet still lighthearted satiric effect that way. In this connection, it is useful to remember that Shakespeare's own name was also sometimes printed as hyphenated, as on the title-page of the *Sonnets* and after the conclusion of the *Threnos* section of "The Phoenix and the Turtle."[36]

To begin, this comedy is known as one of the master dramatist's most topical theatrical scripts. He seems to have taken a keen delight in subliminally indulging in allusions to contemporary society, often taken in a satiric light, and even to himself and his mother behind the general pastoral façade. Thereby not so

---

[36] In a separate note on that poem (*Notes and Queries,* NS, XXXV, 53–54), I have dealt with the import of plausible codification (though not to the point there of inverted cryptography), however subtextual, and the present essay also deals with this aspect.

unexpectedly was he looking ahead to an even more recognizably topical adventure, *Love's Labour's Lost,* especially if the 'school of night' purportedly alluded to there included Marlowe (as has often been thought)—though this coterie has also been questioned, and its existence can scarcely be entirely proved. Aside from entering into the onomastic maze of the Forest of Arden itself in *As You Like It,* we can cite a few examples of name-play. *Arden* itself is commonly thought to be a shortened form not only of *Ardennes* as Anglicized to *Arden* (though now switched back to *Ardenne* in the new *Oxford Shakespeare*), a name extant in Camden's *Remaines*, but also of Mary *Arden* Shakespeare. Recent studies have faced the problem of whether, for instance, a character called William appears briefly because the playwright assumed that role (as well as presumably doubling by taking that of Adam earlier), thereby allowing for in-house amusement based on their having the same Christian forename (see Jones). Although the antiquarian Oldys had written of how one of the dramatist's younger brothers saw him in the role of Adam, William enters only later when Adam is off-stage, allowing the author as actor to engage in fashionable doubling of parts. (This may be rather speculative but it is itself engaging.)

Likewise scholarship has pondered whether Touchstone would have reminded alert playgoers of Marston (see Viswanathan). For notice the clear onomastic similitude of *Mar-text, Marston,* and then *Marlowe. Does Touchstone mar* the *ston*(e), too, that is *Rock* in the spiritual sense, thus tying him in with *Mar*-text? It could be thought of that way. But the main critical concern in this regard is whether Marlowe and his work are alluded to many times throughout this part of the comedy. Agreed, he is recalled in at least a subtle, two-fold capacity: not merely for his creative, poetic writings, which are then memorably 'echoed,' as is well known, but also because of his untimely but in itself dramatic death in an abrupt altercation at an eating place over the "recknynge," alluded to in Touchstone's line "it strikes a man more dead then a great reckoning in a little roome" (3.3.14–16). Augmenting Leslie Hotson's discovery of new data relating to the premature demise of Marlowe are recent studies by Lawless and Holdsworth. Further, Phebe in the play specifically cites a work by the late poet in quoting from "Hero and Leander" (3.5.80-81), which is alluded to again in the next scene (4.1.90-96). The comparison there of a loved object with a nun harks back to the same analogy twice made in the Marlowe poem (I.45, 319).

Kay Stanton, in her paper for the first International Marlowe Conference (University of Sheffield, 1983), now included in the *New Essays,* contended that the "recknynge" in the comedy did allude to Marlowe, not to the continuation by Chapman as has sometimes been thought. Certainly the leading case for Marlowe as the Rival Poet has recently been strengthened (Levin, "Another Possible Clue . . .").

Should it be queried at this point whether such allusiveness would have been at all still effective on the stage several years after Marlowe's unfortunate death, we might bear in mind that Shakespeare was surely *au courant* about such matters in that he likewise alluded to the public figure of Dr. Lopez not only by way of the character of Shylock, but also in the so-called *lupus*/"wolf" onomastic quibble in *The Merchant of Venice* (4.1.134) some years after the physician was executed on a presumably trumped-up charge, yet that later reference was evidently no less effective even then. No one to speak of, moreover, questions the main allusions to Marlowe and his achievements in *As You Like It*. Hence an additional one secreted in the name and character of Mar-text would fit the bill as well, providing for us more of a "recknynge" in deed.

In any event, of late several new allusions to this Kentish poetic rival (more likely by a long shot the Rival Poet than was, say, Chapman) have been set forth in print. Because these poets were so very different, it appears doubtful that they would have at any time successfully collaborated, even in the curious case of *Arden of Faversham* (see Ch 9), though there may be circumstantial basis for this insofar as their plays were put on by Pembroke's Men, and *Arden* had been associated with that acting company. (However, *The True Tragedy of Richard III*, which contains reference to a key character in *Arden* called Black Will, was in the repertoire of the Queen's Men, not Pembroke's. In contrast, *The True Tragedy of Richard Duke of York*, which then lent itself to *2 Henry VI,* belonged to Pembroke's.) Some connection between Shakespeare and Marlowe, at any rate, is hardly surprising when scholars have long accepted Marlovian 'echoes' as being fairly extensive and representative in the former's work, for example in the case of Shylock, indebted to the ignominious Barabas in *The Jew of Malta;* that of Hero in *Much Ado* (or *Won*), whose name again refers back to "Hero and Leander"; and *Richard II*, which exhibits well-recognized overlappings with both *Edward II* and at least the Helen section of *Dr. Faustus.* Moreover, onomastic echoes from *Dr. Faustus* are resonant in *Hamlet.*[37]

In the light of such a spate of old and new analogies, therefore, although we would be modish we could still appear somewhat brash in deigning to promote yet another topical intrusion of the so-called "mighty," if at times all-too-shadowy, Marlovian camp. It is only with some trepidation, then, that I invite the verdict that one of the more obscure, minor figures in the romantic comedy evokes, among other matters, to be sure, a further veiled allusion to the Canterbury giant and thereby to his renowned maverick reputation. After all, he was known not only as a dangerous overreacher, but also a brawler (as in his well-known fracas involving Thomas Watson), a presumed (but hardly proven) deviate, likewise a reputed atheist, and then at times *flippant* Ovidian poet of love. (Phebe extols Marlowe as a true love poet but is hardly authoritative.) In any event, the characters he created reached well beyond their progenitor and have mythopoeic status. With luck, such a hit as here proposed, if palpable, ought at least to serve to befuddle again any desperate anti-Stratfordian hangers-on, providing new grist as well for the evolving Marlovian mill in the industry of contemporary criticism. Let us pose our problem technically as follows: Does Mar-text turn out to be also a valid Marlowe-*Figur*?

In answer, the very hyphenated surname of this over-sensitive Vicar, who offers to officiate at the proposed rustic marriage of Touchstone and Audrey until Jaques 'pessimistically' intervenes (3.3.63), serves to register clear textual multivalence. Elsewhere I have broached the issue of whether the talk in the play about the ineptness of Sir Oliver might not reflect a certain autobiographical relevance (see my correspondence in *Shakespeare Quarterly* XXV, 285), yet that proposal was admittedly meant only as a 'query,' thus without offering extensive supportive evidence. As for whether Marlowe and his Rival might have been personally familiar with each other, the chance is small, though not improbable,

---

[37] See my book on the subject, *The Prince and the Professor* (1986), Part I, whereby the first titular figure stands for the Dane, the second for the professing German. Further, Shakespeare's title originally embracing the unusual term *Tragical History* is taken over from Marlowe's title, and Cornelius and Voltemand early in the Danish tragedy hark back to Cornelius and Valdes, magicians in *Dr. Faustus* (*Voltemand* suggesting *voler* and *main,* and hence *sleight-of-hand*). But the main onomastic link is with the name of the university, *Wittenberg.*

given the size of London at that time. If they had at all collaborated, they may well not have been considered Rivals, however, but all that suggests is that they probably did not collaborate.

A few circumstantial clues as to the *Mar-text/Marlowe* name-play gradually filter in. For instance, the Vicar's allegorical surname bespeaks an anomalous individualist who, whether deliberately or not, would "mar" the biblical "text" either by brazenly misquoting Scripture, by misinterpreting (taking passages out of context the way Faustus does), or both, plausibly also with a recondite, agnostic, or even atheistic rationale. As a prominent name for such a rebel, that of *Marlowe* would easily have come to mind. He was said to have done this sort of thing, making fun of the dogma of the Virgin Birth, for instance, mainly according to the accusations of Kyd and Baines. Thus the Marlowe name might have been maligned, albeit the main Marlowe reference in *As You Like It* may be taken as affectionate. True, the Variorum and other commentaries since 1876 have traditionally invoked only the analogous name of *Marprelate* in this Mar-text connection. As Peter Milward has summed up this consensus: "The peculiar name was evidently suggested by that of Martin Marprelate, whose attacks on the episcopacy in the late eighties had been answered by several of the 'university wits.' In that controversy, the prefix *mar-* had been commonly bandied about, both by Marprelate and by his opponents; and Thomas Cooper, in his *Admonition to the People of England* (1589), speaks of 'not only Mar-prelate, but Mar-prince, Mar-state, Mar-law, Mar-magistrate and all together!'" (146).

Such mocking names are in unison indeed, but the probable genesis of a made-up name like *Mar-text* can scarcely be fully accounted for in terms of the author's broad aesthetic application or transformation of such a Marprelatous occasion. Two logical fallacies easily come to mind in our defense: the Genetic Fallacy, so dubbed by W. K. Wimsatt, and Occasionalism, as specified by Richard L. Levin, a major pet-shibboleth debunker. The main point behind both of these caveats is that literary meaning, in its fullest sense, ought never to be primly equated simply with an immediate source, which itself is often relatively speculative. Cooper's work, then, hardly need be taken as the main or only source for Mar-text's name. Or, to put it another way, what started out as an obvious enough Marprelate allusion could have ended up as a rather more meaningful one to Marlowe, for *Marprelate* was no more than pseudonym.

Further, the nonce-name *Mar-law*, as cited by Cooper, happens to be itself relatively close in sound and form to that of *Marlowe*, so that the hint of Marlowe may also have indirectly come by way of Cooper. In any case, since it was precisely the University Wits, among whom Marlowe was a mainstay, who involved themselves in the Marprelate affair, why should not Shakespeare have seen a tie-in between the two names? Certainly it was not unheard of for a name he made up to enjoy more than one etymological antecedent. For a parallel, Sir John Falstaff's name easily comes to mind as a prime analog; it has been said not only to 'echo' that of Sir John Fastolf but also to hark back obliquely to the dramatist's own. Unduly fatuous though the punning understandably strikes certain critics nowadays, clearly a *spear* that *shakes* is as intimidating as a *staff* which *falls*, and this association is confirmed through similar name-play on the subliminal level in *The Tempest:* "I . . . shake" (5.1.47) and "I'le breake my staffe" (54). Camden listed the names of *Breakspear* and *Shotbolt* as a few variants of *Shakespeare*, whose coat of arms showed a falcon shaking a spear (for more on this, see Ch 9). This is not to deny other possible connotations as well.

True enough, the main Marprelate link may be held as critical in that Mar-text's name may also involve Puritanical associations. Yet, in point of fact, Oliver is actually not a Puritan as such but a rustic Anglican; he figures as a Vicar with perhaps a slight, unorthodox Puritan taint. Subsequent stage figures whose names start with *Mar-* such as Marall in *A New Way to Pay Old Debts* would recall for us Mar-text as well as Marprelate, whereby a dual debt would again be evident. No doubt a plethora of marrers of the text then abounded.

At this juncture, mention might be made of the presidential paper by Dr. Jean Jofen at the first International Marlowe Conference aforementioned (which I happened to attend), a paper which offered the curious but provocative position that Martin Marprelate *himself* could have represented Marlowe—in disguise, no less. This unusual contention led to much stimulating debate, not to mention expected animadversions. Granted, the results of the evidence, which she chose then to reveal only to a limited extent, were neither here nor there, thereby not totally convincing the participants who engaged in scholarly give-and-take afterwards such as Kenneth Muir (who also professed then modestly to being only an avid "interloper," however). In any case, no substantial counter-argument was presented which fundamentally *dis*proved her contention. Her argument happens to tie in conveniently with the thesis of this present chapter, which in no way is meant to be based on it, though, for its chief points were formulated before hers were offered.[38] As to the anticipated unreadiness that a Mar-text/Marprelate association seems adequate enough without our also having to marshall the name of Marlowe, the answer is that surely such a double effect as the one proposed would have lent itself to greater wit on the stage, thereby indirectly recalling Marlowe as a prime University Wit. The more wit, the merrier.

But let us return to the play itself and consider the satire involved. In his customary deft manner, the late Alfred Harbage glossed the Vicar's precipitate entrance and exit as follows: "Poor proud Oliver Mar-text—we remember him always, although he is only given three speeches and then elbowed into oblivion" (239–40). This is a pathetic retrospection indeed. Because he fails to qualify as a "good Priest" (3.3.74), Sir Oliver has to be abruptly alerted to his being no longer in the running for presiding at the ensuing marital service, signifying that his rendering of Scripture was deemed too idiosyncratic. Nowadays, with our purportedly more enlightened sense of toleration, which also allows for accepting multiple meanings, we may escort him genteelly back out of such oblivion.

But is, then, the key issue specifically or merely "some Puritan taint," as Harbage then tentatively inferred? True enough, Mar-text's memorable Parthian shot in taking his leave may easily call to mind Shakespeare's major eccentric 'Puritan,' Malvolio, and *his* last words; for a bad text (Mar-*text*) and a bad will (Mal-*volio*) can be etymologically correlated.[39] In this connection, it might be mentioned, if only in passing, that the late Calvin Hoffman was well-known for his anti-Stratfordian bias that Marlowe wrote the plays accredited to Shakespeare and based his case partly on presumed wordplay on *Mar-text* as insinuating (*mirabile dictu*) Marlowe's text! That clearly is taking any implicit codification much too far. To infer that Marlowe was responsible for the script itself is

---

[38]Dr. Jofen then proposed to present a follow-up paper at the second International Marlowe Conference (1988), for a session which I happened to have been asked to moderate, but one which she decided regrettably to withdraw from at the last moment (though not until after her arresting submission had been studied by the respondent). Unfortunately I cannot cite its content here without her express permission.

[39]It might be contended that Malvolio is not truly a Puritan in that he dons yellow cross-garters, yet, as an outsider, he has often been related to Shylock, himself frequently taken as a 'Puritan' (as well as a Jew of course).

irresponsible. Still, Hoffman may have been partly on the right track to begin with, at least in seeing a hint of Marlowe's name in Mar-text's. In any case, in response to Harbage, if Shakespeare was indirectly reminding his receptive audience about his former Rival Poet, using the veneer of a 'fashionable' Marprelate backdrop, such intense coloration would have taken pointed precedence over a mere 'taint,' Puritan or otherwise.

With this greater chroma in mind, hearken again to the controversy over Sir Walter Ralegh's purported atheistic coterie, in which the Canterbury Rival was said to be darkly enrolled, for this unique gathering probably did exist in some fashion regardless of whether or not it has any bearing upon the 'school of night' purportedly cited textually in *Lost* (4.3.250), where that reading is sometimes considered suspect. Because the name *Oliver* was conventionally abbreviated as *Ol.*, and because one variant spelling of Marlowe's name was the shortened form of *Marlo,* the form *Ol. Mar* suggests easily metathetic name-play on the surname of the playwright. For what it may be worth, a rumor current then about the atheistical group was that it indulged in frequent name-play of just this kind, daring even thus to spell God's name backwards.

Admittedly such onomastics is more orthographic than phonological, involving what critics would now cite as text-play rather more than, for example, speech-play (both forms still being valid facets of wordplay), the reversal of syllables and a couple of letters causing no real problem because such turnabouts were common enough in so much Renaissance literature and nomenclature, thereby, in effect, being also fair play. Would not such relatively elementary reversal have come across well enough to the average Elizabethan spectator who would give it a moment's thought, as well as to readers?

Analogously, as has often been noted, Moth's name in *Lost* seems similarly abbreviated and anagrammatic, a shifting of letters in the shortened forename of *Thomas* Nashe, upon whom the character of Moth is a satire. Whether Holofernes' name in the same context hinted at John Florio's, as has at times been surmised, the name *Berowne* there clearly intimated that of Giordano *Bruno* (as pronunciation would already suggest), thus providing us with an arresting formula: Berowne is to Bruno *and* to Shakespeare even as Mar-text is to Marprelate *and* to Marlowe.

Certainly analogous letter-shifting is discernible enough in the *Malvolio/Olivia/Viola* playful codification ("M.O.A.I.") in *Twelfth Night* (2.5.100), as it is in the name of *Caliban*, based as that is on a variant spelling of *cannibal*, in *The Tempest*. Comparable also is Othello's name as a transposed form of *Otho/Thorello/Leo*, briefly discussed in the opening chapter.

Reverting now to *As You Like It*, we can discern Orlando's name as being a partial shifting of letters in that of the familiar epical hero's name, Roland's. Again it so happens that the first two letters change places (*Or/Ro*) as in the case of Ol. Mar-text's first two letters taken as a reversal of Marlo(we)'s 'last' two (*Ol/lo*). Granted, such displacement or turnabout need not have been in any way deliberate. Mar-text's name surely would suggest more than the pseudonymous *Marprelate*, if only because the latter represented a furious assailant of the bishops, a description that would hardly fit the case of the meek Sir Oliver, his impetuous, final Parthian shot notwithstanding. Mar-text's name may well have been meant to stand for more than a relative nondescript's like *Marprelate*. Overall, Marlowe's name fits the slot better, at least on the connotative, subtextual level, though admittedly it *would* help if Marlowe and Marprelate turned out to be the same. But this is a long shot, I am afraid.

But what then, we might venture to inquire, would be the benefit of a veiled gibe at this Canterbury poet—one time more—in this otherwise fairly straightforward pastoral romance? In response, if we retain the commonplace verdict that Shakespeare and Marlowe were chief poetic rivals (and Chapman, it is generally conceded, had much less genius), a point staunchly upheld by Muriel Bradbrook, A. L. Rowse, and most recently by Paul Ramsey, then any such verbal dueling could have been altogether *de rigueur,* quite in line with the celebrated wit-combats at the Mermaid between the Stratford "upstart" and his more classically minded colleague Jonson. Ironically enough, with regard to the Canterbury candidate, the twitting could have had no ill effect, the Rival having been fatally impaled long before such a verbal fracas began. Still, that pathetic happenstance need scarcely have diminished the impact on the remembering audience, Marlowe having been such a thoroughgoing drawing card for the stage (his *Doctor Faustus* rivaled only by *Hamlet*).

Evidently a prime basis for such name-play was anticipated in the Faustus drama when the would-be magus claimed that "Within this circle is Jehovah's name / Forward and backward anagrammatized" (1.3.8–9), being another allusion to the atheistical group surrounding Ralegh. In the very next line, Marlowe tells of "abbreviated names," almost as if proleptic of Shakespeare's manipulation of Oliver's shortened name as an in-house throwback to his own. What is more, intriguingly enough the idea of Marlowe being the notorious blasphemer marring the scriptural text probably had its main basis in this tragedy. Marlowe and Faustus, after all, were one-time students who abandoned theology and thereby both classifiable as notorious overreachers, and the Wittenberg of the play was based to a considerable extent also on Marlowe's Cambridge (see Gill). (This does not mean that the two figures are exactly identifiable of course.)

Clearly enough, Shakespeare was indebted to the play palpably elsewhere, specifically in *The Merry Wives* with its trio of magicians cited, "Doctor Faustuses" (4.5.69), and notably in *The Tempest,* where the magus's renunciation of magic at the end, "I'll drown my book" (5.1.57), is analogous to Faustus' express last-minute oath and willingness to incinerate his. The parallel of Prospero, a 'white' magician, set alongside Dr. Faustus as a dabbler in the black arts, both sorcerers contemplating the destruction of their conjuring books at the end, has become a commonplace, anticipating Goethe's Faust righteously foregoing magic for social and humanitarian betterment at the end of *Faust II*.

Thus it can be affirmed that the metaphoric water of Shakespeare in effect quenches the Marlovian fire. At any rate, the main literary marrer of Holy Writ known at the time was Faustus, the protagonist of one of the two most popular plays, in that he cites passages from the New Testament (Romans 6.23, John 1.8) perilously out of context in order to pander to his wayward rebelliousness (1.39–43; see Roma Gill's ed.). The often accepted dates for final composition of both *Dr. Faustus* and *As You Like It* (1595 and 1599) deftly correlate. Although, agreed, parts of the latter may have been written shortly after Marlowe's death in 1593 (otherwise, some critics reasonably enough argue, they would have lacked sufficient topical point), many Shakespeareans, including John Dover Wilson, have sensed that it was revised and published (significantly with a few Touchstone scenes dubbed in) a few years later.

Finally, the question emerges about Marlowe himself signifying a kind of Faustus figure reveling in the modish, at times daringly anti-authoritarian, knowledge pursued by the restless Renaissance Man. His tragedy may validly enough be seen as partially open-ended, even heterodox, in that in his brash, nonconformist manner, he seemingly fails to fear the doctrine of hell's required existence, at least as being exigent for *mortal* beings who have sinned and not been forgiven. Is therewith more marring of the biblical text involved? Some animadversion, for example, lingers in scholars' minds, both those officially in as well as those outside the tragedy, as to whether the hero's *soul* as well as body is to be transported finally to the nether regions. For this, Marlowe had a fine precedent in that only God, after all, it is universally believed, has the final jurisdiction over the destination of the soul anyway. Further, at a key point late in the play Mephostophilis affirms that his power extends over a person's physical being only, not truly his soul. Then, surprisingly enough for one supposedly destined for hellfire, Faustus is to be given "due buryall" (Scene 13A.17—Gill's ed.)—not, let us aver in contrast, any of those "maimèd rites" such as reserved for the questionably sanctified Ophelia in *Hamlet*. Most of these points were made by Max Bluestone in his distinguished presentation for the English Institute, where I heard him and engaged in debate, and published afterwards in the *Annual*. In his contribution to the new collection of essays of Marlowe edited by Roma Gill and others, Norman Rabkin called Bluestone's contribution "one of the few truly indispensable pieces of Marlowe criticism" (21). At the tail end, the Scholars are actually rather too pedantic, so to speak, not to be somewhat in the right about Faustus' remains, the concluding didactic Chorus notwithstanding. Bluestone had something. (Still, did the doctor's fellow scholars know about the devil's pact?)

On the other hand, if the tragedy somehow fits into the reverse Morality Play framework, as many critics, though by no means all (e.g., see Ornstein) infer, Marlowe would hardly be marring the Bible in urging that Faustus, owing largely to his sins of pride and implied demoniality with Helen, is to be condemned forever. He is no Everyman, though. But it has been also posthumously suggested by William Empson that Helen originally stood for Minerva, goddess of Wisdom (an affiliation espoused by Bruno in a key oration at Wittenberg), so that Faustus' union with her had idealistically symbolic meaning. Whatever the generic verdict regarding the Morality-Play structure, Mar-text's name would also fit this tradition in symbolizing or personifying a vice. Further, it could obliquely suggest even the name of *Faustus* himself, who would again mar his own label (meaning *lucky*), whether he finally, ironically, does so being in this context beside the point.

Another parallel that should not be discounted is that even as Sir Oliver, as a bush-priest, is abruptly disqualified in the comedy, so the tragedy, although written with the trappings of the orthodox medieval tradition, happens to have been composed by a purportedly non-conformist atheist. Agreed, a strict dichotomy between person and *persona* can be made, for it is plausible that a miscreant might write an orthodox Christian play—even as it is, contrariwise, acceptable that a purported Christian, like Shakespeare, wrote in a classical, largely pessimistic tradition (as in *King Lear*). Yet the burden of proof is on the nay-sayer. Psychology initially suggests that a certain connection exists between a writer and what he composes; the main peril in speculating on the precise nature of this correlation is legalistic—hardly apt to apply to the estate of Shakespeare long after his death. At any rate, whatever the textual ambivalence implied by Mar-text's name, its multivalence is further evident in the complexity of its intriguing topicality. If the satiric portrayal was scarcely meant as a critical thrust of the utmost gravity (thus, let us say, was more Horatian than Juvenalian), it would still have been recognizable as poking fun at a spokesman for the Bible who was himself at times deemed not much of a witness to the faith. Faustus' becoming a discreditable shapeshifter in his tragedy, moreover, lends itself to the unhappy Mar-text's being onomastically allied in the comedy: The first changes his own shape, the second the shape of what he reads and interprets, presumably using preacher's license.

Were it not for the often-held admission that many characters in this comedy have unusually resonant names (see Tannenbaum, H. Levin), the proposed additional onomastic reverberations here might seem forced, perhaps as themselves nearly marring the Shakespearean text. Further, since what we see of the Vicar's character is scant, it would not tell us very much of Marlowe's. On the other hand, for the very reason that he says so little, such evidence does not work *against* the present thesis either. Because the overall effect of Mar-text's few lines, and the adverse reaction they produce, makes him out to be an incompetent, one unsuitable to officiate even at a wedding for a rustic and court fool, such a critical point would hardly have been lost on an audience which recalled Mephostophilis' notorious scoffing at the sacramental marriage rite as but a "ceremoniall toy"

(5.154–55) or which was privy to the news that Marlowe was seemingly on record as having admitted to deviate behavior (i.e., liking boys). So when the little minister took his exit with his line of sheer bravado, "Ne're a fantastical knave of them all shal flout me out of my calling" (3.3.93–94), an audience justifiably suspecting that he was, subliminally at least, a would-be Marlowe, however disguised, would have hooted in derision at the petulant suggestion that such a titmouse would dare to reflect on Old Kit as deliverer of the "mighty line." If not those in the pit, surely some of the acclaimed "wiser sort" in the galleries would have guffawed. In any event such gruff intemperance on a Vicar's part is not very Christian and more befitting the non-believer. An indirect allusion to Marlowe here would be to him as a person and not a criticism (hence not at variance with Phebe's extolling Marlovian poetry elsewhere).

All in all, a sense of Marlovian rhetoric is being touched on quite pertinaciously in the comedy. Not only does Phebe refer to the "mighty line" proleptically with her allusion to the dead author of "The Passionate Shepherd" ("Dead shepheard, now I find thy saw of might"—3.5.80), but a prominent cluster of vital allusions to the Rival Poet is discernible throughout: (1) to his death (3.3.14–16, 3.4.27–29, 3.5.80); (2) to "Hero and Leander" (3.5.81, 4.1.90–96); (3) even plausibly to androgyny or bisexuality when Rosalind, disguised as Ganymede, is pursued by Phebe; for the passage reflects back not only on the Ganymede of Lodge's *Rosalynde,* but on Marlowe's striking use of the myth of Ganymede evidently to exploit bisexual sensationalism in "Hero and Leander" (1.69–70, 83, 128; 2.155–75, 192–96), not to mention Jupiter dandling Ganymede on his knee in *Dido*.

It may, however, be asked: Would Shakespeare allude to Marlowe as an illegitimate minister in the same play in which he has Phebe elegiacally extolling his poetic reputation as a commentator on love? The answer would appear to be that, in truth, Marlowe represented a complex Rival Poet for Shakespeare, one sometimes standing for a poetic authority on love, at other times representing an atheist and marrer of the text. What counts here are his *personae*. In addition, Shakespeare was probably making fun of Marlowe's line which Phebe quotes, because its meaning in context is un-Christian, amoral if not immoral: "Where both deliberate, the love is slight; / Who ever loved, that loved not at first sight?"

(1.75–76). That certainly represents a pagan attitude (based only on Ovid).[40] In any case, Phebe's reference to the "Dead shepheard" is evidently more an allusion to Marlowe's "The Passionate Shepherd" than to him as a person.

What finally supports the case for Mar-text as partly a Marlowe-figure, then, is that the Vicar appears right in the midst of these other, more prominent (or at least more obvious) Marlovian textual resonances. Hence, whether Shakespeare himself was or was not conscious thereof, the two initial syllables in the Vicar's full name (*Ol* and *Mar*) clearly spell out *Marlowe*'s last two syllables in slightly variant form, as we have seen. Yet they also happen to relate to Bassanio's speech at Belmont in *The Merchant of Venice:*

> In Religion,
> What damned error, but some sober brow
> Will blesse it, and approve it with a text,
> Hiding the grosenesse with fair ornament .... (3.2.77–80)

Whatever one cares to believe, whether or not one prefers to think of the play solely in terms of the stage without any orthographic byplay warranted, this cardinal fact still emerges: Sir *Ol. Mar*-text "Forward and backward anagrammatized," as Faustus would have it, does spell out the variant *Marlo,* as found for example in the dedicatory epistle for *The Jew of Malta,* and his first name (like that of Oliver) is also abbreviated at times, for example on the title-page of *Dr. Faustus.* Thus *si una eademque res legatur duobus,* to quote the magus himself, which, when accommodated from Justinian, would mean that Mar-text's name was "bequeathed" to both a Marprelate-*Figur* and a Marlowe-*Figur.* And, after all, when Dr. A. L. Rowse can find Marlowe behind the character of Mercutio, whose death may be symbolic of Marlowe's having been killed only in the previous year, why not also recognize him in *Mar*-text? Half-anagrams abounded (see Appendix A). Rowse should not too often be belittled.

---

[40]It *is* arguable that Shakespeare was not really making fun of Marlowe here, even in a well-intended manner, because nothing in Christian teaching forbids love at first sight. Indeed, such love would appear to tie in with Aquinas' stress on knowledge arriving through the senses and not being *a priori.* Yet essentially such love is more in the pagan courtly love tradition (often related to a mockery of Mariology, or so it has been thought), and in any event it is absurd to believe literally that *all* love, including love of the Spirit, comes as a mere matter of sense impressions. That would be sheer empiricism.

As a kind of postscript, let us consider an analogous topical allusion that has been detected by Lionel Cust in his Faversham Society paper on the reference to "the widow Chambley" (*Arden of Faversham*, 15.1). He saw an in-joke here in reference to a certain Richard Cholmley, who had accused Marlowe of disseminating irreligious doctrines (Cust 126, as cited by Wine 133–4). The point would again be one to wit emerging, recalling Marlowe's role as a University Wit perhaps. Cust felt that this pointed to Marlowe's being "in some way responsible" for the play, for otherwise the joke would have no purpose, but editor Wine himself claimed that "of all the cases presented for and against various known playwrights that for Shakespeare emerges as the strongest" (lxxxviii), a point then brought out in the *Shakespeare Newsletter* (XXVI, 47) announcement of his edition. (Wine, however, wavered in making any final assertion.) Although some collaboration is at least feasible (see Ch 9), in any case the *Cholmley/ Chambley* correlation seems a bit dragged in.

Last of all, a critic may choose to raise the issue whether concern with an additional Marlovian resonance in this play illuminates the larger issues. This charge is, however, somewhat impertinent if only because such "larger issues" were simply not the topic of interest here. Before minor matters are taken care of, larger concerns cannot be fully explicable. More damagingly, an *advocatus diaboli* might urge that satire on Marlowe's character after his decease would have been beneath Shakespeare, yet was the Rival Poet from Stratford truly deprecating his former competitor when all is presented in the spirit of good-natured fun?

PART V
TWO KEY CRUXES IN THE MOST TRAGIC OF PLAYS

Chapter 7

The "Base-Born" Connection:

The Bastard in *King Lear,* Shakespeare's Brother Edmund and His Son

—Baptism of "Edward Shakesbye the sonne of Edward Shakesbye" on 12 July 1607

—Burial of "Edward sonne of Edward Shakespeere Player base borne" on 12 August 1607

—Burial of "Edmund Shakespeare, a player ... in the Church with a forenoone knell of the great bell" on 31 December 1607

Was it merely a striking coincidence that Shakespeare's brother Edmund fathered a bastard son, also conceivably so designated, who shortly died in Cripplegate, and that Edmund in *King Lear* is the name of another son born out of wedlock who dies young too? Because relatively little is known of the first brother, our ability to rely on factual correlations is diminished somewhat, but several valid enough propositions in this regard may still be worth seriously considering. The purpose of this chapter is to investigate these objectively and, in the process, to compare possible etymological source-material operative on another level as well.

It is convenient to start by citing recent scholarship which has offered startling new proof concerning Shakespeare's brother Edmund, whether cogent or not. The parish registers of St. Leonard's, Shoreditch, record the baptism of one "Edward Shakesbye the sonne of Edward Shakesbye" on 12 July 1607 and thereby would seem to indicate that the allusion is to Edmund's son (Phelps 422–3). But, if so, then much of this chapter would initially appear to be for naught, for the date indicates that the baptism occurred only *after* the composition of *King Lear*.

Yet how believable is this piece of evidence? True, one of the numerous variant spellings of the surname *Shakespeare* happened to be *Shàkesbye;* and, true again, the record of the death of the brother's son oddly likewise *mis*cites the name as *Edward* instead of *Edmund* for at least the father if not also the son. Still, these records are, in fact, in themselves suspect. The point is that *Shakespeare* was not such an uncommon name at the time; I came across one from the earlier part of the sixteenth century in London, for example. Further, *Shakesbye* did not have to stand for *Shakespeare*. Now the argument is that the parish clerk who registered the birth of Edward Shakesbye (*not* recorded as 'base-born,' kindly take note) chanced possibly to make the same clerical error in citing the first name of the son as well as the father as did the clerk in the parish of St. Giles, Cripplegate.

Yet the odds against such an identical mistake being made with both names at the same time are surely enormous. Nonetheless, such incidental, new information was published as valuable, hard, primary source material relating to the Shakespeare family. In a sense, perhaps it may be worth having, in that any novel datum which can somehow relate to family connections of the world's chief dramatist deserves a hearing; but, if that is so in such a tentative case, then the plausible ramifications of family ties as related in *King Lear* also should not go by the board (if art is not confused with life in the process thereby). Hence this chapter.

It is a commonplace, as we have seen, for the plays to contain key topical allusions from time to time. In some instances, these have gained special interest because of plausible references to the dramatist's family though historians have often been reluctant to take them very seriously. The most obvious play in this respect is *Hamlet* with its titular figure having the same forename as that of Shakespeare's son Hamnet (a variant form as can be seen from his being named after Hamlet Sadler, with both spellings cited in the playwright's will). Ophelia may conceivably owe something to a certain Katherine Hamlett, who happened to drown, as did Ophelia, in the river. But this correlation has scarcely been proved.

We might also note that Shakespeare's father had died a short time before, so that the father-son relation in the tragedy could have reflected a special poignancy for the dramatist, who then chose to play the part of the ghost on the stage, according to tradition. Although these associations seem valid enough to ponder, no one to my knowledge (save Joyce) has pertinaciously considered what scholarly bearing they may have upon the play itself. Yet might it be otherwise with *King Lear*? Perhaps a family or genetic connection can be found to have had more significant psychobiographical value there.

True, certain figures in *Lear* apparently had a topical basis, at least in part. Cordelia, for example, probably had some bearing on Cordelia Annesley of a famous law court case (a well-recognized parallel); the Duke of Albany likewise may prompt our recalling that the English king in Shakespeare's time was also titular Duke of Albany. The name of Edmund, however, has come in for rather more selective attention. The leading source-chaser for the tragedy in this onomastic respect has been Kenneth Muir, who has firmly advocated that Edmund's cognomen stems from Harsnett's anti-prelatical *Declaration of Egregious Popish Impostures,* which "contributed more to *King Lear* than the source-play, Holinshed, Spenser, or Sidney" ("Samuel Harsnett and *King Lear*" 11). Because other names in the play seem to derive from Harsnett, conceivably also "the name of Edgar's wicked brother, who is called Plexirtus in Sidney's *Arcadia* [the main source for the subplot], was derived from the Edmunds and the Edmund Peckham who figure so prominently in Harsnett's *Declaration*" (12). Here we have a little dispute in the offing because the leading source-chaser of them all, Geoffrey Bullough, revised these references as being rather to Edmunds (and Edmund *Campion*) instead (VII, 301). Yet Campion is not called *Edmund* in Harsnett but *Edmundus.* So the names in Harsnett are not always exactly the same as those in the tragedy. The question now is not whether Muir and Bullough are wrong, for they are most likely in part right, but whether certain other debts are not also validly operative and even more likely in some ways.

Shortly after Muir's article appeared, a case was in fact established for another source of Edmund's name. A new Edmund chanced to appear right next to the name of another Edgar and in Camden's *Remaines.* In drawing due attention to this correlation, the discoverer was cautious, asserting that "this significance in the name Edmund does not, of course, prevent us from agreeing with K. Muir . . .

that it was suggested also by Harsnett's book" (Musgrove 295). True, but the problem is then whether the glosses provided by Camden in turn could have influenced the Stratfordian "upstart." Notably, Edmund's name, derivative of the Saxon *Eadmund,* means "happy, or blessèd, peace," an association that would scarcely apply to the bastard's ignominious role in the play unless ironically. The rebel's familiar credo, "Yours in the rankes of death" (4.2.25), may sound devilishly happy, but it is hardly thereby blessed, though he *is* loved by two queens. Still, that need not totally discount the Old English etymology; elsewhere I happen to have considered Lear's own name as (connotatively, hardly etymologically) correlating with the Old English *lǣre* ("empty"), as suggested earlier, but that made most sense only when the word was still found in Renaissance English spelled *lear(e)*. Analogously, Oswald also appears to have an Old English name and is a bastard too.

Now to explain away the discrepancy between Edmund's Old English meaning and his function in the tragedy as merely rank "evidence of Shakespeare's carelessness in reading" (Musgrove 295) does not really help much. Yet at the same time Camden remarks that "King *Eadgar* was called the Peaceable . . . king *Edmund* for his Valour, *Iron-side*" (295), and these overall character descriptions do tally with what we expect in the play. King Edmund was known for having blinded the sons of the former king of Scotland, and we think of Edmund lining up with Lear's evil daughters to put out Gloucester's eyes, not to mention the controversial 'sight pattern' discernible throughout the play. King Edmund's son was then King Edgar (A.D. 959–75), who (traditionally) rid England of wolves, whereupon we recall Lear's reference to Goneril's "wolvish visage" (1.4.297). But then the sons of Edgar Atheling were also Edgar and Edmund, and a recent scholar has noticed parallels involving the latter's suddenly getting religious and dying a monk, a hint of bastardy again being involved (Burelbach 134). So Shakespeare was clearly somewhat indebted to English history as well as to his contemporary religio-political milieu. Yet since these sources are themselves relatively far apart from each other, could he not also have been, at least on the subliminal level, indebted to something much closer, even his own family life?

If so, as with the Harsnett parallels, more than one Edmund may have been available upon whom he could have drawn. The first and more important was his youngest brother, who came to London to become an actor and follow in his buskin. Evidently he worked at the Globe with the King's Men because, when he died, a lavish funeral was held for him, and it was in the morning presumably so that fellow actors at the nearby Globe Playhouse could easily attend. This point seems to be at variance with the Edward Shakesbye business, since arguably this man's son's birth was in Shoreditch, which intimates that he would have acted where once was the Curtain, not the Globe.

It is likewise worth bearing in mind that, although Edmund "appears to have attained no distinction as a player, he was interred with much dignity and expense" (Brooke 56–7). No doubt his rather more successful brother footed the bill. It would have been in keeping with such a tribute for the latter to have already honored his kinsman if only by bestowing on him a special role, for which he could even have borrowed the brotherly name, in a play often considered the acme of his career. One problem that arises is whether such an assignment would rightly have amounted to such a compliment, but then Shakespeare would hardly have generally indulged in, or even allowed for, the largely amateurish tendency of casting to type. (After all, he may himself once have played the roguish role of Shakebag in *Arden of Faversham,* on which see Ch 9.)

In any case, in providing the only critical observation on the presumed kinship between the two Edmunds available, "Joyce erected a considerable biographical speculation upon Shakespeare's aversion from the name Edmund" (Bradbrook 264). Yet was Joyce correct in finding such a psychological "aversion"? The modernist's notion, as calmly put into Stephen Daedalus' mouth in *Ulysses,* is that two of Shakespeare's three brothers, Richard and Edmund, were transformed in his plays into stage villains, Richard Crookback and the bastard Edmund, the two happening to be remarkably alike in their vindictive attitudes regarding nature having done them an ill turn. Why so? The hint is that he was purportedly haunted by the thought of brotherly usurpation and banishment: "The note of banishment, banishment from the heart, banishment from home, sounds uninterruptedly" (209). But what then about the other brother Gilbert? He was exonerated if only because Stephen accepted the tradition that Gilbert was the one who came to London not to compete but to applaud William's work, for example witnessing his role as Adam in *As You Like It*. "The playhouse sausage filled Gilbert's soul," according to Stephen Daedalus.

But how correct was he? Granting his fictional context, Joyce still reveled in a notable error of fact when he had Stephen observe that *Lear* "was written or being written while his brother Edmund lay dying in Southwark." For unless brother Edmund took two years to perish, the tragedy was written that many years before his death. So we might consider whether Stephen was also most probably mistaken in suggesting that the dramatist turned Edmund 'psychologically' into a dire villain. After all, this brother had made an effort to follow in talented footsteps. If the villainy of Edmund in the tragedy connects with the character of the author's youngest brother at all, the kinship was most probably not the result of an unconscious aversion but more understandably a consequence of something factual in real life. That something could readily have been Edmund's rumored promiscuous behavior, which then presumably led to the birth of another Edmund, born a bastard, who would then be the second Edmund in the Shakespeare entourage to be duly considered. (It all depends on whether the clerk made a double entry error.) The point is that brother Edmund's misbehavior could, in effect, have fostered more than one bastard.

Here is the evidence. First, brother Edmund's son is not called Edmund in the church register, but then neither is the father; instead we have the burial on 12 August 1607 of "Edward, son of Edward Shakespeere, player, base-born" (Fripp II, 687). E. G. Bentley offered a standard apologia for this discrepancy by affirming that "the difference between Edmund and Edward was not very significant for the parish clerk at St. Giles Cripplegate, who, in other entries in his register, makes no distinction between Jone and Joanna, Eleanor and Helen, Orton and Horton, Morgan and Martin, and Shanbrooke and Shambrooke" (81). If the clerk for St. Leonard's, cited earlier, made similar or, in this case, identical misassignments, that would be curious; but we have not been informed of such. In any event, the odds may well be that Edmund's son could also have been called Edmund, that the clerk made the same mistake carelessly, in that it was natural for the brother to have thus named his only son after himself, at least as natural as to relegate the repetition of the name in the register *merely* to thoughtless reiteration, which could explain one error but not two (namely the mistake with the father's forename). However, it might seem more likely that the bastard's son was called Edward and that the clerk made a simple error in repeating the name for the father thereafter in the register. Still, as David George, a specialist in REED work and

Renaissance paleography, told me, the error(s) might have resulted from misreading the abbreviation(s) "Ed."

The circumstance surrounding both the son's birth and death are of special, vital interest apropos of *Lear*. The term "base-born" in the register evokes for us also the character Edmund's notable diatribe in the drama: "Why Bastard? Wherefore Base? Why brand they us / With Base? With baseness Bastardie? Base, Base?" (1.2.6–10). Now we may have an answer. The reference to branding suggests the designation already in the register of births. Although, strictly speaking, etymologically the word *bastard* need not derive from *base* at all, the Jacobeans apparently thought otherwise, and at least this bastard character did (Draper 65). Shakespeare, at any rate, had a biographical precedent to go by.

Edmund Shakespeare's son's death in infancy does not tell us much more than that he was probably not still-born, and so he could have lived several years, not died only one month later as "Edward Shakesbye." The likelihood is that, as a bastard, he would have understandably been maltreated and unwanted, leading to or plausibly accounting for his early demise; or the father, who himself died shortly thereafter, was unwell or relatively penniless, unable to care for the two of them. Although the child could simply have acquired some nameless disease, naturally, if he was a product of brother Edmund's loose living his early demise would take on a particular poignancy in any case.

Why would Shakespeare not have had a special avuncular concern for his brother's illegitimate child? Several formats present themselves: (1) He had been careless in these matters himself, for his own wife had almost given birth to their first child herself prior to wedlock, and he had married her only in the nick of time. If he was flexible this way in his own family, he could have been the same with regard to a nephew. (2) If he had been influenced at all by the untimely death of his own son in writing *Hamlet,* as has been considered, he might as easily have been indebted to thoughts of the passing of his nephew in writing *King Lear.* The two tragedies would complement each other in this biographical respect. (3) In partial support, presumably young Arthur's death in *King John* was similarly influenced by Hamnet's untimely passing. (4) The only other possible autobiographical tie-in with Edmund's name does not appear very convincing but rather in the Joycean line. W. Nicholas Knight has recently contended that the playwright's brother-in-law, Edmund Lambert, was behind the name; for, like the

Edmund of the play, he withheld inheritance—from Shakespeare himself. Possibly both Edmunds were in the background, for Edmund Shakespeare got his name from Lambert; but, given a choice, the nephew sounds more likelier and certainly was more immediately related to the circumstance at hand, at least in terms of the stage.

Because brotherhood itself is truly a central focus in the subplot of the tragedy, instead of expressing an unnatural aversion to his brother, as Joyce and Daedalus suggest, Shakespeare most probably wrote with a certain familial respect, plausibly with the idea reserved in his mind that his brother could take the part on the stage. We think of how William in *As You Like It* could have been played by William himself (see Jones again), not to mention *Arden* as reflective of his mother. One advantage of this theory is that it, in effect, would help answering Edmund's question about bastardy: "Why brand they us / With Base?" Edmund could answer that without help, in a sense, in showing that the player himself had a son who was so branded, that *he* was branded that way in his character role even because of his son.

Consider now a suitable analogy, that between the death of brother Edmund and the famous "Tomorrow" soliloquy in *Macbeth:* "We are not far away from the death of the poor player, Shakespeare's young brother, and the knelling of the bell at St. Saviour's, Southwark for him" (Rowse, *William Shakespeare* 383). The point is that a connection exists between life's being like a "poor player," who is fairly destitute with a short span of life working for the stage, and Edmund Shakespeare, *literally* a poor player in that he did not succeed and probably had little wherewithal, passing from the theatrical scene at the youngish age of twenty-eight. To consider, therefore, that Shakespeare was anticipating in *Macbeth* the fate of his brother is speculative but still intriguing. Further, since *OED* registers several meanings for *poor* (B, 2, 5) that point to the moral as well as economic factor, a "poor player" could also have been the sort who led a dissolute life, easily enough leading to a son born out of wedlock and an early death both for him and the child.

Two centuries ago Malone said that he had considerable material available on Shakespeare's youngest brother, but he then never brought it to press. That seems odd. He was an excellent scholar, and it is hard somehow to believe that he would have misplaced such vital information in spite of (or because of?), say, his own first name being a variant of Edmund's. What is more likely is that he could have decided against releasing rumors that could tarnish the Shakespeare name. Some bitter stories might better remain hidden away.

Psychologically, various supportive studies may be brought to bear, notably those by Norman Holland: "Dr. A. André Glaz says his reading of *Hamlet*... in view of the intensity of Edmund's lines about bastardy in *King Lear* shows that Shakespeare was deeply concerned about illegitimacy" (95). Once again these two seminal tragedies are brought together. Traumatic circumstances could have thus been responsible for Shakespeare's having provided Edmund with a respectable, expensive funeral "with a forenoon knell of the great bell" (Fripp II, 687). On another psychological level, if the poet felt guilty about not doing enough for his youngest brother when he was alive, a costly funeral was at least one recognized way of paying some final obeisance. Also Holland cited a study which claims that the crimes of the Oedipal child are personified in Edmund (85). This view does not at least make of him an out-and-out villain, the sort whom Shakespeare would have allowed his own brother to perform on stage only with a measure of abhorrence. To sum up, it simply will not do to cast out the whole bag of psychological interpretations altogether, as C. J. Sisson tried to in his British Academy lecture so often cited, "The Mythical Sorrows of Shakespeare," by parodying the problem as follows: "in 1607 Shakespeare's brother Edmund died, an event which helped to infuriate him" (9). On the contrary, commonsense suggests that the expense the dramatist must have sustained at the funeral means he experienced a profound and respectful sense of pity, not fury. Sisson simply set up a straw brother in this case.

Evidently, the real Edmund was born when times were bad and therefore was, or at least felt, unwanted, and such a circumstance might account for his trying to succeed where his oldest brother had, but without his having the brotherly talent or stamina to endure. True, times *were* bad for the Shakespeares when Edmund arrived on the scene, whereby one development pertains directly to his name: He got it from his uncle Edmund Lambert, to whom his father had mortgaged property (the Asbies estate). Because of his debts during bad times, John could not regain the property, and later Lambert's son did not help, refusing to restore Asbies. As mentioned previously, some of this internal family conflict could have rubbed off on brother Edmund, but less likely on the dramatist's attitude toward him.

In any event, Edmund had his problems. "The youngest of Will's brothers had probably led an impetuous and irregular life which cost the poet some worry" (Hill 339). But, if the brother saw no need to apologize for his renegade life, he could have taken a spirited role like that of his namesake in *King Lear* with aplomb. At least so Shakespeare may have thought. And did not the character have some reasonably likeable qualities too? For all his viciousness, he stands up on the natural level for the earth goddess (1.2.1). That at least gives him some obvious affinity with human nature in general; it humanizes him. Further, he is an exponent of Renaissance individualism (see Bauer), even though ostensibly substituting pagan nature-worship or simple self-assertion for doctrinal, God-like devotion. Yet the individualist was still to be admired. In renouncing astrology, he still is indirectly thereby approving of basic patristic guidance. As the Natural Man (somewhat akin to Caliban), he provides much ambivalence, but also the nagging afterthought that he is indeed 'naturally related'—even in some way to the playwright, ironically enough.[41]

Clearly Edgar's brother, if not exactly an enticing figure, is forceful, fascinating, and aesthetically challenging, and he has some *insouciant* lines, however they be interpreted. For instance, Levin L. Schücking, in commenting on

---

[41] Recent reassessments of certain positive elements in Edmund's character cannot so easily be shunted aside as merely modern romanticism. At a most successful conference on *Lear* I had the good fortune to direct at Central State University, Ohio (the first of the regular, annual Ohio Shakespeare conferences), no less than two solid papers were delivered in favor of this complex character: Charles Dean's "The Bastard as Stranger" (an approach admittedly owing much to Leslie Fiedler's innovative critical study *The Stranger in Shakespeare*) and Claude Summers' "'Stand Up for Bastards!'" (subsequently published in a special Shakespeare issue of *College Literature*). Dean's position, with which strict historicists would basically disagree, was that, if Shakespeare did not overtly *intend* to make Edmund heroic, that is irrelevant because the current emotions of the play are what count in today's world. Still we might now try to reconcile Dean's radical approach with historicism by interpreting Edmund's behavior as not heroic essentially but in keeping with valid *heroics*. In any case, the modern audience, he felt, is bound to reinterpret Shakespeare in reference to its own idiom and hence may even approve, if only in a limited manner, of Edmund's often gross rebelliousness, Shakespeare's characters so often being multivalent anyway. This approach tallies with the admission that "present day Edmunds are likely to excite admiration" (French 258). It has to be remembered, a point not stressed by critics like Bald and Danby, that Edmund does repent at the end (or at least makes a stab at it like Caliban), for "some good" he means yet to do. (Summers' paper was similar to Dean's, if more concerned with ambivalence as such in Edmund's complex character.)

Edmund's referring to Edgar as "A Brother Noble, / Whose nature is so farre from doing harme, / That he suspects none" (1.2.199), has stated flatly, "We ask ourselves why Shakespeare has put this impartiality, which is quite inconsistent with the rest of his character, into the mouth of the villain" (62). Although this may simply be typical of Shakespeare's method, one answer stands out: Was not the real brother Edmund somehow behind this? If so, in a very true sense indeed, "Edmund was belov'd!" (5.3.239). Yet another critic demurs: "There are all the materials here for a complex characterization. It is as though Shakespeare had recalled his forfeited opportunity in *Richard III* and was more on the brink of giving a worthy role to an unloved, but talented and ambitious, man" (Jorgensen, *Lear's Self-Discovery* 86); yet he then felt obliged to disclaim this observation in that it was morally unappealing to him. Here again Edmund and Richard are associated. Evidently the dramatist felt somewhat guilty about what he had done to Richard and so was somehow seeking to make amends with Edmund; his own brothers come into play without the layman, on the popular-culture level, having to resort to Joyce's suspect analysis. The notion that the author was "on the brink of giving a worthy role" would also imply that he wrote the Edmund part for his youngest brother, who apparently was leading an *un*worthy life and was himself truly unloved, if his having a base-born son is any indication. The brother was likewise ambitious in trying to follow the dramatist's lead (Shakespeare having started out as an actor too), but questionably talented if only because no role which he took on the boards of the stage has come down to posterity.

In sum, the new light to be shed on Edmund I (the brother) and Edmund II (the character) means that, far from being a Joycean scapegoat type, the family Edmund was duly commemorated in *Lear*. A somewhat different approach has been invoked by W. Nicholas Knight: "The play reveals ... fears: that of the patrimony being stolen from the son in the subplot of Edmund's stealing inheritance from his legitimate brother Edgar, recapitulating Shakespeare's experience of *Edmund* Lambert's holding from his brother-in-law what was to have been Shakespeare's inheritance" (177). As for brother Gilbert, Joyce, from his Modernist viewpoint, so to speak, was very probably wrong again. Oldys, who reported the story of one of the dramatist's brothers having come to London to see the plays, was obviously incorrect in asserting that Gilbert lived to a ripe old age. Moreover, if this tradition has, as Halliwell-Phillips had felt, "a glimmering of truth," then the real facts, not a mere glimmer, could well have been that it was Edmund, and not Gilbert, who formally made his *début* in this manner. So, to accommodate the character Edmund's own challenge, let *us* stand up for him—even as he himself at least stood up for Nature.

Now, granted, some readers might be scolding that much of this discussion of Edmund apropos of Shakespeare the man has been actually extra-literary after all; in response to such a demurrer I would gladly concede the point, my penchant being for a historicist approach more than a merely aesthetic one. Opinions about literature *as literature* will differ as long as subjective minds concern themselves with it, so a certain objectivity about the factual person behind the *persona* can be salutary. In a word, biographical interpretation can have a sanity, old-fashioned though it may be, which is often missing from modern structuralism, which pays scant heed to intention or subliminal meanings. Seeing a biographical hint in Edmund the character may even support aesthetic fascination with his role, but that has not been my principal concern, which is more down-to-earth in its stance. Should some critics balk at my approach as not pertaining enough to what comes across in performance, my only rejoinders are as follows: First, I have both acted in and directed a number of stage productions; secondly, *which* spectator do such critics have in mind? Surely the more knowledgeable onlookers (or readers for that matter) should be given more credit and return for their money than the run of the mill, and it is a truism that the more the former know about the background of the author, the more knowledgeable they should become. The important thing is to bear in mind that a tragedy like *King Lear,* its familiar wordplay on Cordelia's "nothing" throughout notwithstanding, was hardly written *in vacuo.*

Chapter 8
"And my poore Foole is hang'd?"—Figuratively or Literally?

Even as our age owes a legacy to nineteenth-century Romanticism, so King Lear's wise and witty jester has won the hearts of audiences through what Romanticists call a natural sympathy, so that the very idea of dying for his master or as a scapegoat has seemed hard to bear or consider. Still, if his plausible demise be taken as overly heartrending, let us recall that the hanging of Cordelia affected Dr. Samuel Johnson much the same way. Yet when the tragedy was originally enacted, the antic was seen as so faithful to his sovereign that the evidence suggests he could have been so up to the end and even have perished in his defense. Whereas, granted, no contextual evidence is extant indicating that he had to be in the company of Lear and his youngest daughter in prison, one reasonable assumption is that they witnessed his being hanged when they got there. For the Fool's succumbing has been critically accepted much more often than many scholars realize. If rejection of it is frequent enough these days, that may be based on misinterpretation of the telling line "And my poore Foole is hang'd" (5.3.306).

Regrettably, uncritical acceptance of such a straightforward necrological announcement as being a gratuitous, added admission of Cordelia's death, thereby not referring to the literal Fool, is at odds with objective exegesis regarding what happened to the court performer. We know already that Cordelia has died, so why should this fact be reiterated? It appears redundant. But then emotions are not always on the same wavelengths with reason.

On the face of it, such recalcitrance concerning the more literal (or obvious) meaning of the line may seem anomalous. The question easily arises as to why the monarch should be obliged to repeat the same obituary, but the further theory that he inadvertently conflates references to both daughter and Fool in a single allusive line, possibly because Robert Armin or more probably Archee Armstrong happened to take both roles on stage (the fad of doubling), may initially appear more plausible, yet also leaves room for doubt. Consider therefore that the sovereign did have his spiritual bodyguard specifically in mind here and that such an assumption amounted to good theater.

I

Let us start with what is foolproof. When Shakespeare used the phrase "Poor Foole" earlier (3.2.72), he designated only his jester. No one has questioned that. (His identification, in this context, of the jester's 'vocation' as that of a court knave is of not much moment.) Although Roger Gard (209) has countered that an earlier allusion by someone else, "My Foole" (4.2.28), refers to Albany, thereby positing a kind of overall Erasmian milieu for 'fool figures' throughout the tragedy, this allusion is itself rather open to question because of the variant textual reading: "My Foote." Whereas the Riverside edition has "A fool usurps my body," thus partly following the Quarto reading, the Folio line reads, "My Foole usurpes my body," and the Pelican edition follows suit. The so-called irregular Quarto reading (the presumed uncorrected state of the Quarto) reads, "My foote usurps my body," which makes better contextual sense than "My Foole" does, at least in that it helps to gloss the Renaissance *topos* of "making one's foot one's hand or face." Thus Tilley's standard dictionary of proverbs has "to make my foot my hand and my servant my superiour" (Thomas Deloney, *The Gentle Craft*) and "the foote should neglect his office to correct the face" (John Lyly, *Euphues and His England*) (item F562). We might compare the modern idiom of putting one's foot into something. At least, the "Foole" reading may sound, in contrast, too modern, though some analogy has been found for it with regard to *Arden of Faversham* (McManaway 139).

Comparable also, at any rate, is the analogous phrase "poore Rogues" (5.3.13), for Lear would hardly be including his one-time favorite daughter in such a lowly grouping, especially when in the same context he anticipates listening to "court news" with her. A rogue was customarily associated only with the fool type and thereby with the presumed nemesis of being in for hanging for mocking misbehavior, as is evident not only from Lear's "Poor Foole, and Knave" reference (3.2.72), but also from such a pointed, analogous one like "You Rogues: give me my Horse, and be hang'd!" (*1 Henry IV*, 2.2.30). Additional allusions can be cited from *The Merry Wives*, 2.2.270, and *Timon of Athens*, 2.2.55.

Another verbal matter worth pondering is that the linking, coördinating connective "And" at the start of the crucial line suggests syntactically that Cordelia was only *in the process* of being executed in accompaniment with the jester. The audience was meant mentally to supply the missing words which would normally precede the elliptical announcement the King suddenly blurts out (an absentmindedness explicable in terms of his poor health and age). His mind is naturally enough errant at this stage (on which, defer to my note on "Lear's 'Poor Fool' as the Poor Fool"). Such a commonsense stress on the import of "And" may, at first, seem like stretching it but is more meaningful, at least, than emphasizing the verb form of *to be* ("And my poore Foole *is* hang'd"), a reading which would imply little more than his aimlessly indulging in a mere rhetorical identification or flourish. Moreover, comparable is the jester's own last speech: "And Ile go to bed at noone" (3.6.85). In spite of that line's proverbial meaning (see M. C. Andrews), some readers have felt comfortable with its more prognosticative effect. John Wain has told of these terse words as conveying "a melancholy prescience, for to go to bed at noon is symbolic of a life cut short in youth" (171). Among others who have thought that the Fool predicts his own demise were Edith Sitwell and Sir John Gielgud. But not much attention, if any, has been paid to how the jester's final words and the King's last speech are introduced in the very same way, by the same conjunction. Does not such clearcut recurrence bespeak verbal echoing, to which at least attentive members of an audience considered as "the wiser sort" might be expected to react positively? (The argument that spectators would simply not notice this repetition is perhaps a bit anti-intellectual.) When so many verbal and structural parallels have been built into this play, not merely in the main plot contrasted with the subplot, yet another verbal link need hardly come as unexpected. It may then prompt overall reinforcement of other parallels.

Evidently one of the jester's main functions was to make meaningful predictions. Apart from his so-called "Fool's Prophecy" interpolation itself ("This prophecie *Merlin* shall make, for I live before his time" [3.2.95–6])—a vision which, by way of psychological counterpoint, could indirectly hint also at the jester's succumbing anterior to *his* scheduled or natural time—at least five anticipations of the antic's forthcoming demise are offered us: 1. "So out when the Candle" (1.4.217); 2. "If my Cap would buy a Halter; / So the Foole followes after" (1.4.320–1); 3. "Tarry, take the Foole with thee" (1.4.315); 4. "least [lest] it breake thy necke" (2.4.73); 5. "Jesters do oft prove Prophets" (5.3.72). In two of the first four, offered by the antic himself, mention is made of a noose for hanging; he asks the King not to part with his close friend in need, but begs to be taken along—even if unto death. In this respect, yet another 'fool' here, though not a professional, can be brought in, one who likewise happens to be "poore" and mentions "Halters," namely Edgar in disguise as Tom o'Bedlam (3.4.54). These proleptic parallels may prove relatively little in themselves but can point ahead to a stronger argument to follow.

II

Particularly relevant to the crux, but hitherto curiously ignored to my knowledge, is the common tradition inherent in the image of a fool's having to be strung up. Already this dire penalty, well-known in folklore, appears in the threat to hang yet another jester, Feste in *Twelfth Night:*

> Maria. . . . my Lady will hang thee for thy absence.
> Clowne. Let her hang me: hee that is well hang'de in
>   this world, needs to fear no colours.   (1.5.3–6)

That *Twelfth Night* as perhaps the best of the comedies is thus generically unlike *King Lear* as perhaps the finest of the tragedies makes no difference with regard to the custom alluded to, which arose from a folk tradition, so to speak, that a jester is susceptible to a kind of hanging if only because of his refusal to communicate properly, his implacable imbecility at times, or (a point possibly indirectly relevant to the problem in *Lear*) his absenting himself. Comparable to the fool getting hanged is the acute description of Despair, allegorized as a form of impossible folly hanging himself out of the sheer desperation which he represents in *The Faerie Queene*.

Worth further scrutiny is the mythic basis for such legendry. The traditional 'fool figure' has been linked, for instance, with the Sun God and the cult of Osiris in ancient Egypt; he was required to succumb if only to be able to be born anew. Various anthropological analogies in other cultures and faiths suggest themselves, too, notably the motif of the dying deity discernible in Nordic pagan beliefs. The popularizer James George Frazer described "the hanging of Odin on the gallows-tree," adding that "Odin was called the Lord of the Gallows or the God of the Hanged, and he is represented sitting under a gallows tree" (II, 290). A *Christus* figure is thereby envisioned as a fool to this world. Frazer further tells of the destruction of the Fool figure on Ash Wednesday during a celebrated rite known as "Burying the Carnival," whereby the clown had to be ritualistically interred "under straw and dung." Occasionally he was immersed in water, a ceremony which, incidentally, might be associated with the mythic background of Falstaff's being similarly dunked in *The Merry Wives of Windsor* (Frye 183). The way a leading Jungian has indicated, "the Fool and the clown, as Frazer has pointed out, play the part of 'scapegoat' in the ritual sacrifice of humans" (Cirlot 106). Another way a major authority on the fool figure, Enid Welsford, has put it is that the "Folk-fool is . . . frequently 'killed,' [and] the central figure of scapegoat rites—whether a living man or an effigy—is often termed a fool" (71).

Consequently this mythical tradition can provide arresting background for probing the jester's fate in *King Lear*. Cathartically, the idea of his possibly 'having to be hanged' is psychologically traceable to man's unconscious urge to castigate the 'fools' harboring within. Still, such an archetypal view does present a problem. Cordelia, for example, has been called a fool figure, in her own right, by critics who choose to find her a female Christ figure, yet she would hardly literally fit the paradigm of Christ—not to mention Mary[42]—if only because her resolute failure to communicate succinctly with her sire at the outset bespeaks a lack of essential royal rapport or at least filial responsibility. True, the sincere motive for her reticence is itself praiseworthy enough, but the final effect is tragic. Although,

---

[42]This was an option I heard suggested in open forum at a session on the Renaissance for the annual Modern Language Association convention not long ago.

granted, one should refrain from equating the King's inordinate sullenness or pride with hers, she is still her father's daughter even in her hurt self-esteem, and some subtle readers may detect a note of primal sin in her implicit, overt failure to "honor [her] father" according to the biblical injunction.[43]

Her deficiency, moreover, may be pointedly labeled one form of the "disobedient sin" found to be the root of the evil in the "Roxburgh Ballad of King Leir," though naturally this form of transgression is *mainly* to be seen in the other daughters, the ruthless ones. All in all, since the play, if Christian at all in its final resolution, is not so in its setting and is hardly, in any case, optimistically Christian (to revert to William Elton's main point), not much basis, if any, supports Cordelia as a true Fool-in-Christ type in spite of a few biblical analogs which may incidentally be culled from her later speeches. In point of judicious fact, a case has been made out for her as in part just as easily symbolic of the spirit of Israel (with bearded Lear then standing for the Lord or Yahweh). Admittedly such an uncommon reading has elicited the sarcastic response in a review that the truly evil sisters might then appear to be Christianity and Islam, but no such secondary implication is imperative to uphold. Cordelia considered as Israel in relation to Lear as the Lord would point mainly to their tensions in getting along over the centuries and not as in opposition to other faiths. And the setting of the play *is* pre-Christian.

How much, then, did Shakespeare draw here upon the folk tradition of the antic who is to be hanged? Although it is hard to be sure, inasmuch as Lear's jester, if in many respects 'wiser' than his master, may be guilty of at least some seeming nonsense (even when ostensibly being ironic), he might be symbolically thought of as a scapegoat victim. To make a long story short, the apparently popular maxim at the time that a fool can be hanged for 'saying nothing' lends itself in a peculiar way to this drama in that, in its echoing aspects of the initial love-test (1.4.130–1, 188, 194, 196), "nothing" is precisely what the Fool literally often does say.

Some substantiation for the dramatist's folk knowledge is evident in such a proverb as "Mumchance, who was hanged for saying nothing," but no firm proof

---

[43] At least one female undergraduate of mine has reacted this way on her own accord, finding no sexism latent.

is extant that such a saying was widespread already in Jacobean England. Nonetheless, consider the jester's self-identification: "I am a Foole, thou art nothing. Yes forsooth I will hold my tongue, so your face bids me, though you say nothing. Mum, mum" (1.4.194-7). Did not the jester stand in for Mumchance? Or look ahead to him?

Another comparable parallel in the hanged-fool tradition is evident in the play *Timon* (not to be confused with *Timon of Athens*), which is an analogy worth citing inasmuch as *Lear* has often been related to the Timon story (the latter taken as a modification of the former but on basically the same theme as in Shakespeare's follow-up drama). The following interchange is worth at least momentary pondering as bearing somehow on the crux:

Gelas. Art though a foole?
. . .
Timon. Bee hang'd!   (4.2.) (Dyce 64)

Whatever the ultimate affinity of King Lear's tragedy to the folk tradition of the hanged jester, observe that the complementary theme of the *wise fool* works even more strongly if considered in counterpoint with it. This conception, a universal one but found to be especially Shakespearean (see Goldsmith), has so frequently been discussed that it seems altogether needless to recount its import in full here. Suffice it to say that even as the King grows more fatuous, his fool paradoxically becomes more sage. The same has been said of the interinvolvement of Don Quixote and Sancho Panza. Yet at the end when Lear has regained a modicum of sensibility, the analogy appropriately had come to an end. And by then the Fool has seemingly expired anyway.

III

At this point, we might confront an opposing, but currently rather fashionable, view, namely that the phrase "poore Foole" alludes to Cordelia and the jester concomitantly. This theory is based on the assumption that the same boy actor doubled in these roles. It is fostered by the nineteenth-century interpretation, first brought out by the critic John Forster, to my knowledge, in a review of Macready's *Lear* at one time ascribed to Dickens (*The Examiner,* 27 Oct. 1849), that in a final moment of "sane madness," so to speak, the King somehow conflated thoughts of his daughter with recollections of his faithful Fool in uttering the seemingly senile line "And my poore Foole is hang'd!" See also Ribner (136), Rosenberg (310).

Now doubling *was* common enough, though it is perilous to be pressured by evidence based on what is theatrical only and hence only presumably more historically relevant than other proof. In any event, the double-role theory in this context was adamantly countered by Alwin Thaler, following the lead of W. J. Lawrence, their argument being carefully documented by Kenneth Muir in his new *Arden* edition. To Thaler, the double-role concept was an intrusion in otherwise sound criticism of the play because it hinged on a tacit improbability: that Shakespeare would have permitted purely theatrical exigencies to "distort his essentially artistic purposes" (Letter, 122). Such a claim may at first seem to be paradoxical in nature, at odds with the dramatist's design, but it is not thereby necessarily self-contradictory. He was writing professionally for the stage, to be sure, but also hardly unilaterally so. It is morally not unfair to him to underscore his concern with cerebration rather than mere empirical sensibility.

In looking askance at the idea of one actor assuming two such roles, because of the obvious difficulty of imagining such "changes in make-up, dress, bearing, and *voice,* required to metamorphose the tempest-tost Fool into the Queen," Thaler proposed that, instead, Shakespeare actually went out of his way to "differentiate between the Fool's voice and Cordelia's." The inference appears tenable enough. For instance, whereas the jester is "always nervous and sharp-tongued," the daughter has her musically soft voice. The antic's voice "out-shrill[s] the storm," noted Thaler, "whereas Cordelia's voice—!" The difference in tonality is clear-cut, her voice being always "soft and low," seen for Lear as such a commendable trait in woman.

Would doubling then not seem like a *tour de force*? Thaler thus validly enough concluded: that "Shakespeare *purposely* made [her voice] ever soft, gentle, and low seems to me as inescapable as the corollary that he would not have done so if he had meant the Fool to pronounce her part, that is, her voice." He then added notably that the jester should likewise be recognized as "faithful to the death"—not, let us add, merely to the monarch's by implication at least in this case, but to his own. The moral of "dust unto dust" would tragically envelop him too.

One point Thaler missed is especially important: the logical inference that the antic, because in his response to the King he echoes Cordelia's initial response and because he parodies Lear's reply, should be presumed to have been most probably present when the sovereign and daughter had their original falling out. Although, admittedly, the stage directions do not refer explicitly to his being there, they need not, obviously cannot, tell us everything. So he could have been meant to be one of the "Attendants" cited in the King's initial entourage. In at least one cinematic production, Edwin Thanhouser's 1916 film, considered one of the best of the 'silents,' the Fool is depicted as present during the banishment scene. But the assumption that he was at hand at the outset need hardly imply that (Kozintsev-fashion) he would also be alive in their company in prison or somehow emerging at the finale. For that may be taking the implicit Erasmian running metaphor throughout this tragedy rather far. Moreover, in Adrian Noble's fairly recent RSC production, the Fool and Cordelia stand together behind Lear's throne at the opening of the play. In any event, the Fool's implicit presence at the beginning would be then out of the question if we have to imagine the same actor having played both roles. So such an interpretation, tempting though it may be because of its presumed vital bearing on theater history, is open to serious animadversion and for purposes of this argument may be discounted. (Granted, of course, the play can be seen somewhat on the mythic as well as literal or figurative level.)

As is often mentioned, the court antic is depicted as closely attached to the youngest daughter. When she had to leave for France, he is reported as having pined away. It may seem at first plausible enough to imagine him as dying in solitary even out of excessive grief for her (or, better, because of his being without her company), though such an inference may finally seem implausible. Was he then summarily executed at the end? For the purely literal-minded, the obvious question that crops up is whether, at least politically speaking, a mere jester would have been worth the hanging. But then again politics does not always rely on commonsense, and scapegoats are legion. The readiest answer is that, although his foes found him to be a cipher, they were still vicious enough to have done away with him out of sheer vindictiveness simply because he symbolized a key part of the Lear-Cordelia circle. Should we call into question such sadism, we might also consider the analogous offhand manner in which his foes apply their peremptory kind of condemnation to the Duke of Gloucester: "Hang him instantly" (3.7.4). What was good enough for the Duke was surely that way for the poor Fool.

Another argument is that Lear would scarcely have wanted to refer to his reginal daughter as a foolish type in the end, his recollection of her initial, seeming obstinacy notwithstanding, for even earlier he had recognized her disagreement with him as having been only a "small fault" (1.4.257). And why, after Lear becomes aware that *he,* after all, is the one who has been the real simpleton, should he in effect apply such a derogatory-sounding epithet back to his once-favored daughter? Senile he was, but at that point, it can be urged, he himself would scarcely have been so foolish. Sir Joshua Reynolds's familiar observation that it would have been unfitting for a queen like Cordelia to be designated a fool, even if used as a term of endearment (one which was not exactly common in the Shakespearean canon), was a keen one. (See the New Variorum edition, 345. The editor, H. H. Furness, conceded that he himself wished that the "poore Foole" crux might "be applied to the faithful fool.") In the Pide Bull Quarto, Cordelia is described as truly reginal and dignified, not at all giving the impression of being essentially Fool-like: "It seemed she was a queene / Over her passion" (2.3.15). We might finally ask: Did not the King at the end know *something* of what he was doing? (For sentimentalizing his feelings to such an extent is a little like over-sentimentalizing those of the Hostess in her describing the death of Falstaff. See Ch 7.)

IV

Because the proverb about "Mumchance, who was hanged for saying nothing" belongs to a later period (Tilley #M1312), we would have to find more support for a literalist reading of the crux in another historical way and not rely on such a maxim. In doing so, let us now consider whether the Fool/Cordelia equation has not been a by-product of the temptation to over-sentimentalize Shakespeare. Granted, this effort my appear heretical to many, but then Romanticism was not always in flower, and it may have been that which colored later audiences' appreciation. The Romantic school naturally tended to dramatize the madness of Lear, for example, living up to their penchant for aberrant emotion at times. For would not only a truly insane monarch call his dearest daughter fatuous, or give that implication, during such a poignant period of reconciliation? Would he have wanted to harp on their quarrel? In short, was he that mad at the end to resort to such an abrasive, lowly tactic? Doubtfully so. And as if to give this reading proper credence, the crucial line capitalizes the word *Foole* as if in explicit contradistinction with any other presumed fool. Barbara Everett (*Young Hamlet* 80) has recently brought this point out well again.

Malone and Steevens were the original sentimentalizers, prompting the Fool/Cordelia identification. But the link-up was given its main impetus early in the succeeding century by Edmund Kean, who restored the tragic ending after Nahum Tate's botched or radical revision, yet he still kept the jester in abeyance. Now, clearly, with the antic missing from the play in such a revision, the line about the Fool being hanged could have had only one significance: It had no choice but to allude to the daughter. But then Kean would have had no objection to that. As an indulgent Romanticist, he wanted to heighten the dramatic effect emotionally by showing the monarch as utterly berserk at the end. Yet he was still prudent. He cautiously waited till his own king, George III, had died before he presented the tragedy in this fashion, and hence the "death of George the Third removed the *taboo* constituted by the applicability of *King Lear* to the mental derangement which clouded the latter days of that firm, just, and equitable prince" (Hawkins II, 116). During our present, often Neo-Romantic, age (which works often in curious counterpoint with professed realistic, Post-Romantic attitudes), we have often enough rediscovered 'the mad Lear,' but the King is simply not always deranged, hardly raving in his last moments. If he is totally out of his mind then, the play would be pathetic rather than truly tragic.

The stress on 'sentiment' in the eighteenth-century sense was already prevalent in Tate's mutilated version of the tragedy. He had the King utter such lamentations as "My poor Cordelia" (a phrase also used by Tate's Edgar) and "My poor dark *Gloster*" (M. Summers 249–50, 252). It was but a relatively short step from such feelings to analogously excessive emotion, and finding "my poore Foole" a reference to the youngest daughter would be a good example. In any event, in an important article, Arthur M. Eastman has cogently pointed out that the so-called 'common' meaning of the expression "poore Foole" as relating to endearment was in fact "genuinely uncommon" in the Renaissance. In a detailed analysis of the crux, he brought ten important parallels into court from other works in the canon, finding only one that corresponded in any vital capacity to the issue in *Lear,* namely "pretty foole" in *Romeo and Juliet* (1.3.31), but observe there the lower-case typography:

> Only in the Nurse's musings on Juliet is "fool" used tenderly and compassionately of someone who, in her innocence, has been made a victim. If we place this fact beside a second—that in his 400-odd other uses of the word "fool" Shakespeare manifestly means merely a victim (without any overtones of tenderness or compassion) or a stupid person or a jester—we can see that the so-called 'common' meaning attributed to "poor fool" is genuinely uncommon. It is, indeed, of such rarity that the remaining arguments in its support must be exceedingly strong.
> (533–4)

But are they? Eastman concluded by stating rather lamely that since one is unable to rely on what Lear says about what happens to the Fool, our accepting an ambiguous reading of the crux is acceptable. But may not such a way out be too facile? If we cannot always trust what the King says about his antic, what *can* we turn to? In general, it is a commonplace that we are to take Shakespeare's characters on faith regarding what they have to say about others. The King is the person closest to the jester, and why would he not be expected to know something of the latter's fate, more so than anyone else? Earlier Eastman made the much more cogent *aperçu* that the argument that "my poore Foole" does not refer to the antic involves a *petitio principii,* begging the question that it is trying to solve. For, obviously enough, we cannot affirm that we do not know what happened to the Fool with any conviction, that is unless the crucial line is itself dismissed as evidence.

The negative argument that Lear would hardly have shifted his train of thought from his favorite daughter to a mere court buffoon is also not very convincing. Steevens argued this way: "That the thoughts of a father, in the bitterest of all moments, while his favourite child lay dead in his arms, should recur to the antick who had formerly diverted him, has something in it that I cannot reconcile to the idea of genuine sorrow and despair" (Variorum 345). But the real point is that King Lear was extremely fond of the Fool, too, who was like a son to him as well as *alter ego.* Steevens's use of "should" is thus ambiguous;

regardless of what any of us subjectively imagine Shakespeare should or should not have composed, the sober reality of what he *did* must take precedence.

Part of the reality is that the play was originally, in the Quarto, a chronicle history play. This description is vital. For F. T. Flahiff has recently worked out a link between *Lear* and *2 Henry IV* on these grounds, one which hinges on ancient English history and legendry and thereby relates importantly to understanding of the tragedy's sources. The inference is that we may not summarily ignore the complete history of a character; from the standpoint of a history play, it was considered instructive to know what happened to a leading personage. The Fool is certainly not minor, at least insofar as he has far more lines than Cordelia herself. As Lear's *alter ego,* he is a leading buttress as well as foil for the King, if not himself exactly a 'little Lear.' Thus, to ignore the Fool's fate is to ignore the play's background as a chronicle history play.

Another point of Eastman's worth recapitulating here is that the play "abounds in 'tautology'" (534). The point, although seemingly pejorative at first (yet note his inverted commas), is well enough taken: Gloucester's death foreshadows Lear's; likewise Cordelia's, the Fool's. Why not then *the Fool's,* Lear's? As has been suggested above, the repetition of the initial conjunction "And" in two key comparable lines, including in the crux, already points the way to the relevance of such "tautology."

Again, as Eastman shows, a relatively long break follows Lear's allusion to Cordelia before his "poore Foole" reference, a hiatus which allows the spectator to believe that the King's mind could easily have wandered from one person to another, as then it certainly did, for example, to Caius, whom he thought dead. Still another natural shift would be from his daughter to the unfortunate jester. Such absentmindedness might suggest a little senility, too, but nothing is wrong in that, so long as he is not thought of as stark raving mad. (He *has* been healed to some extent [Eastman 534].)

Nonetheless, certain critics like to profess that the desperate sovereign's outcry "And my poore Foole is hang'd" is pointless, that he is, in effect, madder than ever at the end. But is it not *in itself* rather pointless to make so much of 'the theme of madness'? After all, at Cordelia's bidding, he was attended to by a physician: soft, therapeutic strains of music alone should have made him regain a certain mental and emotional stability, if not composure. Just as his mind turned from a mirror to a feather, why should it not have wandered from Cordelia to Caius to the Fool—a touching enough *Gedankensprung* not so very exceptional in the elderly? Thus, William Empson has emphatically asserted that Lear "must be utterly crazy to call one by the name of the other" (Bonheim 125), that is, Cordelia by the name of the Fool. He has here hit the nail on its proverbial head: It is for that precise reason that the monarch *did not* call one by the name of the other; when he said "Foole," he knew what he was talking about and meant the jester. He simply had mellowed toward the end. Some twenty-eight lines, after all, occur in the text between the crucial passage and Lear's previous utterance. So what reason is there to deny that his mind should have wandered thus appreciably? He talks of Caius; then we hear of the deaths of the older daughters and Edmund. In the Quarto, notably enough, his mind does *not* return to his favorite at the very end. With no allusion to her *after* the "poore Foole" exclamation, the identification of that crucial phrase as bearing on the jester rather than her is especially clear-cut. In this respect, at any rate, the Quarto has too often been ignored, but here it most probably reveals original intent.

V

The crucial passage now needs to be examined in its full textual, as well as contextual, setting. The First Folio reads as follows:
And my poore Foole is hang'd: no, no, no life?
The Quarto version, however, reads:
And my poore foole is hang'd, no, no life. . . .
Syntactically, to be sure, the Folio has the better overall reading here, but is there any justification for its particular punctuation? Is the question mark truly what is wanted? Although it may be straining things to spend too much time on mere pointing, since we can never be sure whether it was the author's or merely an idiosyncratic compositor's, in this instance it deserves mention simply as a fact of the text. Let us consider it contextually.

As John Dover Wilson once showed, Shakespeare or the printer was at times given more to rhetorical than syntactic effects in his pointing. Hence the colon served as a balancing device rather than in the modern mode whereby what follows that mark so often simply sums up what comes before. What we have is a distinction between rhetorical patterning and mere grammar. Compare a notable analogy. In attempting to discern just how far the Fool/Cordelia equation could be traced back in theater history, I happened to turn up the following reading in an 1800 edition:

> *Albany.* . . . the cup of their deservings.
> *Lear.* O see, see-----
> And my poor fool is hanged: no, no, no life?
> (*The Works of Shakespeare,* V, n.p.)

Such a reworking of the Folio text is clinically of concern because the phrase originally assigned to Albany ("O see, see") is uttered by the monarch. Unless this shift is fortuitous, an unlikely prospect to entertain, it was quite probably done to reveal the editor's wrong-headed belief that "poor fool" referred to Cordelia. Otherwise what would be the point in connecting "see" with "fool"?

But in defending the original reading, we may find it apt for Albany rather than the King to exclaim "O see, see," if for no other reason than that this phrase can then be accommodated to the proposed 'sight pattern' in this tragedy. Albany is, in effect, implying here that it is high time that Lear rid himself of his spiritual myopia, that he regain needful insight into his affairs. Thus, when Lear dies, he can do so content with the thought that Cordelia, though being strung up, was not *fully* hanged. Heroic dignity is enhanced through his last moment of joy. But if he himself says, "O see, see-----," the sight metaphor is lost in favor of romantic pathos. Such an effect was understandable for an edition in 1800, but is hardly fully in keeping with what the dramatist must have wanted. True, the repetition of the imperative form "see" has the effect of a stage direction, in part, drawing our attention back to the stricken sovereign after it has been momentarily deflected by Albany's attempt to deal with practicality, but it is going rather far to say that the 'stage direction' is for the sake of identifying "fool" with Cordelia. Because of both text and context, then, the question mark in the Folio might best be withdrawn. Such an assessment does not, therefore, mean that we should resort to the Quarto, whose punctuation is clearly corrupt in other respects. The main reason for withdrawing the question mark resides in Lear's point that neither Cordelia nor the Fool lives. He therefore does not question that both are victims.

To retain the mark either would prompt the criticism that the King is indulging in a rhetorical flourish, or it is totally misleading.

VI

The vast influence of the misapplied 'term of endearment' reading of "poore Foole" has taken its toll. Thus one specialist, William Elton, has been susceptible to it, has referred to "Lear's daughter, his 'lytel yong fole'" (323), whereby he was correlating a remote passage in *The Interlude of Calisto and Melebea* (hardly an influential playlet) to *King Lear* (323). True, the expression "fole" is one of endearment there, even paralleled by an analogy in *OED* not cited by Elton: "How say ye now by this, little yong fool?" (sb., A, I, 1, c: 1530 *Beautiful Women*), but the contexts are totally diverse. *OED*, incidentally, can be a double-edged sword, for it errs here also, misassigning immediately thereafter a similar passage in *The Winter's Tale,* 2.1.118, "Doe not weepe (Goode Fooles) There is no cause," one which Eastman has conclusively shown is not a term of endearment at all, for the "ladies by their weeping show deficient judgment" (532).

One further approach to grasping the repetition of "no" in Lear's last speech is in that he reflects on multiple deaths, not merely Cordelia's, thereby. Whether he does so deliberately at this sad juncture is really beside the point; the aesthetic effect is obvious enough. The three *no*'s in the Folio ("no, no, no life") thereby cogently tally with the three deaths he takes into account: Cordelia's, Caius', and the Fool's. Since Kent has mentioned, just before, that the elder sisters and Edmund have also perished, the report of the deaths of Cordelia and the jester has the effect of adding to his tragic dirge.

In addition, it is useful to enlist Kozintsev's film version to support the matter of contamination in textual renditions. In his magnificent film of *Lear,* the English subtitle during the crux reads simply "—Hang'd!" Evidently the dash was meant in part to take the place of the deleted words. Although I have been unable to discern whether the line was partly cut first by Kozintsev himself or Pasternak, upon whose text the motion picture was based, I did discuss the crux with the film director following the showing at the first World Shakespeare Congress, in Vancouver (1971). He found the crux a "very interesting" one indeed. Apparently the line was shortened to avoid the misleading ambiguity or false reading that some moderns found inherent in "poore Foole." In a word, he felt that he himself needed to make crystal clear that the King meant Cordelia, not the jester. Yet the consequence, however ingenious, was not Shakespeare. For Kozintsev took the liberty of showing the jester at the film's very end playing disconsolately on his instrument. The effect was that of an interpolated coda. In devising this clever view, he was of course further endorsing the Erasmian or "this-great-stage-of-fools" interpretation of the tragedy as a whole. Although such a *Weltanschauung* is applicable, we might still bear in mind that no definitive evidence exists that Shakespeare ever read *The Praise of Folly,* even in the Challoner translation. The term *fool* is used figuratively in the tragedy, but Shakespeare hardly applied it almost at random or *toto caelo.*

In any case, the film ought to be related to Kozintsev's writings on the tragedy too. There he displayed his ignorance of Thaler's argument against the double-role interpretation, namely that the same boy actor played both Cordelia and the Fool. "In several studies," he casually remarked, " evidence that both roles were played by the same actor is cited" (*Shakespeare: Time and Conscience* 82). Such endorsed vagueness is hardly supportive documentary evidence. He does, however, write more discerningly on the Fool and why the antic left the stage to begin with: "The Fool disappeared as soon as Lear came to understand the meaning of things. . . . When the King became a sage, the shadow with ass's ears wasted away. . . ." Just wasted away? The tragedy's implication is that he died. At any rate, Kozintsev warrantedly found it "shameful to sugar *Lear.* . . ." An excellent point. So let us enumerate the bodies in a respectful way, showing proper condolence without eliminating a requiem for the choric figure who ought to have one too: the jester. Allow for Death having his last snicker.

VII

A final argument in favor of our knowing what happens to the Fool is that it would have been decidedly odd if Shakespeare had created such a sympathetic individual only to assign him to a state of limbo. Does any other major figure, not merely in this play but in the others, disappear without our having some hint of his final destiny? Agreed, this objection has been taken by some critics as in effect reading the play somewhat too literally. "A. C. Bradley, who reasoned only in literal terms," Roy W. Battenhouse has written for example, "was puzzled by the Fool's being dropped from the play in Act III without Shakespeare's informing us as to this character's ultimate fate" (291). Yet good enough reason for such literal puzzlement exists, should we accept the Fool/Cordelia equation. The point is that a tragedy which is also labeled a chronicle history play in Q exacts, by its very nature, a certain commonsense literalness from the spectator/reader. As deplorable as it is that Bradley accepted the Fool/Cordelia equation, his critical decision is at least explicable in that his heritage was simply that of sentimental, nineteenth-century Romanticism. Swinburne, it might be added, likewise maintained, in terms of his own impressionistic background, that "the one great and grave oversight or flaw to be found in this tragic work" was "the sudden and inexplicable disappearance of Lear's only comrade and support" (Bonheim 59). So may we not be comforted at least in knowing that if the antic does not entirely "disappear," that is if his end is in fact told us by Lear, such a flaw would be eradicated?

It might be incidentally recalled at this point how various critics in the past have contended that the Fool does perish, a number of them figuring in the well-known Bonheim compilation: Thaler, as we have seen, would suggest that the jester succumbs, though not at the very end of the play (65); George Orwell observed that "the Fool dangles on a gallows somewhere in the background" (86). Those critics who would steadfastly maintain that the idea of Lear's announcing the death of his Fool does not work on the stage ought to bear in mind that the Fool's decease *has* been taken seriously by some.

It is also arguable that "poore Foole" alludes to the jester's being from the peasant or poor class and that emphasis upon Lear's heartfelt concern for him points toward the monarch's growing sense of social inequality as he mellows. As such, the phrase could relate to the King's likewise famous "Poore naked wretches" speech (3.4.28) and signal a shift from a medieval to a more Renaissance-oriented or money-based society (somewhat like the focus on Brutus rather than on the traditional Caesar, to a certain extent, spelled out a similar switch in *Julius Caesar*).[44]

If we so wish, we may prefer to think of the jester's last line on going to bed at noon as pointing literally to his tucking himself away, but, whatever that verdict, the connotation of concupiscent behavior that has been suggested in the crux (see Andrews) is only questionably germane. It does appear rather too farcical to imagine this imaginative jester leaving his sire only to indulge in frolics in bed.

In any case, why need we believe that the King has to be at all embroidering his final words of woe? It further enhances his dignity at the bitter end to imagine that finally he is *not* deluded, at least with regard to his dear servant. The strong sense of the crucial key line tells us that he *knows* that his jester has been strung up and has had to succumb. The audience is then expected to lament in unison. On the other hand, since he feels shortly thereafter that Cordelia was still alive when she actually was not, some readers and spectators (like Kozintsev in his film) may validly prefer to believe that the reverse may be true with the jester. In other words, the King says the antic is dead, thinking the worst, but he may still be in the background. Still, a major difference is evident. As C. F. Williamson has recently shown, the King thinks he has cut Cordelia down before she has died: "Lear's use of the phrase 'was a-hanging' is thus of the greatest importance: it makes quite clear that the action has not been completed" (416). (This diagnosis, composed by a learned physician, is excellent.) The same is not true of the Fool. Williamson's point is actually more important than the doctor seems to think: It reveals, once again, that the King could not have been referring to Cordelia when he uttered those poignant words about his Fool being hanged, for his daughter, he thinks, has been incompletely hanged whereas the jester appears to have been executed for sure.

---

[44] I explored this possibility in a paper, "Lear's Proletarian Fool," at the "Marxist Understandings of Shakespearean Tragedy" session at the Modern Language Association of America annual meeting in 1976, though one problem with this entire orientation was the unhistorical nature of the tentative approach indicated in the session's title. That did not discourage provocative discussion afterwards.

With regard to Shakespeare's dramaturgical development and the subsequent stage history, the removal of the jester is finally noteworthy if for no other reason than that it marks the gradual eclipse not only of his fools in general—there being no jester after Lear's save Trinculo, hardly one of the 'wise' ones—but of the motley-colored antic in English drama as a whole, because "the later fools contribute little or nothing new to the genre which reaches its supreme expression in the part of Lear's Fool" (Felver 62). The death of the antic in this tragedy therefore signals an ensuing watershed in dramatic history. In this respect, the execution of the Fool would have universal but also historical meaning outside the play itself. His departure thereby provides us with a demise that is prognosticative of more than even what *he,* it may be said, is capable of predicting.[45]

---

[45] As a sort of coda, I should add that after the main part of this chapter was composed in its initial form, I presented a paper, "The Image of the Literal 'Poor Fool' in Jacobean Times," in Seminar V ("Images of *King Lear*") at the International Shakespeare Association Congress in West Berlin (April, 1986). Various points were then made that were inconvenient to incorporate in detail here, e.g., the fact that the word *dead* was added by a later textual editor to the key stage direction "Enter Lear, with Cordelia in his arms," and the idea that a stage director can have Lear momentarily leave his daughter when he states his crucial line, thereby detracting from audience confusion. (In other words, an audience may not be able to fathom why the King would suddenly be talking about his jester when he has his daughter in his arms, naturally, but that problem is resolvable. Numerous actions in Shakespeare are thought to take place on the stage without having explicit stage directions.) Finally Schmidt's standard *Shakespeare-Lexicon* was found to be misleading in supposedly providing many examples of similar 'terms of endearment' relating to "poor fool" in the canon, if only because nearly every one of his references is to dumb animals, and we should hardly wish to lower Cordelia to that genus.

PART VI
THE AUTHORSHIP CRUX

Chapter 9
Elizabethan Hydropathy:
The Domestic Relation of *Arden of Faversham* to *The Merry Wives*

"Fling them in the Thames!" This punitive but primitive threat, found toward the end of *Arden of Faversham* (15. 10), is not without its whimsical thrust also for Renaissance scholars. Although such spontaneous drenching is hardly as effective a means of restoring order as is sedately petitioning the courts of justice, it is still enlivening enough by suggesting an ordered relation in another sense. It points ahead to the amusing misadventures of Sir John Falstaff in *The Merry Wives,* thereby providing a plausibly satirical and thematic correlation between the two leading domestic plays in their genre, a link which has thus far, to my knowledge, been curiously overlooked.

A thorough examination of some of the dominant patterns of imagery in *Arden* may thus prove serviceable in offering a bridge between the early domestic melodrama and the Falstaffian farce (or, better, *comedy* in terms of Jeanne Addison Roberts' recent reassessment). Should these generic associations appear hard to grasp, we might note that the Windsor drama is somewhat like a satyr play thus linked to a classical tragedy. Let us, then, examine whatever cogent basis we have for this kinship, first through some circumstantial, external evidence (consisting of some new clues as to Shakespeare's possible involvement already in the *Arden* tragedy, which would account for his anticipating related effects in the *Windsor* play) and, secondly, through internal evidence, including plots and at times lighthearted characterization.

After also taking into account several parallels between other plays in the canon and the tragedy, in order to arrive at some critical objectivity, we may have a chance to clarify the domestic correlations, hoping to show that if the Stratford "upstart" was hardly involved in his early career as a sole author, certain suggestions of his having plausibly collaborated or of his early apprenticeship ought at least not to be quite ruled out. True enough, his function may have been actually that of kibitzing actor, reviser, or incidental interpolator, but it is also just possible that he had something intrinsic enough to do with a play like this, which, after all, titularly bore the maiden name of his mother, as with Arden in *As You Like It*. Several Shakespeareans have thought that he was indeed involved in some way. In any case, we can aver from the outset that a plausible piece of external evidence associating the *Arden* play with him is a seventeenth-century bookseller's list, Edward Archer's in 1656. W. W. Greg "demonstrated convincingly that [there] is a printing-house error for Shakespeare's name, which appears, wrongly aligned . . . just above" (Wine lxxxiv; see Greg 134–6). This information was not known to many scholars and devotees of the past (including Goethe) who had speculated positively about Shakespeare's possible authorship. Although, granted, we have no hard extrinsic evidence otherwise, a sufficient number of verbal links, which include fairly similar elements in plot-motifs, deserve our full attention. In short, although internal evidence, according to Samuel Schoenbaum at least, falls short of providing here definitive proof for authorship of any kind, it can have its own *raison d'être* and, let us hope, allow us to appreciate the Arden play even better. As a starter, especially memorable is the character Shakebag's remark about being a highway robber and plundering several victims even at Gad's Hill, which was of course the later site of Falstaff's own identical, early misadventures. That, however, would be no justification in itself for purloining *Arden* from the realms of anonymity and imposing it upon the canon.

I

Whatever relevant circumstantial evidence is available has to start with Will Kemp and Robert Greene. When Kemp teasingly fashioned the mockingly commendatory label "My notable Shake*rags*" and at the same time alluded to a certain "Mac*do*beth" in his *Nine Daies Wonder* (1600), he could have meant, in part, to refer to an early version of Shakespeare's Scottish tragedy—if not more. The exact allusion tells of "Macdobeth, or Macsomewhat, for I am sure a Mac it was" (Harrison 30–31). Because he was no longer a member of the Chamberlain's Men, having parted company with them early in 1599, he had nothing to lose by indulging in such satiric lightheartedness. In any case, the recent effort to gloss "Shakerags" as simply an allusion to the *un*kempt or tattered garments from his nine-day virtuoso performance (Parsons 122) is not very convincing, failing to tie in, for example, with standard meanings given in *OED*. At any rate, a good-natured quip here at his "notable" friend William Shakespeare is at least worthy of consideration, for it might also convey indirectly or phonologically the notion of the author Will's having had something to do with the character of Will Shakebag in *Arden*. Self-evidently the very name-play points to similarity.

Is there any basis for this Ardenic correlation, *Shakerags* also linking with *Shakebag* in the play? Yes, for the phrase in Kemp does, in fact, head a section of his report. It implicates someone who is "notable" for being roguish. It is profitable to consider that the author Will may have been humanly drawn to at least the *name* of the rascal Shakebag, could even have assumed the part on the stage (if only as an amusing *tour de force* perhaps) early in his career. If so, then his boon companion, Will Kemp, might as easily have taken on the role of Black Will, Shakebag's accomplice, since his name fits the bill somewhat also. For what it is worth, the very etymology of the name *Kemp* (meaning *wanderer*) could suggest the picaresque, too, hence lending itself to the notion that this actor was living up to his name in a minor way. Indeed, it is possible that Kemp was a bit of a rogue even in another respect by being the "mole" who released texts of plays for publication (see Force). In any case, he wandered off for his 'Wonder.'

Various critics, for example Ivor Brown, have tried to conflate somehow the names of *Shakerags* and *Shakebag*. Aside from Brown's comment to this effect in his study of the women in the dramatist's life (176), another has more recently claimed that "Shakespeare and Greene could be spoofed in the names Greene, Shakebag (a name Greene himself used [or transformed] in referring to

Shakespeare), Black Will, and Arden" (Walz 41).[46] The most enticing hint of all perhaps may be that of Robert Greene's "Shakescene" allusion in 1592, for it too constituted such a portmanteau label, as does *Shakerags*. But it is doubtful whether this *Groatsworth* reference deserves credit for being the initial stimulus for Kemp, that is if he was more likely following a kind of precedent in his career, whereby the name-play in *Shakebag* already had such an effect on him. (For that matter, Greene's allusion may also have been prompted by the Shakebag association.) As we have seen earlier, as with Thomas Thorpe, Master W. H., and the name of *Mar-text,* onomastic playfulness was commonplace enough, at least among some of the *literati*.

What is then the likelihood that Shakespeare might have taken on the role of the renegade Shakebag on the stage, plausibly improvising on it from time to time as may well have been his wont as creative *Johannes fac totum*? Allowing for his having taken to the part with a lively enough flair is scarcely a disrespectful idea, especially if we bear in mind that he could have later given the role of a similar rascal, Edmund, albeit in complimentary guise, to his brother (see Ch 7). Indeed, in a paper delivered to the Faversham Society and subsequently published in the *Archaeologica Cantiana* (1920), Lionel Cust set forth just such a case (Holt 28–29). True enough, a colleague of his then demurred, terming Shakebag's "terribly graphic description of his feelings" an effect that is rather "too 'staged,'" thereby presumably accounting for only a "certain amusing ring of possibility in Mr. Cust's hypothesis" (Holt 28–29). Be that as it may, rumor had it that Shakespeare revealed a certain weakness for his own occasional 'stagey' effects; we need compare only the theatrical tradition that he acted the Ghost in *Hamlet*.

Another problem is that his mother, *née* Mary Arden, with her accepted early religious background, was most probably quite remote in character from Alice Arden in the drama, but such a contrast may invite merely what Keats critically termed negative capability. Most promising of all, current scholarship informs us that the playwright possibly first was affiliated with the Queen's Men, with which *Arden* is also circumstantially, at least, associated, so it is logical to believe he may

---

[46]For that matter, in *Ulysses,* Joyce imaginatively correlated the two names, thereby prompting Burgess' own later, popular identification. (Because, however, Joyce clearly went a bit far in having Daedalus relate Shakespeare's brothers in a cynical fashion to characters in the plays, as we have seen in Ch 7, his authority is hardly recommended.)

at least have performed in the tragedy: "In 1587 an actor of the Queen's Men—the most successful company of the 1580s—died as a result of manslaughter shortly before the company visited Stratford" (Wells and Taylor xvii). Hence it is intriguing to imagine that Shakespeare took the dead man's place (however, see David George on this). Although, true, E. K. Chambers had specified that he saw no link between *Arden* and the Queen's Company, the character of Black Will, as we have seen, happens to be cited in a play produced by the Queen's, and he was also thematically linked to a historical focus that Shakespeare also then adopted. He appears mentioned in *The True Tragedy of Richard III,* a work some critics think was by the Stratford newcomer and may have been a source for the better known history play by him on Richard Crookback.

Now, what hand could Shakespeare have had in *Arden*? Historically, the rogue Shakebag's prototype was a certain *Loosebag,* and the new Stratford recruit could have been involved in the decision in the theater to switch the name to *Shakebag,* thereby endorsing the story in Holinshed (where the shift, or then *erratum,* was already made, if only once). For we know of Shakespeare's use of Holinshed as source material for his many other plays. The Shakebag name would have had a uniquely familial association in accompaniment with the Arden name, thus representing at least an unconscious ring. Further, we observe the printer's convention, presumably, whereby Shakebag's name was sharply curtailed to "Shake" in the line assignments in the Quarto. "Will" was then often set above this curtailed designation, to denote Black Will; so that the ordinary reader cannot help but notice a curious *Will Shake-* association. Underscoring this curiosity is the fact that the play was originally printed with *Arden* and *Will* onomastically side by side on the title-page. Such seemingly covert name-play may prompt the hint that (1) if Shakespeare did not himself act Shakebag on the boards of the stage with gusto, with his faithful companion Will Kemp, say, as his helpmate, (2) he could plausibly have been alternating between the roles, in the process thereby interacting in several ways with his own name. We recall easily enough that doubling was a commonplace in those days. Such a scenario is hardly a displeasing one, speculative though it be. (Of the two suggestions, the earlier one, that Shakespeare alone took the Shakebag role, appears more in keeping with the *Nine Daies Wonder* allusion.)

Whatever the case, whoever wrote the play clearly took a special interest in one George Shakebag, who introduces himself much earlier in the play than in the *Chronicles*. He and his braggart partner Will have been notably humanized, much as other, later, picturesque villains such as Aaron the Moor and Shylock, and they are thereby set up to steal the show. If Will Kemp played Black Will, incidentally, it is amusing to consider how he afterwards might have played the role of braggart to the hilt in real life by dancing all the way from London to Norwich and then writing a report about it.

Keith Sturgess has glossed this stress upon low life by noting that "with Shakespearean generosity the playwright has lavished poetry on the minor characters as well as the major ones" (27). Perhaps so—and in a literal manner as well. Although, in point of fact, Will is actually the more dominant of the two rapscallions (thus the principal Braggadochio), the Shakebag role, too, is considerably enlarged over that in Holinshed. Most telling of all, in light of the plausible Shakespearean association, Shakebag's name and role obviously anticipate those of Falstaff, the latter's analogous portmanteau name being that of yet another *miles gloriosus,* the chief of them all. To put it in popular terms, if the spear shakes, so may the bag, before the staff falls (compare Falstaff on "pick . . . purse" in *Wives,* 1.1.134). However tediously obvious to us, puns like that were common enough at the time; Shakespeare could not help succumbing to them from time to time, and so Johnson called them his "fatal Cleopatra."

Especially tantalizing is the likelihood that Greene, in branding Shakespeare a pilfering "Shakescene," was himself at least unconsciously inspired by Shakebag, as I have suggested earlier. For *Shakebag* was a petty thief's name suggesting a cutpurse, and it fits the scene well. And is it not logical that Greene, himself a well-known rakehell, as was said, composed the Shakescene allusion in 1592 only after being provoked earlier in the same year by witnessing Shakebag in *Arden*? Following him, others took over such name-play, too, whereupon we have Ben Jonson's familiar punning later on "shake a Lance" and "shake a stage" in his 1623 eulogy. One other source for such name-play worth citing is the theory that Shakespeare took upon himself the pseudonym of a certain Shakeshafte in Lancashire, a theory promulgated in 1982 by E. A. J. Honigmann. That analogy has its problems (there being, for example, so many other Lancastrian

Shakeshaftes available), but it is not impossible, and if so, need not conflict with the Shakebag connection but simply provide a precedent for it.

Finally, a striking sort of correlation emerges between the playwright *Robert* Greene and the emergence of *Richard* Greene in the drama. Let us consider four salient points of contact: 1. "Master Greene" in the play, by the very formality of that designation, would have brought to the alert spectator's mind the dramatist Greene, if only because he was at times known and referred to as a Cambridge "Master" (of Arts). 2. Both Greenes, moreover, were ostensibly religiously oriented persons, though with a strong secular side too. Thus Mosby remarks, "You know this Greene. Is he not religious? A man, I guess, of great devotion" (1.586–7). In terms of the irony involved, it is easy to think again of the wayward Falstaff, whose references to the Bible surpass all others in Shakespeare (McCanles 171), yet who is hardly a truly religious type. 3. Paradoxically enough, these two seemingly devout Greenes, in their rapscallion manner, cavorted with the underworld as well as with the disadvantaged, Arden's Greene being familiar not merely with Faversham riffraff but that of London, even as Robert, in turn, was in league with London rogues, notably allied to a certain "Cutting Ball." Let us consider this point in a bit more detail.

Being petty varlets, such so-called "cutters" were incidentally cited along with Greene in *Arden*. In the context of his "Shakerags" passage, we recall, Kemp also told of notorious cutpurses, alluding specifically to a certain "Cutting Dicke" (Goldsmid 25). In representing one of the play's villainous characters accompanying the Shakebag-Will team, Richard Greene would himself recall this daring cutter named Richard for us, namely the notorious renegade pickpocket who is also cited in Wither's *Abuses Stript and Whipt* and by Henslowe. As for Robert Greene, his *Repentances* ought to speak for itself. It has been reiterated by no less a Shakespearean than Muriel C. Bradbrook (*Shakespeare: The Poet in His World*) that a "country" author "seduced him," the culprit being, it is fancied, the Stratford "upstart" (50), but that is mere ribald speculation. Whatever the case, the parallel with brother Edmund is easily recalled.

4. A particularly valuable affinity between the two Greenes is the way both complained bitterly of having themselves been, oddly, the victims of pilfering. This correlation is not only reminiscent of the rumor that Shakespeare himself once did some deer-poaching, but proleptic of what is then said of Sir John in

Wives, 1.1.134. (Again *Arden* looks ahead to the Falstaff plays.) Even more than that, Richard and Robert in their complaints together chose to make contrasting use of analogous *ornithological* imagery in conjunction with standard Aesopian fable: Richard, in his complaint about "this weary bird" (9.39); Robert, in turn, regarding the "upstart Crow." (Whereas one animal is worn out, the other is ready to undertake new flights.) This unmistakable brotherhood in irony thereby made them, metaphorically, of one feathered flock, but also in some ways literally, for Robert's lament concerning the "upstart's" encroachment on him parallels Richard's charge that Arden made off with the former's property.[47]

Were the charges of robbery fully justified in terms of the play? Let us see. (Arden himself is depicted in a much worse way in the *Chronicles;* from what Holinshed's Greene says, the Master was an absolute tyrant, but no such despotism is shown in the play.) What is chiefly of interest is how animal imagery recurs. Employing this for his descriptive purposes, Richard Greene purportedly refers to Aesop, to canine allusions (as in "two stout dogs were striving for a bone" and "the longing water-dog") along with the previously cited ornithological imagery. Analogous animal imagery is iterative throughout the play's texture: "A network of inverted or distorted images of nature and religion—of animals, hunting, and entrapment . . . pictures a world of nature tooth and claw" (Wine lxxxi). In comparison, Robert Greene, as a devotee of classical lore, admitted to his penchant for Aesop as well; we aptly call him to mind in hearing Richard: "I pray you sirs list to Esops talk" (9.30). Granted, Aesop's famous fables were commonly grist for the literary mill, Shakespeare later embroidering Plutarch with Livy and Aesopian fable in his well-known metaphor of the belly in *Coriolanus* (Thomson 31–32; also see Hale), but hardly ruling out the plausibly connecting import of the bird figure. In a word, *Arden* links with the *Groatsworth* in this key respect. The references in both works are to theft, and Richard's addressing Shakebag adumbrates Robert's analogous "Shakescene" accusation. Even the dramatist's falcon on his coat of arms appears to serve as a further reverberation of

---

[47]True enough, it has been claimed that the *Groatsworth* accusation could have rather been leveled at Shakespeare as upstart *actor* rather than playwright, yet that less damaging identification is not allowed by John Dover Wilson ("Malone and the Upstart Crow") and by many historians today. In any case, the general charge of theft of some kind would still serve as an overall parallel between Robert and Richard.

or analogy with the ornithological device, having a bearing on the relevance of heraldry, since the Shakespeares gained the privilege of impaling the arms of Arden—again a resonance of the play's title—on their own badge (see also the next chapter).

Because the present scholarly consensus scarcely supports the inference that Robert Greene himself had a hand in *Arden,* we need not take the correlation with him here too seriously. Robert was hardly charging William with having stolen from him with regard to *this* play. A more cogent view is that the former, as a rival of the latter, became envious and was thus getting even in the *Groatsworth* for apparently satirical thrusts at him in the Greene allusions in the domestic tragedy. In support of this, let us recall the play's dominant irony, a kind so striking that its genre has been specially categorized as that of tragical satire (Walz).

As was then well enough recognized, the "upstart" later paid the *Groatsworth* critic back twice in *Hamlet* in his own coin. First, he mocked the Greene allusion to him as an "upstart Crow, beautified with our feathers" by way of Polonius' throwaway gloss, "beautified is a vilde Phrase" (2.2.111); secondly, he also replied to the charge that he would "bombast out a blanke verse" by having the Prince strategically advise the traveling players to express themselves "trippingly on the Tongue" (3.2.2). Now, rhetorical bombast is already an essential ingredient in *Arden,* thus presumably partly prompting the *Groatsworth* reaction, but it is used there for an overall ironic effect, not merely a sign revealing amateurish style.

Remembering that Greene also castigated Marlowe in the *Groatsworth,* we recall that one of the leading proposed authors of *Arden* is Marlowe himself, who, according to Kyd, once shared a room at Cambridge. Certain critics, such as Fleay and Boas, also once found Kyd to be the true author of *Arden,* though that is a view now in disrepute (Wine lxxxii). If Shakespeare had any hand in the play, would he have been manipulating Marlovian material, even as he did in later dramas as well (Bakeless II, 285–90)? In any event, the topical echoes of the shire of Kent in this play may at first appear to bespeak some close familiarity with the region (Marlowe having hailed from Canterbury in Kent). As Louis Ule posited in 1988 in a paper at the Second International Marlowe Conference, at the Oxford Polytechnic, the Kentish data might have originated by way of Marlowe's father.

Cust, for one, felt that *Arden* revealed the hands of *both* Shakespeare and Marlowe (117), and Glyn Pursglove of St. Peter's College, Oxford, and the

University of Swansea, provided me graciously in person with the useful suggestion that Alice Arden's line "Such winning and such losing Jove send me" (1.126) approximates Marlowe's translation of Ovid, *Elegy* 5.26: "Jove send me more such after-noones as this." Because the early Shakespeare was clearly indebted to Marlowe (compare the allusions to *Edward II* and *Dr. Faustus* in *Richard II*), it is somewhat difficult to tell whether a passage in this apocryphal play is bonafide Marlowe or simply Marlovian in influence; anyway, as I pointed out in Ch 6, no evidence is extant to prove with any cogency that the two dramatists worked together, even at a very early stage. The parallel from Marlowe just cited, for example, can be offset by one with Kyd, one which Pursglove also kindly called to my attention: that between Francklin's "What dismall outcry cals me from my rest?" (4.87) and Hieronimo's "What outcries pluck me from my naked bed . . . ?" (*The Spanish Tragedy,* 2.4.65). Although Wine himself cites this analogy in an appendix to his excellent edition, he still reasonably contends that Kyd is no longer to be taken seriously as author of *Arden* in any sense (lxxxii).

Returning to the *Groatsworth* charge, we may ask: If *Arden* was not the *cause célèbre* for it, does any other play fit better? Perhaps, it just might be urged, Greene's *A Knack to Know a Knave* does on the grounds that the "upstart" could have tampered with it (Born 166), though the evidence seems to me slight. True, *Henry VI* has at times been brought in as well: "Several critics consider it to be mostly from the hands of Greene and Peele. Shakespeare might have written some of its scenes, but he did not certainly revise it. Its repulsive scenes in which Joan of Arc has been ridiculed undoubtedly did not emanate from his pen" (Chakraborty 21). Yet such a negative view is clearly a minority one, for the Stratford newcomer indulged in plenty of such anti-religious satire elsewhere, even though his slant was seemingly more political than theological. All told, *Arden,* especially with its Shakebag, provides rather more readily a valid basis for the "Shakescene" allusion than do most other conjectures. As for the Shakeshafte connection, it is not clear how, if Shakespeare took the name in the Lancashire countryside, *Londoners* would so easily have known about it, enough so as to appreciate a jest about it. If Greene had indulged in a private jest on this basis, what would have been its point? In answer, the *facetia* would more likely be related to *Arden,* its anonymous publication pointing to Greene's remark having an 'in-house' effect.

II

If "Shakescene" was meant to recall *Shakebag,* then the later Forest of Arden would clearly recall not only the dramatist's mother's maiden name but, at least obliquely, the Arden family name in the Faversham tragedy. It may be that Shakespeare did not make Master Arden out to be so perverse, whatever the share he might have had in writing the play, having respect for his mother's maiden name being involved. For, indeed, the central difference between the historical situation and the drama based on it is that the titular figure is not the utterly negative one that he was in real life (Wine lxviii). In any event, both *Arden* and *As You Like It* provide us with convenient topical allusions, ones which look ahead to a similar well-recognized concern with topicality in *The Merry Wives,* namely the celebrated poaching references, allusions to Count Mömpelgart, and (plausibly on the level of occasion) the renowned Garter festivities in 1597 (though this evidence is inconclusive, the play relating more closely to the time *Henry V* was composed [on which, see Ch 10]).

Most memorable in *As You Like It,* insofar as it relates to Greene's complaint in *Arden,* is the self-pitying lament of the shepherd Corin:

> I am shepheard to another man
> And do not sheer the Fleeces that I graze:
> My master is of churlish disposition,
> And little wreakes to finde the way to heaven
> By doing deeds of hospitality.   (2.4.73–7)

Corin's plight is recognizably much akin to Master Greene's, their mutual problem being the deprivation of what should be theirs by tyrannical landlords; they find themselves loudly lamenting their fates as a consequence of the Enclosure Acts confiscating farm land. Such stress on covetousness and the ensuing moral and social realism in *Arden,* far from being a distraction, is a distinctively artistic element appended to the Holinshed story. Greene's lands appertaining to Faversham Abbey were appropriated by Master Arden, providing the main background for this study in social disenfranchisement and perverse cuckoldry.

Because the tragic events "would not have happened if Arden had not been so ruthlessly ambitious in this business dealings" (Holt 8), not to mention in his being too lax in failing to communicate adequately with his spouse, a certain socio-political basis for both Arden stories (*As You Like It* and that of *Faversham*) is clear-cut enough.

The principal reverberation of the name of the Forest of Arden in *As You Like It* is, nonetheless, not so much the original French name of the wood or the dramatist's mother's maiden name, as has hitherto been surmised, but more likely the Arden of the previous play. It represents an attention-getting re-echo, one which a theater circle or in-group could be expected to figure out. Even though the original, historical French name for the woodland was the *Ardennes,* because Shakespeare pointedly mentions Robin Hood in this context, he would normally have been expected to have accommodated the *English* setting for the forest (namely Sherwood)—were it not, that is, for some fairly compelling external (but also, psychologically, internal) motives. In any event, metaphysically *Arden*'s being a woodland name evidently sets up a dramatic contrast to a former landscape, that of *Eden,* recalling for us that the tragedy of Thomas Arden likewise had markedly postlapsarian features in its gradual movement toward dénouement (Chapman [1956] 15–17; Wine passim). In connection with the Arden Forest, even the Robin Hood allusions recollect, however paradoxically, the thievery and rogue motifs in that other *Arden,* the tragedy. Overall, the sociological link between this tragedy and *As You Like It* serves mainly as a useful one to *The Merry Wives* as well, even as, in a recent socialistic analysis of Falstaff and his unruly cohorts, the theme of social exploitation was also correlated with the theme of the Windsor comedy (Siegel).

In now sizing up some curious points of conjunction between *Arden* and *Wives,* we may notice, first of all, that an outstanding one is the intrigue within a setting of committed or, in one case, merely attempted adultery—the shadow of cuckoldry hovering implacably in the background. Greed rather than carnal lust functions as the main culprit, especially in the comedy, and, if Arden's insensitive exploitativeness is given its due, likewise in the tragedy. In both these studies in domestic tribulations and resolutions, much of the focus is on a form of thievery, specifically what might be called spouse-stealing, with its diverse consequences.

A principal thematic ingredient they share is in their use of illusiveness, the particular mirage image mainly involved assuming the tangible form of deceit. Whereas Sir John indulges in outlandish chicanery in the form of deceptive letter-writing and disguise to accomplish his devious ends, Shakebag and his accomplice Black Will (somewhat anticipatory of Falstaff accompanied by Pistol, the latter being as much of a braggart as Will is) also indulge in whatever rascality can be at their beck and call to achieve their own goals.

To start off, they are all hilariously inept. In both plays the ruffians initially fail a number of times to accomplish their purposes, providing analogous, grotesquely frustrating results. It takes the Shakebag-Will team six plotted maneuvers to effect their malicious designs and to dispose of Arden, and Sir John three momentous efforts to arrange for what he hopes will be an assignation leading to adulterous consummation. With the respective accounts given of the futility of these débacles, a certain backhanded humor emerges, the hoodlums' efforts being circumvented in relatively elementary ways. Even when her husband is finally killed, it is Alice (not one of her hired assailants) who delivers the fatal blow. Thus the ballad based on the legend and play referred titularly to "Mistresse," rather than Master, Arden. In retributive terms, the play is more her tragedy than her husband's, which is another possible reason why Shakespeare would have been attracted to the play on the basis of a female Arden in his own family. After the blow is delivered, Master Arden is not dragged into the cellar in the play (as he was in real life), and that points against the author's complete familiarity with the Faversham or Kentish story, and so is a vital point against the involvement of Marlowe (who came from that area). In contrast to what happens in *Arden,* in any case, Sir John is completely thwarted.[48]

In both these cases of domestic distress, a markedly sportive quality links with the wily perpetrator, almost as if murder and adultery (clinically then designated in popular terms 'cold' and 'hot' sins) involve complicated initiatory rites. Such a ritual effect is notably heightened in *Arden* with the rote assassination occurring while the victim is at home engaged in a formalized routine, a game akin

---

[48] Should any all-too-human readers feel at all *sympatico* with the rascal's mating urges and a bit let down at the end, let them happily add to this story the well-known imaginative eighteenth-century sequel, *Falstaff's Wedding* [1760] by a certain Mr. Kewick.

to present-day backgammon. The use of such an apparently innocent pastime as a dramatic device sets off the adulterous, murderous indoor sport of Arden's pre-Lady-Macbeth-like wife.[49]

Further, the appropriation of a ritual game as a kind of *tableau vivant* in *Arden,* with Alice and her co-conspirators grouped about the players in a manner analogous to the murder gang surrounding Julius Caesar in the most popular of the Roman tragedies, is of theatrical import, adumbrating a similar device, if one used less conspicuously, in *The Tempest,* wherein Prospero 'discovers' Miranda and Ferdinand intently absorbed in chessplay. But there the predicament is reversed. The result of the disclosure provides a tone of amity, not enmity; the magus had counseled his daughter on the desirability of abstaining from pre-marital relations, and so the chess match functions as displacement, being abstractly symbolic of the rightful subordination of passion to reason.

In a similar capacity, as Jeanne Addison Roberts has recognized in several studies, the dénouement of *Wives* is also akin to apt sportive activity, even conjuring up typological Hallowe'en masquerading; Bryant and Frye having also discussed mythic elements in the play as archetypally related to changing seasons of the year. Yet *which* ritual would then be involved, fall or spring? The folk theme of "Carrying out Death" could be accommodated to *Wives,* but unless Hallowe'en be figuratively seen as heralding All Saints' Day, that occasion would hardly call for such a mythic label, one more appropriate for the demise of winter (as seen in Laroque's review of Roberts). For what it is worth, Shakebag, Will, and Falstaff all indirectly summon up characteristic and similar ritual folk traditions.

Next in the order of stage business comes a particular aspect of the domestic designs: the similar use of props. In *Arden,* two letters are essential to the plot, even as two are in the Windsor comedy, both cunningly being sent by the varlet. In the earlier play, Greene writes to Mistress Arden regarding the murder plot (8.153–60). More importantly, Michael wants to send a love letter to win Susan, hoping to "finde a fellow / That can both write and read, and make rime too" (1.155–6). The comic effect in this letter-writing business (which also enforces a

---

[49]It is worth glancing at how Middleton employed another game, chess, as a similar stratagem in *Women Beware Women* and *A Game of Chess.*

serious point) (see Ian and Heather Dubrow Ousby, the latter now known as Heather Dubrow) is similar to the effect of Sir Paunch's outrageous epistolary manipulation in *Wives*. Although "the gross attempt at seductive language clearly parodies ... more sophisticated rhetoric," yet it is obvious that "Michael is as much the seducer as the seduced" (Ousby and Ousby 50). So the duper is duped.

Are we not apt to recollect the braggart from The Boar's Head as likewise the trickster being scored upon, a variation on the earlier theme of the plunderer being plundered in *1 Henry IV*? With his customary bravado, Falstaff plays what would now be termed the male chauvinist by underestimating the other sex, having the presumptuous gall to try to seduce two spouses concomitantly with the disingenuous plan of writing them identical love-missives. His curiously naïve machinations, going awry, cause the Windsor wives their titular merriment. But the main hypothesis is that it is an *Arden*-induced gaiety apparently as well. That is, it is if the earlier play was at all instrumental.

In both dramas the addressees are plainly thought to be gullible ladies. Hence the letters are laden with intrigue. Not so surprisingly, an epistolary analog has already been studied as a source for *Wives,* yet in terms of a different domestic drama, namely the farcical *Ralph Roister Doister* (Bennett).[50] Jean Roberts has rightfully enough considered that the Windsor play might better be promoted from the dubious cubbyhole of low comedy; the proposed Ardenic background for it would offer a more appropriate comparison than that of Udall's roistering farce, a rather more slapstick *divertissement.*

In terms of a major episode and a passing allusion to *Arden* which looks verbally ahead to the comedy, the psychological use of water therapy or hydropathy, as it once used to be called, stands out prominently enough. The proposed punitive measure of getting the corpulent rascal thoroughly dunked in the Thames works cathartically to link the comedy with a remarkable prose source in Boccaccio dealing with the misadventures of Frate Alberto.[51] One criticism of

---

[50] Although sometimes designated the earliest English comedy, this play is replete with doggerel and not, to my mind, on a high enough level otherwise to be considered a true comedy.

[51] For Boccaccio considered as a hitherto unrecognized source of *Wives,* see my study "The Malleable Knight and the Unfettered Friar," which has a precedent in the further Shakespearean analogies with Boccaccio in general as cited in Bullough's standard work on Shakespeare's narrative and dramatic sources. See Ch 1 n19.

the Boccaccio/Shakespeare connection here has been that it ignores too much what were stock devices—thus helpfully paving the way for the present non-Boccaccian treatment. The main similarity in my previous article, the so-called 'water therapy treatment,' though seemingly slapstick in some respects, may go somewhat beyond what is 'stock,' in any case. (The very idea of the therapeutic is a cathartic principle beyond the merely commonplace.)

The humor of it is that even apparently staid clerics can have their all-too-human foibles. As a follow-up to this interconnection, let us notice how the very hydropathic device was then anticipated in the Faversham tragedy. For Shakebag's amusing (not to mention bemused) anti-climactic threat, "now I am going to fling them in the Temes" (Thames) (15.10), provides not only verbal similarity but stands in ironic counterpoint to what the rotund rapscallion will himself finally experience. Should such a droll effect seem merely farcical, let us recall that, at least in its satiric aspects, farce paradoxically does have its serious import as well and was hardly designed merely for the sake of slapstick. A similar effect later, though without comic meaning, is then evident in Jack Cade's instruction "throw them into Thames" (2 *Henry VI,* 4.8.2), which is plausibly enough yet another echo of *Arden,* Cade's import also having its own socialistic overtones. (True, it could have been a common enough saying in those days.)

In another sense, the water-therapy device points ahead to what the portly reprobate would like to have said after he got literally all wet and feared to divulge—discretion once again conveniently proving to be "the better part of valor." In contrast, in the *Decameron,* Frate Alberto thrusts *himself* head foremost into the Grand Canal in Venice. Hence, to accommodate our watery metaphor, Shakespeare could have acquired some hint for his ideas in symbolically osmotic fashion, as it were, from the Ardenic tragedy. What Shakebag warned of, Shakespeare then accomplished. Turnabout being fair play, the *Wives* acquire their *Arden*(t) revenge (to accommodate a little title-play).

Still another comical association is evident in the attempt to dupe Ford. In the Faversham play, the line "I am by birth a gentle man of bloode" and the phrase "my deare wyves chastitie" following hard upon (1.36,38) are proleptic of similar references to ethics in the duper-duped comedy: "Sir, I am a Gentleman" (2.2.146), "You are a gentleman of excellent breeding" (205–6), and especially the audacious piece of devilish irony, "as I am a Gentleman, you shall, if you will, enjoy *Fords* wife" (229–30). Such verbal comparisons with courtesy and cuckoldry offer a useful overlap between the plays, one surprisingly hitherto unnoticed, especially with regard to the Windsor comedy.

III

Thus far we have scanned some inviting, interconnecting thematic issues between the two plays, but aside from the major correlation between the names *Will, Shake*bag, and *Arden,* have not yet seen the distinctly overt manner by which nomenclature in general supports reasonably close onomatological parallels. Consider now the following table of name-links:

Onomastic Groupings

In *Arden:*	In *Wives:*
Francklin	Frank (Ford)
George (Shakebag)	George (Page)
Alice (Arden)	Alice (Page)
(Black) Will	Will (Page)
Brad(shaw)	Bard(olph)
Fitton	Fenton
Shakebag (Shake bag)	Falstaff (Fall staff)

Are not such labels striking enough to suggest that Shakespeare might be thought of as having had a copy of the former play at his very elbow when he composed the Windsor comedy? A few correlations may appear simply coincidental or vague, but the bulk of them work together. Granted, the dramatist could simply have recollected the same and similar names from the playhouse, his having *acted* in *Arden* for example. Linguistic similarities and transformations need not always be construed only in terms of explicit authorial intent, however, and can be examined objectively in and for themselves.

The names in the Faversham play have not escaped literary skullduggery altogether, having been in part already linked with similar ones in *The Canterbury Tales.* Of primary concern have been the following: *Francklin* (whose epilogue is somewhat like the apologia delivered by Chaucer's Franklin), *Alice* (who has been found "more akin to the Wife of Bath than to Lady Macbeth" [Walz 23–5]), and the painter *Clarke* (whose surname, pronunciation thereof, and final "e" recall Chaucer's *Clerke*). Does *Arden* draw from Chaucer? Let us ponder this parallel circumspectly.

The character of Francklin represents an innovation; he is not found in the main historical source, Holinshed. Faversham, moreover, was "situated on the Chaucerian pilgrimage route" (Walz 29). Ian Ousby and Heather Dubrow in their research relate *Alice* to Chaucer's *Alisoun,* even as Walz does. So the author of the Faversham play may have taken a special interest in the Chaucerian theme of "soverayntee" in marriage. That would bring in the Merchant's tale, too, because it concerns a gullible person being duped by his friends and young wife into overlooking adultery. But is this play satirical in the same way Chaucer is? Hardly so if it is still mainly to be classified as domestic tragedy.

For what it is worth, because Shakespeare himself was at times indebted to Chaucer, any Chaucerian links here could play along with Shakespeare's possible hand in the play. In recent years, the influence of Chaucer in this respect has been taken much more seriously than heretofore, notably by Thompson, Donaldson, Andreas, and Bergeron. Now that *The Two Noble Kinsmen* with its specifically Chaucerian plot is generally recognized as in part Shakespeare's, his use of "The Knight's Tale" elsewhere would follow easily enough. Even *The Merry Wives,* in being to an extent a recognized parody of *amour courtois* manners, looks back to Chaucer's use of courtly love not only in the *Tales,* but also to *Troilus and Criseyde,* which may be a basis for Shakespeare's *Troilus and Cressida.* This Chaucerian romance was a foundation not only for *the* Trojan War drama (this time a satire indeed), but provided an account of how a decent love-letter should be composed. Although the ultimate source for such instruction is clearly in Ovid, such conventionalized instruction is likewise parodied in the letter-writing in both the Faversham and Windsor domestic entertainments.

IV

More specific correlations call for a separate section. The interpolation of a painter in the Faversham story, for one thing, lends itself to a consideration of artistic terms as aesthetic patterns in both *Arden* and *Wives*. In the former, Michael refers to a "painted cloath" (1.153), art work also alluded to in the Falstaff plays, specifically where the Hostess cites such an *objet d'art* around the fat Knight's bed: "'tis painted about with the story of the Prodigall," she claims, recalling the familiar biblical tale of the Prodigal Son in *Wives* (4.5.6–7). Captivatingly enough, similar allusions are also evident in *1 Henry IV* ("you would thinke, that I had a hundred and fiftie totter'd [tattered] Prodigalls"—4.2.31) and *2 Henry IV* ("the Storie of the Prodigall"—2.1.138–9).

Curiously, this imagery can help us to decode the Hostess' quaint description of Falstaff's nose (and surrounding complexion) in his dying moments as a greenish "Table" (*Henry V*, 2.3.16), if the noun be give the Renaissance meaning of *picture* (see Ch 10). It may be that *Arden* can help vindicate this 'crux of cruxes,' owing to these lines: "Because you Painters make but a painting table of a pretty wench, and spoile her beauty with blotting. . . . you Painters, paint lambes" (10.64–8). In both plays, *table* is figuratively related to the picture of a face and is associated with writing with ink ("blotting" in *Arden*, "Pen" in *Henry V*) and incidental bucolic surroundings ("lambs" in *Arden*, "greene fields" in *Henry V*). For our purposes, the main point of such parallels may well be to add another link in the chain associating *Arden* with the world of Falstaff, but, in point of textual fact, they may suggest an immediate source for the unusual imagery in one of the most famous of deathbed scenes (see Ch 10 again and Appendix B).

Because the next chapter relates the crux and Falstaff to heraldry, too, let us consider armorial links between *Arden* and the Windsor comedy. In her 1970 paper for the Faversham Society, Anita Holt observed that "'Evil to him who evil does' or 'To every man his just deserts' might be suitable subtitles to *Arden of Faversham*" (8–9). Now inasmuch as the first of her proposals is a variant of the motto of the Order of the Garter and is ritualistically cited in Old French toward the end of a presumed 'Garter' play, namely *Wives* (5.5.67), in a context which links textually and imagistically with the crux in *Henry V* (see Ch 10), a conveniently parallel *rite de passage* emerges for interrelating these two domestically congruent plays. Further, her allusion to a garter would call forth a main prototype of Falstaff's, Sir John Fastolf. In *1 Henry VI*, Talbot tears the garter from Fastolf's leg because of the latter's cowardice.

Heraldically, *Arden* further alludes to the "Flower-de-Luce," the Anglo-French name of an inn (1.105, 14.345, 411). Similar armorial wordplay, on "a dozen white Luces" and "Lowses," occurs in *Wives* (1.1.14–6), where heraldry might relate to the very occasion of the drama (if performed for an Order of the Garter investiture ceremony). In the New Arden edition of the comedy, we hear that "the Fairy Queen's speech in Act V of the Folio . . . is explained adequately as a direction to the fairies that they must now start getting Windsor Castle, and in particular the Chapel, ready for the installation, by scouring the 'Chaires of Order,' cleaning the coats of arms and other insignia, and 'writing' in flowers the motto of the Order of the Garter, *'Honi Soit Qui Mal-y-Pense'*" (Oliver xlvi). In the Faversham tragedy, the very structure relating to the assassination at backgammon is of the nature of a similar ritual. Further, in that other Arden play, *As You Like It,* heraldry also resonates, the second scene of the fourth act being largely concerned with a song about a father's heraldic crest. Swearing by one's "Honor the Mustard was naught" (1.2.60–1) refracts the parodic motto "Not Without Mustard," often taken as Jonson's gibe at the motto of the Stratford "upstart" on his newly acquired coat of arms, "Non Sanz Droict."[52]

Now let us tackle more mundane matters. The very *grotesquerie* of the Windsor and Faversham plots connects them in terms of at least negative evidence. The brashness of an inveterate scoundrel's being in love is like a parody of true love. In both studies in domesticity (of an irregular sort), the spouses behave in an analogously predatory manner. Those in the comedy look good to some modern feminists rather more than Mistress Arden does (more than one dissertation has claimed that *Wives* was indeed a pro-feminist play), but Alice and Lady Macbeth have been compared often enough before as villainesses.

A few pertinent numismatic, gastronomic, and bio-psychological allusions in the Faversham play warrant some consideration too. Passing references to angels (gold coins stamped with the device of the archangel Michael) in both *Arden* and *Wives* are of good value in providing us with further ironic overtones,

---

[52]On this resonance, see my essay *"Brassica Hirta: Non Sanz Droict* Re-Echoed." For further research on the relevance of heraldry to the play, see S. Viswanathan (1980) and especially William Green, who relates the heraldic motto to the dating of the play, and the book by Jeanne Addison Roberts, Ch 2: "The Date: A Major Revision." (Yet R. S. White has now questioned this date.)

coincidental though they may appear. Michael in the tragedy, for example, is no angel, and the fat knight as a demoted angel in the comedy puns on such coinage: "Now, the report goes, she has all the rule of her husbands Purse: he hath a legion of Angels" (1.3.48–9). True, in the tragedy the monetary reference offers no obvious wordplay (2.88–9), yet the hint that fallen angels of *some* kind are at work is calculated. Fascinatingly, Shakespeare punned on "angels" in *King John* as well, this time in conjunction with what seems to be a haunting recollection of *Arden:* "shake the bags / Of hoording Abbots, imprisoned angells / Set at Libertie" (3.3.7–9). *Shake the bags / Shakebag.* If, as has been suggested earlier, Shakespeare himself enacted the role of Shakebag (with Will Kemp playing Black Will), would not the phrase "shake the bags" followed at once by "angells" have had an ironic effect upon knowledgeable members of the Elizabethan audience? Perhaps not: Memory and internal parallel-chasing are a scholar's occupation primarily; but, as a sign of conscious or unconscious verbal associations in Shakespeare, they do make some sense.

Regarding gastronomics, let us take note, with yet another nod to Sir John, his gluttony notwithstanding, that the most famous allusion to nutrition in the canon is probably Pistol's to making the world one's "Oyster" (*Wives*, 2.2.2). The literary gourmet should be more than nourished, then, by the braggart Black Will's mentioning the same shellfish in the Faversham tragedy (17.5–7). For such a reference is scarcely inconsequential there. In his pamphlet on the play, C. E. Donne called due attention to the renown of Faversham's succulent seafood (still in repute today), observing that "the Dutch give a preference to these oysters of the Faversham grounds before all others along the coast" (17). Is not what is behind that superlative also thereby a pitch for Pistol's notorious "worldly oyster" throwaway remark to Sir John? If not 'the world,' therefore, at least the locale of Faversham laid profitable claim to making the dual oyster association palatable not only for tourists but also for avid scholars and theatergoers.

With apt psychology, we then venture upon Galenic allusions to temperament in Elizabethan times. Already the opening lines of the tragedy introduce the somber note of melancholia, thus setting forth the macabre tone of events in Faversham. Francklin tells Arden to rid himself of his unhealthy complexion:

Arden, cheere up thy spirits and droup no more. . .
Leave this melancholy moode (1.1–8)

The most immediate parallel to such despondency occurs at the beginning of *The Merchant of Venice*, where again the titular figure admits of gloomy thoughts: "In sooth I know not why I am so sad, / It wearies me; you say it wearies you" (1–2). In this respect, Venice is the location for such similar lines as with Faversham. Falstaff has his disconsolate moments as well, admitting to being "as Melancholly as a Gyb-Cat, or a lugg'd Beare" (*1 Henry IV*, 1.2.68). The old ruffian is finally said by others to die in a sad way, too, of a broken heart (its being "fracted and corroborate"), telling at least superficially of a form of melancholia (see Ch 10). In *Wives*, Mistress Ford accosts her husband in a manner also reminiscent of *Arden:* "How now, (sweet Frank) why art thou melancholly?" (2.1.136).

In sum, given these parallels as valid, evidently Shakespeare would have seen the Faversham tragedy, may easily have acted in it, and so could have been more deeply involved, even plausibly to a certain extent in its construction, and we shall consider this from an evaluatory standpoint in the next section.

V

Let us now try to judge the overall critical framework in which *Arden* has been at times said to be related to the Shakespearean canon. The objective will finally be to show that the most important parallels are with *Wives*, not so much with other dramaturgy (*Macbeth* being a partial exception), especially because of its similar imagery relating to roguery. To my knowledge, this kinship has heretofore been overlooked by the scholarly world, i.e., no one has carefully correlated *Arden* and *Wives* as containing rogue imagery before. But we can also turn to other dramas. Parallels with additional plays can then make the association with *Wives* more plausible.

First, does the Faversham tragedy in any respect herald *Titus Andronicus* as another early play? For an *entrée*, strong parallels have also been discerned between *Titus* and *Edmund Ironside*, leading to the general critical conclusion that the author of the latter was very likely indebted to the former. A certain use of Seneca in both *Titus* and *Arden* is obvious enough, but these connections are very general. With regard to the notorious dismemberment of the human body in *Titus*, Wine tells us in his introduction to the best edition of *Arden* that "one of the play's most recurrent images is that of the maiming and destroying of the human body" (lxv). The most helpful aspect paradoxically is negative: *Titus* shows that Shakespeare was capable of producing an artistic horror show; *Arden* reveals an author who did not shirk from introducing even as controversial an item as a poisoned crucifix. The latter bit of seemingly anti-clerical trapping may appear alien to Shakespeare's general style and more reminiscent of Marlowe or later of Webster. But fear is indeed raised also in *King John* (5.6.23) that the monarch has been poisoned by a monk—likewise an irreverent suggestion. And Juliet has a similar fear. Of course, attacks on corruption in the Church were common throughout this time period. Yet Shakespeare evidently muted the strong anti-Romanism of *The Troublesome Raigne* in writing *King John,* as is usually recognized. Hence let us consider that both the poisoned painting and crucifix in *Arden* were not Shakespeare's original idea, but that he could finally manage putting up with them.

Further, both *Titus* and *Arden* happen to contain *Lamentable* in their titular descriptions (as, for that matter, does *Romeo and Juliet* in its original form). If *Arden* represents a collaboration (a view we may be inclined to uphold), it is intriguing that another, somewhat later domestic tragedy had a similar title and *was* truly a collaboration: *The Lamentable Tragedy of the Page of Plymouth.* (Were these authors plausibly following the lead of *Arden* as then an earlier collaboration?) What strikes us principally about *Arden, Titus,* and *Romeo and Juliet* is their relative *naïveté,* their emotional stress on sheer pathos rather than more dignified awe. Although any alliance between *Arden*'s ritualistic paradox, "And holy church rites make us two, but one," and Friar Laurence's "Till Holy Church incorporate two in one" (2.6.37) may merely be in the nature of a unitive *topos,* such verbal collocation is at least momentarily arresting. A relatively unusual term, "over-plus," happens to occur only thrice in the known canon of Shakespeare but happens also to be present in *Arden*. Other such curious verbal parallels can be adduced.

Some Shakespeareans have correlated the Faversham play as well to the Great Tragedies, a debatable enterprise since it does lack a certain maturity (in spite of what has been deemed its structured "warp and woof"). The Penguin editor feels confident in correlating *King Lear* and *Arden,* especially because of their similar "poise" and a memorable parallel in *Arden* with the familiar "flies to wanton boys" lamentation. Both tragedies, moreover, make telling topical reference to exorcism; both deal with Kent; both reveal certain socially conscious themes. (Because of the references to Kent, mention can be made again of the counter-argument that Marlowe was the sole author because of a certain Kentish atmosphere, that playwright having come from Canterbury. But then the touches of anti-Romanism in the play need not recall Marlowe, albeit Hotson's research has made clear that Marlowe was an anti-Catholic spy, but rather would pre-echo *Lear,* again in terms of Shakespeare's source material and his probable use of Harsnett's *Egregious Popish Impostures* and its study of exorcism [on which see Muir].)

What may be of greater moment is not the Faversham tragedy's relation to any of the great plays alone, but indeed to *at least three of them concomitantly.* (We might once more compare Robert Ellrodt's finding Shakespeare's use of three of Montaigne's essays in their original sequence evidence of his use of Florio's translation when he wrote *Hamlet.*) Thus *Arden* connects not only with *Lear* but *Othello* and *Macbeth,* the Moorish tragedy being the innovative Stratford genius' best domestic tragedy. In accusing not his wife of adultery but the rival who cuckolded him, Master Arden becomes virtually the antithesis of the Moor in this respect.[53] Swinburne is memorable for finding Alice Arden akin to Lady Macbeth "by right of weird sisterhood" (Bullen xv); he playfully mocked the idea of Shakespeare as author by a coy reference to "Black *Will Shake*bag" Wine lxxxviii—italics added). One link between the two tragedies is the presumed witchcraft, Alice's incantation on washing away blood which "will not out" that foreshadows Lady Macbeth's oft-cited malediction: "Out, damned spot!" (5.1.32).[54] Still, this language and incident were not recorded in Holinshed; it took someone with a little innovative genius to introduce it into the Faversham play. Was that Shakespeare? Hardin Craig, for one, unhesitatingly confirmed *Arden* as representing "a masterpiece of psychological interpretation, which foreshadows *Macbeth*" (81-2).

---

[53] Here *Arden*'s plot resembles better *Macbeth,* an analogy documented by Charles Knight, Allen, Craig, Youngsblood, and incidentally later by me.

[54] To be fair, though, bloodstains which will not wash away are traceable also to folk legendary in reference to the 'magical' detection of a homicide (Marsden).

In yet another sense, though, *Arden* may relate to *Hamlet* (making the link with consecutive tragedies four rather than three in number). Wine comments on how the dramatist(s) "prepared with obvious care the lengthy delay leading to Arden's murder" (lxxv). Is there a foreshadowing here of the Danish Prince's long procrastination in killing Claudius? Would then the *-ham,* say, in *Arden's* full title look forward (invertedly) to *Ham-* in *Hamlet*? (We might again compare how Hamlet's name derived from Shakespeare's son's and that the *Arden* of the title also connects with his mother.) All this may be fascinating on a certain level, but it is rather speculative.

Returning to *Macbeth,* we notice that the two professional varlets, Black Will and Shakebag, are not infrequently set alongside the hired assassins in the Scottish tragedy. They all expound on their devious designs in elevated poetic style, one a bit too high-flown for a purely 'naturalistic' effect, thereby revealing not only a negative parallel but presumed lack of skill in the writing of a relatively inexperienced playwright. True, *Arden* is sometimes eulogized for its "intrinsic merit and *maturity* at a time when Elizabethan dramatic form was still a thing of experiment and trial and error" (Sturgess 21), but much of the characterization is not very developed, and certain discrepancies in style are all too evident. If the famous Alice-Mosby quarrel is in high enough style, the use of terse wit much of the time is on a pretty lowly or lighthearted level. Naturally such contrast enlivens the drama somewhat and may not be essentially a defect, but it is nonetheless rather rarely found in the most accomplished masterpieces, though compare, for example, the rowdy *Henry VI* family quarrels. Much is made of this point in the early eighteenth-century criticism of *Arden* by Henry Collyer, to which we shall return in due course.

Now if the play was at all by Shakespeare, how can we explain its exclusion from the Folio? The answer that comes most readily to mind is that Heminges and Condell probably decided not to include doubtful collaborations or may well have lacked access to copy. To take an analogy, *Edward III* is sometimes nowadays thought to be at least partly in Shakespeare's hand, but it was also excluded. In fact, the 1623 collection likewise excluded *Pericles* and *The Two Noble Kinsmen,* also collaborations, so exclusion was hardly a solid criterion for denying Shakespeare part authorship. Another answer that makes a certain amount of good sense is that it was an 'actors' play' (or showpiece) (Sturgess 25). Such an inviting label could explain a limitation of the characterization, why Arden's character is not drawn forcibly enough to offer cogent motivation for his wife and others in wanting him disposed of. For Arden's real-life villainy, as depicted in Holinshed, is much clearer. Let us not discount the verdict of A. H. Bullen: "Even if we do not admit the theory of Shakespeare's authorship, it is in the highest degree probable that *Arden* was one of the plays which received correction and revision from Shakespeare's hand" (xvi). He felt that the Stratford genius was especially responsible for Alice's "passionate entreaty" in the quarrel and reconciliation scene with Mosby, that commencing with "Look on me *Mosby,* or Ile kill my selfe. . . ." Bullen may have been too sanguine for our tastes, but he did have a valid vision, cautious though it was.

Then there was A. F. Hopkinson's position that "scant use of rhyme in *Arden*" suggests not only a novice's hand but paradoxically ties in with analogous effects in Shakespeare's *mature* drama: "It is singular that the first and last of Shakespeare's plays should exhibit a distaste for rhyme: the works of no other dramatist can show the same peculiarity" (xxxiii). However, when Hopkinson then said that this singularity suggests Shakespeare's sole hand in the apocryphal play, he was going rather far. True, he had a point in citing the earliest known allusion to Shakespeare as his being able to "bombast out a blank verse" like the best of poets. With insufficient supportive evidence from comparison with other playwrights, however, the blank-verse argument is too thin to sustain much weight. It could, for example, also be used as a criterion in favor of Marlowe's authorship.

A. C. Swinburne credited Marlowe with being both the "creator of English blank verse" and the "father of English tragedy," so it might seem natural for the Canterbury author to be the originator also of the first English domestic tragedy. But then Marlowe, so far as is known, had no links with the Queen's Men. True, Bakeless' standard biography makes out a strong case for a Shakespeare-Marlowe connection. The subject-matter here, though, does not appear at all akin to what would have attracted the inventor of the "mighty line." It is scarcely grandiose. As noted earlier, the *Arden* playwright's failure to make use of a trapdoor at the end shows that he was uncognizant of local tradition, and hence was probably not a Kentish man.

The modern Revels editor, M. L. Wine, has accumulated some arresting evidence in favor of Shakespeare as possible author, but he prudently stopped short of making any positive claim, citing the understandable difficulty in working with what he considered to be a contaminated text. Yet we may ask whether the text of this play *is* conclusively contaminated. The theory that it constitutes a memorial reconstruction has hardly been proved. (Nor has the theory of memorial reconstructions as a whole, though many conservative scholars still adhere to at least a modified form of it.) The introduction to the Scolar Press edition, for example, draws the prime conclusion that the general coherence of this text is suggestive of a 'good' quarto set by a single compositor whose most disconcerting habit was that of setting prose as verse. So unless someone can clearly come up with some identifiable and distinguishable characteristics by which the theory of such reconstruction can be tested, how can one tell whether a given text is a short play made long by revision, or a long play shortened by some other undefined process? If the current fashion for accepting such reconstruction as a valid principle is thought of as canceling believable parallels with Shakespeare's text, the same mode could be blamed for singling out too many parallels. One logical position could then be that if the parallels are not exact, they still are close *enough,* although in the 'original' text they would presumably be even closer. Wine's reluctance to follow through with his belief that *Arden* is the play from the Apocrypha that most closely approximates Shakespeare's work thus is revealed in a questionable apologia, in his acceptance of the reconstruction theory; although it can be applied, as I have tried now to show, to reach the opposite conclusion. (That *Arden* is clearly already the *best* of the apocryphal plays has been an accepted conclusion critically for many years.)

Several other scholars who have linked *Arden* to the Stratford newcomer can also be cited. MacDonald P. Jackson wrote an Oxford thesis on the subject; it argues directly in favor of Shakespearean authorship on the basis of verbal patterning, but this approach is now commonly thought to be inconclusive in itself. In his flat dismissal of Shakespeare as author, Schoenbaum overlooked Jackson's thesis, as Wine has already pointed out in passing. As for the uncompromising ascription of the tragedy to the "upstart," that view dates back to Tieck. What has not been so well remembered is that Goethe, too, claimed the play as Shakespeare's, and he had an understanding of style at least in the finer sense of that word, if at the same time he was hardly a textual authority.[55]

The best reading of the available evidence leads us to conclude the probability of some kind of multiple authorship, even though, admittedly, that assignment would at first appear to compound the problem. Still, the play was published anonymously, and one good reason for that lack of identification could well have been that the play was a collaboration of actors' efforts involving several hands as well as apprentice work among them. Let us recall once again another anonymous *Lamentable Tragedy,* which clearly was also a well-recognized collaboration, namely that of *The Page of Plymouth.*

VI

In summing up *Arden* in relation to *Wives,* we now return once again to the domestic patternings. As the first domestic drama of Elizabethan times, the Faversham tragedy bears clear relation to a play which Jeanne Addison Roberts in her fine, recent book on the subject has dubbed "domestic comedy," following Leggatt's term, 'citizen drama' (56, 143), namely the Windsor comedy. For that matter, it happened to be also the Avon bard's *first* such comedy in the domestic mode. Thus, in key respects, *Arden* is to *Wives* as first domestic tragedy is to first domestic comedy. Inauguration indeed.

Secondly, the *Arden* style has its affinities with Shakespeare's regular mode, though it is also different in various respects. But we should bear in mind that a play like *Henry VI, Part I* also shows some major discrepancies with Shakespeare's style as found elsewhere and still is generally thought to be entirely his. Thus, "the main body of the play, especially the opening act, is in a style unlike anything of Shakespeare's that we know" (Mincoff 287). For that matter, *The Phoenix and the Turtle* is also far removed in format from other poetry he wrote.

---

[55] Such an attribution by a fellow humanist and genius has been given short shrift if only because later German belletrists have felt less leonine, notably Warnke and Pröscholdt in their edition and Miksch in his Breslau dissertation.

Thirdly, to say that Alice Arden is such a nefarious type that the son of Mary Arden would have *avoided* wordplay on her name if only for self-conscious reasons seems basically fatuous. For if we wish to do so, we could also find a close parallel with his mother's original Catholic faith in Alice's final lines: "And let me meditate upon my Saviour Christ, / Whose bloode must save me for the bloode I shed" and "Let my death make amends for all my sinnes" (18.10–11, 33). In themselves, of course, such grandiose parallels may seem a bit *too* theatrical. Although the overall tragic effect is retributive, however, the outcome is steadfastly Christian.

True, as editor Wine points out, the play notably omits Holinshed's point that Alice "received the sacrament" with Mosby before the murder of Arden. And that, taken by itself, is hardly very respectful of Christian ritual. Still, although the Eucharist in question presumably was not Roman Catholic, its deletion in this context could be taken as at least an oblique token of respect for the Old Faith. If to make much of religion in this context is doubtful, at any rate we can defend ourselves against those who might use the religious issue as an argument *against* any valid Shakespearean association.

In a similar manner, Shakespeare need not have been held back in accepting at least nominal affiliation of the Will-Shake(bag) team and his own name, especially because variants of his surname had been common anyway. If he accepted an 'echo' of his Arden family name in the subject-matter of the play, even if only coincidental, he could have also gone along with 'echoes' of his own name in other characters. After all, he later did not refrain from looking lightheartedly at himself when he had Sir Hugh Evans, in *Wives,* put little Master William through his paces with the latter's mother keeping watch (see William Jones). The same sort of case, again involving the effect of a woman kibitzing on the sidelines, would be evident with *Arden.* In any event, the titles of the two plays, as if to clinch the point, already convey a prepositional correlation: "of Faversham" / "of Windsor." Hence one locale, so to speak, became a literary suburb of the other.

A final demurrer is in order. We need hardly go so far as did G. B. Kuitert, who daringly asserted, "Struck with the thought that his mother, an Arden of Wilmecote, might have been a kinswoman to the gentleman of Feversham, Shakespeare joined with the unknown dramatist" (Warnke and Pröscholdt xx). It is difficult to believe, for example, that the taste of the Stratford genius was responsible for introducing the painter Clarke. We have but to consider the negative criticism of Henry Collyer (1739), some of which is very just:

> As to the play of *Arden* ... it is supposed to have been writ a Hundred and Fifty Years; and when it was wrote, it was done by several ... Hands, for the lowest ruffianly Parts speaks in the same Stile as the best Characters. Besides, they have added so many base and false Things to the True, that, in short, they have almost destroy'd the Whole; such as a Painter, to paint a Picture that should poison him with looking at it. All through the Story they have represented [Arden as] a very just, mild, good-temper'd Man; and in the Wills of Feversham it is said, but one Year before he was kill'd, he gave great Gifts to the Poor, which the Town now enjoys. ... (5)

This accusation, so to speak, which was mainly concerned with a puppet show based on *Arden* rather than the play itself, suggests a plot not entirely befitting Shakespeare's talent, to say the least, but still does not interfere with the notion that several hands were at work. The key passage "it was done by several ... Hands, for the lowest ruffianly Parts speaks in the same Stile as the best Characters," though a bit exaggerated, presents one of the best cases for multiple authorship on the apprentice level. The tendency to avoid considering the play as the work of more than a single hand derives probably from overreaction to the so-called 'disintegrators' like Fleay of the last century. It was thought that assigning a work to multiple authorship was an easy way out which tended to 'disintegrate' the structure of the work by way of explaining discordant styles. Yet, in the present case, the argument for Shakespeare's possible (though hardly proven) involvement would point rather to integration (that is, in the canon or in terms of his being the guiding spirit which would have shaped it up).

Whatever our final verdict on the nature of the play and its authorship, *Arden* ought to be taken seriously. It is well recognized, for example, that it had a solid dramatic influence later, for instance on *A Warning For Fair Women* (Sturgess 19), so why not also more immediately on the Avon genius? Indeed, Hopkinson provides an imposingly lengthy list of parallels in his edition, one too specialized to consider in detail here. What counts mainly in the overall parallel with *The Merry Wives* is the shared domestic realism, something new at the time. As editor Keith Sturgess has suggested, "the best internal evidence of Shakespeare's authorship is the realistic characterization of the play, quite unlike that of *The*

Spanish Tragedy or of most of Marlowe's work" (21). *The Merry Wives*, in providing similar domestic realism on the level of comedy rather than tragedy, indicates that this Stratford "Crow" would not have been out of his field in sharing in the creation of the very "best of the apocryphal plays" (Muir, as cited by Wine lxxxiii), not to mention the creation of the first domestic tragedy. In summing up, the main purport of this chapter has been to reveal the aesthetic interplay between *Arden* and *Wives*, in particular, so that one drama can be seen as leading to the other—not to find a skeleton key for unlocking the complicated authorship question altogether. Moreover, the influences upon *Arden* may be correlated with the influences upon the Stratford bard, so that in effect two things akin to the same thing may be related to each other. For even as the debt of Shakespeare to Spenser's *The Faerie Queene* has occasioned book-length treatment by Potts, so "the composition of *Arden* was influenced by *The Faerie Queene*" (Coyle 146–7).

As a coda, it might be mentioned that a fairly recent production of *Arden* has proposed Shakespearean authorship, namely that presented at the Globe Playhouse, Los Angeles, by the Shakespeare Society of America, July–August 1985. According to the review in *Shakespeare Quarterly*, "Producer Thad Taylor suggested in his advertising and notes that the young Shakespeare had indeed had a hand in the writing or rewriting of the play" (245). The reviewer, Joseph H. Stodder, like myself, was still skeptical yet felt, nonetheless, that some kind of Shakespearean involvement was at least prudentially worth entertaining.

Brief Synopsis

1. *Arden* was an 'actors' showpiece.'
2. Such a practical play suggests actors' involvement in its composition.
3. Circumstantial evidence suggests that the company was the Queen's Men. *The True Tragedie* also links with them.
4. Shakespeare's early company was probably the same. The notion that he worked with Pembroke's Men and so could have written sonnets to young William Pembroke does not tally with Sonnet 13 and its reference to the Youth's father's decease.

5. Shakespeare could thereby have had a hand somewhat in the composition and thus could have more easily 'echoed' this work in *The Merry Wives* especially, not to mention *Macbeth,* etc.
6. A seventeenth-century bookseller's list now corroborates this affiliation. It was not known to most previous attributors.
7. An eighteenth-century critic argues convincingly for multiple styles extant here and thus multiple authorship. So probably Shakespeare, if he was involved, was only collaboratively so.
8. Parallels in name-play and other wordplay are too striking to be entirely coincidental, so that Shakespeare must have at least *acted* in the domestic tragedy. If so, the least he would have done was to interpolate some characteristic lines or images.

PART VII
THE CRUX OF CRUXES

Scene 3

Enter Pistol, Nym, Bardolph, Boy, and Hostess.

HOSTESS 'Prythee, honey-sweet Husband, let me bring thee to Staines.
PISTOL No: for my manly Heart doth ern. —Bardolph, Be blithe. —Nym, rouse thy vaunting Veins.
—Boy, bristle
Thy Courage up. For Falstaff he is dead,
And we must ern therefore.
BARDOLPH Would I were with him, wheresome'er he is, either in Heaven or in Hell.
HOSTESS Nay sure he's not in Hell. He's in Arthur's Bosom if ever man went to Arthur's Bosom: 'a made a finer end, and went away and it had been any Christom Child; 'a parted ev'n just between Twelve and One, ev'n at the Turning of the Tide. For after I saw him fumble with the Sheets, and play with Flowers, and smile upon his Finger's end, I knew there was but one way: for his Nose was as sharp as a Pen, and a Table of Green Fields. "How now, Sir John," quoth I, "what Man, be a' good Cheer." So 'a cried out, "God, God, God!" three or four times. Now I, to comfort him, bid him 'a should not think of

Excerpt from *The Guild Shakespeare,* Volume 6, edited by John F. Andrews. Copyright ©1989 by Doubleday Book & Music Clubs, Inc. Reprinted by permission of Doubleday Book & Music Clubs, Inc., New York, N.Y. 10167.

Chapter 10

The Submerged Heraldic Emblem in Falstaff's Last Moments

With all the ado concerning the most time-honored textual crux in literary history, namely in the report of Falstaff's death, which in the First Folio of 1623 sums up his sere complexion in such a seemingly curious or Mannerist fashion, namely "his nose was as sharpe as a Pen, and [it was] a Table [i.e. picture] of greene fields" (*Henry V,* 2.3.16–7), it is curious that a major source of the problem in Shakespeare has been overlooked until fairly recently. The crucial line has been glossed in Joseph Rann's eighteenth-century edition as "his nose was as sharp as a pen—and as green as grass" (Fogel 491). Rann retained *babbled* in some form in his text, referring to "Table" only in a footnote, but Nicholas Rowe accepted the "Table" reading in his text proper. It was Lewis Theobald, a notorious emendator, who was responsible for the modern *babbled* reading. (Yet the primal word, used long in the theater, has now been restored in the Guild Shakespeare edition. See the reproduction on the opposite page.)

What has been bypassed till recently is the connection with an analogous passage in another Shakespearean play, also involving the rotund rogue and plausibly written before *Henry V,* though not necessarily so, namely *The Merry Wives.* Phyllis N. Braxton's note on the subject, which does not specifically deal with the crux as such, now deserves a follow-up. True, the previous small-talk of the emotional reporter of Sir John's death, the Hostess, as found in the other Falstaff plays, had been considered in a general way, for example by F. W. Bateson. Some analogous pictorial allusions have also been enlisted (for instance, the word "Table" in the crux as meaning *picture*). Bardolph's and

Falstaff's complementary nasal features, as it were, have come in for comparison, as by Gary Taylor in an Appendix to his recent Oxford edition of the play. Most telling of all, perhaps, Dame Quickly's decided penchant for pre-Malapropisms (what Leslie Hotson has dubbed *bienapropisms*) has been duly noted in relation to her exaggerating; this was done by Ephim Fogel, the leading conservative adherent of the Folio reading, and Andrews includes "Table" in his Guild edition of *Henry V*. But Phyllis Braxton is the first, to my knowledge, who has happened to recognize the import of the proximity of the parallel between the reported scene in *Henry V* and the scenario at the end of *Wives*, 5.5.68–71. We might scrutinize that correlation once more (see also a documentary summary in Ch 1).

Stressing the close juxtaposition of several basic words—*green, field(s), flowers*—in both dramas, Phyllis Braxton plainly showed how they occur in approximately the same time and space sequence. Taken in themselves, naturally, these simple pastoral words may appear to be all too commonplace and even coincidental; but she then added to them several more pieces of astute, factual, textual evidence which provide substantial weight. First, she found *Pen* in the Henry play a virtual, unconscious (at least thereby also orthographic) echo of "PENse" (her capitalization) in the Windsor comedy, issuing as it does from the familiar motto of the Order of the Garter, *'Honi soit qui mal y Pense,"* as found at the end also of *Sir Gawayne and the Grene Knight*.[56] Secondly, she observed that the concatenation of the four terms reappears, even more curiously, in the later drama, though in reverse order. Such a 'mirror effect,' too, could have had an unconscious basis. Thirdly, as if this were not noticeable enough, she offered yet a further (highly probable, because so unusual), textual connection: The somewhat less common phrase "fingers' end" in the deathbed scene likewise has become, in effect, an 'echo' of the analogous collocation "finger end" in *Wives* (and not many lines later than the Garter speech), the Hostess adding, "With trial fire touch me his finger end" (5.5.85).

Other fascinating correlations, moreover, were evident. Not only do both scenes involve the Hostess and Knight as principal subjects, but the action happens to occur "at the identical hour—between midnight and one in the

---

[56] As I have relevantly posited in a paper in *Arthurian Interpretations*, I, 35–8, Shakespeare could have been indebted to this romance in other respects.

morning." Finally, the inherent symbolism in the two episodes is compared in some detail, but that need not be recapitulated here. Clearly any true student of Falstaff's dying moments would be seriously remiss in not taking into strict account these new, provocative findings, ones which ought to have been examined closely long ago. Although Falstaff's final humiliation in the comedy has been accepted before as a mode of symbolic death anticipating his physical one as reported in *Henry V*,[57] Phyllis Braxton's analysis is still useful for further analysis. Even the somewhat tangential points that she makes, such as finding the characters in the comedy also somehow transposed from their historical setting to fit into a later one, "to be present at Windsor during the reign of Queen Elizabeth I," can have a bearing on the celebrated crux in the history play, as we shall shortly observe. Even the name *Falstaff* is to be seen as heraldic wordplay on Shakespeare's armory (whereby a falling staff would lightly 'echo' crossed spears), no doubt influenced by Jonson's well-known heraldic punning ("Not Without Mustard" as bearing on *Non Sanz Droict*). Some self-irony was doubtless healthily involved.

One matter that Phyllis Braxton did not take into account must presently be confronted, if only because most readers would be inclined to inquire about its plausible relevance as an added effect. The issue is whether the implications of her notable parallels have any bearing on validating the Folio reading of the crux of cruxes. Yet this problem she apparently declined here to consider, for she interpolated instead the more or less standard Theobald emendation (*babld*), modernized in the Pelican edition as "babbled," even though no evidence exists that Shakespeare ever used this word (however spelt) in print. (Nor, as Leslie Hotson showed, did he write *babble of*. His few usages of the noun *babble* in *Twelfth Night,* where it is preceded by "vain bibble-," and once similarly in *Henry V,* 4.1.71, are extremely negative in tone.) Thus the eighteenth-century emendation is at least open to question once again. As Oliffe Richmond suggested, if the fat rogue were contentedly babbling away about green fields or pastureland, either those of his youth or from the twenty-third psalm, why would the Hostess

---

[57]I have pointed this out in my preliminary study, "Falstaff's Green Sickness Unto Death." See Ch 1 n3. But I was anticipated.

have had to arouse him with "what man? be a good cheare"? Logically, that makes sense.

Now if Mistress Quickly's long speech in the comedy formally praising the Order of the Garter, its accouterments, and its motto (a key caveat incidentally bearing on the latent theme of the play) basically relates to her description of Sir John's demise as likewise containing heraldic overtones, however metaphorically, then her espousal of the term "Table" there, if partly then meant in the acceptable sense of picture (or tableau) of armorial effects, would clearly, in turn, hark back to her earlier, pictorial, crest-like account in the history play. Such a correlation, after all, represents more than mere circumstantial evidence; it amounts to external (as opposed to simply internal) proof insofar as it would reflect on an *occasion* for the former play; it vindicates her having sophistication enough earlier to employ a more or less élitist phrase later. Along with this might be mentioned the quaint fact that the rotund rascal himself indulged in heraldic allusion, as in his well-known reference, in his familiar soliloquy on honor, to "a mere scutcheon" (5.1.139). Because this technical term signified a coat of arms borne at a funeral, it subliminally could adumbrate the heraldic effects in the account of his own death. Compare also the well-received viewpoint that Falstaff's reference to "I in the clear sky of fame" (*2 Henry IV*, 4.3.49) was so similar to Horace's *Odes*, I, xii, 46–49, that A. H. Gilbert considered that Shakespeare might have come upon the concept in a collection of *imprese*, mottos associated with emblems with possible heraldic connections. (In May 1613 Shakespeare helped his good friend Burbage devise an *impresa* for the Earl of Rutland, a friend of Southampton's.)

This is not to imply that the entire meaning of "Table" in this context was simply heraldic; probably to many members of the audience the common substantive would have had its more obvious, ordinary overtones (perhaps, though, with a connotative hint of the geographical meaning, as in *table-land,* for which see *OED, table,* sb. 13b) and suggested that the corpulent old rapscallion was, in effect, a veritable picture (or 'spitten image' in the later idiom) of green, if not gangrenish, death. That condition plausibly was due to an acutely jaundiced complexion brought on by cirrhosis of the liver (due to his alcoholism), as has been suggested more than once, notably by two scholarly physicians, Dr.

Chambers Davidson and (more prominently of late) Dr. Henry Janowitz.[58] Other psychological and even theological connotations may truly be considered as well to enrich the meaning if one likes, for example the green effects associated with unrequited love, presumably here Platonic (the standoffish King it was, after all, who in his prudence was said in the play to have been responsible for having 'killed' Falstaff's heart, hence aesthetically accounting in part for his greenish makeup or seeming iron-deficiency anemia). This is not even to mention the common biblical apothegm that "All flesh *is* grasse" (and, in the same context incidentally, "of the field") from Isaiah 40.6. This biblical allusion is a far cry from that to the twenty-third psalm usually enlisted with the standard "babld" emendation. (For good measure, other psalms, 37.2 ["like grass they quickly wither"] or 102.5 ["like grass is my heart"], may be better accommodated here instead.) Even this biblical echoing could easily have been derived from an emblem. For example, in Sir George's 'Palace' in Curloss, Scotland, appears a ceiling of emblems, a collection which I have seen, including one with the first line of a *subscriptio* "All flesche is grasse, and withereth lyk the haye" (dated ca. 1597); it is also found in the familiar Whitney emblem collection of 1586, where contextual reference made to laughing and dying links also with Falstaff (217).

On the level of popular culture, a ballad-like song then common with the refrain about death being even "greener than the grass" can be enlisted.[59] Indeed, authorities from Greek and Egyptian times on down, notably Hippocrates, had associated a greenish (usually yellowish-green) pallor with a dying complexion, one that could then easily be taken hyperbolically on the stage. The Hippocratic account involves the commonplace that Greeks have a somewhat greenish complexion traditionally to begin with. Rather than a greenish Greek, as it were, Falstaff on his deathbed happened to represent a jaundiced Briton. (But, among others, J. D. Wilson has still related him to a Greek, Socrates.)

---

[58]Although the medical term *cirrhosis of the liver* is post-Renaissance, Shakespeare did make reference to jaundice, and liver ailments were legion. See my clustered papers on the general subject cited in Ch 1 n3. Jaundice could be not merely yellow, but greenish-yellow.

[59]I have suggested this association elsewhere in my *Shakespeare Jahrbuch* (East) contribution.

Yet what may have set off this whole chain reaction of associations could well enough have amounted to something fairly factual and simple, but still involving a certain sophistication: the submerged heraldic suggestion. The close parallel with the passage in *Wives* shows that such urbane terminology need not have been too remote for the Hostess. Because the argument that the elliptical "Table" reading would have been too complicated for her is one that I have heard cited as an objection to accepting the Folio reading (though the commonly elided expression "it was" might well be thought of as a single, more dialectal, "'twas"), knowledge of her as previously having shown a certain sophistication really can help. The notion that ellipsis was such a commonplace in Renaissance times was a major point in Fogel's original defense of the Folio reading. For almost anything was then accommodated elliptically. The closest parallel with the crux is the Hostess' comparison of the human body to greenery before, in *2 Henry IV*, specifically in a passage which offers the dialectal contraction in a slightly different form: "an [as if] 'twere an aspen leaf" (2.4.100–1).

In sum, the basic argument supporting a heraldic reading of the crux of cruxes has been aptly set forth already by Hilda Hulme in reference to the Hostess: "she sees the pen as a device on a coat of arms, the field vert translated into green fields, and . . . she expected her hearers to pick up some topical reference to an actual coat of arms or an inn sign" (*Explorations* 142). Then, in her helpful documentation, Hilda Hulme noted that "*Table* is found as a 'surface on which a picture is painted' [see *OED* sb 3], sonnet 24, 2; *field*, common enough in its heraldic sense from c. 1400, has this meaning in *Lucrece* 58." Admittedly, she boldly proposed then still another, variant reading of the "Table" context, one which seems rather problematical; she evoked the image of a pen on a writing desk, suggesting a mixed metaphor (which Taylor in his aforementioned Appendix recognized as a bit of nonsense), and that can be dispensed with here as simply stretching things. Compare John Andrews' gloss in his annotation at the end of this chapter. Worth retaining in mind is the Renaissance commonplace that a literary figure was often a 'speaking figure,' even as a painting could be a dumb poem. Shakespeare alluded to that in *The Taming of the Shrew*, Induction, 45; *The Rape of Lucrece*, 1366–1456; *Timon of Athens*, 1.1.26–38; *Cymbeline*, 2.4.66–79; and *The Winter's Tale*, 5.2.89–98. Also sonnet 2 relates a "field" to the human face, thus tying in with the allusion to "table" in sonnet 24.

Further, Hilda Hulme's heraldic emblem is based on an altogether new emendation; she inferred that the dramatist meant "on a Table" rather than "and a Table"; but the preceding comma, for one thing, would bring the prepositional substitution into question. (The ordinary rationale for the comma certainly would be to set off a parallel simile, to start off a new independent clause or, rhetorically, to preclude misreading.) She thus retained the controversial Folio reading of "Table" but only to supplant Theobald's emendation with a brand new one of her own. Nevertheless, it appears now, with Phyllis Braxton's evidence, that on at least the submerged level Hilda Hulme was most likely *otherwise* on the right track. In other words, Falstaff's nose was pointed like a pen and distinguished by being greenish in its pallor (as could be said then of some of the rest of his complexion), the comma in the crux providing a requisite pause and incidentally also preventing misreading. (Evidently his *nose* was not also "as sharpe as . . . a Table." No zeugma need be read in here.)

Something from the heraldic imagery in the prototypical scene in the comedy, then, had worked its way into the deathbed scene in the history play. Whereas Hilda Hulme had queried what precise "Table" (picture) would have come to the dramatist's or the Hostess' mind, and in so doing deigned to posit a plausible inn-sign as a sort of random referent, the more clear-cut pictorial effect at the back of Shakespeare's psyche would evidently have been the linked heraldic emblem or insignia in *Wives*. After all, with a 'Garter' play, such details would have technically stood out for him, providing external evidence in behalf of the Folio interpretation.

In support of this armorial connection, notice once again that Falstaff connects with heraldic devices even elsewhere as well, notably when he referred to a knightly coat of arms in *2 Henry IV,* as pointedly claimed by the leading expert on Shakespeare and heraldry, Guy Cadogan Rothery (20). That the comedy was part of a Garter investiture ceremony has been such common belief that it was formerly at least taken to be part of the catechism. The very first scene deals with the "rollicking drolling of Justice Shallow's armorial bearings, a passage full of meaning and requiring comment" (Rothery 20). What is more, we have already seen in the last chapter how *Wives* tallies with *Arden* specifically on the level of heraldic imagery.

Additional points can relate, for heraldry links quite closely with the Arthurian tradition in which perforce Falstaff obliquely or parodically participates, as in Mistress Pistol's alluding to "Arthur's bosom" (by which is meant Avalon) in the deathbed scene. A clear-cut connection, moreover, exists in popular culture between heraldry and the word *Table* as associated with the Round Table, a standard treatise of the time being entitled *The auncient order, society, and unitie laudable, of Prince Arthure, and his knightly armory of the Round Table* (1583). Somewhat comparable was Henry Peacham's *The compleat gentleman* (1627), which, in its subtitle, annexed the term *field* heraldically.

A further point is that *Wives* was traditionally a play for Queen Elizabeth I, the Virgin Queen, who desired to see the fat knight in the throes of love (if only in that he would get his comeuppance that way), and so it may be of at least some passing import that the Queen's printer happened to bear "vert three fleurs de lis of the field" (Moran 81). In a word, the *flowers/green/fields* conjunction was thereby adumbrated in Elizabeth's own armory, the "field vert" being thereby implied (Hulme 142)—thus, owing to the connection with royalty, a memorable enough table or picture indeed. Because Phyllis Braxton made something of the comedy as being updated to accommodate Windsor in Elizabethan times, this additional, closely knit heraldic correlation likewise has its provocative effect.

As for the cause of Falstaff's death itself, all the play directly tells us is that he succumbed to a broken heart. Yet now we can at least also affirm from the immediate context of the Folio text that his end was Hippocratic. Comparable then would be the description of Thomas of Woodstock's death in *Richard II*. After an extensive vegetative metaphor involving branches and root, he is "hackt downe, and his summer leaves all faded" (1.2.20). Even more related would be Macbeth's well-known comment on himself: "I have liv'd long enough: my way of life / Is falne into the Seare, the yellow Leafe" (5.3.22–3). From leaves to grass: Is there that much difference? In answer, the shift is not merely an abrupt one from yellow to green when we consider that jaundice commonly involves a conflation of both these colors. For Falstaff's nose easily was deeply jaundiced *owing to,* most likely, cirrhosis of the liver, his having been such an imbiber. On the physical level, at least, that appears to have been his particular "green sickness."

After this chapter was composed, Giles E. Dawson's paper on "Shakespeare's Handwriting," which is largely devoted to a discussion of

Falstaff's death appeared (following up a note on the subject he had published some years before in *TLS*), and because of his authority as a paleographer, it deserves comment. The difficulty is that Dr. Dawson bypasses what has to be proved: He indicated that *if* "Table" is a misprint, then it is explicable in terms of the dramatist's handwriting, evidently misread by the compositor. Yet the capitalization of the noun surely indicates that it was not set accidentally (compare the capitalization of "poore Foole" in *Lear*). For years the Folio reading was understood as intentional. Need we change our course? Bearing in mind that *and* (or *an*) often had then the meaning of *if* (or *as if*), as in Bully Bottom's "I will roar you an 'twere any nightingale" (*A Midsummer Night's Dream*, 1.2.45), on the modern stage we might better emend the Hostess' crucial, exaggerated series of images to read as follows: "his nose was as sharp as a pen—an 'twere a table of green fields." (For more on the crux in terms of its influence on later authors, notably Heywood and then Milton, see Appendix B.)

HENRY V ACT II, SCENE 3

II.iii *This scene takes place on a street in London.*

2 Staines *a small town on the Thames between London and Southampton.*

3 ern *grieve.*

9-10 Arthur's Bosom *The Hostess is thinking of Abraham's bosom (Luke 16:22), a symbol of Heaven. The soul of the legendary King Arthur was said to reside in Avalon, another paradisal realm.*

11-12 and . . . Child *as innocently as a just-christened child.*

12-13 just between . . . Tide *The time of Falstaff's death recalls 2 Henry IV, III.ii.228-29, where Falstaff says "We have heard the Chimes at Midnight, Master Shallow."*

17-18 as sharp . . . Fields *This famous passage is here rendered as it appears in the First Folio. Since the middle of the eighteenth century most editors have adopted Lewis Theobald's emendation and substituted " 'a babbl'd" for "a Table." But "Table" and "Pen" can be related in various ways. The Hostess could be referring to a pen on a decorated writing tablet, for example; or she could be referring to a pen (enclosure) on a picture (tabula) of green fields. Or, more simply, she could be thinking of a writing pen on a table covered with green baize (a coarse cloth often used to protect flat surfaces). If so, both objects could be equally distinct to her, the pen with its fine point, the table with its keen edges and sharp corners.*

Professor Andrews presupposes the emendation of *on* for *and*.

Excerpt from *The Guild Shakespeare*, Volume 6, edited by John F. Andrews. Copyright ©1989 by Doubleday Book & Music Clubs, Inc. Reprinted by permission of Doubleday Book & Music Clubs, Inc., New York, N.Y. 10167.

APPENDICES

Appendix A
"New tricks":
Special Effects in the *Odcombian Banquet*, *Volpone*, and the *Sonnets*

Is there additional evidence that Thorpe indulged in name-play to support our reading of his fulsome dedication to the *Sonnets*? Aside from his previous 'dedication' to another one-time stationer's assistant and procurer of neglected copy, Edward Blount (with its opening, rather silly pun on having to be "blunt"), the best proof is in his printing a pirated, learned burlesque, Thomas Coryate's *Odcombian Banquet,* which was apparently a theft by Thorpe and Blount together of Coryate's yet-to-be-published *Crudities*.

In her very thorough, if not always easy-to-believe study of printing of the *Sonnets,* Katherine Duncan-Jones called attention to this curious piracy but finally chose to give it short shrift, considering it, by and large, uncharacteristic of Thorpe as the serious printer on whom Ben Jonson relied. But the *Banquet* deserves careful reappraisal here if only because of what she failed to mention: its modish use of puns, anagrams, acrostics, and macaronic verse, including many more oversized spaces between the first letter in a name and what follows, thus correlating with the "W. H. ALL" typographical curiosity discussed in Ch 3.

Let us consider, for example, the inclusion of an acrostic poem by Jonson on the very name of Coryate. After each letter in both first and last names a line of poetry follows, but only after a notable *em* space. The effect is exactly like that in the "M[r]. W. H. ALL. HAPPINESSE . . ." problem. Now this same effect is also found in Thorpe's printing of Jonson's *Volpone,* where at the start once more, as in the *Sonnets,* the use of extra spacing becomes dramatically evident—

not merely once but seven times. (This can then be compared with such repetition even thirteen times with Coryate's name in the *Banquet.*) This so-called "Argument" was set up by Thorpe as follows:

    V olpone, childlesse, rich, faines sick, despaires,
    O ffers his state to hopes of severall heyres,
    L ies languishing; His *Paradise* receaves
    P resents of all, assures, deludes: Then weaves
    O ther cross-plots, which ope' themselves, are told,
    N ew tricks for safety, are sought; They thrive: When, bold,
    E ach tempt's th'other againe, and all are sold.   (1607 ed., sig. A2)

Because the allusion to the weaving of cross-plots and new tricks here was also obviously intended as a valid, if oblique, one to the use of this very acrostic, which certainly may be said to involve its own sort of 'cross-plot' (the very kind of puzzle implying such crisscrossing), we have another clue to the "W. H." business. Such games people played.

One unreadiness which may come to mind is doubt as to whether this acrostic was not simply Jonson's rather than Thorpe's invention—in terms of the typographical effects on display. The latter can be shown to be most probably the contribution of the manager of the printing house, Thomas Thorpe, again. Now carefully examine how this can be proved, because the argument is tricky.

Katherine Duncan-Jones provided a major piece of evidence but then may have somewhat misinterpreted it. She indicated that the use of the Senate's proclamation in Act V of Jonson's *Sejanus,* which Thorpe set up after the manner of a Roman inscription (that is, with a full-stop after each word), has a precise parallel in the style of his 'dedication' to the *Sonnets.* So far so good. But then she contended that the capitals (and presumably the end-stops) were evidently part of Jonson's original intent, not Thorpe's. Yet, as she admitted, these idiosyncratic features disappeared when the poet supervised the 1616 Folio of his *Works.* Apparently he felt then that Thorpe's innovative printing was too eccentric.

The same argument could then hold for the extra spacing in Jonson's two acrostics which Thorpe printed (one in *Volpone,* the other in the *Banquet*). More likely than not, they included typographical curiosities added by Thorpe's publishing house of its own accord. True, it is easy to suppose that Jonson originally wrote these poems with a certain slight pause of the pen after each capital letter in order to set off the acrostic more easily for the unwitting (or lazy) reader. But it was then Thorpe who deliberately must have chosen to capitalize on this feature for his own purposes. He evidently made the gap pronounced, not merely looking like an accidental, but abruptly obvious. Perhaps he took his cue from the section of the bizarre mélange entitled "To Topographicall Typographicall Thomas." He evidently set out to do all he could out of sheer typographical bravado, which included word-games and extra spacing. The effect was sheer eccentricity, but it was typical of him.

The acrostic in *Volpone* is remarkable because, as Katherine Duncan-Jones showed, a passage in this play is set out like a lapidary inscription remarkably similar to the curious manner in which the 'dedication' to the *Sonnets* is organized. One of her points is that Thorpe somehow directed that the use of capitals and stops in the 'Roman' passage in *Sejanus* be fused with the inscription from *Volpone* (both plays having been printed within a few years of each other) to arrive at his novel way of setting up the inscription for Shakespeare's poems. The result was surely an odd kind of collage. But she did not go far enough because she neglected to involve the evidence in the *Banquet* here as well.

At least four 'anagrams' stealthily announce themselves in the *Banquet,* one of which, the first, is not in the *Crudities* and thus was most probably Thorpe's own invention. All playing upon a name, that of Thomas Coryate, they read as follows:

1. Thomas Coriatus: Homo Christatus
2. Thomas Coriatus: Tu cos amatoris vel
3. Thomas Coriatus: Tuta cos amoris
4. Thomas Coryate: Ca, ho, Maitre.

(Aside from the first anagram, which is conspicuously on the reverse side of the title-page and hence probably Thorpe's own, the second is on sig. N3^v, as is the third; the fourth, on sig. O4^r.) A fifth anagram may appear in the Latin name of the contributor Glareanus Vadianus (Strachan 290). Although to some perfectionists, this wordplay is suspect, because the anagrams are incomplete, they are specifically submitted in the *Banquet* as examples of this form of codification. Hence we are led to conclude that, in inventing further name-play in the "W. H. ALL" inscription, Thorpe was projecting or anticipating a kind of conflation of the anagram and the acrostic formats, as he would see them. For want of a better designation, his invention might be called an *anacrostic*.

Admittedly such innovativeness appears highly eccentric, yet it was no more so than other such anomalies in the *Banquet*. They buttress, in effect, a series of oddities already in the inscription to the *Sonnets:* the oddity that the manager of a printing house rather than the poet would dedicate these seemingly very personal poems; the curiosity that Thorpe would, in effect, 'invent' a name with his extra spacing in the inscription (thus looking ahead to Coryate, who was himself a specialist in inventing words); the religious punning on the Nicene Creed, "onlie begetter . . . sonnets" echoing "only begotten" / "Son," a quasi-devout allusion spiritually correlated with words like "eternity" and "ever-living." (As implied earlier, he could be thought of as having had a precedent in Christ's founding His Church on wordplay involving *Peter* and *petra* or *rock*.)

True, the idea of his setting forth his go-between's name twice (first as plain Master W. H. and then as "W. Hall" to the initiated in-group) may smack of a certain redundancy, and yet the 'dedication' was rampant with similar redundancy or rhetorical repetition (as in "eternity" and "ever-living" and the cloying phrase "wisheth the well-wishing"). Because the contextual meaning of "onlie begetter" is thus clearly derivative of the Creed, thereby signifying the procurer (or the one and only person who gave birth to the sonnets for the printing house), it would really have been pushing matters for him to have wanted the *application* of "begetter" to be also derivative in meaning. In other words, it is more reasonable to presume that the term had a significance in the inscription which was very closely associated with that in the Creed. Hence, because Christ was not merely *inspired* by the Father, but rather *proceeded* from Him traditionally, it is logical and consistent to believe here that the sacred canon of the sonnets, too, proceeded from (in the sense of being produced or procured by), and was not inspired by, Master W. H.

In all fairness, possible objections ought to be considered as well. The *Banquet* contains an Incipit which has its own example of extra spacing: "Incipit Glareanus Vadianus / A Sceleton or bare Anatomie" (sig. P2^r). This glaring gap seems entirely accidental because of the unimportant context; it might have been the result of the printer having to 'justify' a short line in that the Incipit as a whole is shaped in the extremely exacting form of an inverted pyramid. On the other hand, the extra spacing in the inscription for the sonnets would have been unaccidental especially if Thorpe had his printer follow Roman lapidary inscriptions to the letter. Such lapidary passages occasionally had abbreviations (comprehensible from the words being spelled out elsewhere) and gaps deriving from names being left out; so he was in effect following protocol.

For a good example of a Roman inscription containing a notable oversized space after a set of abbreviations and initials, see the excerpt from the "Fasti Consulares of the First Punic War" as duplicated in Sir John Edwin Sandy's *Latin Epigraphy I:*

AP·CLAVDIVS·C·F·AP·N   CAUDEX   (171).

Most gaps in Roman inscriptions resulted from names being omitted (often chiseled out for political reasons and the like). Because Thorpe followed Roman convention here, it stands to good reason that his own gap might be thought of as involving his own kind of practical politicking.

Another minor point that could be tentatively advanced against the candidacy of W. Hall is that Thorpe published a work by yet another Hall as well, Bishop Joseph Hall's allegorized *Discovery of a newe World,* the same year. The coincidence of the identical surnames is, however, nothing more than misleading. If anything, such an association could well have been an auxiliary reason prompting the printing house manager to wish partly to 'cover up' the conflicting or confusing surname of the seemingly undistinguished one-time stationer's assistant, who had then only recently, as Sir Sidney Lee pointed out, risen a little in his profession and thus deserved the title of *Master* ("Mr.") before his printed initials. Thorpe, after all, would readily have found no sense in confusing two Halls for the general reader, particularly, let us presume, when the poems were often enough scarcely the sort of reading which would appeal to a devout man of the cloth like the Bishop. As for the *Discovery* title, it is true enough that Shakespeare had discovered a "newe World" for himself (that is, the realm of his immortal poetry), but not exactly the more-than-geographical kind purportedly documented by the good Bishop. *Sic transit gloria mundi.*

Appendix B

Retabling Green Fields: Submerged Resonances in Milton and Heywood

If to arrive at Shakespeare's leading *miles gloriosus* in journeying to Milton is historically acceptable toursmanship, Milton can, in turn, tell us more of Sir John Falstaff—even of his controversially reported death. Hence the trip is worth taking here, but we must hang on to our seats.

As an *entrée*, some years ago I had the fortunate opportunity to query a visiting actress at the Antioch College theater, after she had publicly recited the Hostess' account of Falstaff's demise as a set piece, why she had so blithely retained Theobald's Falstaffolatrous emendation of *babbled* for the Folio reading, *Table*. (Editor Gary Taylor found the original spelling of the conjectured reading to be *babeld,* but this word, let alone this spelling, is not found elsewhere in Shakespeare. It is sometimes assumed that for *Table* to be a plausible misprint, the original spelling was rather *babld*.) Momentarily disconcerted, she hesitatingly responded that the Folio's famous phrase, "Table of greene fields," was simply too obscure in meaning for her. At such a sensitive point it would probably have been supererogatory to try to explain how, for example, *OED* provides, as one of the derived meanings of *Table,* 'picture,' and that that way pictorial sense could have been symbolically made of the text, for she appeared already quite set in her ways. But the main question before us now is this: Would that conventionalized attitude not have been uncalled for prior to Theobald, that is before the mid-eighteenth century? Did not "Table" previously make some sense in this context to a seventeenth-century Hostess?

To answer such queries, we can muster some new data. Thus far one drawback to uncovering a satisfactory reply has been that no one, to my knowledge, has yet pointed out some of the vital analogs to the Folio reading of what we might choose to call the Great Crux in non-Shakespearean seventeenth-century literature. The need for so doing is compelling. Otherwise Theobald's version will become so accepted that scholars may find themselves accommodating well-known lines from Tennyson: "'babeld,' 'babeld'; our old England may go down [with Theobald's emendation] at last" (from "Locksley Hall Revisited"). Alack and alas. Or, from the popular culture perspective, they might resort to a parody of the emendation in Conan Doyle's "The Adventure of the Three Students": "the landlady babbled of green peas at seven-thirty." Surely it is helpful here to be reminded that the time of Sir John's dinner is not quite time for his death. Yet the Hostess does converse with the Knight about being "ill for a greene wound" (2 *Henry 4*, 2.1.93). So why not see if the Folio reading of the Great Crux could have been influential on seventeenth-century readership?

I

Because one of the writers closest to Shakespeare in genius who has shown large-scale documented indebtedness to him was Milton, we may scrutinize some of the latter's own general *table* references to see if they might help us understand the kind of context suggested in *Henry V*—regardless, at first, of whether or not they might reveal any clear-cut Shakespearean leftovers.

First of all, evidently he read his predecessor's works thoroughly both in Quarto and Folio, so that he was probably well enough aware of the memorable account of how Sir John expired. As one commentator has observed:

> Milton's encomium on Shakespeare had been composed in 1630 before the publication of the Second Folio, and he could not have read *Pericles* in either the First or Second Folios as it was only included in the corpus in the second impression of the third printed in 1663. There cannot have been many of his learned contemporaries who cared enough for Shakespeare to follow him in the Quartos as well as in the Folio which established his literary fame, but Milton's acquaintance with *Pericles* must have come from these. (Trickett 26)

Now, one might ask, what is the point of quoting that if the issue at stake is Milton's reading the Folio, not the Quartos? The answer is that if he was aware of both Q and F versions of Falstaff's final moments, he would most probably have noticed that the "Table" reading in F represents part of an addition not found in Q and hence not readily explicable at the outset as a simple misprint. After all, since Milton was aware of such a relatively minor allusion to death in the Q version of *Pericles* as "humming water must o'erwhelm thy corpse," which was subsequently transformed into the *Lycidas* line "Where thou perhaps under the humming tide" (157) (Trickett 25), it is at least plausible that he could also have made good, transformed use of the "Table" passage from the epic-like *Henry V* in some subliminal manner. Where else but in his *own* epic poem? Consider the evidence.

After referring to "this Table" as one belonging to Adam and Eve, he described its terrestrial composition memorably thus: "of grassy turf / Thir Table was" *(Paradise Lost,* V, 391–92). Now, scholars have vigorously debated what such an unusual "Table" could have been; it has stirred some controversy akin to the problem in *Henry V*. It was evidently one formed of green sod, but almost everything has been suggested from a picnic spread out on the grass to an actual makeshift outdoor piece of furniture.

Most likely the best description of the object is a raised surface of some sort, one with a grassy top and surrounded by mossy seats. Analogously, an outdoor amphitheater on May Day (Otten 260), like that of Wells College nearby, where I am writing, comes to mind. On the other hand, if we concern ourselves rigorously and literally with tables of green sod in a *textual* manner, the obvious Shakespearean parallel would appear to emerge:

Table of greene fields	*(Henry V)*
of grassy turf / Thir Table	*(Paradise Lost)*

Granted, these contexts are altogether diverse, so that any labored consideration of possible, conscious influence here would quite obviously be rather *recherché*. Nonetheless, it is tempting to imagine how Milton, who must have read and later remembered with avid pleasure the vivid account of Falstaff's passing (as one of the most famous deathbed descriptions in world literature), would have puzzled over Shakespeare's curiously inventive (or Mannerist) turn of phrase in the Folio.

In support of such a presumption, recall that his masque *Comus* was itself partly, but strikingly, based on an analogous Shakespearean model. Although owing to the element of magic, as has often been pointed out (Major, Blondel), the leading precursor of the titular figure is the conjuror Prospero, old Falstaff clearly anticipates Comus, too, in likewise being a gluttonous rapscallion out to ensnare young women and, in general, wreak havoc. On this specific aspect of gluttony (which Chaucer and Spenser stressed as even prior to the deadly sin of lust in import), see Joan Larsen Klein's recent observations about Milton's demonic Bacchus. As a Vice figure, one based on the Devil of morality play tradition, Falstaff looks ahead, moreover, to Milton's Satan—a parallel which John Dover Wilson has pointed out in his book on Sir John (23). So, given these other Falstaffian parallels in Milton, it is scarcely too much to add to them the likelihood that the fat knight's death could also have been influential, even in terms of an oblique textual 'echo,' as the picture suggests. The humanity of Falstaff was thus evident already in Adam and Eve. This is the major consideration.

II

Yet one more Miltonic textual analogy, one at least indirectly also reminiscent of the "Table of greene fields," is the "Table in this Wilderness" of *Paradise Regained* (II, 384), itself the sequel to the epic. Although, true enough, editors customarily gloss the allusion here as basically one to Psalm 78.19 ("a banquet in the wilderness"), a hint of Shakespeare could also manifest itself. The striking Shakespearean allusion would be no less than to *The Tempest* again. What clues us in is that Milton's outdoor table then "Vanish'd quite" (II, 402). Also comparable is a noted stage-direction in the thaumaturgical romance (with italics added): "Ariell (like a Harpey) claps his wings upon the *Table*," whereupon "the Banquet *vanishes*" (1583–85) (Hinman text). One histrionic disappearance has, it would seem, prompted another.

It goes without saying that were it not for the astonishing number of allusions to Shakespeare throughout Milton's works, such a stagey, parallel effect might appear to be, on the surface at least, itself almost evanescent. Magicians have been prone from time immemorial to make things seem to disappear; so it might seem initially extraneous to adduce magically the parallel in the magian romance. On the other hand, one supportive point is that such a Miltonic "Table" effect would tie in with another example of Milton's conflation of two main sources: the Bible and the master dramatist.[60] This example also involves verbal or textual quibbling. Let me recapitulate the point again: Eve's retort to Satan, "Serpent, we might have spar'd our coming hither, / Fruitless to mee, though Fruit be here to excess," puns on "Be fruitful" in Genesis 1.28 but likewise recalls "all this derision / Shall seeme a dreame, and fruitless vision" (*A Midsummer Night's Dream,* 3.2.370–71), where the term *fruitless* has been cogently and authoritatively glossed as a "submerged Eden pun" (Garber 51). Why, then, not also a submerged *Shakespearean* quibble in the work of the Puritan poet?

These Miltonic "Table" passages in *Paradise Lost* and *Regained* hardly in themselves conclusively intimate that Milton was already cognizant of what might now be called the Great Crux and that he inadvertently anticipated that formidable phrase, let us say, by inaugurating his own cruxes, but it is no longer so easy to shunt aside this plausibility with a mere casual shrug. We cannot be certain that he even favored the Folio reading, though he might have avoided the undignified action of babbling (and not only for puritan reasons). If only because he made use of some analogous Shakespearean floral allusions, specifically the "flowers o' the spring" amid the "vernal flowers" of *Lycidas* (Sims), we might care to bear sensibly in mind that, on the level of metaphor at least, it does not take so many steps to make a scholarly excursion from a garden plot into "greene fields." The path is a natural one anyway.

After all, is it really so unusual that Milton artfully referred to his own tables in connection with greenery of some sort? We know that John Donne had proleptically made an analogous allusion in "Th' earths face is but thy Table; there are set / Plants" (from his "Elegie on M[ris] Boulstred"). The referent of "thy" is Death personified. Hence once more a literary analogy with the "Table of greene fields"—this time as likewise depicting Death's verdant countenance—is worth due contemplation as, let us confirm, offering an aesthetic as well as spiritual

---

[60]I have briefly discussed such paronomasia elsewhere (*AN&Q,* XVI, 119–20).

tonic. Likewise, Milton's "Table" references are open to similar accommodation. Therefore the Donne-Milton connection serves as final support of subliminal seventeenth-century usage of the crucial Folio reading, which need hardly have been the misprint it has so often be called. In any case, compared with most of the plays in the Folio of 1623, *Henry V* was more tolerably free of misprints, and the capitalization of *Table* is more than a compositorial idiosyncrasy if it strongly indicates, as I infer, that the transcriber felt certain that he was setting up the type for a noun (nouns being frequently capitalized in those days) and that such a substantive reading made enough sense in context. After all, this reading was presumably used on the stage from the beginning of the seventeenth century through the middle of the next. So let us no longer table the Folio here but allow for the reading of *Table* itself.

III

Finally a more convincing immediate influence of the Folio reading of the crux can be seen in a familiar passage in Thomas Heywood's *A Woman Killed With Kindness*. Oddly, the analogy has not been cited before in this connection, to my knowledge, although T. S. Eliot has expounded on it in his well-known essay "Thomas Heywood" (1931), duplicated in his *Selected Essays,* where he called the passage "one of the best known of quotations" (153). After citing the pertinent lines and their context in full, he commented on their significance stylistically. Here is part of the significant portion (his citation):

> O speak no more!
> For more than this I know, and have recorded
> Within the red-leaved table of my heart.

Afterwards Eliot had his qualms about it: "The image at the beginning of this passage does not, it is true, deserve its fame. 'Table of my heart' is a legitimate, though hardly striking, metaphor; but to call it *red-leaved* is to press the anatomical aspect into a ridiculous figure." He then ventured to assert that "a conceit" is not really involved, "merely the irreflective grasping after a fine trope." But, in this respect, Eliot again showed that he was more of a critic than a historical scholar. For the pertinent figure is again obviously Mannerist, thereby straining for effect simply in the usual mode of this style. Eliot would rather have it protometaphysical, but we may doubt that explanation.

Clearly, the notion of recording something in a table of red leaves relating to a bodily organ recalls Falstaff's nose or facial feature depicted as a table of foliage as well, not red but having the complementary color of green. It would appear then that Heywood could even have been indebted to the description of Falstaff's death, famous as it was, as well as Sonnet 24.2. Leslie Hotson, one noted defender of the Folio reading (if only from the pretty much discredited position of the allusion being to Sir Richard Grenville, whose name was sometimes, but very rarely, referred to as Greenfield), related Heywood's play *The Captives* already to the crux in a letter to the *TLS* on 30 May 1958. The parallel is not so striking as the present one. Further, considerable evidence is extant that Heywood was much indebted to Shakespeare.

For the latter point, the entry in the *Dictionary of Literary Biography* may best be consulted. Even this thorough study by Peter Davison (University of London) is incomplete, for though it mentions that the play *Sir Thomas More* may have been revised possibly by Shakespeare and also Heywood, it does not cite the latter's presumed hand in *The Jew of Malta,* a work generally believed to have influenced, in turn, Shakespeare in *The Merchant of Venice.*

In any case, Davison refers to "Charles Lamb's description of Heywood as a 'prose Shakespeare'" (105), the duplication of numerous characters in *Edward IV* which appeared in *Richard III* (108), and notably to the dramatization of *The Rape of Lucrece.* Indeed, "Shakespeare's influence is apparent very early in the play—in the third line" (118). *The Iron Age,* moreover, looks back at the model ("whereas Shakespeare treated only part of the story in *Troilus and Cressida*") (125). Further, like his mentor, Heywood made use of the bed trick device, in *A Maidenhead Well Lost,* the title of which obviously adds an extra dimension to that of *Love's Labour's Lost.* Hence it is surely not at all surprising that Heywood would also have taken over a key image from *Henry V* in his best known play. The image is closer even than the one Hotson thrice repeated in print from Thomas Bastard, "Yet breathing tables sweetly thee resemble," a quotation cited mainly to show that *table* had the meaning of *picture* and not merely of *tablet* in those days. The best known analogy, again in Shakespeare, "Drawne in the flattering table of her eie" (*King John,* 2.1.503–4), the line there being pointedly repeated for effect, has been criticized on the grounds that *table* could simply have meant "the canvas of a picture," not the image itself. In the light of the other evidence, however, even that criticism is suspect.

Certainly Heywood's use of an image so similar to that in *Henry V* strongly supports the Folio reading, even more than the rather more speculative parallel in Milton.

Conclusion

The problem with having a conclusion to a work concerned primarily with literary history is that it would appear to defeat the basic purpose: to see the facts as they have come down to us without prejudgment nor in terms of a philosophic or theological stance. From time to time I have tried to present some isolated conclusions regarding technique and import at the end of separate chapters, and some of these thoughts are worth summarizing more concisely now. In brief, because aesthetics as such is often still considered subjective ('beauty being in the eyes of the beholder,' not even thought of Thomistically as a Transcendental as such), my principal precedent has been for the objective approach, for the outer reality enclosing the inner spirit (not that the latter is not highly important, too, in its own way).

Still, my approach was not meant to be construed as nihilistic in the least way, diverse or relativistic though its aspects are. For example, although the evidence makes me decline to want to accept the time-worn interpretation that Falstaff was babbling away the twenty-third psalm in his dotage, that does not make me find him irreligious; as was pointed out, allusions in this context to more relevant psalms (nos. 37 and 102) can be textually more profitable. Likewise, although I should prefer to see resonances of the name Edmund in *King Lear* less related to anti-papal tracts (or to the name of the saint for that matter), the setting being pre-Christian, than to what some biographical evidence tells us, Shakespeare's subliminal allusions to his brother and nephew in this context are highly charitable in the best Judeo-Christian sense.

As for the "poor Fool" in *Lear* relating to the actual jester and not to Cordelia as a Christ figure (or symbolic, for that matter, of the spirit of Israel in the Old Testament), such a reversion to what appears to be original intent scarcely detracts from universal belief in the brotherhood of humankind, to which a genius of Shakespeare's caliber (here I would rather not add "that of the Upstart Crow") surely would have paid tribute.

Regarding the lack of implementation of the Golden Mean in *Romeo and Juliet,* such innocence ought at least to instruct the onlooker wisely enough; much that is positive can be learned from a relatively unsophisticated tragedy of young love like this, and Juliet's conative yearning for some semblance of the Mean is at least fairly instructive. In this instance, of course, what mainly counts is not the textual crux as such but how it reflects on intellectual history, of which the play is a microcosm.

The fun made of Mar-text in the pastoral comedy likewise demotes the label of Vicar no less than the text-play on "meane" in the Venetian tragedy demotes that of the Friar, for the point is that true lovers still want a "good priest" (3.3.74) to help them along. The genius of Marlowe as satirized, at least in part, in Mar-text symbolizes the perils of worldly intrusiveness.

Further, stress on *Love's Labour's Won* as a more adequate label than one dealing with *Nothing* certainly conjures up the hallmarks of the Judeo-Christian tradition more than anything else insofar as "God is Love" spells this out. My rejection of the *Nothing* label then is, in essence, *anti*-nihilistic.

It would be possible to go on and on, showing how concern with cruxes and their solutions ought to have a deeply beneficial and thereby moral effect upon Shakespearean scholarship, readership, and the playgoers themselves. But even saying this much may appear like special pleading, and it would be best to leave most conclusions up to the individual perceptive reader/spectator as much as possible. More concentrated analysis would doubtless need to probe the psychological depths of the unconscious mind and determine how it formulates creative tags and thoughts in general; the nature of textual cruxes and other conundrums would appear to depend on inchoate resolutions at times. At other times, psychology might best be dispensed with, for instance apropos of the familiar problem of whether Hamlet's flesh is dirtied or rather healthy and "solid." Aesthetically, or psychologically, the first inclination might be to prefer the second, later reading, but in terms of Pauline theology, the "sullied" exegesis has its distinctive merits, one sometimes all too hard to believe in during our day and age when belief in the effects of primal sin are no longer considered so dominant.

Granted, new scholarly information suddenly may shift our understanding of a particular crux, especially if it is textual in nature. For example, as I write these lines, news has come to me that a reference to *Iudian* in the works of Robert Greene may shed more light on the "base Indian/Iudean" crux in *Othello,* possibly predisposing the reader in favor of the later reading, which I find at least metrically less effective. (I am not at liberty to dwell on this more deeply at the present time.) But that is merely one of the expected pains—but, indirectly at least, also hidden pleasures—of my profession. Because of this, I was advised by one reader of the book in manuscript that perhaps I ought to forego a conclusion altogether and leave everything up to the knowledgeable reader. (At the same time he admitted that my leaving one out would be surprising.) I am not that kind of a pessimist that I believe truth is so relative, however, and hope that the culling of these final thoughts may be deemed not too obvious or pretentious and might even be of some small service.

As the epigraph of the book indicates, I have been influenced by Arnold's familiar poem on Shakespeare and formerly even considered dubbing the work *That Inscrutable Smile* in honor of the enigmatic earlier poet's smile, which like the sphinx symbolized in his Cleopatra does not inform us whether greatness there ends in tragedy or triumph. For the nature of cruxes is always going to be, to some extent, unfathomable, and that may well ironically be part of the enjoyment that they have continually engendered for us. Hence in eschewing the aesthetic for the moral element in these concluding remarks, I have not intended to be setting up a didactic tone, and certainly was not prompted by the special pleading of personal religious beliefs, which attempt to be more tolerant than apodeictic.

Select Bibliography

Adams, John Quincy. *A Life of William Shakespeare*. Boston: Houghton, 1923.

Alexander, Peter. *Shakespeare's Life and Art*. London: Nisbet, 1946.

Allen, Percy. *Shakespeare, Jonson, and Wilkins as Borrowers: A Study in Elizabethan Dramatic Origins and Imitations*. London: Palmer, 1928. (Ch on "*Arden of Feversham* and *Macbeth*.")

Andreas, James. "From Festivity to Spectacle: *The Canterbury Tales, Fragment I*, and *A Midsummer Night's Dream*." *The Upstart Crow* 3 (1980): 19–28.

Andrews, Michael Cameron. "'And I'll Go to Bed at Noon.'" *Notes and Queries* NS 25 (1978): 149–51.

Anshutz, H. L. "Cordelia and the Fool." *Research Studies* (Washington State U) 32 (1964): 240–60.

Anonymous. *The Lamentable and True Tragedy of M. Arden of Feversham, 1592*. Menston, Yorkshire: Scolar, 1971.

Aquinas, Thomas. *Basic Writings*. Trans. Laurence Shapcote, O.P. Ed., rev., and corrected by Anton Pégis. 2 vols. New York: Random, 1945.

---. *Commentary on the Nicomachean Ethics*. Trans. C. I. Litzinger, O. P. Chicago: Regnery, 1964.

Baillie, William M. "*Henry VIII:* A Jacobean History." *Shakespeare Studies* 12 (1979): 247–66.

Bakeless, John. *The Tragicall History of Christopher Marlowe*. 2 vols. Westport: Greenwood, 1970.

Bald, R. C. "'Thou, Nature, Art my Goddess': Edmund and Renaissance Free-Thought." In *Joseph Quincy Adams Memorial Studies*. Eds. James G. McManaway et al. Washington: Folger, 1948. 337–49.

Baldwin, T. W. "Shakespeare's Jester: The Dates of *Much Ado* and *As You Like It*." *Modern Language Notes* 39 (1924): 447–55.

---. *Shakspere's "Love's Labour's Won": New Evidence from the Account Books of an Elizabethan Bookseller.* Carbondale: Southern Illinois UP, 1957.

Bartenschlager, Klaus. "*Romeo and Juliet:* Werkintention versus Publikumserwartung. Zur Figur des Friar Laurence." In *Sympathielenkung in den Dramen Shakespeares: Studien zur Publikumsbezogenen Dramaturgie.* Ed. Werner Habicht et al. Munich: Funk, 1978. 93–102.

Bateson, F. W. *The Scholar-Critic. An Introduction to Literary Research.* London: Routledge, 1972. 126–33.

Battenhouse, Roy W. *Shakespearean Tragedy: Its Art and Its Christian Premises.* Bloomington: Indiana UP, 1969. 119–27.

Bauer, Robert J. "Despite of Mine Own Nature: Edmund and the Orders, Cosmic and Moral." *Texas Stud. in Lang. and Lit.* 10 (1968): 359–66.

Bennett, A. L. "The Sources of Shakespeare's *Merry Wives.*" *Renaissance Quarterly* 23 (1970): 429–33.

Bentley, Gerald E. *Shakespeare: A Biographical Handbook.* New Haven: Yale UP, 1961.

Berg, Sarah van den. "'The Paths I Meant Unto Thy Praise': Jonson's Poem for Shakespeare." *Shakespeare Studies* 11 (1978): 207–18.

Bergeron, David. "*King Lear* and John Hall's Casebook." *Shakespeare Quarterly* 23 (1972): 206–7.

---. "The Wife of Bath and *The Taming of the Shrew.*" *U Review* (Kansas City) 36 (1969): 279–86.

Berry, Ralph. *Shakespeare's Comedies: Explorations in Form.* Princeton: Princeton UP, 1972.

Beyersdorff, Robert. *Giordano Bruno und Shakespeare.* Oldenburg: Stalling, 1889.

Birkhoff, G. D. *Aesthetic Measure.* Cambridge: Harvard UP, 1933.

Blake, E. Vale. "The Impediment of Adipose." *Popular Science Monthly* 17 (1880): 60–71. (Rpt. in *Hamlet: Enter Critic* [1960].)

Blondel, J. "From *The Tempest* to *Comus,*" *Revue de Littérature Comparée* 49 (1975): 204–16.

Bluestone, Max. "*Libido Speculandi:* Doctrine and Dramaturgy in Contemporary Interpretations of Marlowe's *Doctor Faustus.*" In *Reinterpretations of Elizabethan Drama.* Ed. Norman Rabkin. New York: Columbia UP, 1969. 33–88.

Boe, John. "Mr. W. H.: A New Candidate." *Shakespeare Quarterly* 37 (1986): 97–8.

Bonheim, Helmut W., ed. *The King Lear Perplex.* Belmont: Wadsworth, 1960.

Booth, Stephen, ed. *Shakespeare's Sonnets.* New Haven: Yale UP, 1977.

Born, Hanspeter. *The Rare Wit and the Rude Groom: The Authorship of "A Knack to Know a Knave" in Relation to Greene, Nashe, and Shakespeare.* Bern: Francke, 1971.

Bradbrook, Muriel C. *Shakespeare and Elizabethan Poetry.* London: Chatto, 1965.

---. *Shakespeare: The Poet in His World.* London: Weidenfeld, 1978.

Brandes, George. *William Shakespeare.* London: Heinemann, 1920.

Braxton, Phyllis N. "Shakespeare's *Merry Wives of Windsor* and *Henry V.*" *Explicator* 48 (1989): 8–10.

Brenner, Gerry. "Shakespeare's Politically Ambitious Friar." *Shakespeare Studies* 13 (1980): 47–58.

Brooke, Tucker. *Shakespeare of Stratford: A Handbook for Students.* Freeport: Books for Libraries, 1970.

Brooks, Alden. *Will Shakspere: Factotum and Agent.* New York: Round Table, 1937. (Anti-Stratfordian)

Brown, Ivor. *The Women in Shakespeare's Life.* New York: Coward, 1969.

Bruyne, Edgar de. *L'Esthétique du Moyen Âge.* Louvain: Éditions de l'Institut Supérieur de Philosophie, 1947.

Bryant, J. A. "Falstaff and the Renewal of Windsor." *PMLA* 89 (1974): 296–301.

Bryant, James C. "The Problematic Friar in *Romeo and Juliet.*" *English Studies* 55 (1974): 340–50.

Bullen, A. H., ed. *Arden of Feversham, A Tragedy: Reprinted from the Edition of 1592.* London: Jarvis, 1887.

Bullough, Geoffrey, ed. *Narrative and Dramatic Sources of Shakespeare.* 8 vols. London: Routledge, 1957–75.

Burelbach, Frederick M. "Names of Supporting Characters in *Hamlet, King Lear,* and *Macbeth.*" *Names* 35 (1987): 127–38.

Bush, Douglas. *English Poetry: The Main Currents from Chaucer to the Present.* New York: Oxford UP, 1963.

Butler, Samuel, ed. *Shakespeare's Sonnets.* Rpt. New York: AMS, 1968.

C., B. H. "Othello." *Notes and Queries.* 2nd Ser. 10 (1860): 269–70.

Cassirer, Ernst. *The Philosophy of Symbolic Forms.* Trans. Ralph Manheim. 2 vols. New Haven: Yale UP, 1955.

Chakraborty, S. C. *Shakespeare the Manouverer: English "Histories."* Calcutta: Firma KLM, 1980.

Chambers, Sir Edmund. *Shakespeare: A Survey.* London: Macmillan, 1925.

Chambrun, Clara Longworth de. *Shakespeare: A Portrait Restored.* Freeport: Books for Libraries, 1970.

Champion, Larry S. *Evolution of Shakespeare's Comedy: A Study in Dramatic Perspective.* Cambridge: Harvard UP, 1970.

Chapman, Raymond. "*Arden of Feversham:* Its Interest Today." *English* 11 (1956): 15–17.

---. "'Twelfth Night' and the Swan Theatre." *Notes and Queries* 196 (1951): 467–70.

Cirlot, J. E. *Dictionary of Symbols.* Trans. Jack Sage. New York: Philosophical Library, 1962.

Clayton, Thomas. "'Is this the promis'd end?' Revision in the Role of the King." In *The Division of the Kingdoms: Shakespeare's Two Versions of "King Lear."* Ed. Gary Taylor and Michael Warren. Oxford: Clarendon, 1983. 121–41.

Colie, Rosalie L. "'Nothing is but what is not': Solutions to the Problem of Nothing." In her *Paradoxia Epidemica.* Princeton: Princeton UP, 1966. Ch VII.

Collyer, Henry. *A Short Account of Lord Cheyne, Lord Shorland, and Mr. Thomas Arden.* Canterbury: Privately Printed, 1739.

Cox, C. B. "Bisexual Shakespeare?" *The Hudson Review* 40 (1987): 481–6.

Coyle, Martin. "*Arden of Faversham* and *The Faerie Queene.*" *Notes and Queries* NS 28 (1981): 146–7.

Craig, Hardin. *The Literature of the English Renaissance, 1485–1660.* New York: Collier, 1962.

Crispin, Edmund. *Love Lies Bleeding.* Middlesex: Penguin, 1984.

Curtius, E. R. *European Literature and the Latin Middle Ages.* Trans. W. R. Trask. Princeton: Princeton UP, 1953.

Daly, Peter M. "A Note on Sonnet 116: A Case of Emblematic Association." *Shakespeare Quarterly* 28 (1977): 515–6.

Dansby, John F. *Shakespeare's Doctrine of Nature: A Study of "King Lear."* London: Faber, 1949.

Davidson, Chambers. Correspondence in the *TLS,* 30 May 1958: 297.

Davidson, Clifford. "'My poor fool is hang'd!'" *Universitas* (Wayne State U) 1 (1963): 57–61.

Davison, Peter. "Thomas Heywood." In *Dictionary of Literary Biography, Vol. 62: Elizabethan Dramatists.* Ed. Fredson Bowers. Detroit: Gale, 1987. 101–35.

Dawson, Giles E. "Shakespeare's Handwriting." *Shakespeare Survey* 42 (1990): 119–28.

---. "Theobald, *table/babbled,* and *Sir Thomas More.*" *TLS,* 22 April 1977: 484.

Dewey, John. *Art as Experience.* New York: Minton, 1934.

Dobbins, Austin C., and Roy W. Battenhouse. "Jessica's Morals: A Theological View." *Shakespeare Studies* 9 (1976): 107–20.

Doebler, John. "A Submerged Emblem in Sonnet 116." *Shakespeare Quarterly* 15 (1964): 109–10.

Donaldson, E. Talbot. *The Swan at the Well: Shakespeare Reading Chaucer.* New Haven: Yale UP, 1985.

Donne, C. E. *An Essay on the Tragedy of "Arden of Feversham."* London: Russell, 1873.

Donne, John. *The Poems of John Donne: Edited from the Old Editions and Numerous Manuscripts.* 2 vols. Ed. Herbert J. C. Grierson. Oxford UP, 1912.

---. *The Songs and Sonets of John Donne: An 'Editio Minor' with Introduction and Explanatory Notes.* Ed. Theodore Redpath. London: Methuen, 1956.

---. *The Songs and Sonets of John Donne.* 2nd ed. Ed. Theodore Redpath. New York: St. Martin's, 1983.

Dowden, Edward. "Introduction" to *The Histories and Poems of Shakespeare.* Ed. W. J. Craig. Oxford: Oxford UP, 1936.

Draper, John W. *Stratford to Dogberry: Studies in Shakespeare's Earlier Plays.* Pittsburgh: U of Pittsburgh P, 1961. Ch V.

Dubrow, Heather. *Captive Victors: Shakespeare's Narrative Poems and Sonnets.* Ithaca: Cornell UP, 1987.

---. "Shakespeare's Undramatic Monologues: Toward a Reading of the *Sonnets.*" *Shakespeare Quarterly* 32 (1981): 55–68.

Duncan-Jones, Katherine. "Was the 1609 *Shake-speares Sonnets* Really Unauthorized?" *Review of English Studies* NS 34 (1983): 151–71.

Dyce, Alexander, ed. *Timon: A Play.* London: The Shakespeare Society, 1842.

Eastman, Arthur. "King Lear's 'Poor Fool.'" *Papers of the Michigan Academy of Science, Arts and Letters* 49 (1964): 531–40.

Eccles, Mark. *Shakespeare in Warwickshire.* Madison: U of Wisconsin P, 1961.

Edmonds, Charles. Correspondence in *The Athenaeum* no. 2400, 25 Oct. 1873: 528–9.

Edwards, Philip. "Shakespeare and the Healing Power of Deceit." *Shakespeare Survey* 31 (1978): 115–25.

Ehrlich, Avi. "Ambivalence in John Donne's 'forbidding mourning.'" *American Imago* 36 (1979): 357–73.

Eliot, T. S. "Dante." *Selected Essays.* New ed. New York: Harcourt, 1932. 199–237.

---. "Thomas Heywood." In his *Selected Essays, 1917–1932.* New York: Harcourt. 149–58.

Ellrodt, Robert. "Self-consciousness in Montaigne and Shakespeare." *Shakespeare Survey* 28 (1975): 37–50.

Elton, William. *King Lear and the Gods.* San Marino: Huntington, 1966.

Empson, William. *Faustus and the Censor: The English Faust-Book and Marlowe's Faust.* Ed. John Henry Jones. New York: Blackwell, 1987.

Engle, Lars. "Afloat in Thick Deeps: Shakespeare's Sonnets on Certainty." *PMLA* 104 (1989): 832–43.

Euclid. *Elements Geometricall, Mathematicè, Physicè, et Pythagoricè.* Trans. H. Billingsley. London: Daye, 1570.

Evans, Willa McClung. *Henry Lawes, Musician and Friend of Poets.* New York: MLA, 1941.

---. Rev. of Harriet Joseph's *Shakespeare's Son-in-law: John Hall, Man and Physician. Shakespeare Quarterly* 17 (1966): 431–3.

Everett, Barbara. *Poets in Their Time: Essays in English Poetry from Donne to Larkin.* London: Faber, 1986.

---. *Young Hamlet: Essays on Shakespeare's Tragedies.* Oxford: Clarendon, 1989.

Everitt, E. B. *The Young Shakespeare: Studies in Documentary Evidence.* Copenhagen: Rosenkilde, 1954.

Felker, William. "La Dama Negra en la Poesia de William Dunbar." *Káñina* (U of Costa Rica) 5 (1981): 111–4.

Felver, Charles S. *Robert Armin, Shakespeare's Fool: A Biographical Essay.* Kent: Kent State UP, 1961.

Fiedler, Leslie. *The Stranger in Shakespeare.* New York: Stein, 1972.

Flahiff, F. T. "Edgar: Once and Future King." In *Some Facets of "King Lear."* Ed. Rosalie L. Colie and F. T. Flahiff. Toronto: U of Toronto P, 1974. 221–37.

Fleissner, Robert F. For entries, see the notes to Ch 1 *et passim.*

Fogel, Ephim. "'A Table of Green Fields': A Defense of the Folio Reading." *Shakespeare Quarterly* 9 (1958): 485–92.

Force, James H. "The 'Mole' in Shakespeare's Company." *Selected Papers* (Shakespeare and Ren. Assn. of West Virginia) 13 (1988):39–47.

Foster, Donald W. "Master W. H., R. I. P." *PMLA* 102 (1987): 47–54, 840–1 (*"Forum"*).

Fowler, Alastair. "Leontes' Contrition and the Repair of Nature." In *Essays and Studies 1978.* London: Murray, 1978. 36–64.

---. *Triumphal Forms: Structural Patterns in Elizabethan Poetry.* Cambridge UP, 1970.

Franson, J. Karl. "Numbers in Shakespeare's Dedications to *Venus and Adonis* and *The Rape of Lucrece.*" *Notes and Queries* NS 38 (1991): 51–54.

Frazer, James George. *The Golden Bough: A Study in Magic and Religion.* 3rd ed. 12 vols. London: MacMillan, 1922.

Freccero, John. "Donne's 'Valediction: forbidding mourning.'" *ELH* 30 (1963): 335–76.

French, Carolyn. "Shakespeare's 'Folly': *King Lear.*" *Shakespeare Quarterly* 10 (1959): 523–29.

Fripp, Edgar I. *Shakespeare: Man and Artist.* 2 vols. Oxford: Oxford UP, 1938.

Frye, Northrop. *Anatomy of Criticism.* Princeton: Princeton UP, 1957.

Funck-Hellet, Ch. *Composition et Nombre d'Or dans les Oeuvres Peintes de la Renaissance.* Paris: Fréal, 1950.

Furness, H. H., ed. *A New Variorum of Shakespeare: "King Lear."* 3rd. ed. Philadelphia: Lippincott, 1880.

---. *A New Variorum of Shakespeare: "Love's Labour's Lost."* Philadelphia: Lippincott, 1904.

---. *A New Variorum of Shakespeare: "Much Ado About Nothing."* Philadelphia: Lippincott, 1899.

---. *A New Variorum of Shakespeare: "The Winter's Tale."* Philadelphia: Lippincott, 1898.

Garber, Marjorie B. *Dream in Shakespeare: From Metaphor to Metamorphosis.* New Haven: Yale UP, 1974.

Gard, Roger. "The 'Poor Fool.'" *Essays in Criticism* 14 (1965): 209.

George, David. "Shakespeare and Pembroke's Men." *Shakespeare Quarterly* 32 (1981): 315–323.

Ghyka, Matila. *The Geometry of Art and Life.* New York: Sheed, 1946.

---. *Le Nombre d'Or.* Paris: Gallimard, 1931.

Gilbert, A. H. "Falstaff's Impresa." *Notes and Queries* 164 (1933): 389.

Giroux, Robert. *The Book Known as Q: A Consideration of Shakespeare's Sonnets.* New York: Vintage, 1983.

Glaz, A. André. "*Hamlet,* or, The Tragedy of Shakespeare." *American Imago* 18 (1961): 129–58.

Goldsmid, Edmund, ed. *Kempes Nine Daies Wonder, Performed in a Journey from London to Norwich.* Edinburgh: Privately Printed, 1884.

Goldsmith, R. H. *Wise Fools in Shakespeare.* East Lansing: Michigan State UP, 1955.

Gorlier, Claudio. "Il poeta e la nuova alchimia." *Paragone* 16.172 (1965): 55–78; 16.174 (1965): 43–80.

Green, William. *Shakespeare's "Merry Wives of Windsor."* Princeton: Princeton UP, 1962.

Greg, W. W. "Shakespeare and *Arden of Feversham.*" *Review of English Studies* 21 (1945): 134–6.

Grosart, A. B., ed. *The Complete Poems of Robert Southwell, S.J.* London: Robson, 1872.

Gurr, Andrew. "Shakespeare's First Poem: Sonnet 145." *Essays in Criticism* 21 (1977): 221–6.

Hale, David G. "Aesop in Renaissance England." *The Library* 5th Ser. 27 (1972): 116–25.

Halliday. F. E. *A Shakespeare Companion, 1564–1964*. Baltimore: Penguin, 1964.

---. *Shakespeare*. New York: Yoseloff, 1961.

Harbage, Alfred. *A Reader's Guide to William Shakespeare*. New York: Farrar, 1963.

Harcourt, John B. "'Children of divers kind': A Reading of *Romeo and Juliet*." *The Upstart Crow* (U of Tennessee, Martin) 3 (1980): 76–80.

Harrison, G. B., ed. *Nine Daies Wonder*. New York: Dutton, 1923.

Hartwig, Joan. *Shakespeare's Analogical Scene: Parody as Structural Syntax*. Lincoln: U of Nebraska P, 1983.

Hawkins, F. W. *The Life of Edmund Kean*. 2 vols. London: Tinsley, 1869.

Heffner, Jr., Ray L. "Hunting for Clues in *Much Ado About Nothing*." In *Teaching Shakespeare*. Ed. Walter Edens et al. Princeton: Princeton UP, 1977. 177–277.

Heilman, Robert B. *This Great Stage: Image and Structure in "King Lear."* Baton Rouge: U of Louisiana P, 1948.

Heninger, Jr., S. K. "The Pattern of *Love's Labour's Lost*." *Shakespeare Studies* 7 (1974): 25–33.

---. *Touches of Sweet Harmony: Pythagorean Cosmology and Renaissance Poetics*. San Marino: Huntington, 1974.

Hill, Frank Ernest. *To Meet Will Shakespeare*. New York: Dodd, 1949.

Hinman, Charlton, ed. *The First Folio of Shakespeare*. New York: Norton, 1968.

Hockey, Dorothy C. "Notes, Notes, Forsooth . . ." *Shakespeare Quarterly* 8 (1957): 353–8.

Hodges, C. Walter. *Playhouse Tales*. London: Bell, n.d.

Holdsworth, R. V. "Touchstone's Little Room." *Shakespeare Quarterly* 33 (1982): 492–3.

Holland, Norman. *Psychoanalysis and Shakespeare*. New York: McGraw, 1966.

Holt, Anita. "*Arden of Feversham:* A Study of the Play First Published in 1592." *Faversham Papers* no. 7 (Published by the Faversham Society, 1970): i–v, 1–40.

Honigmann, E. A. J. *Shakespeare's Impact on His Contemporaries*. Totowa: Barnes, 1982.

Hopkinson, A. F., ed. *Arden of Feversham*. London: Sims, 1898.

Hopper, Vincent Foster. *Medieval Number Symbolism: Its Sources, Meaning and Influence in Thought and Expression*. New York: Columbia UP, 1938.

Horne, R. C. "Two Unrecorded Contemporary References to Shakespeare." *Notes and Queries* NS 31 (1984): 218–20.

Hotson, Leslie. Correspondence in the *TLS,* 30 May 1958: 297.

---. *Mr. W. H.* London: Rupert Hart-Davis, 1964.

---. *Shakespeare's Sonnets Dated and Other Essays.* New York: Oxford UP, 1949.

Hubler, Edward. Rev. of Hotson's *Shakespeare's Sonnets Dated. Shakespeare Quarterly* 1 (1950): 78–83.

Hulme, Hilda M. *Explorations in Shakespeare's Language: Some Problems of Lexical Meaning in the Dramatic Text.* New York: Barnes, 1962.

---. "Sonnet 145: 'I Hate, From Hathaway She Threw.'" *Essays in Criticism* 21 (1971): 427–9.

Iyengar, K. R. Srinivasa. *Shakespeare: His World and His Art.* London: Asia, 1964.

Jackson, MacDonald P. "Editions and Textual Studies." *Shakespeare Survey* 37 (1984): 202–19.

---."Material for an Edition of *Arden of Feversham.*" Diss. Oxford, 1963.

---. "Punctuation and the Compositors of Shakespeare's *Sonnets,* 1609." *The Library* 5th Ser. 30 (1975): 1–24.

Jacobs, Richard. Rev. of Giroux's *The Book Known as Q. Review of English Studies* 35 (1984): 372–3.

Jahn, J. D. "The Eschatological Scene of Donne's 'A Valediction: forbidding mourning.'" *College Literature* 5 (1978): 43–7.

Janowitz, Henry D. "Falstaff's Nose *Was* 'a Table of green fields': A Footnote to Ephim Fogel's Defense of the Folio Reading." *Cahiers Elisabéthains* 33 (1988): 53–55.

Johnson, Samuel. "Cowley." In his *Lives of the English Poets.* 2 vols. Oxford: Milford, 1906. I, 1–54.

Jones, William M. "William Shakespeare as William in *As You Like It.*" *Shakespeare Quarterly* 11 (1960): 228–31.

Jorgensen, Paul. *Lear's Self-Discovery.* Berkeley: U of California P, 1967.

---. "Much Ado About *Nothing.*" *Shakespeare Quarterly* 5 (1954): 287–95. Rpt. in *Redeeming Shakespeare's Words.* Berkeley: U of California P, 1962. 22–42.

Joseph, F. S. C. "Donne's "A Valediction: forbidding mourning,' 1–8." *Explicator* 16 (1958): no. 43.

Joyce, James. *Ulysses.* Rev. ed. New York: Random, 1961.

Kemp, William. *Nine Daies Wonder.* Ed. G. B. Harrison. New York: E. P. Dutton, 1923.

Kermode, Frank. "Shakespeare for the Eighties." *New York Review of Books,* 28 April 1983: 32.

Kinnear, Benjamin Gott. *Cruces Shakespearianae.* London: Bell, 1883.

Klein, Joan Larsen. "The Demonic Bacchus in Spenser and Milton." *Milton Studies* 21 (1986): 93–118.

Knight, W. Nicholas. "Patrimony and Shakespeare's Daughters." *U of Hartford Stud. in Lit.* 9 (1977): 175–86.

Knolles, Richard. *The Generall Historie of the Turkes*. 5th ed. London: Islip, 1638.

Køkeritz, Helge. *Shakespeare's Pronunciation*. New Haven: Yale UP, 1953.

Kozintsev, G. *King Lear: The Space of Tragedy*. Trans. Mary Mackintosh. London: Heinemann, 1977.

---. *Shakespeare: Time and Conscience*. Trans. Joyce Vining. New York: Hill, 1966.

Landry, Hilton. "The Marriage of True Minds: Truth and Error in Sonnet 116." *Shakespeare Studies* 3 (1967): 98–110.

Laroque, F. Rev. of Roberts's *Shakespeare's English Comedy*. *Cahiers Elisabéthains* 17 (1980): 117–9.

Lee, Byung-Eun, and David Shelley Berkeley. "The Evil Number Five: Numerological Symbolism in *Paradise Lost*." *English Language Notes* 27.4 (1990): 33–8.

Lee, Sidney. "John Hall (1575–1634)." In *Dictionary of National Biography* 63 vols. London: Smith, 1885–1901. XXIV, 70–1.

---. *A Life of William Shakespeare*. New York: Macmillan, 1899.

Leech, Clifford. "Shakespeare's Life, Times, and Stage." *Shakespeare Survey* 4 (1951): 148–53.

Lees, F. N. Correspondence in the *TLS*, 28 March 1958: 169.

Levin, Harry. "Shakespeare's Nomenclature." In *Essays on Shakespeare*. Gen. ed. G. W. Chapman. Princeton: Princeton UP, 1965. 59–90.

Levin, Richard L. "Another Possible Clue to the Identity of the Rival Poet." *Shakespeare Quarterly* 36 (1985): 213–4.

Levith, Murray. *What's in Shakespeare's Names*. Hamden, CT: Archon, 1978.

Lewis, B. Roland, ed. *The Shakespeare Documents: Facsimiles, Transliterations, Translations and Commentary*. 2 vols. Oxford: Oxford UP, 1941.

Lippincott, H. F. "*King Lear* and the Fools of Robert Armin." *Shakespeare Quarterly* 26 (1975): 243–53.

Macey, Samuel L. "The Naming of the Protagonists in Shakespeare's 'Othello.'" *Notes and Queries* NS 25 (1978): 143–5.

Mackerness, E. Rev. of Milward's *Shakespeare's Religious Background*. *Modern Language Review* 69 (1974): 842–3.

McCanles, Michael. *Dialectical Criticism and Renaissance Literature*. Berkeley: U of California P, 1975.

McDonald, Russ. "Othello, *Thorello,* and the Problem of the Foolish Hero." *Shakespeare Quarterly* 30 (1979): 51–67.

McGinn, Donald J., and George Howerton, eds. *Literature as a Fine Art.* Evanstown: Row, 1959.

McGuire, Philip. "On the Dancing in *Romeo and Juliet.*" *Renaissance and Reformation* NS 5 (1981): 87–97.

McIntosh, William A. "A Note on Will Kemp." In *Studies in English and American Literature.* Eds. John L. Cutler and L. S. Thompson. Troy: Witson, 1978. 58–9.

Major, John M. "*Comus* and *The Tempest.*" *Shakespeare Quarterly* 10 (1959): 177–83.

McLeod, Randall. "Spellbound: Typography and the Concept of Old-Spelling Editions." *Renaissance and Reformation* NS 3 (1979): 50–65.

McManaway, James G. "A Reading of *King Lear.*" *Notes and Queries* NS 14 (1967): 139.

Marlowe, Christopher. *The Complete Works.* Vol. II. Ed. Roma Gill. Oxford: Clarendon, 1990.

Marotti, Arthur F. *John Donne, Coterie Poet.* Madison: U of Wisconsin P, 1986.

Marsden, Michael T. "The Otherworld of *Arden of Feversham.*" *Southern Folklore Quarterly* 36 (1972): 36–42.

Meller, Horst. "An Emblematic Background for Shakespeare's Sonnet No. 116—And More Light on Mr. W. H." *Archiv für das Studium der Neuren Sprachen und Literaturen* 217 (1980): 39–61.

Metz, G. Harold. "Wonne is 'lost, quite lost.'" *Modern Language Studies* 16.2 (1986): 3–12.

Miksch, Walther. "Die Verfasserschaft des *Arden of Feversham:* Ein Beitrag zur Kydforschung." Diss. Breslau, 1907.

Milton, John. *Complete Poems and Major Prose.* Ed. Merritt Y. Hughes. Indianapolis: Odyssey, 1957.

Milward, Peter. *Shakespeare's Religious Background.* Bloomington: Indiana UP, 1973.

Mincoff, M. "The Composition of *Henry VI, Part 1.*" *Shakespeare Quarterly* 16 (1965): 279–87.

Monaghan, Forbes J. *A Breakthrough to Shakespeare.* Tuscaloosa: Portals, 1979.

Moran, James. *Heraldic Influences on Early Printers' Devices.* Leeds: Elmete, 1978.

Mossman, Thomas Wimberley, ed. *The Primacy of S. Peter: A Translation of Cornelius à Lapide, upon S. Matthew XVI.17–19 and St. John XXI.15–17.* London: Bell, n.d.

Muir, Kenneth. "The Order of Shakespeare's Sonnets." *College Literature* 4 (1977): 190–96.

---. "Samuel Harsnett and *King Lear*." *Review of English Studies* NS 2 (1951): 11–21.

Munro, John, ed. *The London Shakespeare*. 6 vols. London: Eyre, 1958.

Musgrove, S. "The Nomenclature of *King Lear*." *Review of English Studies* NS 7 (1956): 294–8.

Neely, Carol Thomas. "Detachment and Engagement in Shakespeare's Sonnets: 94, 116, 129." *PMLA* 92 (1977): 83–95.

Novarr, David. *The Disinterred Muse: Donne's Texts and Contexts*. Ithaca: Cornell UP, 1980.

Oliver, H. J., ed. *The Merry Wives of Windsor*. London: Methuen, 1971.

Ornstein, Robert. "The Comic Synthesis in *Doctor Faustus*." *ELH* 22 (1955): 165–72.

Otten, Charlotte F. "'My Native Element': Milton's Paradise and English Gardens." *Milton Studies* 5 (1973): 249–67.

Ousby, Ian, and Heather Dubrow Ousby. "Art and Language in *Arden of Faversham*." *Durham U Journal* 37 (1976): 47–54.

Parsons, R. D. "Shakespeare the Shake-scene." *Notes and Queries* NS 28 (1981): 122.

Peacham, Henry. *The compleat gentleman. . . . Whereunto is annexed a description of the order of a maine battaile, or pitched field, eight severall wayes*. London: Constable, 1627.

Pearce, T. M. "*Romeo and Juliet* as Situation Ethics." In *Shakespeare in the Southwest: Some New Directions*. Ed. T. J. Stafford. El Paso: Texas Western P of the U. of Texas, 1969. 1–15.

Pequigney, Joseph. *Such Is My Love: A Study of Shakespeare's Sonnets*. Chicago: U of Chicago P, 1985.

Phelps, Wayne H. "Edmund Shakespeare at St. Leonard's, Shoreditch." *Shakespeare Quarterly* 29 (1978): 422–23.

Pinciss, G. M. "Shakespeare, Her Majesty's Players, and Pembroke's Men." *Shakespeare Survey* 27 (1974): 129–36.

Piper, W. B. "Evaluating Shakespeare's Sonnets." *Rice U Stud.* 65 (1979): 18–20, 50, 68–70.

Pohl, Frederick J. *Like to the Lark: The Early Years of Shakespeare*. London: Davis, 1972.

Potter, Lois. Rev. of Giroux's *The Book Known as Q*. *Shakespeare Survey* 36 (1983): 173–4.

Potts, Abbie Findlay. *Shakespeare and "The Faerie Queene."* Ithaca: Cornell UP, 1958.

Praz, Mario. *The Flaming Heart: Essays on Crashaw, Machiavelli, and Other Studies in the Relations Between Italian and English Literature from Chaucer to T. S. Eliot*. Garden City: Doubleday, 1958.

---. *Studies in Seventeenth-Century Imagery*. London: Warburg Institute, 1939.

Pyles, Thomas. "Ophelia's 'Nothing.'" *Modern Language Notes* 44 (1949): 322–3.

Quennell, Peter. *Shakespeare: A Biography*. New York: Avon, 1963.

R., R., trans. *The auncient order, society, and unitie laudable, of Prince Arthure, and his knightly armory of the Round Table*. London: Wolfe, 1583.

Rabkin, Norman. "Marlowe's Mind and the Heart of Darkness." In *"A Poet and a Filthy Play-maker": New Essays on Christopher Marlowe*. Ed. Kenneth Friedenreich et al. New York: AMS, 1988. 13–22.

Ramsey, Paul. *The Fickle Glass: A Study of Shakespeare's Sonnets*. New York: AMS, 1979.

Ribner, Irving. *Patterns in Shakespearian Tragedy*. New York: Barnes, 1960.

Richmond, Oliffe. Correspondence in the *TLS,* 27 April 1956: 253.

Richmond, Hugh M. "Much Ado About Notables." *Shakespeare Studies* 12 (1979): 49–63.

Roberts, Jeanne Addison. *Shakespeare's English Comedy: "The Merry Wives of Windsor" in Context*. Lincoln: U of Nebraska P, 1979.

---. "*The Merry Wives of Windsor* as a Halloween Play." *Shakespeare Survey* 25 (1972): 107–12.

Roessner, Jane. "The Coherence and the Context of Shakespeare's Sonnet 116." *JEGP* 81 (1982): 331–46.

Rollins, Hyder E., ed. *A New Variorum Edition of Shakespeare: The Sonnets*. 2 vols. Philadelphia: Lippincott, 1944.

---. *The Renaissance in England*. Boston: Heath, 1954.

Rosenberg, Marvin. *The Masks of King Lear*. Berkeley: U of California P, 1972.

Rostenberg, Leona. "Thomas Thorpe, Publisher of 'Shake-speare's Sonnets.'" *Publications of the Bibliographical Society of America* 54 (1960): 16–37.

Røstvig, Maren-Sofie. "Ars Aeterna: Renaissance Poetics and Theories of Divine Creation." *Mosaic* 3 (1970): 40–61.

---. "Structure as Prophecy: The Influence of Biblical Exegesis upon Theories of Literary Structure." In *Silent Poetry: Essays in Numerological Thought*. Ed. Alastair Fowler. New York: Barnes, 1970. 32–72.

Rothery, Guy Cadogan. *The Heraldry of Shakespeare: A Commentary with Annotations*. London: Folcroft, 1930.

Rowse, A. L. *Discoveries and Reviews: From Renaissance to Restoration*. New York: Harper, 1975.

---. *William Shakespeare: A Biography*. New York: Harper, 1963.

Sams, Eric. *Shakespeare's Lost Play: "Edmund Ironside."* New York: St. Martin's, 1985.

Sandys, John Edwin. *Latin Epigraphy I: An Introduction to the Study of Latin Inscriptions*. Chicago: Ares, 1974.

Schoenbaum, Samuel. "On the Page and on the Stage." *TLS,* 11 July 1975: 756.

---. *William Shakespeare: A Compact Documentary Life*. New York: Oxford UP, 1977.

---. *William Shakespeare: A Documentary Life*. New York: Oxford UP, 1975.

Schücking, Levin L. *Character Problems in Shakespeare's Plays: A Guide to the Better Understanding of the Dramatist*. New York: Holt, 1922.

Shakespeare, William. *The Complete Pelican Shakespeare*. Gen. ed. Alfred Harbage. Rev. ed. Baltimore, Penguin, 1969.

---. *Henry IV, Part 2; Henry V*. Ed. John Andrews. The Guild Shakespeare. Garden City: Doubleday, 1989.

---. *Henry V*. Ed. Gary Taylor. Oxford: Clarendon, 1982. Appendix II, 292–95.

---. *Sonnets*. Ed. Martin Seymour-Smith. London: Heinemann, 1976.

Shapiro, Susan C. "The Originals of Shakespeare's Beatrice and Hero." *Notes and Queries* NS 25 (1978): 133–4.

Shawcross, John. "Poetry, Personal and Impersonal: The Case of Donne." In *The Eagle and the Dove: Reassessing John Donne*. Ed. Claude J. Summers and Ted-Larry Pebworth. Columbia: U of Missouri P, 1986. 53–66.

Shullenberger, William. "Linguistic and Poetic Theory in Milton's *De Doctrina Christiana*." *English Language Notes* 19 (1982): 262–78.

Siegel, Paul N. "Falstaff and His Social Milieu." *Shakespeare Jahrbuch* (East) 110 (1974): 138–45.

Sims, J. H. "Perdita's 'Flower o' the Spring' and 'Vernal Flowers' in *Lycidas*." *Shakespeare Quarterly* 22 (1971): 87–90.

Slater, Eliot. "Word Links with *All's Well that Ends Well*." *Notes and Queries* NS 24 (1977): 109–12.

Southwell, Robert. *The Complete Poems of Robert Southwell, S.J.* Ed. A. B. Grosart. Westport: Greenwood, 1970.

---. *The Poems of Robert Southwell, S.J.* Ed. James H. McDonald and N. P. Brown. Oxford: Clarendon, 1967.

Spencer, Theodore. *The Art and Life of William Shakespeare*. New York: Harcourt, 1940.

Stageberg, Norman C. "The Aesthetic of the Petrarchan Sonnet." *Journal of Aesthetics and Art Criticism* 7 (1948): 132–7.

Stanton, Kay. "Shakespeare's Use of Marlowe in *As You Like It*." In*"A Poet and a Filthy Play-maker" : New Essays on Christopher Marlowe*. Eds. Kenneth Friedenreich et al. New York: AMS, 1988. 23–35.

Steadman, John M. "Falstaff's 'Facies Hippocratica': A Note on Shakespeare and Renaissance Medical Theory." *Studia Neophilologica* 29 (1957): 130–35.

Stephen, Leslie. "Did Shakespeare Write Bacon?" in *Men, Books, and Mountains: Essays by Leslie Stephen*. Collected and introd. by S. O. A. Ullmann. Minneapolis: U of Minnesota P, 1956. 74–80.

Stevenson, David L. "Among His Private Friends, John Donne?" *Seventeenth Century News* 12 (1954): 7.

Stevenson, Robert. *Shakespeare's Religious Frontier*. The Hague: Nijhoff, 1958.

Stodder, Joseph H. Rev. of recent Shakespearean productions in *Shakespeare Quarterly* 38 (1987): 243–8.

Stokes, Francis Griffin. *A Dictionary of the Characters and Proper Names in the Works of Shakespeare*. New York: Peter Smith, 1949.

Stoll, E. E. "Not Fat or Thirty." *Shakespeare Quarterly* 2 (1951): 295–301.

Strachan, Michael. *The Life and Adventures of Thomas Coryate*. London: Oxford UP, 1962.

Stroup, Thomas. "Cordelia and the Fool." *Shakespeare Quarterly* 12 (1961): 127–32

Sturgess, Keith, ed. *Three Elizabethan Domestic Tragedies: "Arden of Faversham," "A Yorkshire Tragedy," "A Woman Killed With Kindness."* Baltimore: Penguin, 1969.

Summers, Claude J. "'Stand up for Bastards!' Shakespeare's Edmund and Love's Failure." *College Literature* 4 (1977): 225–31.

Summers, Montague, ed. *Shakespeare Adaptations*. London: Cape, 1922.

Tannenbaum, Samuel A. "The Names in *As You Like It*." *Shakspere Association Bulletin* 15 (1940): 255–6.

Taylor, George Coffin. "Shakespeare and Milton Again." *Studies in Philology* 23 (1926): 189–99.

Thaler, Alvin. Correspondence in the *TLS,* 13 February 1930: 122.

---. *Shakespeare and Our World*. Knoxville: U of Tennessee P, 1966.

---. "The Shaksperian Element in Milton." *PMLA* 40 (1925): 645–91.

Thomas, Sidney. "On the Dating of Shakespeare's Early Plays." *Shakespeare Quarterly* 39 (1988): 187–94.

Thomson, J. A. K. *Classical Influences on English Prose*. New York: Collier, 1962.

Thompson, Ann. *Shakespeare's Chaucer: A Study in Literary Origins*. Liverpool: Liverpool UP, 1976.

Tilley, M. P. *A Dictionary of the Proverbs in England in the Sixteenth and Seventeenth Centuries*. Ann Arbor: U of Michigan P, 1950.

Tobin, J. J. M. "Nashe and Othello." *Notes and Queries* NS 31 (1984): 202–3.

Trickett, Rachel. "Shakespeare and Milton." *Essays and Studies 1978*. London: Murray, 1978.

Tung-chi, Lin."'Sullied' is the Word: A Note in *Hamlet* Criticism." *Waikuoyu. Fuden English Stud.* (Shanghai) 1 (1980): 1–11.

Viëtor, Wilhelm, ed. *"King Lear": Parallel Texts of the First Quarto and the First Folio.* Marburg: Elwet'sche, 1982.

Viswanathan, S. "*As You Like It*, I.ii.55–72." *American Notes and Queries* 18 (1980): 70–2.

---. "Is Touchstone Marston?" *American Notes and Queries* 10 (1971): 99–101.

Veen, Otto van. *Amorum Emblemata.* Introd. Stephen Orgel. New York: Garland, 1979.

Wain, John. *The Living World of Shakespeare: A Playgoer's Guide.* New York: St. Martin's, 1964.

Walker, D. P. "Kepler's Celestial Music." *Journal of the Warburg and Courtauld Institutes* 27 (1964): 228–50.

Walton, Izaak. *Izaak Walton's Lives.* Introd. Henry Morley. London: Routledge, 1888.

Walz, Eugene P. "*Arden of Faversham* as Tragic Satire." *Massachusetts Stud. in English* 4.2 (1973): 23–41.

Ward, B. R. *The Mystery of Mr. W. H.* London: Palmer, 1923. (Anti-Stratfordian)

Warnke, Karl, and Ludwig Proescholdt, eds. *Arden of Feversham.* Halle: Niemeyer, 1888.

Weber, C. O. "The Aesthetics of Rectangles and Theories of Affection." *Journal of Applied Psychology* 15 (1931): 310–18.

Weckermann, Hans-Jürgen. Rev. of Levith's *What's in Shakespeare's Names. Shakespeare Quarterly* 34 (1983): 510.

Wells, Stanley. *Shakespeare: An Illustrated Dictionary.* London: Kaye, 1978.

Wells, Stanley, and Gary Taylor, eds. *William Shakespeare: The Complete Works.* Oxford: Clarendon, 1986.

Welsford, Enid. *The Fool: His Social and Literary History.* New York: Farrar, 1935.

Wentersdorf, Karl P. "The 'Fence of Trouble' Crux in *Arden of Feversham.*" *Notes and Queries* NS 4 (1957): 160–1.

Wertheimer, Max. "Untersuchungen zur Lehre von der Gestalt." *Psychol. Forsch.* 4 (1923): 301–50.

White, R. S. "The Date of *The Merry Wives of Windsor.*" *Notes and Queries* NS 38 (1991): 57–60.

Whiting, Anthony. "Donne's 'A Valediction: forbidding mourning.'" *Explicator* 31 (1973): item 56.

Whitney, Geoffrey. *A Choice of Emblemes* (1586). Introd. Frank Fieler. New York: Blom, 1967.

Williams, George Walton. "Textual Studies." *Shakespeare Survey* 36 (1983): 181–95.

Williamson, C. F. "The Hanging of Cordelia." *Review of English Studies* 34 (1983): 414–8.

Wilson, F. P. *Elizabethan and Jacobean.* Oxford: Clarendon, 1945.

Wilson, John Dover. *Shakespeare's Happy Comedies.* London: Oxford UP, 1962.

---. *The Fortunes of Falstaff.* New York: Macmillan, 1944.

Wine, Martin L., ed. *The Tragedy of Master Arden of Faversham.* London: Methuen, 1973..

Wither, George. *A Collection of Emblemes, Ancient and Moderne.* Introd. Rosemary Freeman. Columbia: U of South Carolina P, 1975.

Wood, H. Harvey, ed. *The Plays of John Marston.* 3 vols. London: Oliver, 1938.

Woudhuysen, H. R. "*King Henry VIII* and 'All is True.'" *Notes and Queries* NS 31 (1984): 217–8.

Yates, Frances. *The French Academies of the Sixteenth Century.* London: Warburg Institute, 1947.

---. *A Study of Love's Labour's Lost.* Cambridge: Cambridge UP, 1936.

Youngblood, Sarah. "Theme and Imagery in *Arden of Feversham.*" *Studies in English Literature* 3 (1963): 207–18.

Index

(Names of principal authors, critics, works, and other historical figures)

Key Abbreviations:
All's Well = *All's Well that Ends Well*
Arden of F = *Arden of Faversham*
Much Ado = *Much Ado About Nothing*
R&J = *Romeo and Juliet*
Shak = Shakespeare
The Shrew = *The Taming of the Shrew*
Wives = *The Merry Wives of Windsor*
Won = *Love's Labour's Won*

Adams, J. Q., *beget* as *inspire*, 75

Adamson, J. H., Milton on creation *ex Deo* rather than *ex nihilo*, 47

Aesop, iterative animal imagery, 204

Alberti, 134

Alexander, Peter, printer-publisher William Hall's 1608 marriage as inspiration for Thorpe, 76

Andreas, James, Shakespeare and Chaucer, 214

Allen, Percy, *Arden of F* and *Macbeth*, 220n

Andrews, John F., 230, 232, 236, 240, 306

Andrews, M. C., the Fool's last line as proverbial, 177; bawdiness, 193

Annesley, Cordelia, possible source for Cordelia in *King Lear*, 165

Aquinas, Thomas, 131–32, 139; astral influence on human lives, 127

Arden, Mary, allusion to her in "Arden . . . merry," 8–9

Aristotle, *Poetics*, 52; on moral virtues relating to a Mean, 132

Armin, Robert, 60, 176

Armstrong, Archee, 176

Arnold, Matthew, on Shakespeare as sphinx-like or inscrutable, 3
Aurelius, Marcus, 141

Bacon, Francis, cites Otho I, 11
Bähr, W., golden proportionality in the sonnet form, 133
Baillie, William, status of *All Is True*, 61
Baines, Marlowe accused of irreverence, 149
Bakeless, John, Shak-Marlowe connection, 205, 222
Bald, R. C., 172n
Baldwin, T. W., 58, 60; *Won* seen as alternative title of *All's Well*, 25
Barclay, 140
Barnfield, Richard, Shak as ever-living, 74
Bartenschlager, Klaus, apologia for Friar Laurence, 139
Bastard, Thomas, "tables" as pictures, 255
Bateson, F. W., 231; different compositors making similar mistakes, 6
Battenhouse, Roy, 135–36, 192
Bauer, Robert J., Edmund in *King Lear* as exponent of individualism, 172
Benedicte and Betteris, imposed subtitled for *Much Ado*, 42
Bennett, Josephine Waters, *Much Ado* as expressive of indifference, 41; *Wives* apropos of *Ralph Roister Doister*, 211
Berg, Sarah van den, Jonson apropos of Shak, 28
Bergeron, David, 97; Shak and Chaucer, 214

Berry, Ralph, critical of Folio order, 26–27; *love* as running metaphor in *Much Ado*, 54
Beyersdorff, Robert, 31
The Bible, 7, 46, 55, 75, 127, 134, 138–39, 154, 156, 180, 203, 233, 235, 252–53, 257-58
Birkhoff, G. D., 141
Blondel, J., 252
Blount, Edward, 75, 78, 80, 99, 243; picker-up of neglected 'copy,' 94
Bluestone, Max, ambivalence in Faustus' end, 155
Boas, Frederick, Kyd as author of *Arden of F*, 205
Boccaccio, G., Frate Alberto as source for Falstaff in *Wives*, 211–12
Bonaventura, St., 55, 127
Bonheim, Helmut W., 88, 192
Booth, Stephen, 98–99, 115; vs. Mr. W. H. as necessarily the printer-publisher William Hall, 93; "writ" in sonnet 116 connoting 'writ of error,' 107; sonnet 116 misnumbered, 110; sonnet subgroups "overlap confusingly," 119; sonnet 116 akin to Donne's "Valediction," 120
Born, Hanspeter, Shak's hand in Greene, 206
Bowers, Fredson, 17; defense of "sallied" (sullied) flesh in *Hamlet*, 5-6
Bradbrook, Muriel, 167; Shak and Marlowe as the Rival Poets, 153; Shak as "seduced," 203
Bradley, A. C., literalist reading of *King Lear*, 192
Bradock, Richard, the former employer of W. Hall (2), 94

281

Brae, A. E., *Won* associated with *Much Ado*, 54

Brandes, George, *begetter* as a farfetched term of Thorpe's, 74

Braxton, Phyllis N., 231–33, 237–38

Brenner, Gerry, 135

Brooke, Arthur, 167; determinism stressed in main source for *R&J*, 127; anti-Romanism, 137

Brooks, Alden, the perspicuous gap between "W. H." and "ALL," 67

Brown, Ivor, Shakebag's name related to *Shakerags*, 199

Brown, John Russell, the running metaphor in *Much Ado* is love, 54

Browne, Thomas, the pentad's spiritual import, 133

Bruno, Giordano, name related to Berowne's, 31, 152; Helen of Troy as a Minerva figure, 155

Bruyne, Edgar de, humans reflect the harmony of the universe, 66

Bryant, J. A., 135; mythic elements in *Wives*, 210

Bullen, A. H., 220, 222

Bullough, Geoffrey, Don John not villainous enough to cause such ado, 41; source for character of Edmund in *King Lear* in Edmund Campion, 165

Burelbach, Frederick M., Edgar Atheling's sons correlating with names in *King Lear*, 166

Burgess, Anthony, Dark Lady as non-Caucasian, 19; Shakebag's name related to Shak, 200n. *See also* The Dark Lady

Bush, Douglas, 102

Butler, Samuel, 'dedication' to *Sonnets* related to Nicene Creed, 74–75

C., B. H., Othello's name based on *Othelio*, 13

Camden's *Remaines*, 146; Edmund's name found next to Edgar's, 165–66

Castiglione, 37, 140

Cervantes, Shak's lack of interest in, 24

Chakraborty, S. C., *Henry VI* a collaboration, 206

Chambers, Sir Edmund, 93; rejection of *Won* as *All's Well*, 57; *Much Ado* acknowledged as leading contender for *Won,* 64; no link between *Arden of F* and the Queen's Men, 201

Chambrun, Clara Longworth de, 87, 93–95, 200; W. H. as William Harvey, 82

Champion, Larry S., relevance of wordplay on *nothing* questioned, 45

Chapman, Raymond, 57, 208

Charles II, King, subtitled some of Shak's plays, 40

Chaucer, Geoffrey, 133, 140, 213–14, 252

Cholmley, Richard, Marlowe accused of irreverence, 159

Cibber, Colley, *Love's Last Shift* titularly related to *Love's Labour's Lost,* 55

Cicero, 140

Cirlot, J. E., Jungian approach to scapegoat 'fools,' 179

Clayton, Thomas, 109

Colie, Rosalie L., Renaissance love of paradox, 45

Collyer, Henry, 221; puppet show based on *Arden of F,* evidence of collaboration in the play itself, 226

Conan Doyle, Sir Arthur, parody of *babbled* emendation, 250

Constable, Henry, 42, 89; Shak's sonnet 145 as a recantation à la Constable, 110

Cooper, Thomas, 149

Coryate, Thomas, 243–46; his unauthorized text printed for Thorpe by Eld, 72

Cossi, Michael, historical source for Michael Cassio's name in *Othello*, 8

Covell, William, 85, 99

Cox, C. B., 111

Coyle, Martin, *Arden of F* indebted to Spenser, 227

Craig, Hardin, *Arden of F* foreshadowing *Macbeth*, 220

Crispin, Edmund, his mystery novel on the finding of *Won*, 25

Curtius, E. R., 127

Cust, Lionel, 159; Shak in the role of Shakebag, 200; Shak and Marlowe as both in *Arden of F*, 205

Daly, Peter, connections between one of van Veen's emblems and sonnet 116, 111

Danby, John F., 172n

Dante, Alighieri, 115; source for Donne's "Valediction," 102; circle imagery in the *Paradiso* related, 103

Dark Lady, The, 18–19, 68, 82–83, 87, 110, 117–18

Davidson, Chambers, Falstaff's cirrhosis of the liver, 235. *See also* Janowitz

Davies, John, epigram on Shak, 28

Davison, Peter, 255

Dawson, Giles, relevance of Shak's handwriting to Falstaff's death, 18; defense of *babbled* paleographically, 238–39

Dean, Charles, Fiedlerian approach to Edmund in *King Lear*, 172n

Dee, John, Elizabethan Pythagoreanism, 135

Dekker, Thomas, disappearance of his collaboration with Jonson, 25

Deloney, Thomas, 176

Dewey, John, 134n

Dickens, Charles, 181

Doebler, John, sonnet 116 relating to the compass device, 114

Donaldson, E. Talbot, Shak and Chaucer, 214

Donne, C. E., Faversham's seafood, 217

Donne, John, 4, 16; paradox on nothingness, 45; Mannerist appeal, 47; "Table" related to "Plants," 253-54. *See also* Ch 4

Donne, Jr., John, influenced by Shak's Dark Lady sonnets, 116

Dorn, Alfred, 'inventor' of Golden Section structure in poetry, 134

Double Fals[e]hood, questionably based on *Cardenio*, 24

Dowden, Edward, *begetter* as *obtainer* or *producer*, 75

Draper, John W., Renaissance understanding of *bastard* and *base*, 169

Dryden, John, his *All For Love . . . Lost* related titularly to the *Won/Nothing* collocation, 39

Dubrow, Heather, 119. *See also* Ousby

Duncan-Jones, Katherine, 78, 97, 118, 243–45; argues Shak saw the *Sonnets* to press, 33

Dyce, Alexander, 64

Eastman, Arthur, 185–87, 190

Eccles, Mark, William Hall uncovered in Dr. Hall's family, 78; evidence of Dr. Hall's acquaintance with Covell, 85

Edmonds, Charles, 92–93

Edmund Ironside, 14, 24, 29, 61–62, 218. *See also* Sams

Edwards, Philip, 135

Eliot, T. S., Othello trying to cheer himself up, 7; highest praise for the *Paradiso,* 103; stressed Heywood's use of a "Table" that is "red-leaved," 254

Ellrodt, Robert, 220; evidence of consecutive effects as a basis for influence, 109

Elton, William, Christian pessimism in *King Lear,* 10, 180; Cordelia seen as fool by analogy with an interlude, 190

Elyot, Sir Thomas, 132; the Mean in dancing, 129

Empson, William, Thorpe's eccentricities, 83; Helen in *Dr. Faustus* as a Minerva figure, 155; Lear is completely berserk if he calls his Cordelia a fool, 188. *See also* Bruno

Engle, Lars, sonnet 116 related to weddings, 120–21

Erasmus, Desiderius, 140, 191; overall context for fool figure in *King Lear,* 176

Estienne, Henri, author of book in Susanna Hall's library, 90. *See also* Schoenbaum

Euclid, 134–35

Everett, Barbara, 102; the Fool in *King Lear* as truly hanged, 16; William Hathaway as Mr. W. H., 72; capitalization of "Foole" points to the jester, 185

Everitt, E. B., 61

'Faithful Wife,' The, 15, 83, 88, 105, 114. *See also* Shakespeare, Anne Hathaway, and Ch 4

Felver, Charles S., 194

Fibonacci, mathematics and rabbit propagation, 133

Flahiff, F. T., historical sources of *King Lear,* 187

Fleay, Kyd as author of *Arden of F* (a disintegrationist view), 205; disintegration theory, 226

Fletcher, John, his sequel to *The Shrew,* 59

Florio, John, 53, 80–81, 152

Fogel, Ephim, authorship and internal evidence, defense of F in *Henry V,* 18; "Table" as picture, 231–32; ellipsis as a Renaissance commonplace, 236

Ford, John, supposed author of *The Golden Meane,* 140

Force, James H., Kemp as "mole," 199

Forster, John, 181

Foster, Donald, 68–69, 72n, 74–75, 88, 93, 120

Fowler, Alastair, 77; number lore in the *Sonnets,* 32; the pentad functional in Spenser, 134

Franson, J. Karl, numerology apropos of Shak's narrative poems, 30; numerological evidence indicates Shak as author of dedications, 77

Freccero, John, spiral effect preferred to circle in the "Valediction," 102

French, Carolyn, Edmund in *King Lear* is today exciting admiration, 172n

Fripp, Edgar I., Shak's sonnets related to the house of the deceased Earl of Oxford, 87

Frye, Northrop, 63; mythic basis for the Fool's death (or immersion in water, as with Falstaff), 179; mythic elements in *Wives*, 210

Funck-Hellet, Ch., 111

Furness, H. H., 184

Galen, 47, 217

Garber, Marjorie, 253

Gard, Roger, 176

George, David, scansion of crucial line in *Othello*, 6; paleographical confusion possible in a clerk's entry, 168–69; vs. theory that players recruited from the provinces, 201

Gervinus, Georg, 139

Ghyka, Matila, 125, 129, 134

Gielgud, Sir John, the Fool as predictive of his own death, 177

Gilbert, A. H., Shak's familiarity with heraldic and emblematic mottoes, 234

Giroux, Robert, 83–84; vs. Thorpe dedicating the *Sonnets* to their author, 74; Thorpe as cryptic, 78

Glaz, A. André, Shak's deep concern with bastardy, 171

Goethe, Johann Wolfgang, 223–24; Prospero akin to Faust, 154; Shak as author of *Arden of F*, 198

Goldsmid, Edmund, Kemp on cutpurses, 203

Goldsmith, Robert Hillis, 181

Gorlier, Claudio, Donne possibly among Shak's "private friends," 109

Greene, Robert, 198–99, 200, 203–6, 259

Green, William, heraldry apropos of *Wives*, 216n

Greg, W. W., Jonson seen as author of prefatory letter attributed to Heminges and Condell, 28; proof for the attribution of *Arden of F* to Shak, 198

Grierson, H. J. C., compass effect traced to Persia, 102

Guarini, Giovanni, 102

Gurr, Andrew, 110, 117, 119–20

Hale, David G., 204

Hall, Dr. John, 85–89, 90, 97, 99. *See also* Ch 3

Hall, Joseph, 247; introduction of compass simile prior to Donne's, 103

Hall, Susanna, 90, 95. *See also* Susanna Shakespeare

Hall, William (1) (brother of Shak's son-in-law), 71–72, 80, 82, 85–89, 98–99

Hall, William (2) (printer and then publisher), 80–81, 91, 93–95, 98–99; his import considered by Lee, 76

Hall, William (3) (of Hackney), 85, 91

Halliday, F. E., 96, 208; *Much Ado*, the first registered play by Shak, 32; Pembroke's Men and son William, 84; Dr. Hall presumably leaving Nash, his son, some of

Shak's books, 90; vs. Mr. W. H. as (necessarily) the printer-publisher W. Hall, 93

Halliwell-Phillips, J. O., on one of Shak's sons coming to London, 174

Hamlett, Katherine, possible source for Ophelia, 164

Harbage, Alfred, the serious titular meaning of *As You Like It* accommodated, 50; Mar-text's "Puritan" taint, 151–52

Harcourt, John B., 135, 139

Harrison, G. B., 199

Harsnett, Samuel, 165–66, 220

Hartwig, Joan, Friar Laurence's problems, 52–53

Harvey, Gabriel, 48

Harvey, Sir William, 81–82, 93, 97. See also Chambrun, Rowse, Stokes

Hatcliffe, William, 73, 82. See also Hotson

Hathaway, William, 72, 87. See also Everett

Hawkins, F. W., George III's death removes taboo, 185

Heffner, Jr., Ray L., *Much Ado* designed as 'throwaway,' 50

Heninger, Jr., S. K., 132, 135

Henslowe, Philip, "Cutting Dicke," 203

Herbert, George, "Judas-Jew," 7; 'shape' poetry, 30

Herbert, William, 79, 97, 117. See also Pembroke

Hill, Frank Ernest, Edmund Shak's renegade life, 172

Hippocrates, 47, 235, 238

Hobday, C. H., Shak as possibly involved with *Arden of F*, 17

Hockey, Dorothy, wordplay on *nothing* in *Much Ado* in context, 45

Hodges, C. Walter, parody of the *Much Ado* titular crux, 41–42

Hoffman, Calvin, *Mar-text* supposedly standing for "Marlowe's text," 151–52

Holdsworth, R. V., Marlowe's death and *As You Like It*, 146

Holinshed, 214, 220, 222, 225; Loosebag once renamed Shakebag, 201–2; Greene more tyrannical here than in the play, 204; less moral and social realism than in *Arden of F*, 207

Holland, Norman, Edmund in *King Lear* apropos of Freudianism, 171

Holmes, William, 98–99

Holt, Anita, 200, 208; proposed 'subtitles' for *Arden of F*, 215

Homer, Hector compared to Romeo in terms of determinism, 126

Honigmann, E. A. J., *Othello*'s two presumed arch-texts, 6

Hopkinson, A. F., 226; distaste for rhyme seen in both *Arden of F* and Shak's dramaturgy, 222

Hopper, Vincent, 127; the pentad as "the type of nature," 133

Horace, 131, 133, 234; stress on the Golden Mean in the *Odes*, 125–26

Horne, R. C., wordplay on Shak's name uncovered, 79

Hotson, Leslie, *Won* an "imprecision," 27; evidence of Shak's link with host of Mermaid Tavern, 30; disagreement with Leech, 36; *Two Gentlemen of Verona* related to *Love's Labour's Lost*, 53;

critical of E. K. Chambers on *Won*, 57; *Won*, being excellent, is surely not lost, 60; labored codification of W. Hatcliffe's name in Mr. W. H., 73; Marlowe's death, 146; Marlowe, an anti-Catholic spy, 220; Shak's avoidance of *babbled* or *babble of*, 232–33; green fields linked with Grenville's name, 255

Howard, Philip, 76, 92, 94–95, 99. *See also* Southwell

Hubler, Edward, the *Won* title considered an error, 25

Hulme, Hilda, "dram of eale" apropos of beer yeast, 8; cruxes as lexical problems, 20; no. 145 as a 'faithful wife' sonnet, 117n; "Table" as heraldic and pictorial, 236, 238. *See also* The 'Faithful Wife' and Gurr

Iphis and Iantha, a questionably Shakespearean drama, 26

Irenaeus, 133

Isle of Dogs, vanished play by Jonson and Dekker, 25

Iyengar, K. R. Srinivasa, W. H. related to John Hall's family, 77

Jackson, John, member of the Mermaid Tavern 'fraternity,' 30

Jackson, MacDonald P., Thorpe's accountability, 68; Donne's "Valediction" related to Shak's love poetry, 109; Oxford thesis on *Arden of F* as Shak's, 223

Jackson, William, host of Mermaid Tavern, 30

Jacobs, Richard, Thorpe as cryptic, 78

Jahn, J. D., circular imagery in Donne related to necrological imagery, 104

Janowitz, Henry, Falstaff and cirrhosis of the liver, 235. *See also* Davidson

John, Don (of Austria), linked politically with Don John in *Much Ado*, 23

Jonson, Ben, 27–29, 46, 69, 71, 81, 153, 202, 216, 233, 243–44; Thorello as source for Othello's name and character, 12; disappearance of his collaboration with Dekker, 25

Jofen, Jean, Marprelate related to Marlowe, 150–51

Johnson, Dr. Samuel, 102, 118, 175

Jones, William, 170, 225; Shak doubling as William and Adam, 146

Jordan, Wilhelm, the Dark Lady as black, 19. *See also* The Dark Lady

Jorgensen, Paul, crucial words as running metaphors in plays, 20; relevance of wordplay on *nothing*, 45; Edmund in *King Lear* as almost worthy, 173

Joseph, F. S. C., Brother, Donne among Shak's "private friends," 109

Joseph, Harriet, 85

Joyce, James, 167–70; speculations on autobiographical relevance of Shak's relatives to characters in plays, 165; confusion as to relation of brother Edmund to *King Lear*, 168; scapegoat image, 173; Shak in the role of Shakebag, 200n

Justinian, 158

Kemp, Will, 200, 203, 217; *Nine Daies Wonder,* 42; played role of Dogberry, 47; his withdrawal related to date of *Much Ado,* 60; alluded to Shak as "Shakerags," 198–99

Kepler, Johannes, the Mean, time, and music, 129

Kermode, Frank, negative review of Giroux's book on *Sonnets,* 84

Kinnear, Benjamin Gott, early book on cruxes in Shak, 20

Kittredge, George Lyman, sonnet 116 as addressed to a woman, 119

Klein, Joan Larsen, 252

Knight, Charles, *Macbeth* and *Arden of F,* 220n

Knight, W. Nicholas, Edmund in *King Lear* based on Edmund Lambert, 169–70

Knolles, Richard, his history of Turkey as source for *Othello,* 7–8

Kökeritz, Helge, relevance of wordplay on *nothing* questioned, 45

Kozintsev, G., 193; crucial line curtailed in film version, 190–91

Kuitert, G. B., Ardens of Wilmecote and of Faversham related, 225

Kyd, Thomas, 226–27; as author of *Arden of F,* 17; accused Marlowe of impiety, 149; authorship of *Arden of F* disputed, 205–6. *See also* Baines

Landry, Hilton, marital metaphor in sonnet 116, 114

Laroque, F., 210

Lawes, Henry, rewording of sonnet 116, 117

Lawless, Marlowe's death and *As You Like It,* 146

Lawrence, W. J., opposed to double-role (Cordelia-Fool) theory, 182

Lee, Byung-Eun, and David Shelley Berkeley, pentad as evil, 133

Lee, Sir Sidney, 77–78, 80, 86, 93–94, 98, 247; on Thorpe's idiosyncrasies, 68; W. H. related to printer-publisher William Hall, 76

Leech, Clifford, disagreement with Hotson, 36

Lees, F. N., *Won* seen as *As You Like It,* 54

Leggatt, A., 224

Levin, Harry, resonant names in Shak, 156

Levin, Richard L., opposes 'two-audience' theory, 48; Marlowe considered Rival Poet, 147; vs. Occasionalism, 149

Levith, Murray, Shakespearean etymology, 10–11

Lewis, B. Roland, 85, 90; no entry on William Hall as member of Dr. Hall's family, 77

Lipsius, 140

Litzinger, C. I., 132

Livy, 204

Lopez, Dr., 147

Love Lies Bleeding, mystery novel based on finding of 'lost' *Won,* 25

Lyons, Clifford, tacit acceptance of *Much Ado* label, 44

Lyly, John, 47, 176

Macey, Samuel L., Othello as an Italian name of Teutonic origin, 13

Mackerness, E., 95

Maclean, significance of full titles of Shak's plays, 62

Macready, W., 181

Major, John M., 252

Malcontent, The, Malevole related to Malvolio, 34

Malone, E., 57, 204n; his data on Edmund Shak missing, 170

Marlowe, Christopher, 72, 99, 126, 205–6, 209, 219–20, 222, 227, 258; Mar-text's name related to his, 4; possible connections with *Arden of F,* 17. See also Ch 6

Marotti, Arthur F., attempt to redate sonnet 116, 120

Marprelate, Martin, 15, 145. See also Ch 6

Marsden, Michael T., 220n, 221

Marston, John, 34–35; his *What You Will* derives from Shak's subtitle to *Twelfth Night,* 33; Touchstone possibly modeled after him, 146

McCanles, Michael, Falstaff knowledgeable on the Bible, 203

McDonald, Russ, kinship of *Othello* and *Every Man in His Humour,* 12

McGinn, Donald J., and George Howerton, 48

McGuire, Philip, 129, 132, 135

McLeod, Randall, Thorpe's accountability, 68

McManaway, James G., 176

Meller, Horst, connections between van Veen's emblems and sonnet 116, 111–18

Meres, Francis, 23, 25–29, 38, 40, 47–48, 58, 60, 63

Metz, G. Harold, 60; disputes contention that some of Shak's plays had 'flippant' subtitles, 26

Middleton, Thomas, 210n

Miksch, Walther, vs. *Arden of F* as Shak's, 224n

Milton, John, deterministic Satan compared to Romeo, 126; "Table" image, 249–54

Milward, Peter, parallels between Southwell and Shak found "convincing" by a reviewer, 95; Mar-text and Marprelate, 149

Mincoff, M., 224

Mirandola, Pico della, poetry to reproduce order of universe, 131

Mömpelgart, Count, 207

Monaghan, Forbes J., 119

Montaigne, Michel, Shak's acquaintance with Florio's trans., 80; Shak indebted to him in *Hamlet,* 109

Moran, James, Queen Elizabeth's own armory related to Shak, 238

Mossman, Thomas Wimberley, Greek and Aramaic name-play on *Peter,* 138

Muir, Kenneth, 150, 182, 220, 227; acclaimed numerological order of *Sonnets,* 32; moral basis in the comedies, 38; *Sonnets* considered as unauthorized, 77; Edmund associated with nomenclature in Harsnett, 165

Musgrove, S., 166

Nash, Thomas, the T. N. initials in the Aldine Ovid not his, 89

Nashe, Thomas, 90; source of *Othello* crux, 6; source of Moth's name, 152

Neely, Carol Thomas, sonnet 116 seen as detached from Young Man sonnets, 119

Novarr, David, questions Freccero's reading of Donne's "Valediction," 102

Oldys, rumor as to Shak in role of Adam, 146

Oliver, H. J., 'Garter' ceremonies in *Wives,* 216

Ornstein, Robert, 155

Orwell, George, 192

Otho, Marcus Salvius, analogies with Othello's career, 11–12

Othoman, 8, 11–12

Otten, Charlotte F., 251

Ousby, Ian, and Heather Dubrow Ousby, 210–11; *Alice* in *Arden of F* and Chaucer's *Alisoun,* 214. *See also* Dubrow

Ovid, 28, 206, 214

Oxford Shakespeare, 109; appropriation of *All Is True* label titularly, 61; Falstaff's name changed to Oldcastle, 64; Arden name in *As You Like It* changed to *Ardenne,* 146

Pacioli, Fra Luca, 134; the Divine Proportion, 56

Palladis Tamia, meaning of title, 29; its arrangement related to that in Folio, 65. *See also* Meres and Ch 3

Parsons, R. D., *Shakerags* suggesting Kemp as unkempt, 199

Passionate Pilgrim, The, 78

Patrides, C. A., 122

Peacham, Henry, 238

Pearce, T. M., application of 'Situation Ethics' to *R&J,* 138–39

Peele, George, 206

Pelican Shakespeare, sonnet 145 found displaced apropos of Dark Lady sonnets, 110. *See also* The Dark Lady

Pembroke, Earl of, 76, 82, 84, 97, 111; played up to by Lawes, 117. *See also* Herbert, William

Pequigney, Joseph, sonnet 116 seen reductively in terms of the Young Man only, 110–11

Peter Martyr, 136

Phelps, Wayne H., 164

Plantin, Christophe, printer with compass device, 103

Plato, 134

Plautus, 140

Plutarch, 204

Piper, W. B., "remover" in sonnet 116 as recalcitrant magistrate, 107

Pohl, Frederick J., Shak's mother's predicted objections to sonnet subject-matter, 82

Potter, Lois, positive review of Giroux, 84

Potts, Abbie Findlay, 227

Praz, Mario, 102, 114

Pursglove, Glyn, parallels between *Arden of F* and Marlowe and Kyd, 205–6

Pyles, Thomas, bawdy meaning of *nothing,* 49

Quennell, Peter, *begetter* as *obtainer* or *producer,* 76

Rabelais, François, 34

Rabkin, Norman, 155

Ralegh, Sir Walter, 152, 154

Ramsey, Paul, male initial *W.* almost always meant *William* then, 92; Shak and Marlowe as the Rival Poets, 153

Rann, Joseph, 18th-century gloss on "Table" as picture, 231

Reage, Pauline, *Story of O,* 30

Redpath, Theodore, 102–3, 108; questions if Donne's "Valediction" is about his wife, 104; sonnet 116 related to "Valediction," 120

Reynolds, Sir Joshua, Queen Cordelia not to be construed as a poor fool, 184

Ribner, Irving, 182

Richmond, Hugh M., linking the two Don Johns, 23; Berowne and Benedick related to figures in French court, 31; historical bases for characters in *Love's Labour's Lost,* 36–37

Richmond, Oliffe, 233–34

Rival Poet, The, 83, 114, 145, 147–48. *See also* Chs 3 and 6

Roberts, Jeanne Addison, 216n, 224; *Wives* seen as domestic comedy, not farce, 197; *Wives* related to Hallowe'en, 210

Roessner, Jane, 115–16, 119

Rollins, Hyder, 140; danger of reading *Sonnets in vacuo,* 84

Rosenberg, Marvin, 310

Rostenberg, Leona, argues Shak did not see *Sonnets* to press, 33; Thorpe considered as large-scale punster, 68

Røstvig, Maren-Sofie, the mystical and occult separate, 130–31

Rothery, Guy Cadogan, 237

Rowe, Nicholas, 231

Rowley, William, 61

Rowse, A. L., 81, 95, 111; Emilia Bassano Lanier as the Dark Lady, 19; *onlie begetter* not as one and only inspirer, 76; Shak and Marlowe as Rival Poets, 153; Mercutio based on Marlowe, 158; Edmund Shakespeare relates to passage in *Macbeth,* 170

"Roxburgh Ballad of King Lear, The," daughters show "disobedient sin," 180

Sams, Eric, 14, 25, 61

Sanderson, Robert, 136

Sandys, John Edwin, 247

Schoenbaum, Samuel, 72, 89; on authorship and internal evidence, 18; challenges tradition that Jonson was involved in F order, 28; reaction to *Won* as *Much Ado,* 35; *Won* as a possible lost script, 60; Lee cited creditably, 76; item in Susanna Hall's library, 90; overlooked MacD. P. Jackson's Oxford thesis, 223

Schücking, Levin L., 172–73

Seneca, influenced both *Titus Andronicus* and *Arden of F,* 218

Seymour–Smith, Martin, 116; *begetter* not *inspirer,* 76

Shakesbye, Edward, 163–164, 167, 169

Shakeshafte, William, 202, 206

Shakespeare, Anne Hathaway. *See* Ch 4 and 'Faithful Wife'

Shakespeare, Edmund, 15. *See also* Ch 7

Shakespeare, Gilbert, 167; story of his coming to London to see plays, 173–74

Shakespeare, Hamnet, named after Hamlet Sadler, 164; his untimely

passing related to Arthur's, 169.
See also Ch 7

Shakespeare, Mary Arden, allusion to her in "Arden . . . merry" in *As You Like It*, 8–9. *See also* Chs 4 and 6

Shakespeare, Susanna. *See* Hall, Susanna

Shakespeare, William, *Works*
Plays
All's Well that Ends Well, 25, 40, 50–51, 53, 57, 65
Antony and Cleopatra, 131
As You Like It, 4, 8–9, 11, 15, 17, 48, 50, 54, 57, 59, 130, 133, 145, 170, 198, 207–8, 216. *See also* Ch 6
Comedy of Errors, The, 40, 65
Coriolanus, 204
Cymbeline, 236
Hamlet, 5, 8, 48–49, 75, 109, 148, 153, 155, 169, 205, 220–21, 258
1 Henry IV, 38–39, 141, 150, 177, 211, 215, 218
2 Henry IV, 187, 215, 234, 236–37, 250
Henry V, 5, 18, 37, 130–31, 215. *See also* Ch 10 and Appendix B
1, 2, 3 Henry VI, 58, 206, 212, 215, 221, 224
Henry VIII, 38, 59, 61, 108
Julius Caesar, 126, 193
King John, 169, 219, 255
King Lear, 5, 10, 15–16, 46, 49, 69, 156, 219–20, 239, 257–58. *See also* Chs 7 and 8
Love's Labour's Lost, 31, 36, 38, 47, 49, 54, 56, 58, 63, 65, 96, 131, 146, 152
Macbeth, 17, 138, 170, 214, 216, 218, 220–21, 228, 238
Measure For Measure, 131
Merchant of Venice, The, 10, 26, 38, 65, 139, 147, 218, 255
Merry Wives of Windsor, The, 26, 53, 65, 154, 177, 179, 184. *See also* Chs 9 and 10
Midsummer Night's Dream, A, 65, 239, 253
Much Ado About Nothing, 14, 30, 64–65, 108, 147, 258. *See also* Ch 2
Othello, 6–8, 12, 62, 131, 137, 153, 220
Pericles, 28, 97n, 221, 250
Richard II, 101, 147, 206, 238
Richard III, 173, 255
Romeo and Juliet, 4, 9, 16, 32, 52, 186, 219, 258. *See also* Ch 5
Taming of the Shrew, The, 23, 25, 65, 58–59, 236
Tempest, The, 12, 29, 65, 101, 119, 135, 153–54, 210, 252
Timon of Athens, 236
Titus Andronicus, 54, 218–19
Troilus and Cressida, 29, 57, 214, 255
Twelfth Night, 26, 33–34, 38–40, 57, 61, 65, 151, 153, 178, 233
Two Gentlemen of Verona, 53, 65
Winter's Tale, The, 32, 65, 141, 190, 236

Poetry
Lover's Complaint, A, 75
Phoenix and the Turtle, The, 145, 224
Rape of Lucrece, The, 30, 77, 236, 255
Sonnets, 4, 14–16, 145, 236, 255. *See also* Chs 3 and 4 and Appendix A
Venus and Adonis, 30, 77, 96

Apocrypha (or Possible Collaborations)
Arden of Faversham, 5, 11, 15–17, 147, 159, 167, 176. *See also* Ch 9
Cardenio, 24, 29
Edward III, 221
Sir Thomas More, 118n, 255. *See also* Dawson
Two Noble Kinsmen, The, 59, 214, 221

Shapiro, Susan C., the date of *Much Ado,* 47

Shawcross, John, Donne's "Valediction" about John and Ann (on one level), 105

Shullenberger, William, 47

Sidney, Philip, *Astrophel and Stella*, 42; *Arcadia* source for subplot of *King Lear*

Siegel, Paul N., social exploitation in *Wives*, 208

Sims, J. H., 253

Sir Gawayne and the Grene Knight, 232

Sisson, C. J., anti-psychological approach to *King Lear* (and to biographical interpretation), 171

Sitwell, Edith, the Fool predicts his own death, 177

Slater, Eliot, 57

Socrates, Falstaff compared, 235

Southampton, Earl of, 79, 82–83, 95, 97, 111, 117, 234. See also Ch 3, Appendix A, and Wriothesley, Henry

Southwell, Robert, 76, 91–92, 94–97, 99; his own dedication to W. S. (plausibly William Shakespeare), 88; as a remote cousin of Shak's, 101; parallels with Donne's "Valediction" in *Saint Peter's Complaint*, 103. See also Howard, Philip

Spencer, Hazleton, vs. Thorpe as dedicating *Sonnets* to their author, 74; vs. W. H. as Henry Wriothesley's initials in reverse, 82

Spencer, Theodore, *All Is True* as another alternate title, 61

Spenser, Edmund, 139–40, 165; Despair as Fool hanging himself, 178–79; Shak's debt to, 227; gluttony, 252. See also Coyle

Stanton, Kay, "recknynge" in *As You Like It* relating to Marlowe, not Chapman, 147

Stageberg, Norman, the Golden Mean and the aesthetic of the sonnet form, 133

Steevens, George, 186

Stephen, Leslie, key riposte to anti-Stratfordians, 73

Stevenson, David, Donne among Shak's "private friends," 109

Stevenson, Robert, 135

Stodder, Joseph H., possibility of Shak's hand in *Arden of F*, 227

Stokes, Francis Griffin, Othello's name from the Morea, 13

Stoll, E. E., 141; Hamlet not "solid" in the sense of obese, 4

Stopes, Charlotte, 95; W. H. as William Harvey, 82

Strachan, Michael, 290

Sturgess, Keith, 221; *Arden of F*'s "Shakespearean generosity," 202; *Arden of F* very influential on other plays, 226

Summers, Claude, rehabilitates Edmund in *King Lear*, 172n

Summers, Montague, 185

Swinburne, A. C., 222; Lady Arden in *Arden of F* allied to Lady Macbeth, 220

Tannenbaum, Samuel, resonant names in Shak, 156

Tate, Nahum, 185

Taylor, Gary, 249; vs. Folio reading of Falstaff's death, 18; evidence of Shak revising sonnets, 78; sonnet 145 as a 'Faithful Wife' sonnet, 109; sonnet 145 as unsequential,

111; Appendix on the "Table" crux, 232

Taylor, Jeremy, 136

Taylor, Thad, argues that Shak "had a hand in writing or rewriting" *Arden of F*, 227

Tennyson, Alfred Lord, Theobald's emendation accommodated, 250

Terence, 140

Thaler, Alwin, 191–92; countered double-role (Cordelia-Fool) theory, 182–83

Theobald, Lewis, 231, 233, 249–50. See also Ch 10 and Appendix B

Thomas, Sidney, *Won* seen as "probably an alternate title," 38

Thompson, Ann, Shak and Chaucer, 214

Thomson, J. A. K., 204

Thorpe, Thomas, 67–72, 200. See also Ch 3 and Appendix A

Tieck, Johann Ludwig, 223

Tilley, M. P., 176, 184

Tillyard, E. M. W., Shak's transition period, 48

Trickett, Rachel, Milton's familiarity with Shak in Q and F, 250–51

True Tragedy of Richard Duke of York, The, 147

True Tragedy of Richard III, The, 147; reference to Black Will, 201

Tung-chi, Lin, favoring the "sullied" reading in *Hamlet*, 130. See also Bowers, Fredson

Udall, Nicholas, 211

Ule, Louis, Kentish data in *Arden of F* connected with Marlowe's father, 205

Valéry, Paul, 125, 134

van Veen, Otto, 111–20

Vinci, Leonardo da, 134

Viswanathan, S., 146, 216n

Wain, John, the Fool's last words as prescient, 177

Walker, D. P., 129

Walton, Izaak, 119; "Valediction" related to Donne's spouse, 104

Walz, Eugene P., names of Shak and Greene alluded to in *Arden of F*, 199–200; *Arden of F* as "tragical satire," 205; *Arden of F* as based on Chaucer, 214

War Hath Made All Friends, subtitle for *Edmund Ironside*, 61

Ward, Col. B. R., evidence of four William Halls, 91n

Warnke, K., and Ludwig Pröscholdt, vs. *Arden of F* as Shak's, 224–25

Watson, Thomas, 148

Weber, C. O., conation and the Mean, 137

Webster, John, 219

Wells, Stanley, Knolles as a source for *Othello*, 7; *Won* considered as *The Shrew*, 58; transcript of *Sonnets* not directly from Shak, 89; sonnet 145 as a 'Faithful Wife' sonnet, 109; sonnet 145 as unsequential, 111. See also Taylor, Gary

Welsford, Enid, folk-fool 'killed,' 179

Wertheimer, Max, conation and the Mean, 137. See also Weber, C. O.

What You Will, 33

White, R. S., 216n

Whitney, Geoffrey, 235

Williams, George Walton, the em space as rhetorical pause, 67

Williamson, C. F., Lear not thinking that Cordelia has died, 16, 193

Wilson, John Dover, 154; on a subtitle used as a main title, 33–34; *Won* as possibly "the lost twin," 37; rhetorical rather than syntactic pointing, 188; Shak as "upstart" playwright, not actor, 204n; Falstaff linked with Socrates, 235; Falstaff anticipating Milton's Satan, 252

Wimsatt, W. K., 149

Wine, M. L., 159, 198, 205–8, 218, 220, 223, 225, 227

Wither, George, compass emblem, 116; "Cutting Dicke," 203

Wood, H. Harvey, 34–35

Woudhuysen, H. R., status of *All Is True,* 61

Wright, Leonard, 136

Wriothesley, Henry, 82. *See also* Southampton

Wyatt, Thomas, 140

Yates, Frances, 131; relates Berowne to Bruno, 31

Youngblood, Sarah, *Macbeth* related to *Arden of F,* 220n

Zeising, Adolf, 141